Mastering Azure Security

Implementing Zero Trust, compliance, and threat protection with Azure security tools

Arnav Sharma

www.bpbonline.com

First Edition 2026

ISBN: 978-93-65891-317

LIMITS OF LIABILITY AND DISCLAIMER OF WARRANTY

The information contained in this book is true and correct to the best of author's and publisher's knowledge. The author has made every effort to ensure the accuracy of these publications, but the publisher cannot be held responsible for any loss or damage arising from any information in this book.

All trademarks referred to in the book are acknowledged as properties of their respective owners but BPB Publications cannot guarantee the accuracy of this information.

www.bpbonline.com

Dedicated to

Avin and Aveer
My wonderfully mischievous boys,
whose curiosity, chaos, and endless energy
remind me why learning, building, and securing the future matter.
You make life louder, brighter, and infinitely better.
This one is for you, with all my love.

About the Author

Arnav Sharma is a principal security architect with over a decade of experience in cloud computing, cybersecurity, and enterprise IT transformation. His career has spanned a diverse range of industries, helping organizations modernize their infrastructure, implement secure cloud architectures, and align security practices with real-world business needs.

Arnav specializes in Microsoft Azure and brings deep expertise in identity and access management, cloud governance, infrastructure automation, and threat protection. He holds more than 30 industry-recognized certifications, reflecting his commitment to continuous learning and hands-on mastery of evolving technologies.

He is a proud **Microsoft Certified Trainer** (**MCT**) and a Microsoft **Most Valuable Professional** (**MVP**) — acknowledgments that highlight his contributions to the global tech community. As a trainer and mentor, Arnav is known for breaking down complex technical topics into practical, relatable guidance for learners at all levels. He has delivered countless workshops, webinars, and corporate training sessions, helping professionals across the world skill up in cloud security and automation.

Outside of his professional role, Arnav is passionate about writing and sharing knowledge. He regularly publishes technical blogs, industry insights, and tutorials focused on cloud security, DevSecOps, and identity management on his personal website. His content has reached a wide audience of security practitioners, engineers, and technology leaders who value clarity, depth, and real-world relevance.

Arnav also mentors aspiring professionals through community programs and initiatives, believing strongly in giving back and empowering the next generation of cybersecurity leaders.

He lives in Sydney, Australia, with his wife and two sons, who keep him grounded, curious, and constantly inspired. When he is not immersed in the cloud, you can find him exploring the latest in AI, teaching, or reflecting on how technology can be a force for good in an increasingly connected world.

About the Reviewers

- **Navneet Kumar Tyagi** is a seasoned IT professional with over 18 years of experience in software architecture, data engineering, and cloud-native development. He has contributed to technology solutions across the healthcare, energy, and finance sectors, with a strong focus on scalable system design and enterprise data platforms. Navneet specializes in building modern data ecosystems using Azure/AWS services.

  As a technical architect, Navneet brings deep expertise in full-stack development, system integration, and governance-focused data solutions. He is passionate about enabling intelligent data sharing and has led initiatives that transformed legacy data workflows into secure, high-performance analytics platforms.

  When he is not architecting cloud solutions, Navneet enjoys mentoring emerging developers and exploring advancements in AI-driven data engineering.

  He is currently working with finance of America and is part of the enterprise integration team working on the latest Azure/AWS services integration with the company's financial products.

- **Harvendra Singh** is a distinguished technology leader specializing in cloud engineering, architecture, automation, and AI-powered solutions. He designs and implements scalable, secure systems utilizing Azure, .NET, C#, Python, GCP, Kubernetes, Databricks, and other cutting-edge technologies. With expertise in cloud-native applications, microservices, event-driven architectures, and distributed systems, Harvendra drives innovation in cloud and AI ecosystems, delivering high-impact solutions that drive business value and sustainable growth.

- **Shivaprasad Sankesha Narayana** is a Microsoft Certified Senior Cloud and Solution Architect with two decades of experience leading enterprise-scale digital transformation across the oil and gas, insurance, and healthcare industries. Currently contracting with BP in Houston, Texas, he drives the design and implementation of cloud-native solutions that integrate Azure, AWS, AI/ML, and digital twin technologies to modernize operations, strengthen security, and improve business agility.

  He is widely recognized for architecting secure and scalable hybrid cloud platforms, delivering impactful solutions in cloud migration, predictive maintenance, and enterprise data governance. Beyond industry leadership, Shivaprasad actively contributes to the professional and academic community as a peer reviewer for international conferences and as a technical reviewer.

  A senior member of IEEE and fellow member at Threws, a contributor to multiple forthcoming book chapters, Shivaprasad is committed to advancing innovation at the intersection of cloud computing, artificial intelligence, and enterprise architecture.

Acknowledgement

I would like to express my sincere gratitude to all those who supported me in completing this book.

First and foremost, I extend my heartfelt thanks to my wife, Antima Sharma, for her love, patience, and constant support. Your willingness to manage everything, especially the kids, gave me the time and space to focus. I could not have done this without you.

To my father, Ashok Kumar Sharma, and my mother, Sarita Sharma, thank you for always encouraging me to work hard and believe in myself. Your belief in me made a big difference.

To my boys, Avin and Aveer, your energy, curiosity, and endless questions kept me inspired. This book is for you.

I am grateful to BPB Publications for their guidance and support in making this book a reality. A special thanks to the editorial and publishing teams for their expertise and assistance throughout the process.

I would also like to thank the wider Azure, Microsoft MVP, and cybersecurity community for the knowledge and inspiration shared through forums, blogs, and conversations. Your work helped shape the ideas in this book.

Finally, to all the readers, thank you for your interest and support. I hope this book serves as a useful guide on your journey through Azure security.

Preface

We live in a time when the cloud powers everything, from small startups to big enterprises. While Microsoft Azure brings agility, scalability, and innovation to the system, it also introduces new security challenges that require more than just traditional IT knowledge. Securing cloud environments is not just about ticking boxes; it is about understanding how every decision you make, from identity design to data protection, shapes your organization's security posture.

Mastering Azure Security was written for professionals who want to go beyond surface-level advice. Whether you are a system administrator transitioning to the cloud, a security architect responsible for cloud governance, or simply someone curious about building safer systems in Azure, this book is for you.

The content is based on my real-world experience working with cloud and cybersecurity teams across various industries. I have seen firsthand the complexities organizations face when it comes to balancing security, usability, and speed. My goal with this book is to simplify those complexities and present security as something that is not only essential but approachable and easy to manage.

Each chapter focuses on a specific area of Azure security, structured to take you from foundational concepts to practical implementation:

Chapter 1: Introduction to Azure Security- We begin by looking into the core principles of cloud security. This includes the shared responsibility model, key threat vectors, and Microsoft's approach to security and compliance. You will gain a clear understanding of Azure's security foundations and how it differs from traditional on-premises thinking, which is the foundation for everything that follows.

Chapter 2: Securing Identity and Access- Identity is the new perimeter. This chapter covers Entra ID (formerly Azure Active Directory), RBAC, Conditional Access, multi-factor authentication, and how to enforce Zero Trust principles. We will also look at **Privileged Identity Management** (**PIM**), identity lifecycle automation, and how attackers often exploit identity misconfigurations.

Chapter 3: Securing Networks- We explore how to design secure network architectures using virtual networks, **Network Security Groups** (**NSGs**), Application Security Groups, firewalls, Private Endpoint, and custom routing strategies. From segmentation to inspection, this chapter will help you build resilient Azure network topologies that support both isolation and scalability.

Chapter 4: Securing Compute- Focused on virtual machines and compute workloads, this chapter walks through secure VM deployment, **just-in-time** (**JIT**) access, endpoint protection, and workload hardening techniques. You will also learn about VM extensions, patch management, and best practices to minimize the attack surface of compute resources.

Chapter 5: Securing Data- Data is a prime target for attackers. Learn how to protect it using encryption (at rest and in transit), access control, data masking, backups, and secure database practices across Azure Storage and SQL. We will also examine identity-based access for storage accounts, backup vault protections, and how to detect suspicious access attempts.

Chapter 6: Security Governance- Security without governance is a mess. This chapter introduces Azure Policy, management groups, Blueprints, and compliance tooling to help you enforce and audit security consistently. You will learn how to design and implement guardrails that prevent misconfigurations and align your Azure environment with regulatory requirements.

Chapter 7: Security Posture- Here, we will deep-dive into Microsoft Defender for Cloud, Secure Score, and continuous assessment tools to measure, monitor, and improve your overall security health. This chapter helps you build a proactive security culture by identifying risks early, automating remediation, and benchmarking your progress.

Chapter 8: Workload Protection- Every workload has unique risks. This chapter covers how to secure key Azure services such as App Services, Containers, Key Vaults, and more using Microsoft Defender's workload protection capabilities. We explore threat detection strategies tailored to each service, with real examples and tips for reducing false positives.

Chapter 9: Security Monitoring- You cannot protect what you cannot see. Learn how to monitor security events using Log Analytics, Azure Monitor, and Microsoft Sentinel, and how to respond with playbooks and automation. This chapter also covers alert customization, incident response workflows, and how to build a centralized security operation.

Chapter 10: Security Best Practices- We wrap up with tried-and-tested best practices, hardening checklists, and real-world tips to help you maintain a strong and evolving security posture in Azure. You will walk away with actionable guidance, covering both technical controls and operational strategies to keep your environment secure long-term.

Writing this book has been a journey, one that would not have been possible without the support of my family, especially my wife Antima, who managed the chaos at home so I could focus on finishing every page. My parents, Ashok Kumar Sharma and Sarita Sharma, have always inspired me to pursue knowledge and share what I learn. And my boys, Avin and Aveer, remind me daily that curiosity and energy are at the heart of learning.

Let us get started.

Coloured Images

Please follow the link to download the
Coloured Images of the book:

https://rebrand.ly/6c4d86

We have code bundles from our rich catalogue of books and videos available at https://github.com/bpbpublications. Check them out!

Errata

We take immense pride in our work at BPB Publications and follow best practices to ensure the accuracy of our content to provide with an indulging reading experience to our subscribers. Our readers are our mirrors, and we use their inputs to reflect and improve upon human errors, if any, that may have occurred during the publishing processes involved. To let us maintain the quality and help us reach out to any readers who might be having difficulties due to any unforeseen errors, please write to us at :

errata@bpbonline.com

Your support, suggestions and feedbacks are highly appreciated by the BPB Publications' Family.

Piracy

If you come across any illegal copies of our works in any form on the internet, we would be grateful if you would provide us with the location address or website name. Please contact us at business@bpbonline.com with a link to the material.

If you are interested in becoming an author

If there is a topic that you have expertise in, and you are interested in either writing or contributing to a book, please visit www.bpbonline.com. We have worked with thousands of developers and tech professionals, just like you, to help them share their insights with the global tech community. You can make a general application, apply for a specific hot topic that we are recruiting an author for, or submit your own idea.

Reviews

Please leave a review. Once you have read and used this book, why not leave a review on the site that you purchased it from? Potential readers can then see and use your unbiased opinion to make purchase decisions. We at BPB can understand what you think about our products, and our authors can see your feedback on their book. Thank you!

For more information about BPB, please visit www.bpbonline.com.

Join our Discord space

Join our Discord workspace for latest updates, offers, tech happenings around the world, new releases, and sessions with the authors:

https://discord.bpbonline.com

Table of Contents

1. Introduction to Azure Security 1

Introduction 1

Structure 1

Objectives 2

Threat landscape 2

Understanding the current threat environment 2

Cloud and associated threats 2

Azure's threat intelligence 4

Key features of Azure's threat intelligence 5

Shared responsibility model 6

The core principle 6

Microsoft's responsibilities for cloud security 6

Customer responsibilities for cloud security 6

Responsibility distribution across cloud service models 6

Shared responsibility in practice 8

Misconceptions and clarifications 8

Cloud security posture management 9

The tools that make CSPM work in Azure 9

Zero Trust security model 11

Understanding the Zero Trust security model 12

Core principles 12

Implementing Zero Trust in Azure 13

Zero Trust architecture example 16

Deploying Zero Trust 16

Zero Trust principles 17

Threat protection with Microsoft Defender for Cloud 18

Defense-in-depth 19

Understanding the defense-in-depth security strategy 19

Layers of defense 19

Best practices 21

Advantages of defense-in-depth 23

Conclusion....26

2. Securing Identity and Access....27
Introduction....27
Structure....27
Objectives....28
Introduction to Entra ID....28
Overview of Entra ID....28
Importance of identity in security....29
Key features of Entra ID....30
Microsoft Entra ID authentication....32
Understanding authorisation....32
Comparison of password-based vs. passwordless authentication....35
Authentication flows....35
Implementing authentication best practices....37
Microsoft Entra ID authorisation....40
Understanding authorisation....40
Comparing RBAC vs. PIM....42
Privileged Identity Management....42
Types of roles....43
Best practices for authorisation....44
Microsoft Entra ID Secure Score....46
Understanding what Secure Score is....47
How Secure Score works....47
Importance of Secure Score....48
Components of Secure Score....48
Improving your Secure Score....50
Microsoft Entra ID tenant security....52
Securing the Microsoft Entra ID tenant....52
Appropriate use of security use....54
Best practices for Microsoft Entra ID tenant security....54
Microsoft Entra ID identities and protection....55
Types of identities....55
User accounts....55

Guest accounts 56
Service principals 57
Managed Identities 58
Identity protection features 58
Enhancing identity security in Microsoft Entra ID 60
Microsoft Entra ID secure application access 61
Securing access to applications with Microsoft Entra ID 61
Single sign-on for seamless and secure authentication 61
Conditional Access for intelligent security enforcement 62
Securing on-premises applications with Azure AD application proxy 64
Enhancing application security with Microsoft Entra ID 65
Managed Identity-based secure authentication 65
Updating applications helps to reduce vulnerabilities 65
Session management and monitoring 65
Risk-based access management and identity protection 65
Ensuring compliance and governance with identity access reviews 66
Conclusion 66

3. Securing Networks 67
Introduction 67
Structure 68
Objectives 68
Overview of virtual networks 68
Network segmentation 69
Network Security Group vs. Application Security Group 70
Simple Azure network architecture 70
Traffic filtering and protection 72
NSG vs. Azure Firewall 77
Best practices for securing Azure Virtual Networks 77
Securing private access to Azure resources 78
Introduction to private access 78
Key features 79
Private Link vs. Service Endpoints comparison table 82
Hybrid connectivity 82

Hybrid connectivity decision matrix......83
Enhancing security with ExpressRoute private access......83
Azure VPN Gateway......84
Types of Azure VPN Gateway connections......84
How Azure VPN Gateway works......85
Benefits of Azure VPN Gateway......85
ExpressRoute......86
Types of ExpressRoute circuits......87
ExpressRoute connectivity models......88
Working of ExpressRoute......89
Benefits of Azure ExpressRoute......90
Azure Virtual WAN......90
Types of Azure Virtual WAN......90
Working of Azure Virtual WAN......91
Best practices......92
Securing public access to Azure resources......93
Public Access considerations......93
Tools for securing public access......94
Azure Application Gateway......94
Azure Front Door......96
Web Application Firewall......100
Predefined rules and custom policy configurations......100
Azure DDoS protection......102
How Azure DDoS protection works......102
Two tiers of Azure DDoS protection......102
Endpoint security......103
Azure Traffic Manager......103
How Traffic Manager boosts endpoint security......104
Custom DNS and Azure DNS......105
How Azure DNS enhances endpoint security......105
Certificates......107
How certificates enhance security in Azure......108
Managing certificates in Azure......108
Azure Key Vault for secure certificate storage......108

Automating TLS certificate rotation with Azure Key Vault.. 108
Best practices *109*
Conclusion.. 110

4. Securing Compute.. 111
Introduction..111
Structure...111
Objectives 112
Securing Azure Virtual Machines 112
Overview of Azure Virtual Machines *112*
Key security features for Azure VMs.. *113*
Best practices for securing virtual machines.. *114*
Azure Virtual Machines baseline architecture.. *116*
Securing Azure Container Services 118
Overview of container services.. *118*
Best practices... *120*
Baseline architecture for an Azure Kubernetes Service Cluster *122*
Securing Azure App Service... 124
Overview of Azure App Service.. *124*
Key security features of Azure App Service.. *124*
Securing Azure Serverless... 127
Overview of serverless security.. *128*
Key security features *128*
Best practices for securing serverless applications.. *129*
Securing Azure API Management 130
Overview of API Management *131*
Key security features of Azure API Management *131*
Best practices for securing Azure API Management.. *134*
Baseline architecture for APIM.. *136*
Conclusion... 138

5. Securing Data... 139
Introduction.. 139
Structure.. 139

Objectives 139

Access control for storage services 140

Overview of storage access control 140

Access control methods for storage 140

Managing access policies for storage services 142

Best practices for securing Azure Storage access 143

Data protection for storage services 145

Introduction to data protection 145

Key features 146

Governance and data classification 147

Best practices 149

Encryption for storage services 151

Overview of encryption 151

Encryption methods 151

Encryption methods comparison 152

Key management 153

Best practices 154

Security of database services 156

Overview of Azure database security 156

Authentication and access control 156

Auditing and monitoring 158

Data protection techniques 160

Best practices for securing Azure database services 162

Comparing security capabilities 164

Conclusion 165

6. Security Governance 167

Introduction 167

Structure 167

Objectives 168

Cloud Adoption Framework 168

Overview of CAF 168

CAF Governance Model 169

Best practices for CAF 171

CAF sample architecture 172
Well-Architected Framework 172
Overview of WAF 172
Comparing CAF and WAF 173
Best practices for WAF 174
WAF review tool 175
Microsoft Purview data governance 176
Overview of Microsoft Purview 176
Key features 176
Best practices for Purview 177
Purview sample architecture 179
Azure management groups 180
Overview of management groups 180
Key features 180
Best practices for management group 181
Azure management groups sample architecture 182
Azure Blueprints 183
Overview of Azure Blueprints 183
Key features 183
Best practices for Blueprints 184
Azure Blueprint Sample 184
Azure Landing Zones 185
Overview of Landing Zones 185
Key features 186
Best practices for Landing Zones 186
Azure Landing Zone Architecture 187
Azure Resource Graph 189
Overview of Resource Graph 189
Key features of Resource Graph 189
Best practices for Resource Graph 190
Azure Resource Graph homepage 190
Azure Policy 191
Overview of Azure Policy 191
Key features 191

Best practices for Azure Policy ... 192
Azure Policy homepage ... 193
Azure Key Vault ... 193
Overview of Key Vault ... 194
Key features ... 194
Best practices for Key Vault ... 195
Azure Key Vault sample ... 195
Azure Locks ... 196
Overview of Azure Locks ... 196
Key features ... 196
Best practices for Azure Locks ... 197
Azure Resource Lock sample ... 198
Conclusion ... 198

7. Security Posture ... 201
Introduction ... 201
Structure ... 201
Objectives ... 201
Azure Advisor ... 202
Overview of Azure Advisor ... 202
Key features of Azure Advisor ... 203
Using Azure Advisor effectively ... 205
Best practices of Azure Advisor ... 206
Microsoft Defender for Cloud ... 207
Overview of Microsoft Defender for Cloud ... 208
Key features of Microsoft Defender for Cloud ... 210
Secure Score ... 210
Inventory management ... 210
External Attack Surface Management ... 211
Compliance monitoring ... 212
Hybrid and multi-cloud support ... 213
Agentless and agent-based scanning ... 213
Threat detection and alerts ... 213
Recommendations Engine ... 213

Implementing CSPM with Microsoft Defender for Cloud........214
CSPM best practices with Microsoft Defender for Cloud........216
Conclusion........217

8. Workload Protection........219
Introduction........219
Structure........219
Objective........220
Microsoft Defender for Cloud CWPP services........220
Defender for Cloud homepage........220
Overview of CWPP........221
Key features of CWPP........221
Benefits of cloud workload protection platform........223
Microsoft Defender for Servers........224
Overview of Defender for Servers........224
Enabling and configuring Defender for Servers........225
Key features of Defender for Servers........226
Best practices of Defender for Servers........228
Microsoft Defender for Storage........229
Overview of Defender for Storage........230
Enabling Defender for Storage........230
Key features of Defender for Storage........231
Best practices of Defender for Storage........232
Microsoft Defender for Databases........235
Overview of Defender for Databases........235
Enabling Defender for Databases........236
Key features of Defender for Databases........236
Best practices of Defender for Databases........238
Microsoft Defender for Containers........240
Overview of Defender for Containers........241
Enabling Defender for Containers........241
Key features of Defender for Containers........242
Best practices of Defender for Containers........243
Microsoft Defender for App Service........245

Overview of Defender for App Service 246
Enabling Defender for App Service 246
Key features of Defender for App Service 247
Best practices of Defender for App Service 248
Microsoft Defender for Key Vault 249
Overview of Defender for Key Vault 250
Enabling Defender for Key Vault 250
Key features of Defender for Key Vault 250
Best practices of Defender for Key Vault 251
Microsoft Defender for Resource Manager 253
Overview of Defender for Resource Manager 253
Enabling Defender for Resource Manager 254
Key features of Defender for Resource Manager 254
Best practices of Defender for Resource Manager 256
Microsoft Defender for DNS 257
Overview of Defender for DNS 257
Enabling Defender for DNS 258
Key features of Defender for DNS 258
Best practices of Defender for DNS 260
Conclusion 261

9. Security Monitoring 263
Introduction 263
Structure 263
Objectives 263
Azure Monitor 264
Overview of Azure Monitor 264
Azure Monitor homepage 264
Key features of Azure Monitor 267
Security event monitoring in Azure Monitor 268
Best practices of Azure Monitor 269
Microsoft Sentinel 270
Overview of Microsoft Sentinel 270
Microsoft Sentinel homepage 271

Log Analytics for Sentinel 273
Key features of Microsoft Sentinel 273
Configuring data collection in Microsoft Sentinel 274
Threat hunting and response automation in Microsoft Sentinel 275
Best practices of Microsoft Sentinel 276
Traffic Analytics 277
Overview of Traffic Analytics 278
Components of Traffic Analytics 278
Key features of Traffic Analytics 280
Configuring Traffic Analytics 281
Best practices of Traffic Analytics 282
Conclusion 283

10. Security Best Practices 285
Introduction 285
Structure 285
Objectives 285
Concepts best practice guidance 286
Foundational security principles 286
Best practices 287
Workload implementation best practice guidance 288
Identity and access security 288
Network security 289
Compute security 290
Data security 291
Governance and compliance 292
Security operations best practice guidance 292
Monitoring and threat detection 293
Incident response 294
Continual improvement 294
Conclusion 295

Index 297-308

CHAPTER 1
Introduction to Azure Security

Introduction

In this chapter, you will master foundational security principles. First, the threat landscape will be outlined, and you will be introduced to the shared responsibility model, which is a critical understanding of utilizing cloud platform resources.

Next, you will learn about cloud security posture management, which provides risk detection and remediation for your environment's resources. Finally, you will find out what the Zero Trust security model is and the security strategy approach of adopting defense-in-depth.

Structure

This chapter contains the following topics:

- Threat landscape
- Shared responsibility model
- Cloud security posture management
- Zero Trust security model
- Defense-in-depth

Objectives

By the end of this chapter, readers will understand the foundational principles of Azure security, including the evolving threat landscape, cloud security posture management, the shared responsibility model, and the Zero Trust security model. They will also gain insights into key security tools and strategies to protect cloud environments effectively.

Threat landscape

The digital threat landscape is constantly evolving with new attack vectors emerging. Organizations must adapt to protect their cloud environments. As cyber threats become more sophisticated, organizations must continuously adapt their security strategies to safeguard their cloud environments effectively.

According to IBM's *2023 Cost of a Data Breach Report*, organizations leveraging cloud environments faced an average breach cost of USD 4.75 million, emphasizing the need for proactive cloud security measures.

Understanding the current threat environment

In our digital age, all organizations are evolving digitally, regardless of their size, how long they have been in business, or whether they are startups. Additionally, cloud computing has caused a significant shift in business operation methods and dynamics. As systems continue to evolve quickly, the complexity and the threat landscape both rise.

Cyberattacks have become more complex, more common, and more damaging than they have ever been in the past. Cybercriminals do not rely on one attack method; instead, they use various methods, like ransomware, phishing, supply chain attacks, and zero-day vulnerabilities. These vectors make it more and more difficult to detect and mitigate.

The shift to remote and hybrid work post-COVID-19 has broadened the attack surface by introducing risks from home networks and personal devices. At the same time, cybercriminals have embraced AI and automation to deliver large-scale attacks, including AI-generated phishing and adaptive malware. These developments demand more vigilant and adaptive security postures.

Cloud and associated threats

Many companies are moving workloads to the cloud without fully understanding the security risks associated with cloud services. This results in a wide variety of vulnerabilities and an exposed cloud landscape, making it easier for cybercriminals to steal data and attack various systems.

Apart from hosting workloads, many organizations rely on applications from cloud marketplace and external vendors to enhance their cloud capabilities. These connections increase utility but make cyberattacks more likely to occur. If a third-party application or vendor connected to a cloud environment is penetrated and is less secure, it can lead to a cascading impact that exposes sensitive data and affects operations in the primary organization's systems.

Additionally, adhering to global data protection regulations such as the **General Data Protection Regulation** (**GDPR**) and **California Consumer Privacy Act** (**CCPA**) makes handling security in the cloud more challenging. Companies have to make sure that these systems follow the necessary criteria to prevent fines and damage to the company name. Furthermore, one should have a good awareness of built-in compliance technologies to guarantee governance and legal non-compliance. Even accidental non-compliance can have significant operational and financial effects.

Key elements of this landscape include:

- **Advanced persistent threats (APTs)**: Organized groups supported by governments or well-funded NGOs carry out APTs in cyberspace. Targeting specific businesses, government agencies, or groups, these attackers try to damage or steal intellectual property, financial data, or sensitive intelligence information.

  APTs are distinguished by their persistence; they do not simply attack and then go. Rather, they enter networks undetectably for long periods of time, acquiring data or causing damage without being discovered. These attacks seriously affect businesses all around since they are intentional, patient, and highly customized to evade standard security protocols.

- **Ransomware attacks**: In the digital age, ransomware attacks, where attackers encrypt victim data so it can not be accessed until a ransom is paid, are becoming common. Usually targeting organizations, government agencies, and even hospitals, these attacks have become a popular and profitable means of extortion. Usually, in cryptocurrencies, victims are given a deadline to pay the ransom, which helps to restore access to the encrypted data. Ignoring payment might result in the public disclosure of private data or ongoing data loss.

  The ability of ransomware to paralyze whole systems and stop activities makes it so successful. Before launching the ransomware, attackers sometimes enter a network by means of phishing emails, dangerous links, or software flaws. Once within, the malware spreads rapidly, shutting down some services and occasionally whole systems. The rising frequency and sophistication of these attacks have made them a top issue for companies all around, so immediate demand for more robust cybersecurity policies is driven by them.

- **Supply chain vulnerabilities**: Supply chain vulnerabilities are a growing problem in cybersecurity. Instead of attacking a company head-on, hackers are finding ways to exploit weaknesses in the software, hardware, or services provided by third-party vendors. It is like sneaking into a house through a neighbor's unlocked door—they use the trust companies place in their suppliers to infiltrate systems without raising suspicion. These attacks are hard to catch because they rely on relationships and existing access points within the supply chain.

The scariest part is how much damage these attacks can cause. If a single popular tool or system gets compromised, it can affect thousands of businesses at once, as we have seen with incidents like SolarWinds. Attackers may leave behind secret entry points for later use, interfere with regular business operations, or take some data out. Businesses must proactively fight against these techniques by closely vetting their partners, implementing additional security measures, and monitoring for any odd activities. The key is to always be one step ahead.

- **Cloud-specific threats**: As more companies switch to platforms like Azure, cloud-related issues are starting to cause actual worry. One of the main issues is configuration errors, such as unintentionally leaving a database or storage open to the internet and readily exposing private information. Unauthorized access is another big concern caused by weak passwords, poor access controls, weak policies, or not having multi-factor authentication. On top of that, these identity-based attacks, like leaked passwords or privilege misuse, are on the rise as hackers look for ways to exploit how cloud environments handle users and roles.

  The complexity of cloud systems makes these attacks especially challenging. With so many options and capabilities, things might easily slide through the loopholes, especially during rapid growth or cloud migration. Hackers are aware of this, and they are quick to exploit such situations. That is why it is important to maintain fundamental security practices such as frequently reviewing configurations, tightening identity constraints, and inspecting cloud resources. The cloud may accomplish incredible things, but it is not set-it-and-forget-it; maintaining its security requires continual attention.

Azure's threat intelligence

Having explored the evolving threat landscape, the key aspects of these risks, and how the cloud has reshaped security challenges, it is time to focus on Azure and how it helps address these challenges to secure systems effectively.

Azure's threat intelligence is all about helping businesses stay one step ahead of cyber threats. It taps into Microsoft's global network of security signals, billions of them every day, to give organizations a clear picture of the evolving threat landscape. Whether it is spotting suspicious activity, blocking malicious IPs, or analyzing attack patterns, Azure's tools and resources are designed to keep your cloud and on-premises environments secure.

For example, a healthcare provider using Azure Defender and Microsoft Sentinel detected multiple failed login attempts from unfamiliar IP addresses linked to a known malicious actor.

By correlating signals from Azure's threat intelligence feeds, Sentinel automatically triggered a Conditional Access policy that blocked the IP range and alerted the security team. This prevented credential compromise and stopped the attack before sensitive patient data could be accessed.

Handling enormous data using **artificial intelligence** (**AI**) and **machine learning** (**ML**) is one of its greatest strengths. Rather than creating random or false alarms, it points out actual hazards and offers practical advice to help solve the issue. This intelligence and information feeds directly into tools like Azure Defender (now part of Microsoft Defender for Cloud) and Microsoft Sentinel, so you can spot and respond to alerts faster. Plus, its library of threat indicators, like known bad IPs or domains, makes it easier to fine-tune your defences and stop attacks before they get in.

Key features of Azure's threat intelligence

Azure's threat intelligence provides a proactive approach to identifying and mitigating security threats. By leveraging global threat visibility and advanced analytics helps organizations detect potential cyber risks before they escalate. The following are the key features of Azure's threat intelligence:

- **Global threat visibility**: Microsoft gathers threat data from endpoints, apps, cloud environments, and outside networks, among other sources. This worldwide coverage enables it to identify trends of hostile behaviour and provide early warnings regarding new or developing hazards before they cause a major breach.
- **Advanced analytics**: Azure threat intelligence coexists with Azure Defender, which is now located under Microsoft Defender for Cloud. This allows companies to quickly recognize and handle risks since they may gain practical insights from within their security system.
- **Integration with Azure Defender**: Azure threat intelligence works hand-in-hand with Azure Defender (now part of Microsoft Defender for Cloud). This means businesses can get actionable insights directly within their security platform, making it easier to identify and respond to threats quickly.
- **Threat indicators**: Azure offers a library of threat indicators, like known bad IP addresses, domains, and file hashes. These are ready to be used in your security operations, helping you to strengthen monitoring and block malicious activities.
- **Incident response support**: Tools like Azure Sentinel (now Microsoft Sentinel) make responding to threats much smoother. Using data from Azure threat intelligence, Sentinel helps security teams analyze incidents in detail and even automate responses, reducing the time it takes to address risks.

Shared responsibility model

Understanding threats is just one piece of the bigger picture. The next step is knowing who is responsible for protecting cloud environments. That is where the shared responsibility model comes in. In this section, we will have a look at the shared responsibility model and how it is defined.

Core principle

The shared responsibility model in Azure clearly outlines who is responsible for what when it comes to securing cloud environments. It is a partnership between Microsoft and its customers, with responsibilities shifting depending on the type of cloud service—**software as a service** (**SaaS**), **platform as a service** (**PaaS**), **infrastructure as a service** (**IaaS**), or on-premises. This model ensures that both parties know their role in keeping the workloads safe.

Microsoft's responsibilities for cloud security

Microsoft takes care of the infrastructure that supports Azure services, including:

- **Physical security**: Protecting data centres with measures like restricted access, surveillance cameras, and environmental controls.
- **Host infrastructure and virtualization**: Ensuring the safety of the physical servers, networking, and hypervisors from threats.

Customer responsibilities for cloud security

As a customer, your focus is on securing the parts of the system you control, such as:

- **Data, applications, and endpoints**: Ensuring sensitive information is protected, apps are securely configured, and devices are safe from threats.
- **Identity and access management**: Managing who has access to your resources or services, and additionally implementing strong authentication methods like multi-factor authentication, privilege identity management, and Conditional Access policies.

Responsibility distribution across cloud service models

Depending on whether you are using SaaS, PaaS, IaaS, or managing an on-premises environment, the responsibilities shift:

- **SaaS**:
    - Microsoft handles almost everything, including applications, operating systems, and infrastructure.

- You are responsible for your data, devices, and identity management.
- **Example**: Office 365

- **PaaS**:
  - Microsoft manages the infrastructure and operating system.
  - You manage your applications, data, and identity controls.
  - **Example**: Azure App Services
- **IaaS**:
  - Microsoft takes care of the physical hardware and networking.
  - You are responsible for configuring the operating system, securing applications, and protecting data.
  - **Example**: Azure Virtual Machines
- **On-premises**:
  - Everything is on you, from managing the physical data centre to securing applications and data.

Following is the reference to Microsoft's definition of the shared responsibility model and the expectation of each service:

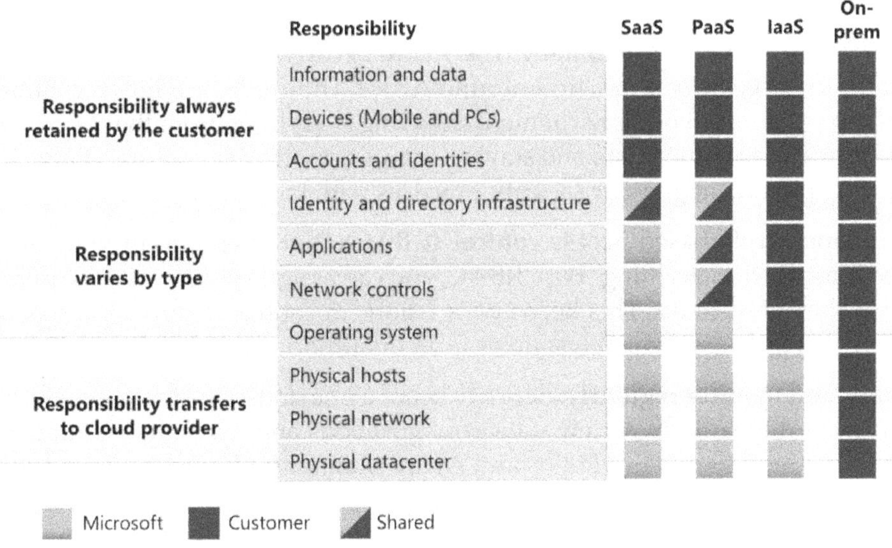

Figure 1.1: Microsoft division of responsibility

The image above illustrates the shared responsibility model for cloud services, which defines the division of responsibilities between the customer and the cloud provider. This model changes depending on the type of cloud service being used: SaaS, PaaS, IaaS, or on-premises.

The further you move toward SaaS, the more responsibilities are handled by the cloud provider, whereas in an on-premises setup, the customer takes full responsibility for everything from physical hardware to applications and data.

In a SaaS model, customers primarily focus on managing their data, devices, and user identities. The provider is responsible for everything else, including applications, operating systems, and physical infrastructure. PaaS increases flexibility, but clients are now responsible for their own apps and identity infrastructure. In IaaS, the cloud provider just administers the physical infrastructure, such as data centres and networks, leaving the client to manage everything else, including the operating system and network controls.

In an on-premises setup, the customer has complete power but must also take full responsibility for everything, including keeping the physical hardware secure, setting up the software, and making sure they follow the rules. The picture uses different shades of blue to show changes in duty, making it clear which tasks belong to the customer, the provider, or are shared between them. This chart helps you see how your duties change as you use different cloud services.

Shared responsibility in practice

To make the shared responsibility model work, it is important to understand your part and take real actions to keep your cloud environment safe. Microsoft takes care of the infrastructure, but you are responsible for using the tools and best practices to keep your data and apps safe.

Here is how to get started:

- **Use Azure Security Benchmark**: The Azure Security Benchmark is a getting started guide and lists the best practices around Azure. The guide provides recommendations to help you secure your environment, covering everything from the start, like securing identities to managing data and staying compliant with relevant standards. It is a great starting point to align your security practices with industry best practices.
- **Implement role-based access control (RBAC)**: Not everyone in your organization needs access to everything. With RBAC, you can assign specific roles to users based on what they need to do. This keeps permissions in control, reduces the risk of misuse, and helps protect sensitive resources from unauthorized and unwanted access.
- **Audit and monitor regularly**: Security is not a one-and-done thing—you need to stay on top of it. Regularly review your configurations and keep an eye out for anything unusual. Tools like Azure Policy and Azure Monitor make this easier by helping you track changes, identify risks, and fix issues before they turn into real problems.

Misconceptions and clarifications

Despite being seemingly straightforward, the shared responsibility model can lead to misunderstandings about who is responsible for what. Since these misunderstandings may result in security breaches, it is critical to resolve any ambiguity, as follows:

- One common belief is that Microsoft manages all cloud security, but this is not the case. While Microsoft oversees the physical and data centre security, you protect your data, apps, and access controls in Azure. If you overlook your side of the tale, you run the risk of leaving your environment open to possible hacks.

  For instance, a financial services firm misinterpreted its responsibility under IaaS and left an Azure Blob Storage container publicly accessible without encryption or access control. The exposure led to sensitive client data being leaked online, representing how ignoring your portion of the shared responsibility can result in serious reputational and regulatory consequences.

- Use products like Microsoft Defender for Cloud to help you prioritize your loopholes and close gaps. They point out possible weak places and offer suggestions for how to fix them. By stressing the particular areas that call for attention, these tools improve your general security and help you to prevent mistakes.

Cloud security posture management

Managing cloud security can be difficult, especially when you have limited time and knowledge and a complex environment to protect; this is where **cloud security posture management** (**CSPM**) can help. CSPM helps in the detection and management of issues such as vulnerabilities, compliance gaps, and misconfigurations. It is about equipping you with the tools and ways to properly handle security issues, not just about finding them. CSPM uses technologies in Azure, including Azure Policy to help you stay compliant and Microsoft Defender for Cloud to help you remain secure.

For example, consider a financial services organization preparing for an ISO 27001 compliance audit. Using Microsoft Defender for Cloud, the CSPM system detects a misconfigured virtual machine missing endpoint protection. Azure Policy flags a storage account lacking encryption at rest. These alerts are surfaced in the Secure Score dashboard, prioritized based on risk, and remediated before the scheduled audit. Compliance reports generated from Defender for Cloud provide auditors with real-time evidence of security posture, making the process smoother and more transparent.

Tools that make CSPM work in Azure

CSPM in Azure relies on a set of powerful tools designed to enhance security, enforce compliance, and detect misconfigurations. These tools provide continuous monitoring and automated remediation to help organizations maintain a strong security posture in their cloud environments. The following are the key tools that make CSPM effective in Azure:

- **Microsoft Defender for Cloud**: Defender for Cloud acts as your security control centre or security hub. It continuously checks your environment, finds potential risks (like unpatched systems or weak configurations), and gives you recommendations to fix them. It does not just tell you what is wrong; it provides actionable steps, so you know exactly what to do.

The following figure shows the homepage for Microsoft Defender for Cloud, giving an overview of the security posture and the state of the environment:

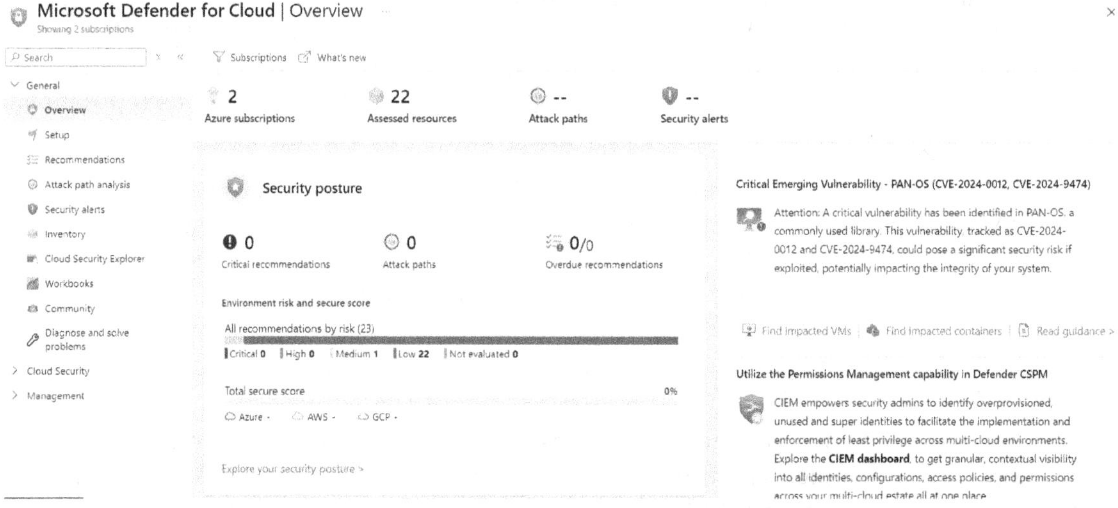

Figure 1.2: Defender for Cloud portal

- **Azure Policy**: Azure Policy, as shown in the following figure, automatically enforces rules such as requiring encryption for all storage accounts or blocking insecure configurations. With Azure Policy, you do not have to manually check every resource—it handles it for you, keeping things compliant and consistent.

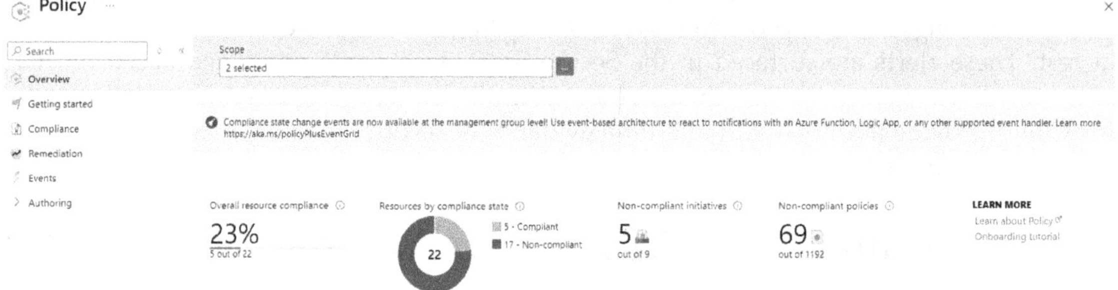

Figure 1.3: Azure Policy

Let us understand how CSPM helps you stay secure:

- **Continuous assessment**: As we know that security is never a set it and forget it thing—your cloud setup is always changing, and CSPM tools continuously monitor it. If someone accidentally opens up a sensitive port or configures permissions the wrong way, CSPM catches it right away, so you can fix it before it turns into a bigger problem.

- **Prioritizing risks**: Not all vulnerabilities are equal. CSPM allows you to prioritize the most serious issues, which could result in a data breach or substantial outage. Prioritizing what is most important allows you to make the greatest use of your time and resources.
- **Clear remediation steps**: Finding a problem is important, but understanding how to solve it is the key. CSPM gives you step-by-step directions for solving security issues, such as strengthening access controls, patching a vulnerability, or rectifying a misconfiguration. They make addressing security weaknesses less unpleasant and more manageable.

Let us understand where CSPM makes a difference:

- **Fixing misconfigurations**: Misconfigurations are one of the most common cloud security issues, like accidentally leaving a storage bucket exposed to the internet or giving overly broad permissions. CSPM tools highlight these problems so you can secure them before an attacker takes advantage.
- **Staying compliant**: If your business needs to follow regulations like GDPR, HIPAA, or ISO 27001, you can use CSPM to manage and monitor your resources. It checks your environment to make sure it follows the standards and makes audits easier by providing clear results that show everything meets the standards.
- **Managing hybrid and multi-cloud environments**: If you are using more than one cloud provider or combining on-premises and cloud systems, CSPM helps you maintain a consistent security posture across all platforms. No more juggling different tools or worrying about gaps—it gives you one clear view of everything.

Let us understand why CSPM is a must-have:

- **Centralized management**: CSPM gives you a centralized view of your entire environment, making it easy to see what is working, what is not, and where you need to act. It is like having a dashboard that shows you the complete picture of your cloud security.
- **Stay compliant without a hassle**: Compliance policies and regulations should not be complicated to maintain and operate. Using automated policies and built-in monitoring, CSPM makes it easy to remain compliant with regulations while focusing on your business.
- **Reduce risks before they become problems**: By identifying issues early and providing clear guidance on how to fix them, CSPM helps prevent incidents like data breaches or downtime. It is a proactive way to stay secure, not just reactive.

Zero Trust security model

Traditional security models operated under the assumption that everything inside the network perimeter could be trusted. However, with the rise of cloud adoption, remote work, and cyber threats, this approach is no longer effective. The Zero Trust security model focuses on a *never trust, always verify* strategy. This section explores the core principles of Zero Trust and how organizations can implement it to strengthen their security posture.

Understanding the Zero Trust security model

The old *castle-and-moat* method of cybersecurity, which trusts everything inside the network, does not work anymore because of advanced dangers and the mixed work settings we have today. Introducing the Zero Trust security model— a new way of thinking about security that does not automatically trust anyone or anything. Every request for entry must be checked and confirmed regularly.

Zero Trust is a security approach that assumes no one, whether inside or outside an organization, can be trusted by default. Every user and device must be verified before being granted access to systems and data. This means always checking and confirming who is trying to access what, instead of just trusting them once off.

Core principles

The Zero Trust security model is based on a simple idea: *Never trust, always check.* Unlike traditional models, Zero Trust works under the assumption that a breach could occur at any time, from any source—whether internal or external. It highlights the need to regularly check users, devices, and systems to make sure that only allowed people or devices can access resources.

This model is important today because many employees, workers, partners, and devices often join from outside the usual network boundaries in cloud-based settings. Zero Trust is a way to help your organization stay safe in today's changing environment.

Zero Trust is built around three guiding principles:

- **Verify explicitly**: In a Zero Trust framework, every access request is treated with suspicion. Authentication and authorization must happen for each request, using all available data points, such as:
  - User identity and role.
  - Device health (e.g., *is it managed and secure?*).
  - Geographic location (e.g., *is it in Australia?*).
  - The sensitivity of the resource being accessed.

  For example, if a person signs in from a new device or a different location, they may need to provide additional verification, like **Multi-factor authentication** (**MFA**). This ensures that access decisions are made in real-time and are not based on assumptions or past results.

- **Least privilege access**: Zero Trust means giving users and systems only the rights they need to do their jobs, nothing extra. This lowers the chances of someone misusing their rights, either by mistake or on purpose.
    - For example, a marketing team member should not have administrative rights to IT systems.
    - Temporary access can be given for certain tasks, but it will only allow limited access and for a limited time interval.

  By limiting access to the bare minimum, you significantly reduce the potential damage caused by a breach.
- **Assume breach**: A key idea of Zero Trust is to act as if attackers are already inside your system and have access to information. This idea creates the need for:
    - **Segmentation**: Breaking your network into smaller zones to limit how far an attacker can move laterally.
    - **Monitoring**: Continuously tracking activity across your environment to detect and respond to suspicious behaviour quickly.

  This proactive approach ensures that even if a breach occurs, its impact is minimized and it is detected faster.

Implementing Zero Trust in Azure

Using the Zero Trust security model in Azure involves utilizing Azure's tools and services to set up a security system that constantly checks who can access resources, keeps those resources safe, and finds threats in real time. Following is a full breakdown of how you can apply Zero Trust principles across your Azure environment:

- **Identity and access**: Identity is key to Zero Trust, because every contact with your system begins with verifying who you are. Entra ID offers many tools to protect and handle identities effectively:
    - **MFA**: MFA makes sure that even if someone gets your password, they still can not get into your account without another step, like a message on your phone, a text code, or a fingerprint scan. It lowers the chance of unauthorized entry or permissions.
    - **Conditional Access policies**: Conditional Access allows you to choose who can access your resources based on different situations. These policies look at things like who the user is, how healthy their gadget is, where they are, and how sensitive the data is that they are trying to access. Examples include:
        - Requiring MFA for access outside normal working hours.
        - Blocking login attempts from high-risk locations.

        - Allowing access only from devices that are compliant with your organization's policies, such as those with updated security patches.

    - **Privileged Identity Management (PIM)**: For accounts with administrative privileges, Azure AD PIM enforces just-in-time access. This ensures that elevated permissions are granted only when needed and automatically revoked after completing a task.

    - **Identity protection**: Identity protection uses AI to find and react to suspicious activities like strange login patterns, hacked accounts, and risky sign-ins.

- **Network security**: The Zero Trust strategy shows that depending on just one secure network is not an effective or the best method. Azure helps to protect your network by keeping resources separate and making it harder for threats to spread within the network.

    - **Azure Virtual Networks (VNets)**: VNets let you divide your network into smaller, separate areas. For example, you can keep production work separate from the testing segment. This way, if one is compromised, it would not impact the other environment.

    - **Azure Firewall**: Azure Firewall is a cloud-native stateful resource that controls inbound and outbound traffic based on the firewall policies. It helps enforce network and application control, ensuring that only allowed traffic flows in and out of your network.

    - **Network Security Groups (NSGs)**: NSGs offer fine-grained control over traffic at the subnet or virtual machine NIC level. NSGs can be used to block IP addresses or ports that are not required for your resources.

    - **Private Endpoint and ExpressRoute**: Private Endpoint and ExpressRoute ensure that the traffic remains within Microsoft or provider backbone, ensuring the data is not exposed over the public internet.

    - **Limit lateral movement**: In the event of a breach, attackers often try to move laterally to other parts of the network. Using Azure Bastion and **just-in-time** (**JIT**) access to limit such lateral movements can be restricted.

- **Data security**: Data security and information protection define Zero Trust as one of its main components. Azure provides solutions to ensure that your data is protected both at rest and in transit.

    - **Encryption**: Azure enables encryption for data at rest and in transit by default.

        - **At rest**: Use Azure Disk Encryption or Azure SQL **transparent data encryption** (**TDE**) to protect stored data.

        - **In transit**: Enforce HTTPS/TLS for all communications between applications, users, and APIs.

- o **Azure Key Vault**: You can store sensitive information like encryption keys, secrets, and certificates in Azure Key Vault, a secure, centralized location. Access to these keys can be tightly controlled and monitored.
- o **Access control for sensitive data**: Use Azure RBAC to restrict who can view or modify resources or data. For example, only specific roles should be able to download customer data from a database.
- o **Data loss prevention (DLP)**: Implement DLP policies in Microsoft Purview to prevent sensitive information leaks, like personal data or financial records, from being shared or sent outside your organization.

- **Application security**: Zero Trust's security is essential since criminals usually exploit the applications in the first place.

  Azure provides tools to efficiently monitor and protect applications:

  - o **Azure Web Application Firewall (WAF)**: WAF protects web applications from common vulnerabilities like SQL injection, **cross-site scripting** (**XSS**), and DDoS attacks. It acts as a filter, analyzing traffic before it reaches your applications.
  - o **Defender for App Service**: Azure Defender for Apps checks your applications for vulnerabilities, misconfigurations, or suspicious activity. It gives suggestions for improving the security of your application.
  - o **Secure development practices**: Using Azure DevOps or GitHub Advanced Security, include automatic scanning in your DevOps workflows together with safe coding techniques. Microsoft Defender for DevOps helps find and fix security issues during the development cycle.

- **Visibility and analytics**: Zero Trust stresses the importance of real-time information and the ability to quickly detect and respond to risks. The following analytics and monitoring tools are provided by Azure:

  - o **Microsoft Sentinel**: Sentinel is Azure's **Security information and event management** (**SIEM**) tool. It gathers, examines records, finds abnormalities, and responds automatically to threats. Like, Sentinel can automatically quarantine a compromised user account or block suspicious IP addresses when it is configured to do so.
  - o **Azure Monitor**: Azure Monitor provides visibility into the performance and security of your workload. Alerts can be set up for unusual behaviours, such as spikes in resource usage or unauthorized access attempts.
  - o **Log Analytics and threat intelligence**: Collect logs from different sources in order to have a single perspective of your environment. You can use built-in threat intelligence to recognize and react to attack patterns that are already known.

- **Proactive threat hunting**: Use tools like Azure Defender to actively hunt for vulnerabilities and threats before they are exploited. Proactive monitoring ensures that you are not just reacting to incidents but preventing them.

Zero Trust architecture example

Implementing the Zero Trust security model requires a well-structured architecture that enforces strict access controls, monitoring, and segmentation across all layers of an organization's IT environment. A Zero Trust architecture ensures that no user, device, or system is inherently trusted, reducing the risk of lateral movement in case of a breach. The following example illustrates how Zero Trust principles can be effectively applied to modern cloud and hybrid infrastructures.

Deploying Zero Trust

Figure 1.4 represents the Zero Trust security model, a modern approach to cybersecurity that ensures no user, device, or system is trusted by default. At its core is the principle of *never trust, always verify*, supported by continuous monitoring, authentication, and authorization. The central shield in the diagram symbolizes Zero Trust as the foundation of security, protecting all aspects of an organization's infrastructure, applications, data, network, endpoints, and users.

Each part around the shield shows an important area where Zero Trust concepts are used. For example, users are protected by identity verification methods like MFA and special access rules. At the same time, devices are checked to make sure they follow the necessary standards before being allowed entry. Data is kept safe using encryption and rules like DLP. The network is also divided into sections to stop risks from spreading. Applications and systems are regularly checked and strengthened to prevent weaknesses, using tools such as firewalls, web security, and tracking services.

The top layer focuses on the key elements of Zero Trust: seeing everything, automating processes, and coordinating actions. Visibility lets organizations see all activities happening in their systems in real-time. Automation helps simplify tasks such as handling incidents and ensuring compliance, which reduces mistakes made by people. Orchestration connects all the parts, making sure that security tools and rules work together effectively for overall safety. This flexible, step-by-step method helps organizations stay strong against changing dangers while keeping a firm grip on their digital spaces.

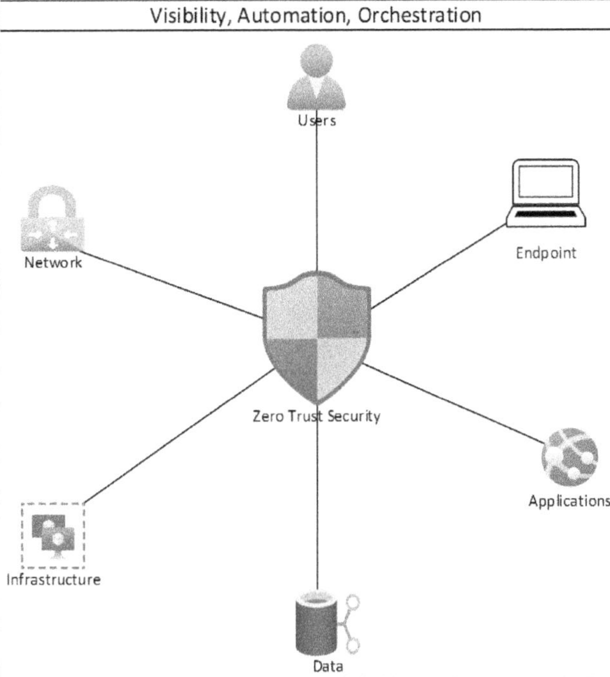

***Figure 1.4**: Components of Zero Trust*

Zero Trust principles

Figure 1.5 shows the three main ideas of the Zero Trust security model, a new approach to cybersecurity that protects organizations from changing threats. The concepts are verified explicitly, use least privilege access, and assume breach. These ideas work together to reduce weaknesses and improve security, in the following ways:

- **Verify**: Emphasizes the need to consistently check and confirm each entry request. Unlike traditional security models that depend on a fixed area of trust, Zero Trust needs to check all relevant information. This includes the user's identity, their position, the condition of their device, the context of their work, how the data is classified, and any unusual activities.
- **Use the least possible access**: Access is about giving users only the rights they need to do their jobs. By using methods like JIT and **just-enough-access** (**JEA**), organizations can provide limited and temporary access. Risk-based adaptive policies change access levels depending on things like where you are or the condition of your device. These steps protect data and help users stay productive, allowing them to work while reducing unnecessary risk.
- Finally, **assume breach** prepares ahead of time for the chance of a hack. This concept aims to reduce the harm of a breach by dividing access according to networks, users,

devices, and applications. It also includes encrypting all sessions from start to finish and using advanced analysis to identify threats, see security status, and strengthen defences. By accepting that breaches will happen, organizations can create systems to limit the damage and stop the spread of threats within the network.

These concepts create the basis for a Zero Trust model, helping organizations protect themselves from current cybersecurity threats. Zero Trust keeps your important data safe by constantly checking who can access it and getting ready for any security problems that might happen.

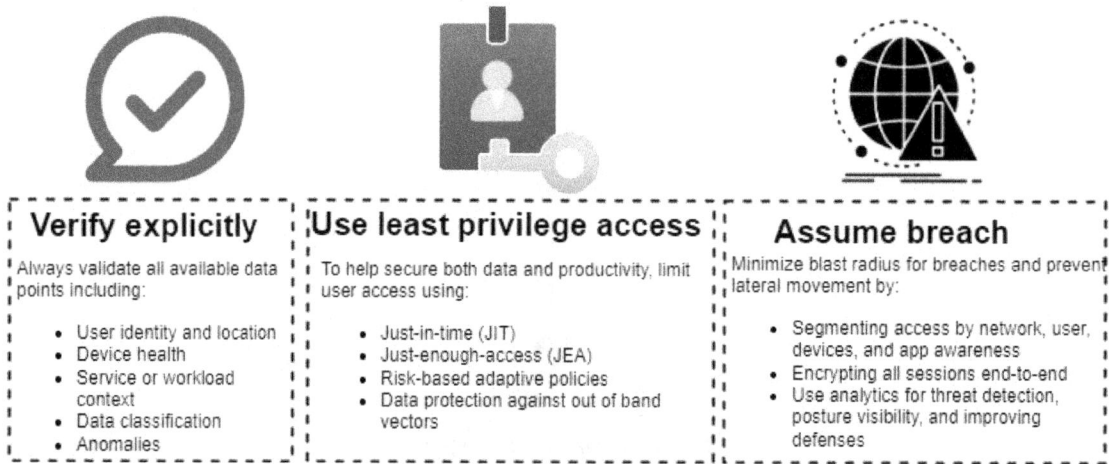

Verify explicitly
Always validate all available data points including:
User identity and location
Device health
Service or workload context
Data classification
Anomalies

Use least privilege access
To help secure both data and productivity, limit user access using:
Just-in-time (JIT)
Just-enough-access (JEA)
Risk-based adaptive policies
Data protection against out of band vectors

Assume breach
Minimize blast radius for breaches and prevent lateral movement by:
Segmenting access by network, user, devices, and app awareness
Encrypting all sessions end-to-end
Use analytics for threat detection, posture visibility, and improving defenses

***Figure 1.5**: Zero Trust principles*

Threat protection with Microsoft Defender for Cloud

Figure 1.6 shows Microsoft's various offerings, including SharePoint, Exchange, and Microsoft Teams, as essential components linked to the Entra ID tenant in the middle of the diagram. These services are absolutely vital since they include important corporate data, including files, emails, and chat records.

Using Microsoft Defender gives these services advanced threat detection, data protection, and compliance tools. The flawless integration guarantees that companies may centrally control access and security regulations, therefore lowering complexity and preserving strong defence systems against contemporary cyberattacks.

Under the Microsoft Entra ID umbrella, the whole methodology shown in the diagram emphasizes the synergy of on-site, cloud, and SaaS contexts. Organizations now have complete tools to monitor, protect, and respond to risks over their whole ecosystem. This guarantees a safe and efficient IT infrastructure that meets the needs of hybrid and cloud-native settings while handling important cybersecurity issues.

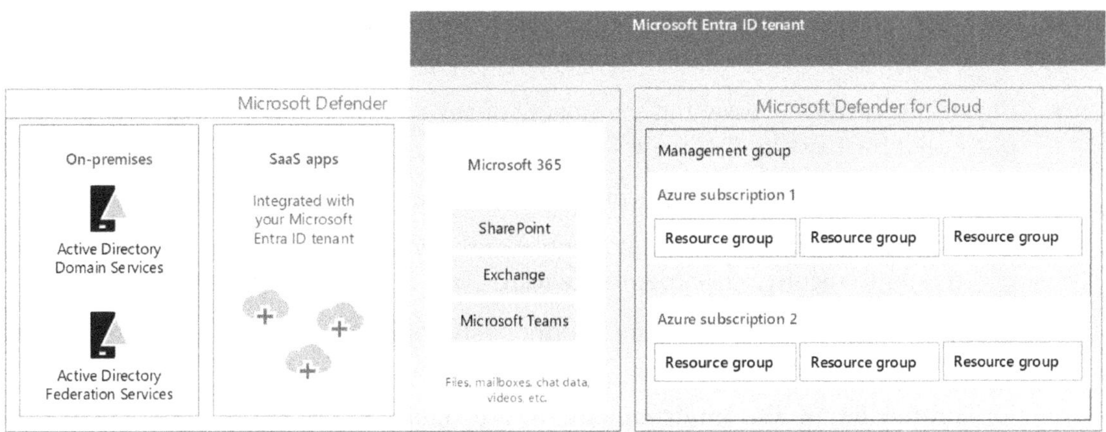

Figure 1.6: *Coverage for Microsoft Defender for Cloud*

Defense-in-depth

Layering security restrictions across several regions is another crucial tactic, even though Zero Trust stresses ensuring access at every stage. Defense-in-depth is useful in this situation.

Defense-in-depth is a comprehensive strategy that layers multiple security measures across all levels of an environment—physical, digital, and human. This redundancy ensures that if one layer fails, others are ready to block, detect, or mitigate the threat, giving organizations the best possible chance of protecting their assets.

Understanding the defense-in-depth security strategy

Defense-in-depth takes the approach of layering security controls throughout an organization's IT infrastructure, from the physical hardware in data centres to the data itself. The idea is simple but powerful: no system is perfect, and breaches are inevitable. This method guarantees that an attacker will encounter more defences even if they manage to get past one layer by implementing overlapping security measures.

This approach is not just about technology—it is also about processes and people. By combining tools, policies, and training, defense-in-depth creates a well-rounded security posture that adapts to modern challenges.

Layers of defense

A security strategy relies on multiple layers of defense to protect systems, data, and networks from evolving threats. Defence-in-depth ensures that if one layer is compromised, additional security measures are in place to detect, mitigate, and contain the impact. The following sections outline the key layers of defense that work together to provide comprehensive protection:

- **Physical security**: An essential component of any security solution is safeguarding the physical infrastructure that drives your systems.

  Azure employs the following techniques to maintain the security of its data centres:

  - **Controlled access**: Azure data centres are only accessible by permitted personnel, thanks to security checkpoints, keycards, and biometric verification.
  - **24x7 surveillance**: Areas are continuously monitored and prepared to prevent any unauthorized access.
  - **Protection of the environment**: Azure data centres are designed to handle unexpected events. If there is a fire, power outage, or natural disaster, they have backup power, temperature control, and fire safety systems to keep everything working well.
- **Identity and access management**: Following physical security, you should make sure your resources—including users and devices, only allowed people and systems may access them. Azure offers several tools to simplify and direct this process.
  - **Entra ID**: It is about verifying users, devices, and applications for access and permission. **Single sign-on** (**SSO**) lets people access different apps with just one login. MFA makes security stronger by asking for a second way to verify your identity.
  - **RBAC**: Not everyone needs access to everything. With RBAC, people get the right level of access based on their job. For example, a developer might be able to test configurations but would not have permission to make changes to live systems. This helps prevent mistakes and reduces security risks.
  - **PIM**: Important accounts, like those with admin rights, need extra security. PIM improves security by giving access only when it is needed and taking it away afterwards. It includes clearance processes and keeps track of all activities, showing how these accounts are used.
- **Network security**: Network security is all about preventing unauthorized access and controlling movement within your environment. Here is how different Azure resources can help keep your network secure:
  - **NSGs**: These act like virtual firewalls, managing inbound and outbound traffic at the subnet or VM level based on set rules.
  - **ASGs**: Make it easier to manage network rules by grouping VMs with similar requirements, ensuring only the right traffic flows between them.
  - **Azure Firewall**: A fully managed security service that inspects and filters traffic, blocks known malicious IPs, and enforces security policies.

  - **VNet peering**: Peering provides a secure connection between Azure VNets while keeping traffic private on Microsoft.

- **Application security**: Applications can serve as entry points for cybercriminals. Ensuring they are secure is critical to preventing exploits:

  - **Azure Application Gateway with WAF**: Protects web applications from common attacks, such as SQL injection, cross-site scripting, etc, by inspecting HTTP/S traffic.

  - **Defender for App Service**: Monitors Azure-hosted applications for vulnerabilities, misconfigurations, and suspicious activity.

- **Data security**: Usually, attackers' main aim is data. Azure presents several means of security for it:

  - Azure defaults encryption of data to guard it from illegal access, even in cases of interception.

  - Azure Key Vault is a safe place to keep passwords, certificates, and encryption keys, among other sensitive data. Access is logged and kept under control.

  - DLP is the identification and safeguarding of private information or financial records from inadvertent distribution or illegal access.

- **Monitoring and response**: The final layer is about detecting, responding and recovering from potential threats:

  - **Azure Monitor**: Tracks performance and logs activity across resources, helping detect anomalies.

  - **Microsoft Sentinel**: A powerful SIEM tool that detects threats in real time, helps investigate incidents, and automates responses to attacks.

  - **Defender for Cloud**: Continuously assesses your environment and provides recommendations to improve security.

Best practices

Using a defense-in-depth approach is about ensuring that the different levels work efficiently. Following these recommended practices will help companies to maximize protection and reduce vulnerabilities:

- **Using a layered method**: Depending on one security mechanism is similar to stuffing all your eggs into one basket—should it fail, your whole system is vulnerable. Rather, mix several layers of protection over several locations, including:

  - Strong authentication methods, including MFA and Conditional Access policies, help to stop illegal log-in access.

  - Azure Firewall, NSGs, and ASGs help to control unneeded traffic.
  - Deploy Azure Defender for App Service and WAF to guard against cyberattacks for your apps.
  - **Data security**: Store credentials safely in Azure Key Vault after encrypting confidential data.

  Each one of these layers enhances the others so that, should one security control fail, others are in place to identify, stop, or lessen the effects of an attack.

- **Regularly test security**: Though attackers are continually changing their strategies, no security solution is flawless. Organizations must so aggressively seek flaws before cybercrime strikes. In this manner:
  - Ethical hackers model real-world assaults to expose security flaws in systems, networks, and identity controls.
  - Cyber teams assess the defences against a simulated attack by posing as hackers in red team exercises.
  - Regular review of access limitations, security settings, and compliance reports lets one identify risks before they become cause for concern.

  By constantly testing and strengthening security policies, companies can keep ahead of cyber attacks.

- **Leverage automation**: Cyberattacks can happen anytime, so security teams need to respond quickly and efficiently. Instead of handling everything manually, organizations can use Azure's automation tools to streamline daily security operations, as follows:
  - **Azure Automation**: Handles routine tasks like patch management, security updates, and compliance enforcement without manual intervention.
  - **Logic Apps**: Automates the workflows to trigger security alerts, like creating incidents, and taking actions on the threats that are detected.
  - **Microsoft Sentinel playbooks**: Investigates and responds to threats in real time, helping security teams focus on critical issues.

  Automation not only speeds up response times but also minimizes human error, ensuring security processes run consistently.

- **Educate employees**: Regardless of how sophisticated your security measures are, human error remains one of the most serious threats in cybersecurity. Employees are frequently victims of phishing scams, weak passwords, and data leaks.

  Technology alone can not stop cyber threats—people play a key role in keeping systems secure. That is why ongoing security awareness training is essential, as follows:

- **Phishing awareness training**: In order to prevent scams, train personnel to identify and report any emails, links, or attachments that seem suspicious.
- **Strong password policies**: Encourage the use of passphrases or password managers to reduce the risk of compromised accounts.
- **Secure device use**: Train staff how to securely use work devices, such as enabling encryption and avoiding public Wi-Fi for sensitive tasks.

Regular training sessions, simulated phishing attacks, and internal security drills can turn employees into a strong first line of defence rather than a security liability.

Advantages of defense-in-depth

Defense-in-depth uses several layers of protection to protect various parts of your IT systems. This means that if one security measure does not work, then other measures will be ready to help prevent and lessen the effect of the attack.

Here is why this approach works well:

- **Redundancy**: Redundancy is a key benefit of defence-in-depth. This helps establish several levels of protection such that even in the event of a system failure, the others can continue to function.

  Consider it like a medieval castle: even if an enemy penetrates the exterior walls, there are guard towers, an inner fortress, and a trench to slow them down. In cybersecurity, if a hacker gets through one security layer, there should be more layers to keep resources safe.

  For example:

  - If someone's login details are stolen, they still can not access the system if MFA is turned on because they need a second form of verification.
  - If a network firewall is breached, internal segmentation through NSGs and Azure Firewall prevents the attacker from moving freely inside the network.
  - If an endpoint is infected with malware, Defender for Endpoint can detect and isolate the affected device before it spreads.

  When several security mechanisms are in place, a single security lapse only activates the next line of defence, preventing a full-scale intrusion.

- **Comprehensive protection**: Cybercriminals use different methods like phishing, malware, social engineering, and brute-force tactics to attack organizations. Defense-in-depth means your security looks at all possible threats instead of just one area.

  For instance:

  - **Identity protection**: Azure Entra ID helps users log in safely, and PIM stops people from gaining higher access without permission.

- **Network security**: Azure Firewall, NSGs, and VPNs help keep the network safe by managing network security and restricting sources that are not whitelisted or required.
- **Application security**: WAF helps to protect web applications from common attacks such as SQL injection and cross-site scripting.
- **Data security**: Encryption ensures that data remains unreadable to unauthorized users, even if they manage to access it. Only those with the correct decryption keys can unlock and interpret the information, making it an essential safeguard against data breaches and unauthorized access.
- **Monitoring and response**: Microsoft Sentinel helps to identify threats in real-time and can respond automatically using its built-in features, making Azure always secure and reliable. It keeps an eye on information from various sources to spot potential risks as they occur.

This method uses different layers of protection, preventing any one type of attack from completely crippling the system.

- **Scalability**: Security requires evolution throughout time. Organizations' security plans have to change as they grow, embrace cloud services, and bring new technology into use. Defense-in-depth is scalable and adaptable enough for companies of various kinds and sectors.

  Here is how defense-in-depth helps with scalability:

  - **Cloud-ready security**: Whether your organization is on-premises, hybrid, or fully in the cloud, security layers can be adjusted accordingly. Azure services like Defender for Cloud provide security recommendations that scale with your environment.
  - **Automated security management**: Tools like Microsoft Sentinel use AI to continuously adapt to emerging threats, so your security posture improves as your business grows.
  - **Access controls**: Azure RBAC ensures that all employees or cloud users have the required level of access without being able to view information that is not relevant to them.
  - **Performance optimization**: Security measures can be fine-tuned based on risk levels or the risk appetite of an organization. For example, a small business might rely on NSGs for traffic filtering, whereas a large enterprise with high security needs could implement Azure Firewall Premium for advanced threat protection.

  Since defense-in-depth is modular, organizations can start with basic security layers and scale up as they grow, ensuring they remain secure without overspending on unnecessary protections.

- **Comprehensive protection**: Cybercriminals do not stick to one method; instead, they use all kinds of methods to infiltrate organizations, from phishing and malware to brute-force attacks and social engineering. That is why focusing on just one area of security is not enough. A defence-in-depth strategy ensures you are covered across all fronts, protecting every possible entry point and making it much harder for attackers to succeed.

  Here is how it works:

  - **Identity protection**: Tools like Entra ID help ensure that users log in securely, with features like MFA and SSO. For sensitive accounts, PIM provides extra safeguards by requiring temporary, just-in-time access, so users do not have more permissions than they need.
  - **Network security**: Network resources like Azure Firewall, ASG, and NSGs act as gatekeepers, managing traffic and blocking untrusted sources. They make it much harder for attackers to move through your network, even if they manage to get into one endpoint.
  - **Application security**: Web apps are a popular target for attackers. Tools like WAF protect against threats such as SQL injection and CSS. On the other hand, Azure Defender for App keeps an eye out for any strange activity.
  - **Data security**: Encryption protects your data by making it unreadable to anyone who does not have the encryption keys. Keys, certificates, passwords, etc, are safely kept in Azure Key Vault, protecting critical information from being accessed by unauthorized people.
  - **Monitoring and response**: Tools like Microsoft Sentinel can help you stay on top of threats. Sentinel can detect and respond automatically to prevent threats from spreading by collecting data from all Azure resources.

  By combining these security measures, you can build a security system that is both comprehensive and resilient. To break through, attackers would have to overcome a series of huddles, and each layer is designed to detect, slow down, or completely stop them.

- **Scalability**: A defense-in-depth strategy has one advantage: it allows your company to scale. Business security needs change with time as companies grow, adopt new technologies, and deal with fresh risks. Designed to react to these changes, defense-in-depth provides security for companies of all kinds and degrees of complexity.

  For example, if your organization begins in an on-premises environment and then migrates to the cloud, the layers of security can adapt to the new infrastructure. Tools such as Azure Defender for Cloud and Microsoft Sentinel automatically change to monitor and defend growing resources, ensuring that your security architecture keeps up with them.

Scalability also requires tailoring security to the amount of risk and size of your activities. A small firm may employ simple NSGs for network security, whereas a larger enterprise may use advanced solutions such as Azure Firewall Premium to provide higher-level protection. Defense-in-depth's modular strategy enables organizations to begin with key layers and build on them as their demands and dangers evolve, delivering constant, dependable protection regardless of how vast or complicated their environments become.

Conclusion

It is essential to stay ahead of risks and build security into daily tasks rather than check boxes or use the newest tools for cloud security. This part talked about how the threat landscape is constantly changing, what CSPM is for, and how the Zero Trust framework helps businesses take a more proactive and cautious approach to security. We also talked about the shared responsibility model, which makes it clear that both users and providers need to work together to keep the cloud safe.

Protection can not just be set up once and then forgotten about. It is an ongoing process that needs to be reviewed, updated, and made better all the time. Tools like Microsoft Defender for Cloud and Azure Policy can be helpful, but our actions and habits are what really make security better.

In the next chapter, *Securing Identity and Access*, we will explore identity management, authentication mechanisms, and access control strategies. You will learn how to protect user accounts, enforce least privilege access, and strengthen security with tools like Microsoft Entra ID and Conditional Access policies.

Join our Discord space

Join our Discord workspace for latest updates, offers, tech happenings around the world, new releases, and sessions with the authors:

https://discord.bpbonline.com

CHAPTER 2
Securing Identity and Access

Introduction

In this chapter, you will learn skills to master securing Azure identity and access solutions. This will be the first chapter to build on the foundation knowledge of the security introduction of *Chapter 1, Introduction to Azure Security*. You will start by understanding the core concepts of Authentication and Authorization, and then you will be introduced to Entra ID as Microsoft's cloud-based **identity and access management** (**IAM**) solution. Then you will learn about identity Secure Score, tenant security, as well as the different identity types and their protection.

Structure

This chapter contains the following topics:

- Introduction to Entra ID
- Microsoft Entra ID authentication
- Microsoft Entra ID authorisation
- Microsoft Entra ID Secure Score
- Microsoft Entra ID tenant security
- Microsoft Entra ID identities and protection

- Microsoft Entra ID secure application access
- Enhancing application security with Microsoft Entra ID

Objectives

This chapter aims to provide readers with comprehensive skills and knowledge for effectively securing identity and access solutions within Microsoft Entra ID. Readers will understand essential concepts of authentication and authorization, master best practices for identity management, learn to utilize security features such as MFA and Conditional Access, and enhance security posture using Microsoft Entra ID Secure Score and Tenant Security tools.

Introduction to Entra ID

Modern digital environments are increasingly secured by IAM. Protecting organisational data and resources from unauthorised use depends on making sure the correct people have suitable access. Designed especially to meet these needs, Microsoft Entra ID provides complete IAM solutions.

Overview of Entra ID

Entra ID is a powerful tool for managing IAM in Azure, but *why is identity security important?* Nowadays, compromised credentials are one of the most common attack vectors. In this section, we will identify the backbone of security strategies and why protecting IAM is important.

Originally called **Azure Active Directory** (**Azure AD**), Microsoft Entra ID is a complete IAM solution meant to help companies control access to their resources across cloud and hybrid environments. The requirement for a centralised and intelligent identity management solution has become more apparent as companies embrace cloud-first approaches. Entra ID offers advanced identity administration, strong authorisation systems, and flawless authentication, forming the backbone of identity security. It guarantees safe access to applications and services for employees, partners, and external users, hence stopping unwanted access. Entra ID streamlines identity management throughout a large ecosystem by connecting thousands of outside apps, lowering friction for end users and internal users.

Following is the homepage for Entra ID showing overall status with the number of users, groups, applications, and devices enrolled into Entra ID:

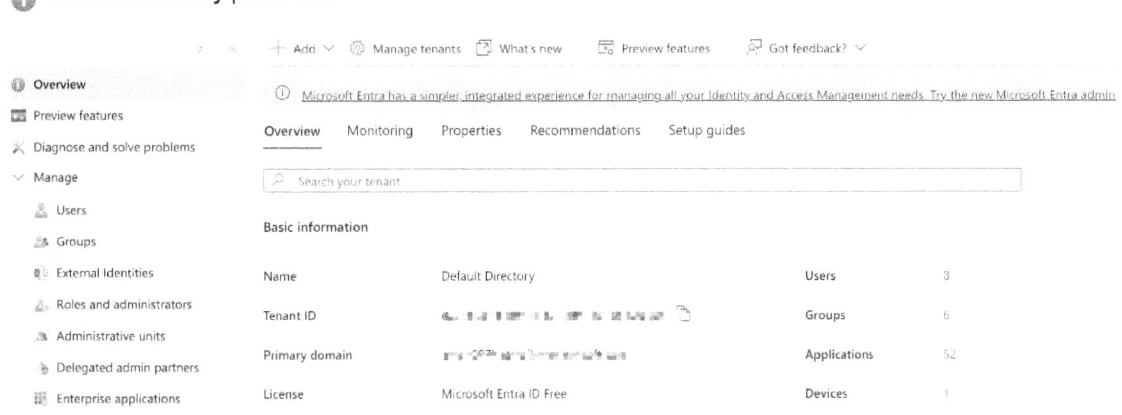

Figure 2.1: Entra ID home page

Strong security architecture distinguishes Entra ID, including MFA, Conditional Access policies, and adaptive risk-based authentication. Implementing dynamic access limits depending on user behaviour, device compliance, and location, these features help organisations reduce risks connected with compromised credentials and phishing attempts. The SSO feature also simplifies login across applications, therefore lowering passwords and increasing output. Entra ID provides PIM, allowing companies to manage sensitive data with fine-grained control over access to critical systems and resources, guaranteeing that elevated permissions are enabled only when needed.

Entra ID also helps to identify irregularities and possible risks, therefore offering proactive security insights. The technology also enables hybrid identity situations, which let organisations expand their on-site Active Directory to the cloud, therefore guaranteeing flawless identity synchronisation. Microsoft Entra ID provides a scalable, intelligent, and safe identity management solution fit for the changing digital environment, whether handling internal IDs or partner access.

Importance of identity in security

Identity forms the basis of security in the digital environment. Maintaining system security starts with confirming who asks for access, whether for sensitive data, business networks, or cloud apps. Strong identity management guarantees that only the correct people, employees, partners, or customers have access to the correct resources at the required time, therefore helping to prevent unwanted access. Security of identity is a significant concern for companies of all kinds since weak or poorly Managed Identities might cause data leaks, breaches, and compliance violations. It is helpful in the following ways:

- **Protection against unauthorised access**: Identity is the first line of defence against cyber threats and unauthorised access. Limiting access to important systems, data, and apps helps one stop illegal access that is capable of compromising systems or causing data breaches. By lowering reliance on passwords, usually the weakest link, strong authentication techniques such as MFA, RBAC, and passwordless authentication improve security. Attackers can use compromised credentials to move laterally within an organisation without appropriate identity protection, causing significant financial and reputational damage.

- **Compliance with regulatory guidelines:** Many industries are subject to strict compliance regulations that mandate proper identity management to protect sensitive data. To reduce security risks, frameworks including GDPR, HIPAA, and SOC 2 demand companies to use least privilege access, keep audit records, and apply safe authentication systems. Ignoring these regulations could lead to significant penalties and judicial actions. Strong identity management helps companies not only guard their data but also show compliance with auditors, authorities, and consumers, so it guarantees confidence and responsibility.
- **Zero Trust principles**: Modern security architecture known as Zero Trust states that, even if resources are inside the company network, none of the users or devices should be trusted automatically. Zero Trust grants access dynamically by constant identity verification and risk-based authentication, therefore replacing conventional perimeter defences and having Conditional Access rules, device compliance checks, and PIM, which guarantees users only have the access they need when they need it. Organisations can reduce attack surfaces, stop lateral movement by attackers, and improve general cybersecurity resilience by first ensuring identities at the core.

Key features of Entra ID

Key features of Entra ID are as follows:

- **Centralised identity management**: Microsoft Entra ID allows organisations to handle user IDs across Azure, Microsoft 365, and hundreds of external apps from one interface by providing a consistent identity and access management solution. This centralised approach ensures that staff, partners, and outside users have the necessary access without complications, thereby cutting administrative overhead and simplifying user provisioning and de-provisioning, and so reducing administrative overhead.

  Consolidating identity management helps companies implement standard security regulations throughout their IT environment.

  Using RBAC, admins can specify exact rights for users, guaranteeing only access to the resources necessary for their positions. Self-service features also let users reset passwords or seek access to programmes, therefore lightening IT demand and increasing efficiency. Entra ID also connects with well-known outside SaaS solutions, which help companies secure and simplify access across their company environment.
- **MFA**: Passwords alone are insufficient to protect against cyberattacks. MFA provides an additional layer of security by requiring users to verify their identity using a different factor, such as a notification from a mobile app, a code sent by SMS, or

biometric authentication. Even if a password is hacked, MFA decreases the chances of unauthorised access. Entra ID guarantees improved security without interfering with production by making MFA policies for all users.

Additionally, providing adaptive MFA, which changes authentication criteria depending on risk, Microsoft Entra ID also, when a user tries to log in from a trusted device or location, for example, they might not be prompted for MFA; on the other hand, an unknown device or high-risk login sets further verification actions. This sync between security and user experience lets businesses minimise disruptions and increase defences. Entra ID also supports passwordless authentication methods, including Windows Hello and **Fast Identity Online 2** (**FIDO2**) security keys, therefore improving security by avoiding the need for conventional passwords.

For example, if a user signs in from their corporate laptop on a known Wi-Fi network, they might bypass MFA. However, if they attempt access from a new device in a different country, adaptive MFA will challenge them with biometric verification or a one-time code.

- **Conditional Access**: Organisations can use Conditional Access, allowing access to systems based on real-time risk considerations, either granting or denying access. Conditional Access assesses parameters such as user location, device compliance, application sensitivity, and login behaviour before allowing access, therefore substituting a one-size-fits-all security strategy. This ensures that high-risk logins, such as those from untrusted devices or unknown locations, trigger MFA or are banned completely.

  Along with Microsoft Defender for Identity, Conditional Access offers real-time analysis of suspicious login attempts. Conditional Access can instantly reject access or force extra authentication requirements if there are attempts to log in using stolen credentials from an unexpected location. Session restrictions let companies further prevent people from downloading private information using public networks or unmanaged devices. These policies help companies guarantee workers can operate securely from anywhere and greatly lower the risk of credential-based assaults.

- **Integration with on-premises directories:** Entra ID provides a flawless connection with on-site systems for companies still depending on **Active Directory** (**AD**). By using Entra ID connect, companies can expand their current AD to the cloud, allowing consumers to access cloud applications with their current credentials. This hybrid identity model guarantees seamless authentication experiences, lowers administrative work, and lets companies quickly move to a cloud-first identity strategy without changing older systems.

  Entra ID enables hybrid join and pass-through authentication, enabling companies to retain on-site authentication systems while progressively implementing cloud-based security controls. Also, organisations can guarantee safe sign-ins across cloud and on-site environments using federated authentication and **password hash synchronising**

(**PHS**). These capabilities guarantee compliance and security in a hybrid IT environment and help companies modernise their identity infrastructure at their own speed.

Microsoft Entra ID authentication

Authentication is the key part of identity security, verifying user identities and ensuring that access to organizational resources is granted only to legitimate users. Microsoft Entra ID offers multiple authentication mechanisms to prevent credential theft and unauthorized access attempts, thereby strengthening the overall security posture.

Understanding authorisation

The first line of protection against cyberattacks with Microsoft Entra ID is authentication, which lets organisations guard against credential theft, illegal access, and identity-based assaults. Entra ID provides several authentication techniques, from conventional password-based authentication to current passwordless solutions, to satisfy the various security needs of companies. By lowering reliance on passwords, which remain a significant target for attackers, these systems not only increase security but also enhance user experience.

Safe and flexible authentication techniques are more critical than ever when organisations choose hybrid and cloud environments. Microsoft Entra ID helps companies apply regulatory standards and authentication policies required for their risk profiles. This lets organisations enforce stricter authentication for high-risk sign-ins and offers a seamless experience for trusted users, supporting risk-based Conditional Access. The main authentication systems accessible in Entra ID are listed as follows, together with how they enable companies to have access to vital resources:

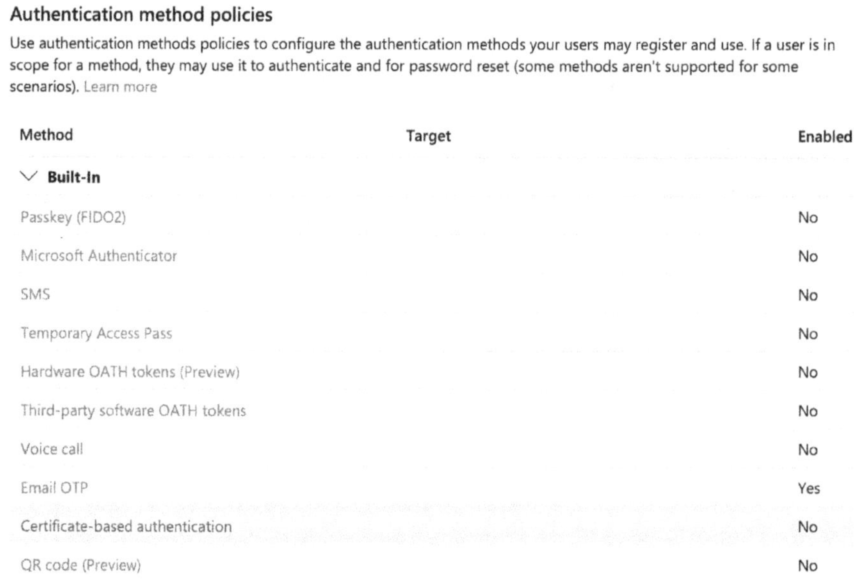

Authentication method policies

Use authentication methods policies to configure the authentication methods your users may register and use. If a user is in scope for a method, they may use it to authenticate and for password reset (some methods aren't supported for some scenarios). Learn more

Method	Target	Enabled
Built-In		
Passkey (FIDO2)		No
Microsoft Authenticator		No
SMS		No
Temporary Access Pass		No
Hardware OATH tokens (Preview)		No
Third-party software OATH tokens		No
Voice call		No
Email OTP		Yes
Certificate-based authentication		No
QR code (Preview)		No

Figure 2.2: *Entra ID portal—Authentication methods*

- **Password-based authentication**: Password authentication has long been the most commonly used technique. Users utilising password-based authentication validate their identity by entering a unique combination of a username and password. Although this approach is simple, it is also most susceptible to attacks, including:
  - o Attackers utilise phishing, that is, false emails or login pages, to get victims to divulge their passwords.
  - o Automated tools use brute force attacks; that is, they try many combinations to guess passwords.
  - o Attackers get illegal access using previously disclosed passwords from other websites.
  - o Keylogging and social engineering allow cybercriminals to collect passwords using malware or manipulative techniques.

  Many companies still depend on password-based authentication for legacy applications, even with its weaknesses. With password restrictions, **self-service password reset** (**SSPR**), and password protection solutions, Microsoft Entra ID helps lower risks. These tools stop users from choosing readily guessable credentials, impose complex password constraints, and find leaked passwords. But in today's cyber world, depending only on passwords is insufficient, so other authentication layers are essential.

- **MFA**: MFA adds a further verification step beyond passwords, strengthening security and allowing users to authenticate their identity using several authentication ways. These elements fit into three groups:
  - o **Something you know**: Passwords, security questions, etc.
  - o **Something you own**: Smart card, security token, mobile phone, etc.
  - o **Something you are**: Biometric data, including facial recognition and fingerprints.

  MFA helps companies greatly lower the danger of weak or stolen passwords, allowing unwanted access. An attacker cannot proceed without the second authentication factor, even if they obtain access to a user's credentials. Microsoft Entra ID supports several MFA techniques, among which are:
  - o Users of the Microsoft Authenticator App can create a **one-time password** (**OTP**) or get a push alert to confirm their identity.
  - o Emails or SMS-based OTPs send a temporary code to the registered phone number or email address.
  - o Hardware security tokens are physical objects that create safe OTPs for authentication.
  - o Windows Hello with fingerprint authentication for safe sign-in and biometric verification.

Adaptive MFA dynamically enforces MFA depending on login location, device compliance, and unexpected behaviour, thereby intelligently assessing login risks. For instance, a sign-in from a trusted device might not cause MFA, whereas a login attempt from a foreign nation calls for more verification. This method minimises authentication difficulty by balancing security with user ease, therefore stopping unwanted access.

- **Authentication without passwords**: Passwordless authentication has become popular as organisations search for better user experiences and more robust security substitutes for more conventional password-based approaches. Passwordless authentication completely removes passwords, therefore lowering the phishing, credential stuffing, and brute force attack risk. Entra ID provides safe and frictionless sign-in choices instead of asking users to recall and enter a password:
    - Users using Windows Hello for Business authenticate using a PIN connected to a particular device or biometrics, facial recognition, or fingerprint scanning. This approach guarantees credentials never leave the user's device, therefore improving security.
    - Hardware-based authentication using USB, NFC, or Bluetooth security keys, FIDO2 Security Keys. These phishing-resistant keys give consumers a safe and practical approach to log in.
    - **Microsoft Authenticator app (Passwordless Mode)**: Users confirm login requests using their mobile devices using push notifications or biometrics rather than typing a password.

    Passwordless authentication dramatically enhances IT efficiency, user experience, and security. It lowers IT support expenses connected to password management by removing the risks connected to resets, password leaks, and reusing. Furthermore, it offers quicker and more practical ways to sign in, which increases staff efficiency while preserving high degrees of security.

    Following are the options for various authentication methods available in Entra ID:

+ New authentication strength   Refresh

Authentication strengths determine the combination of authentication methods that can be used.
Learn more

Type: All   Authentication methods: All   Reset filters

Authentication strength	Type	Authentication methods	Conditional access policies
Multifactor authentication	Built-in	Windows Hello For Business / Platform Credential ...	Not configured in any policy yet
Passwordless MFA	Built-in	Windows Hello For Business / Platform Credential ...	Not configured in any policy yet
Phishing-resistant MFA	Built-in	Windows Hello For Business / Platform Credential ...	Not configured in any policy yet

Figure 2.3: *Entra ID portal: Authentication strengths*

Comparison of password-based vs. passwordless authentication

Take a look at the following table to understand the comparison:

Feature	Password-based	Passwordless
Susceptible to phishing	High	Very low
User convenience	Moderate (must remember passwords)	High (biometric or device-based auth)
Support overhead	High (resets, lockouts)	Low (minimal IT tickets)
Credential reuse risk	High	None
Authentication speed	Medium	Fast
Regulatory compliance support	Partial	Strong (FIDO2, MFA enforced)

***Table 2.1**: Password-based vs. passwordless authentication*

Authentication flows

Microsoft Entra ID defines how users and applications securely Access resources depending on their interaction type and security rules. Multiple authentication techniques handle diverse access scenarios, therefore ensuring usability and security. When a user connects to an automated service, an application, or the Azure Portal, Entra ID provides several authentication methods to fit security and regulatory criteria.

Three methods to categorise these authentication flows are interactive, non-interactive, and Conditional Access integration:

- **Interactive authentication**: This is usually used when a user personally registers into an application or service; interactive authentication is the most often used mechanism. Direct user input is required, including login and password input, followed by MFA sign-in request approval or a passwordless authentication solution like Windows Hello or a FIDO2 security key. Cloud apps, including Microsoft 365, Azure Portal, Teams, and other SaaS apps, are accessible only to authorised users.

  Interactive authentication with Entra ID is distinguished mainly by SSO, which lets users authenticate once and access different applications without re-entering credentials. Entra ID provides federated authentication via connectivity with outside identity providers, including **Active Directory Federation Services** (**AD FS**), *Google*, and social identity providers, for smooth authentication. Adaptive risk-based authentication dynamically changes authentication requirements based on login conditions, user location, device trust, and behavioural anomalies.

- **Non-interactive verification**: Non-interactive authentication is used in automated processes, background services, and system-to-system authentication. Applications, service accounts, and APIs can authenticate without human involvement, ensuring safe and ongoing access to cloud resources.

  Microsoft Entra ID implements non-interactive authentication in the following ways:

  - **Service-to-service authentication**: An application authenticates itself using a certificate or client secret rather than a password using Client Credential flow, usually, in situations like backend API integrations, Azure Functions, and Logic Apps.
  - **Managed Identities**: Azure services can authenticate to other Azure resources, e.g., Azure Key Vault and Azure SQL, without maintaining credentials. This eliminates the need to manage service account passwords or secrets.
  - **Refresh token**: Refresh tokens allow applications to maintain authenticated sessions without using regular logins, hence improving security and performance for long-running background processes. Minimising credential exposure, reducing password dependency, and minimising human involvement in authentication processes.

- **Conditional Access integration**: Integrated with authentication flows, Conditional Access is a tool that enforces context-aware access controls. Conditional Access automatically changes authentication requirements depending on risk signals like user location, device compliance, login behaviour, and session risk, substituting consistent security measures for all users.

  Critical situations where Conditional Access improves authentication:

  - Conditional Access can prevent authentication or demand MFA if a login effort starts from an unknown location or a dangerous IP.
  - Organisations can implement device regulations calling for users to sign in from compliant managed devices before using corporate resources.
  - High-risk actions like administrative-level sign-ins can be gated with extra authentication stages or JIT privileged access controls applied using PIM.
  - Conditional Access policies can limit session lengths, therefore guaranteeing that authenticated sessions automatically cease after a certain period, and so lowering the danger of unwanted persistent access.

The following figure shows the Conditional Access homepage where users or admins can create new policies ot view the existing ones. This also provides a getting started guide for CA Policies, as shown in the following figure:

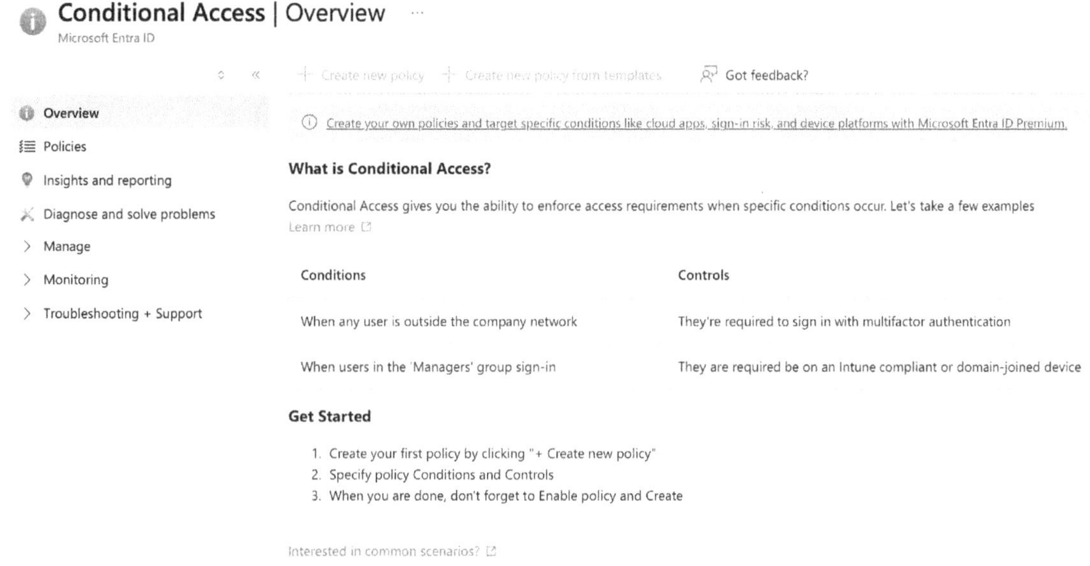

***Figure 2.4**: Conditional Access portal*

Microsoft Entra ID guarantees adaptive, risk-based security by combining Conditional Access with authentication flows, preserving a flawless user experience. Organisations can lower authentication friction for low-risk users and, if necessary, introduce strict verification procedures.

Implementing authentication best practices

The cybersecurity strategy of every organisation primarily focuses on authentication security. Companies have strict authentication policies since identity-based threats keep growing to protect user accounts, apps, and private data. Microsoft Entra ID presents a powerful IAM infrastructure, therefore optimising security and assuring a perfect user experience, which depends on best practices being followed. Tracking authentication logs, enforcing MFA, and passwordless authentication enable significantly increased identity security and reduce the risk of unauthorised access.

Here are the best practices:

- **Enforce MFA for all users**: Since MFA offers an additional verification step beyond simply a password, it is among the most successful means of preventing unwanted access. MFA guarantees that an attacker cannot access without another authentication element, even if they compromise a user's password. According to a Microsoft study, allowing MFA will stop over 99% of identity-related threats, making it a necessary security tool for every company.
    - MFA should be required of all users, including admins, staff, and outside partners.
    - Using security keys or biometrics, enforce more robust MFA rules for privileged accounts, including executives and IT managers.

- Use Windows Hello for Business, FIDO2 security keys, or Microsoft Authenticator push notifications, phishing-resistant MFA techniques.
- Use Conditional Access to provide risk-based MFA, triggering MFA only for high-risk sign-ins, that is, from untrusted devices or unknown locations, to lower user friction.
- Educate users on MFA phishing, including push notification fatigue assaults, in which attackers bombard approved users with approval requests until they unintentionally accept one.

Making MFA required on all accounts can help companies greatly lower the possibility of illegal access, therefore protecting important systems against credential-based assaults.

MFA home page, shown as follows, can be used to configure various options that can be enforced for the users. This allows a step-wise configuration of options, thereby ensuring security and compliance, as shown in the following figure:

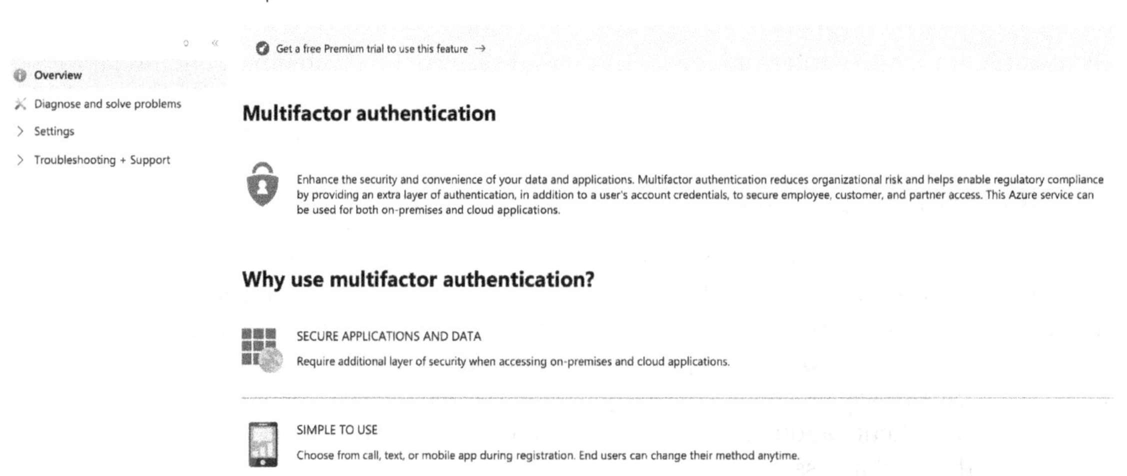

Multifactor authentication | Overview
Get a free Premium trial to use this feature →
Overview
Diagnose and solve problems
Settings
Troubleshooting + Support
Multifactor authentication
Enhance the security and convenience of your data and applications. Multifactor authentication reduces organizational risk and helps enable regulatory compliance by providing an extra layer of authentication, in addition to a user's account credentials, to secure employee, customer, and partner access. This Azure service can be used for both on-premises and cloud applications.
Why use multifactor authentication?
SECURE APPLICATIONS AND DATA
Require additional layer of security when accessing on-premises and cloud applications.
SIMPLE TO USE
Choose from call, text, or mobile app during registration. End users can change their method anytime.

Figure 2.5: MFA configuration page

- **Use passwordless authentication wherever possible**: Password-based authentication is still one of the greatest security flaws in business contexts. Cybercriminals primarily target weak, used, or stolen passwords to cause data breaches and account takeovers. Eliminating the need for passwords completely by passwordless authentication lowers security concerns and improves the login experience.
  - Microsoft Entra ID's passwordless authentication options: Windows Hello for Business, tied to a trusted device, uses biometrics, fingerprint, or face recognition, or a PIN for authentication.

- o Eliminating the need for passwords, Microsoft Authenticator (Passwordless Mode) lets consumers sign in via push notifications, biometrics, or a one-time passcode.
- o Strong, phishing-resistant hardware-based authentication is offered by FIDO2 Security Keys, USB, NFC, or Bluetooth security keys.

Advantages of not using passwords:

- o **More security**: Passwordless techniques lower phishing, brute force, credential stuffing, and danger.
- o **Improved user experience**: Users have a faster and more flawless login experience due to not having to recall difficult passwords.
- o **Reduced IT support expenses**: Lowers password-related helpdesk tickets, including account recovery requests and resets.

Organisations can improve security, lower user annoyance, and minimise attack surfaces connected to conventional passwords by progressively moving to passwordless authentication.

For passwordless authentication, the following page can be used for configuration, and various options can be used to customize the solution:

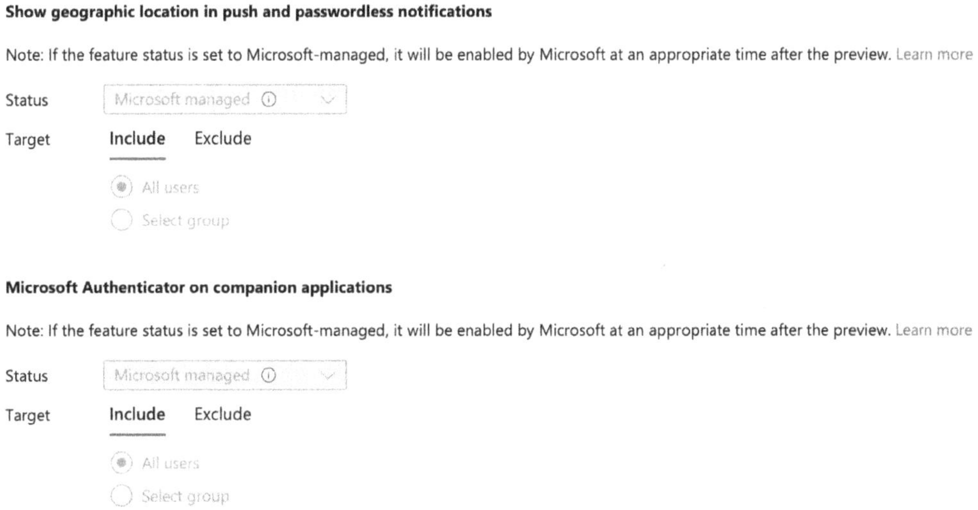

Show geographic location in push and passwordless notifications

Note: If the feature status is set to Microsoft-managed, it will be enabled by Microsoft at an appropriate time after the preview. Learn more

Status Microsoft managed

Target Include Exclude

All users

Select group

Microsoft Authenticator on companion applications

Note: If the feature status is set to Microsoft-managed, it will be enabled by Microsoft at an appropriate time after the preview. Learn more

Status Microsoft managed

Target Include Exclude

All users

Select group

***Figure 2.6**: Passwordless configuration*

- **Monitor authentication logs for anomalies**: Strong authentication policies, nevertheless, constant monitoring of authentication logs is crucial to identify unusual activity and react to possible security concerns right away. Advanced identity protection tools included in Microsoft Entra ID examine login patterns and flag high-risk sign-ins depending on anomaly detection.

Key monitoring strategies:

- o **Turn on Entra ID sign-in logs and audit logs**: Every authentication attempt is recorded in these logs, which let security teams examine login trends, unsuccessful attempts, and odd behaviour.
- o **Microsoft Entra ID identity protection**: This AI-powered security feature detects suspicious sign-ins, including:
    - Impossible travel (logins from two distant locations quickly).
    - Unknown sign-in characteristics—logins derived from untrusted devices or IPs.
    - Unusual authentication requests (high volume of failed logins).
- o **Conditional Access risk policies**: Automatically block or require MFA for high-risk sign-ins detected in authentication logs.
- o **Monitor and respond to risky users**: If a user's credentials are compromised, automatically revoke access and require a password reset or passwordless authentication.
- o **Use Azure Sentinel for advanced threat detection**: Integrating authentication logs with Microsoft Sentinel provides real-time alerts and automated security responses to mitigate threats before they escalate.

By actively monitoring authentication activity, organisations can quickly identify and remove threats, preventing account leaks and minimising the impact of breaches.

Microsoft Entra ID authorisation

Authorisation is essential for deciding what applications and users can access following successful authentication. Microsoft Entra ID offers authorisation controls and systems that let you exactly regulate roles and rights within the environment. Correct use of these restrictions guarantees that users get only the required access, hence greatly lowering security concerns and preserving compliance.

Understanding authorisation

Authorisation directs what one can do once inside; authentication determines who can use an application or resource. While authorisation addresses, *what are you allowed to do*? authentication replies, *are you who you claim to be*? This distinction determines how security policies are implemented, how private data is protected, and how the least privileged access across an organisation is guaranteed.

Strong authorisation mechanisms from Microsoft Entra ID assure users and applications have access to the resources they need and nothing more or less. Two primary technologies in Entra ID that offer control of authorisation are PIM and RBAC:

- **RBAC**: It allocates privileges according to predefined roles instead of giving people instant access to resources. RBAC assigns permissions to groups, users, or apps rather than granting individual users access, enabling more scalable and more manageable maintenance of access management.

  Working of RBAC in Entra ID:

  - **Roles define permissions**: Instead of saying *John can access this file*, you say *Anyone with the 'Reader' role can access this file.*
  - **Users (or Groups) get assigned to roles**: Assigning roles to groups instead of individuals keeps things tidy and scalable.
  - **Access is scoped**: You can give different access levels at the subscription, resource group, or individual resource level.

    For example, an IT admin may have a *Contributor* role that lets them make changes to Azure resources, while an auditor might have a *Reader* role that only allows them to view reports but not modify anything.

    The following figure shows various roles available in Entra ID. Admins can assign built-in roles from this page or create custom roles as per requirement:

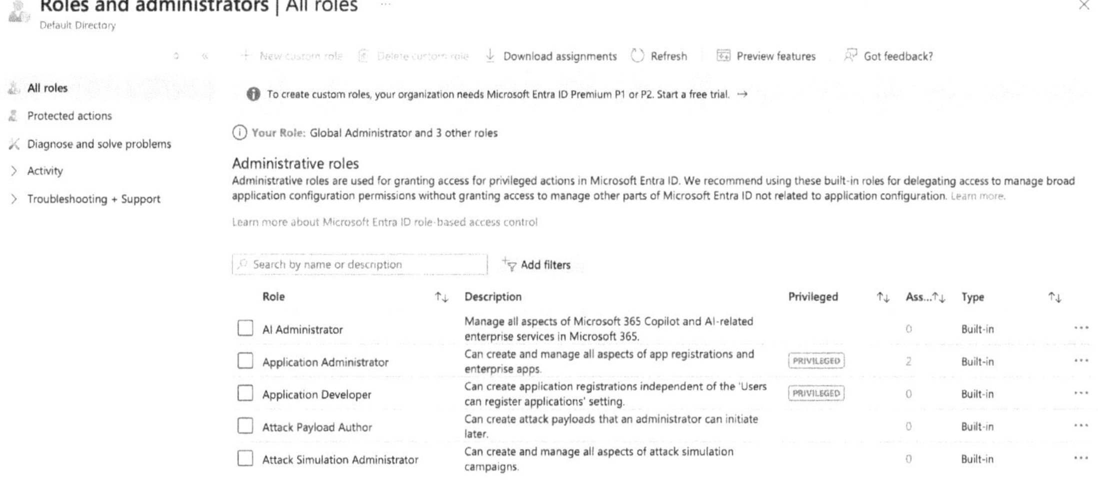

Figure 2.7: Roles and permissions

  Benefits of using RBAC:

  - **Follows the principle of least privilege (PoLP)**: Users only get the access they need to perform their job, reducing security risks.
  - **Simplifies access management**: Instead of managing permissions for each user individually, admins can grant access based on roles.

- o **Reduces security risks**: Minimises accidental or malicious changes by limiting excessive permissions.

Comparing RBAC vs. PIM

Take a look at the following table to understand the comparison:

Feature	RBAC	PIM
Purpose	Assign permanent access based on roles	Provide just-in-time, time-bound access for privileged roles
Access duration	Typically permanent	Temporary, with auto-expiry
Approval workflow	Not built-in	Optional approval before activation
Audit logging	Basic activity logs	Detailed logs and alerts on role activation
Use cases	Daily user tasks (e.g., Reader, Contributor)	Admin or high-risk roles (e.g., Global Admin, Security Admin)
Security risk	Higher if not regularly reviewed	Lower, as access is tightly controlled

Table 2.2: *RBAC vs. PIM*

Privileged Identity Management

Some roles come with a lot of power, and with power comes more significant security risks. Roles like Global Administrators or Security Administrators provide many permissions and access; if their credentials are compromised, an attacker could wreak havoc on the entire organisation.

This is where PIM comes into the picture. PIM helps control and lock down these high-risk roles so privileged access is only given when absolutely necessary, and even then, just for a given amount of time.

In the following figure, the PIM options can be set and configured as per the requirement:

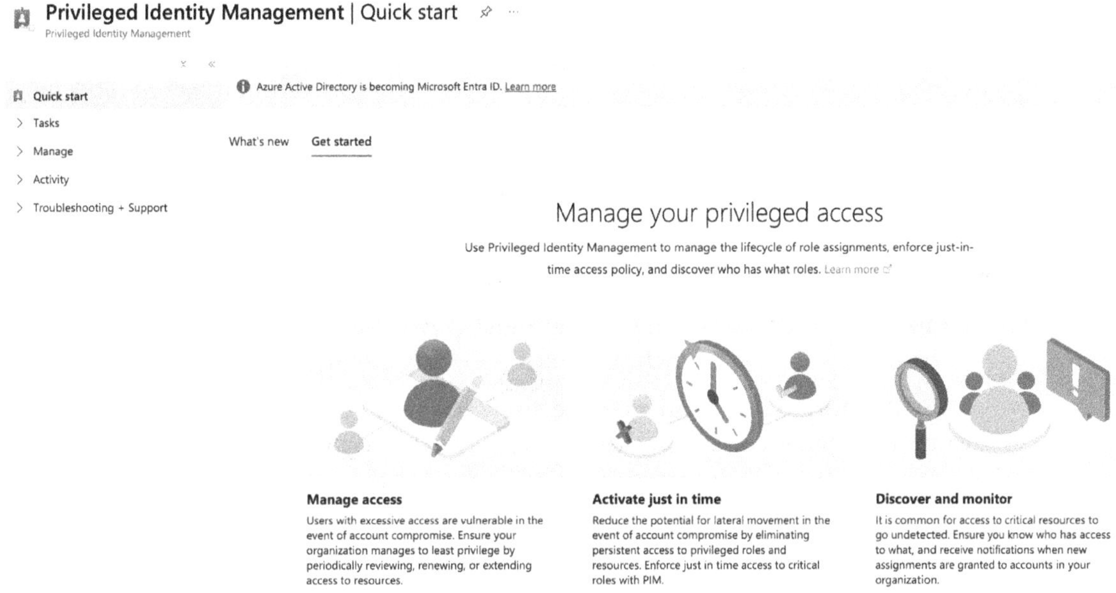

Privileged Identity Management | Quick start
Privileged Identity Management
Quick start
Tasks
Manage
Activity
Troubleshooting + Support
Azure Active Directory is becoming Microsoft Entra ID. Learn more
What's new
Get started
Manage your privileged access
Use Privileged Identity Management to manage the lifecycle of role assignments, enforce just-in-time access policy, and discover who has what roles. Learn more
Manage access
Users with excessive access are vulnerable in the event of account compromise. Ensure your organization manages to least privilege by periodically reviewing, renewing, or extending access to resources.
Activate just in time
Reduce the potential for lateral movement in the event of account compromise by eliminating persistent access to privileged roles and resources. Enforce just in time access to critical roles with PIM.
Discover and monitor
It is common for access to critical resources to go undetected. Ensure you know who has access to what, and receive notifications when new assignments are granted to accounts in your organization.

Figure 2.8: *PIM portal*

How PIM enhances security:

- **Just-in-time access**: Users do not have permanent admin rights. Instead, they request access only when needed, and it is automatically revoked after a set time.
- **Approval-based access**: Some roles require an extra layer of approval before being activated.
- **Time-limited privileges**: Even if access is granted, it expires after a set period, reducing long-term exposure.
- **Audit logging and alerts**: Every action is logged and monitored, so you can always see who accessed what and when.
- **Risk-based security controls**: If PIM detects something suspicious, like an admin logging in from a new location or device, it can require extra verification (like MFA).

Types of roles

Roles in Microsoft Entra ID help to specify what users can and cannot access. Roles combine permissions together to provide access management more securely and effectively than individually providing specific rights to every user. Appropriate job assignment and permissions help restrict security risks, eliminate inadvertent misconfigurations, and enforce the least privilege concept, that is, users only have the access they need.

Two primary kinds of roles are provided by Microsoft Entra ID:

- **Built-in roles**: These are ready-to-use, predefined Permissions. Built-in roles are predefined by Microsoft and cover the most common administrative and user management needs. These roles simplify access control by providing ready-made permissions for common IT responsibilities. Instead of figuring out what access a user needs from scratch, you can assign them a built-in role that already includes the right permissions.
- **Common built-in roles in Microsoft Entra ID**:
  - **Global Administrator**: This is the most powerful role. This role can manage everything in Entra ID, including user accounts, security settings, and policies.
  - **User Administrator:** Can manage user accounts, passwords, and groups, but cannot change security policies.
  - **Security Administrator**: Controls security settings, MFA policies, and Conditional Access, but cannot modify users.
  - **Application Administrator**: Manages enterprise applications and grants application access but does not manage users.
  - **Billing Administrator**: Manages subscriptions, license assignments, and billing details without access to security or user settings.
- **Custom roles**: While built-in roles work well for most cases, sometimes they are too broad or too restrictive for some scenarios. That is where custom roles can be used. Custom roles let organisations create their own permission sets allowing them to grant precise access based on unique business requirements.

  For example, your company has a Help Desk team that needs to reset passwords but shouldn't be able to delete accounts. Instead of giving them User Administrator (which has more power than needed), you can create a custom role that only includes password reset permissions and nothing more.
- Key features of custom roles in Microsoft Entra ID:
  - **Granular permissions**: Choose exactly what actions a user can perform (e.g., reset passwords but not delete users).
  - **Scoped access**: Limit role assignments to specific users, groups, or resources instead of applying them organisation-wide.
  - **Security-first approach**: Helps enforce least privilege access, preventing unnecessary exposure to sensitive data.

Best practices for authorisation

Proper authorisation is essential for keeping your organisation's data and systems secure. If users have too much access, they can unintentionally or maliciously cause harm. If they have too little access, they might not be able to do their jobs effectively. Striking the right balance requires carefully managing roles and permissions while ensuring that access is both necessary and temporary.

To assist organisations in implementing security policies without compromising output, Microsoft Entra ID offers strong tools such as PIM and RBAC.

Following best practices, including least privilege access, JIT access, and routinely monitoring role assignments, helps companies to lower security risks, ensure compliance, and safeguard private information:

- **Using least privilege access**: One of the most basic security techniques, the PoLP ensures that users only have the rights they absolutely need and nothing more. Should a position not call for administrative access, it should not have it. One should not have permanent rights if one merely requires momentary access to a resource.

  Enforcing least privilege access:

  - Use RBAC to allocate permissions based on job responsibilities instead of personal users, therefore enforcing least privilege access.
  - Assign scope roles as precisely as you can (e.g., let particular resource groups access rather than the whole environment).
  - Unless absolutely required, most users do not require complete system-wide access, hence avoid assigning Global Administrator.
  - Apply extra security restrictions using Conditional Access in response to users trying to access sensitive materials.

  Implementing least-privilege access helps you to reduce security breaches, inadvertent changes, insider threats, and risk while nevertheless allowing users to carry out their jobs as needed.

- **Access critical roles using JIT PIM**: Some roles, such as Global Administrator, Security Administrator, or Subscription Owner, have wide access and can be a significant security risk if abused or hacked. Microsoft Entra ID delivers PIM, which gives JIT access to vital roles rather than allowing consumers permanent access to these roles.

  How PIM enhances security:

  - High-privilege accounts are only active as needed, therefore lowering the attack surface and improving security.
  - Provides an approved workflow; before activating certain roles, users may need manager permission.
  - Automatically removes access; access expires after a designated period, therefore avoiding the accumulation of long-term privilege.

- It implements MFA, hence users activating privileged roles have to first confirm their identity.
- Guarantees complete auditing and tracking by logging every role activation, therefore revealing privileged actions.

PIM lets an IT administrator seek temporary access, complete their work, and automatically revoke rights once they are used, for instance, if they require Global Administrator rights to troubleshoot a problem. While preserving operational effectiveness, this greatly lowers security concerns.

- **Regularly review and audit role assignments**: Over time, users shift teams, assign tasks, or leave the company totally. Regular access evaluations help users who have rights they no longer require avoid data leaks, insider threats, or privilege escalation assaults. Therefore, regular auditing and cleaning up role assignments is absolutely essential to ensure that access stays necessary and justified.

  Best practices for reviewing role assignments:

  - Set up automated role reviews using Microsoft Entra ID to schedule regular access checks to confirm that users still need their allocated roles.
  - Get team leads to verify whether users still require specific rights under demand of manager or peer approval.
  - Use Entra ID Audit Logs and sign-in reports to identify attempts at unauthorised access from audit logs displaying anomalous activity.
  - Remove unnecessary roles right away; instead of allowing access to build over time, cancel it if a user no longer needs it.
  - Limit the number of Global Administrators; most companies just need two to four Global Admins for redundancy; others should use PIM for temporary admin access.

Frequent review and audit of role assignments help businesses ensure compliance, reduce the danger of privilege accesses, and maintain a safe access model shifting with business needs.

Microsoft Entra ID Secure Score

Security is about knowing how effectively tools are being utilised, not only about having the correct instruments. Microsoft Entra ID Secure Score then comes in very handy. This built-in security analytics tool lets companies assess their identity security posture, spot hazards, and apply best practices to improve defense against cyberattacks.

By assigning a numerical score based on preset security settings, rules, and identity protection methods, Secure Score offers a basic yet effective method to evaluate security changes. Your identity security is stronger the higher your score, but, more significantly, Secure Score offers specific, doable suggestions on how to do better.

Understanding what Secure Score is

Microsoft Entra ID Secure Score is a security assessment tool meant to check your environment's configuration of identity and access protection mechanisms. It offers the following:

- A numerical security score indicates, depending on best practices, stronger identity security.
- Lists of actions you can take to raise your security posture (e.g., turning on MFA, cutting Global Admins, implementing Conditional Access).
- **Constant monitoring**: Your score changes dynamically with security adjustments.
- **Comparative analysis**: See how your security posture matches industry norms and like companies.

By focusing on genuine threats and vulnerabilities that can affect their company, Secure Score helps IT managers, security teams, and compliance officials prioritise security changes, as shown in the following figure:

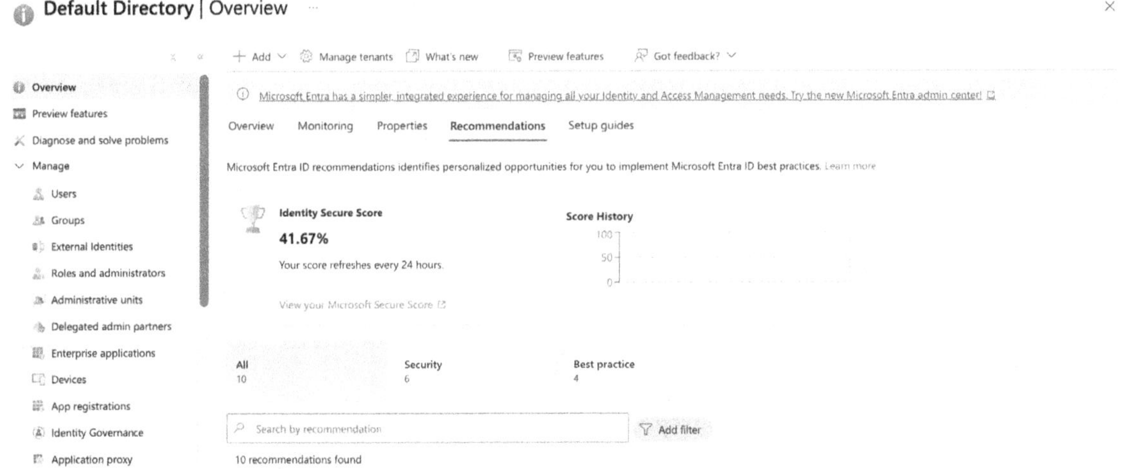

Figure 2.9: Secure Score in Entra ID

Working of Secure Score

Analysing your present identity security settings, Secure Score generates a percentage-based score depending on suggestions followed against possible enhancements.

This is how it operates:

- Microsoft reviews specified security settings after scanning your identity environment.
- It evaluates your settings in relation to optimal standards and rates them depending on the current state of configuration.

- Secure Score emphasises specific advice, including:
  - Every user is enabled for MFA.
  - Reducing the global administrator count.
  - Conditional Access rules for risk-based authentication.
  - Monitoring sign-in risk levels with Microsoft identity protection.
    - You follow the recommendations to increase your security score.
    - Real-time Secure Score updates reflect recently enforced security policies.

Organisations lower their risk of identity breaches, account takeovers, and illegal access by following the advised procedures, therefore strengthening their Entra ID system against cyber threats.

Importance of Secure Score

Microsoft Entra ID Secure Score provides organizations with insights into their identity security posture, enabling proactive risk management and continuous improvement to avoid cyber threats. Secure Score helps organizations by offering the following key benefits:

- **Offers a clear security standard**: Companies may monitor changes in their identity security posture over time.
- **Finds weaknesses before attackers act**: Emphasises areas of weakness in identity security, therefore guaranteeing proactive filling of security vulnerabilities.
- **Gives top priority to the most effective security measures**: Secure Score enables one to concentrate on high-impact enhancements, greatly lowering danger.
- **Governance and compliance**: Helps match industry standards and best practices like ISO 27001, GDPR, and NIST with security policies.
- **Promotes a security-first perspective**: Gives IT managers, security teams, and CISOs visibility so they may continuously improve security.

Components of Secure Score

Microsoft Entra ID Secure Score is meant to help companies clearly grasp their identity security posture. It does this by examining many parts of identity security and providing possible suggestions to improve security. Not only a tool for a static evaluation, Secure Score tracks security settings, user behaviour, and potential risks to enable companies to make data-driven decisions on identity security.

Three main ideas form the foundation of the Secure Score: identity protection recommendations, user behaviour insights, and integration with Microsoft Defender for Cloud.

These elements, taken together, provide a whole picture of identity security concerns and help companies be proactive in order to reduce risks:

- **Identity protection suggestions**: The identity protection recommendations of Secure Score are among its most essential features. These automatic security recommendations target lowering the risk of identity-related attacks, including phishing, credential theft, and illegal access. Microsoft Entra ID constantly evaluates security policies, authentication techniques, and sign-in behaviour to offer suggestions for strengthening defences against cybercrime.

  Standard identity protection suggestions:

  - Turn on MFA for every user to stop account grabs.
  - Cut the global administrator count to limit high-privilege exposure.
  - Enable Conditional Access rules into effect to guarantee context-aware authentication.
  - Utilising Entra ID's risk-based authentication, track and block high-risk sign-ins.
  - Use non-password-based authentication techniques to lessen reliance on passwords.
  - Following this advice can help companies greatly reduce their attack surface and raise their Secure Score over time.

- **User behavior insights:** Strengthening identity security mostly depends on an awareness of user interaction with your systems. User behaviour insights included in Secure Score offer analytics on unsafe sign-ins, odd user activity, and other security hazards. These revelations enable companies to spot and handle identity-based assaults before they start to inflict damage.

  What user behavior insights reveal:

  - Risky sign-ins point to login attempts from untrusted devices, suspicious IP addresses, or uncommon sites.
  - Flags scenarios whereby a person signs in from two far-off sites within a limited period, suggesting possible credential compromise in impossible travel events.
  - Many failed login attempts—Highlights accounts that might be targeted for brute-force assaults.
  - **Role abuse**: Track administrative account activity to find odd access trends.

  Real-time user behaviour allows companies to create automated risk-based responses—such as mandating MFA for high-risk sign-ins, limiting access to critical data, or setting off alarms for IT staff to look into dubious behaviour.

- **Integration with Microsoft Defender for Cloud**: Secure Score operates with Microsoft Defender for Cloud to offer a centralised view of identity security suggestions alongside more general security insights. By allowing organisations to link identity threats with other security issues, this integration helps them to see their security posture holistically.

Key benefits of integration with Defender for Cloud:

- o Unified security ideas aggregate suggestions for cloud security, device, and identity on one dashboard.
- o Cross-domain threat detection helps link identity-based vulnerabilities with other security events, including network invasions or endpoint breaches.
- o Automated attack response lets companies use Microsoft 365, Azure resources, Entra ID, and security rules across for a unified defence plan.
- o Comparative security posture helps companies to evaluate their Secure Score against industry norms and like companies.

Using Microsoft Defender for Cloud helps organisations guarantee that identity security is a component of their more general security plan, lowering attack surfaces and speeding incident response times.

Improving your Secure Score

Microsoft Entra ID Secure Score is a path towards improved security, not only a number. Your identity protection mechanisms are more robust the higher your score. Increasing your Secure Score is about closing security vulnerabilities and shielding your company from risks, and not about pursuing a perfect number.

Organisations can lower the risk of illegal access, strengthen their security posture, and increase general resilience against cyber threats by following advised MFA settings, correcting risky users and sign-ins, and routinely reviewing Secure Score recommendations:

- **Implement all recommended MFA settings**: One of the simplest and most successful approaches to raising your Secure Score is MFA. MFA is a crucial security control since Microsoft research reveals it can prevent over 99% of identity attacks.

  Best practices for MFA implementation:

  - o **Implement MFA for all users**: Every employee, administrative assistant, and outside partner should be obliged to utilise MFA.
  - o **Employ phishing-resistant MFA techniques**: Stronger protection comes from Microsoft Authenticator, FIDO2 security keys, Windows Hello, than from SMS or email-based MFA.
  - o **High-risk activities call for MFA**: Privileged accounts and essential apps should include extra security layers beyond minimum MFA.
  - o Establish policies for Conditional Access that, depending on risk, set off MFA based on sign-ins from new sites, untrusted devices, or anonymous networks.
  - o **Instruct consumers on MFA security**: Educate staff members to identify MFA fatigue attacks where hackers flood authentication attempts until the user unintentionally confirms one.

  - o Organisations dramatically lower identity-based threats and immediately increase their Secure Score by ultimately deploying MFA across all users and systems.

- **Remediate risky users and sign-ins**: Not every attempt at login is real. Microsoft Entra ID tracks user activities constantly in search of compromised accounts, suspicious behaviour, and high-risk sign-ins. Improving the Secure Score means acting proactively to remove dangerous people and stop efforts at illegal access.

  Steps to remediate risky users and sign-ins:

  - o Microsoft Entra ID can automatically find and warn about dangerous sign-ins, like logins from strange IP addresses or unlikely travel occurrences.
  - o **Look at high-risk users**: If an account is recognised as compromised, instantly reset their credentials and demand more confirmation.
  - o **Block highly risky sign-ins**: Use Conditional Access rules to automatically turn off access to dubious login attempts or call for extra authentication.
  - o **Limit access for compromised accounts**: Limit Access until IT verifies it is secure if a user account seems suspiciously acting.
  - o **Watch privileged accounts**: As they are primary targets for attackers, administrators and other high-privilege roles should be under continual examination.

  Frequently addressing problematic users and sign-ins not only increases Secure Score but also helps to stop intrusions before they create damage.

- **Regularly review and act on Secure Score recommendations**: Security calls for ongoing improvement; it is not a one-time endeavour. Based on the most recent threat intelligence, Microsoft Entra ID Secure Score offers real-time security advice. Organisations should routinely go over and apply these suggestions to keep ahead of cyberattacks.

- **How to stay on top of Secure Score recommendations**:

  - o **Visit Secure Score once a week**: The terrain of security is continually shifting, so fresh advice might vary depending on new risks.
  - o **Give high-impact recommendations top priority**: Concentrate on solutions that provide the most protection, such as MFA, Global Admins, and risk-based Conditional Access enforcement.
  - o Enforce policies automatically using Microsoft Entra ID's identity protection and PIM.
  - o **Review and correct role assignments**: Eliminate pointless rights, restrict administrator responsibilities, and guarantee that least privilege access is applied.
  - o Create alerts for security updates and set Microsoft Defender for Cloud to instantly warn IT teams of identity-related concerns.

Regularly including Secure Score in your security plan helps companies always strengthen their defences and lower vulnerabilities.

Microsoft Entra ID tenant security

Securing a Microsoft Entra ID tenant is essential for safeguarding organisational identities, protecting sensitive data, and preventing unauthorised access. Since the Entra ID tenant acts as the central identity hub for applications, users, and services across Azure, Microsoft 365, and integrated SaaS applications, any security misconfigurations can lead to account takeovers, data breaches, and privilege escalation attacks.

A well-protected tenant guarantees only authorised users and applications may access company resources, prohibits unauthorised changes, and enforces security best practices at every level. Microsoft offers various built-in security tools, but companies must implement proactive security policies to safeguard their identity environment completely.

Securing the Microsoft Entra ID tenant

Establishing strong access controls, implementing authentication rules, and limiting unwarranted rights form the first stage in safeguarding an Entra ID tenant. A compromised tenant can cause broad security concerns about:

- Unauthorised use of cloud services, data, and apps.
- Compromised privileged accounts are producing data exfiltration or disturbance.
- Too generous rights given to users raise insider danger.
- Insufficient insight into outside cooperation and guest access.

Organisations should use robust authentication, RBAC, and ongoing security monitoring to help lower these risks.

To guard against identity risks, Microsoft offers a spectrum of security tools to isolate the tenant, validate approved domains, and enforce security policies:

- **Tenant isolation and preventing cross-tenant access**: Tenant isolation guarantees that, unless specifically authorised, individuals and applications from outside organisations cannot access your resources. Entra ID defaults to strictly separating tenants; however, admins can adjust cross-tenant settings for particular business needs, such as B2B collaboration or access to outside applications.

  Best practices for tenant isolation:

  - Until specifically permitted through cross-tenant access settings, block cross-tenant access until absolutely necessary.

- o Control how outside users may join, authenticate, and access corporate resources using Azure AD B2B rules.
- o Limit application rights to stop outside-requesting third-party apps from asking for pointless rights that can compromise private data.
- o Apply Conditional Access rules and force extra layers of authentication for outside users, like MFA for guest accounts.

Strict tenant isolation helps companies to lower the danger of illegal data access, stop identity spoofing, and maintain security limits between different companies.

- **Custom domain verification and preventing unauthorised domain use**: Custom domain verification guarantees that the Entra ID tenant only associates authorised domains with it, therefore preventing attackers from faking corporate identities or phony email addresses. Custom domains (e.g., companyname.com) are often used in organisations for branding and uniformity in authentication; nonetheless, unverified domains might create security concerns.

  Best practices for custom domain verification:

  - o **Before linking any custom domain to Entra ID**: Unverified domains could be used for phishing attempts or domain impersonation.
  - o **Use domain federation wherever feasible**: Set up federated authentication if your company uses on-site login to guarantee flawless and safe access.
  - o **Stop unapproved users from adding domains**: Let Global Administrators change domain settings only to prevent inadvertent security mistakes.

  Organisations can stop identity impersonation and illegal access attempts by making sure the tenant uses just verified domains.

- **Security defaults and enforcing baseline security policies**: Security Defaults offer a set of pre-configured security options meant to enforce necessary identity protection without demanding sophisticated setups. By prohibiting outdated authentication techniques, enforcing MFA, and using identity protection policies, these defaults improve the security posture of the Entra ID tenant.

  Security defaults automatically enable:

  - o Mandatory MFA for all users and managers helps to guard against phishing attempts and stolen credentials, automatically enabling.
  - o Blocking outdated authentication helps stop often-used in brute-force assaults and insecure authentication techniques, including SMTP, POP3, and IMAP.
  - o Strong authentication is enforced for Global Administrators, Security Administrators, and other high-privilege positions, therefore providing extra security for privileged accounts.

Appropriate use of security use

Security Defaults in Microsoft Entra ID offer predefined identity security protections for organizations requiring immediate security improvements without complex configurations. Security Defaults are particularly beneficial in the following scenarios:

- Security Defaults give companies without sophisticated security setups a rapid approach to imposing robust security protections without configuring Conditional Access controls.
- Built-in security measures with low setup effort help **small-to-medium businesses** (**SMBs**) with limited IT resources.
- Security defaults act as a foundation for companies switching to more exacting security policies with Conditional Access, which are then implemented.
- Security defaults let companies rapidly improve tenant security and guard against unwanted access attempts by protecting identities.

Best practices for Microsoft Entra ID tenant security

The following are the best practices:

- **Use security defaults for basic protection**: Enabling security defaults guarantees MFA is applied, legacy authentication is prohibited, and privileged users have extra protections even if an organisation has not set Conditional Access rules. This serves as the fundamental security precaution for safeguarding identification.
- **Turn on self-service password reset (SSPR) to lower IT support risk**: Users of SSPR can safely replace their own passwords without involving IT help. This lowers user productivity and increases the risk of social engineering assaults aimed at IT help desks.

  Let us see how to ensure SSPR for every user:

  - Let users change passwords free from IT's control.
  - **Demand robust authentication for resetting**: Set security questions, Microsoft Authenticator, or phone verification to confirm user identification.
  - **Watch SSPR logs for unusual behaviour**: Review password resetting efforts often to find possible compromise efforts.
- **Restrict guest user permissions using access reviews**: Although guest users are sometimes asked to help with projects, leaving guest accounts with too high access could create security issues. Organisations should restrict guest access and impose access checks to stop pointless disclosure of corporate data.

Best strategies for control of guest access:

- o **Enable access reviews**: Review and delete visitor users who no longer require access on occasion.
- o **Limit visitor user rights**: Stop visitors from sharing resources, changing settings, or accessing directories.
- o **Restrict the guest access's length**: Time-bound access rules help to guarantee that visitors only have access as required.
- o **Review visitor activity logs**: Track unusual behaviour connected to outside users and sign-ins.

Proper control of guest user rights helps companies stop illegal data access and guarantee that teamwork stays safe.

Microsoft Entra ID identities and protection

Entra ID separates identities into four types, each with a particular function in controlling access to resources, therefore maintaining security and control access. Understanding these identity types is essential for enforcing least privilege access, securing sensitive data, and ensuring compliance with identity governance best practices.

The four primary identity types in Entra ID are:

- **Standard accounts** for internal users and staff members.
- **Guest accounts** are used for limited access outside partners.
- **Service principals** enable apps or services needing authentication.
- **Managed Identities** to automatically assign IDs for Azure resources.

Each identity type has different use cases, security considerations, and best practices, which we will explore in detail as discussed in the following section.

Types of identities

The following section is a detailed overview of the different types of identities available in Microsoft Entra ID, each designed to meet specific access and authentication needs across various user and application scenarios.

User accounts

Standard organisational users are the most often identified type in Microsoft Entra ID, which is user accounts. These accounts are for staff members, contractors, or internal users who need daily access to internal systems, cloud services, and corporate apps.

Key features of user accounts:

- Created and under control inside Microsoft Entra ID.
- Applied in interactive logins (such as Microsoft 365, Teams, SharePoint, business apps).
- RBAC lets one assign roles and permissions.
- It can be enabled (for hybrid environments) from the on-site active directory using Entra ID Connect.
- Encourages SSO, therefore enabling users to authenticate once and access several applications without re-entering passwords.

Best practices of user accounts:

- **Implement MFA**: This calls for extra security against credential theft by means of verification of the above passwords.
- **Use policies for Conditional Access**: Limit access depending on user location, device compliance, and login behaviour.
- By letting users reset their passwords, SSPR is enabled, hence lowering IT support costs.
- Passwordless Authentication using Microsoft Authenticator, FIDO2 security keys, or Windows Hello to close vulnerabilities connected to passwords.
- Review and disable inactive accounts often to stop unwanted access by deleting stale accounts.

Guest accounts

Companies sometimes work with contractors, vendors, or partners who need restricted access to corporate resources. Microsoft Entra ID lets companies create guest accounts, therefore giving external users controlled, limited access to particular apps or services rather than whole user accounts.

Key features of guest accounts:

- Designed under Azure AD **business-to-business** (**B2B**) collaboration.
- Connected to the current identity provider of the external user, ie. Google, Microsoft, or another corporate Entra ID tenant.
- Use invitation-based access, meaning external users must accept an invitation before accessing resources.
- Supports Conditional Access rules to regulate visitor signing-in location, time, and method.
- Using access reviews can be automatically deleted following a designated period.

Best practices of guest accounts:

- **Limit guest rights to least privilege access**: Make sure guests have access to what they need, not needless privileges.
- **Refer to access reviews**: Occasionally Review guest accounts and delete those no longer needed.
- **Limit access to sensitive information**: Set Microsoft 365 and SharePoint rules to stop guest users from over-sharing private data.
- **Turn on guest MFA**: Guards against efforts at illegal access and account compromise.
- **Use Conditional Access to restrict access**: Limit outside user access to particular sites, tools, or security-conscious programmes.

Service principals

A service principal is an identity type used for applications, services, and automation processes that must authenticate and interact with Microsoft Entra ID or Azure resources. Unlike user accounts, service principals are not associated with a specific person but are assigned to applications requiring access to resources.

Key features of service principals:

- Used for authentication between applications, services, and cloud workloads.
- Can be assigned specific roles and permissions based on RBAC.
- Verifies using client secrets or certificates rather than passwords.
- Supports OpenID's Connect authentication and OAuth 2.0.

Best practices for securing service principals:

- Use Managed Identities whenever possible (instead of service principals) to eliminate secret or credential management.
- **Limit service principal permissions using least privilege access**: Assign only the permissions required for the application to function.
- **Rotate client secrets and certificates regularly**: Prevents long-term exposure of sensitive credentials.
- **Monitor service principal activity logs**: Detects suspicious behavior, such as unauthorised access attempts.
- **Enable Conditional Access for service principals**: Restricts authentication to specific networks or trusted workloads.

Managed Identities

Managed Identities provide automated, system-Managed Identities for Azure resources, eliminating the need to manage secrets, passwords, or certificates for authentication. Managed Identities are a more secure alternative to service principals for enabling Azure VMs, Functions, Logic Apps, and other cloud services to authenticate securely.

Key features of Managed Identities:

- Automatically managed by Azure, requiring no manual secret or password rotation.
- Can be used to authenticate Azure resources securely (e.g., Azure Key Vault, Azure SQL Database, and Azure Storage).
- Supports two types of Managed Identities:
  - **System-assigned Managed Identity**: Tied to a single Azure resource and deleted when the resource is removed.
  - **User-assigned Managed Identity**: Can be assigned to multiple resources and persists beyond individual resources.
- Uses OAuth-based authentication without needing API keys, client secrets, or passwords.

Best practices for using Managed Identities:

- **Prefer Managed Identities over service principals**: Since Azure manages them automatically, they reduce the risk of leaked credentials.
- **Apply the principle of least privilege**: Assign only the minimum required permissions to each Managed Identity.
- **Monitor Managed Identity usage**: Regularly review audit logs to detect unusual activity.
- **Use system-assigned Managed Identities for single-resource scenarios**: Ensures the identity lifecycle is tied to the Azure resource.

Identity protection features

Securing user identities is one of the most critical aspects of modern cybersecurity. Microsoft Entra ID offers identity protection tools that enable companies to control the identity lifecycle, automate actions, and find hazards thus lowering the possibility of compromised accounts and illegal access.

Among the most regularly occurring risks businesses handle nowadays are identity-based ones include brute force efforts, phishing, and credential stuffing. Microsoft Entra ID identity protection uses machine learning, artificial intelligence-driven risk analysis, and automation to discover and lower these hazards before they lead to security breaches.

Key identity protection features in Microsoft Entra ID:

- **Risk detection**: Tracks possible identity risks and suspicious user behaviour.
- **Risk policies**: These automatically address remedial steps meant to stop security breaches.
- **Identity governance**: It guarantees correct compliance and lifetime management of identity.

These capabilities combine to offer an automated, proactive method of identity security:

- **Risk detection**: It is all about monitoring for suspicious user activity in Entra ID. Microsoft Entra ID's risk detection system constantly monitors user activity to find and alert on compromised accounts. It detects unusual login habits and unauthorised access attempts using AI-driven risk evaluation.

  Types of risks detected by Entra ID:

  - **Typical travel or impossible travel**: Should a user log in from two geographically separated sites in a brief period, the system notes the attempt as suspicious.
  - **Sign-ins from foreign IP addresses or locations**: Should a user login from a rarely used or untrusted IP address, the system could restrict or challenge access.
  - Entra ID detects logins from compromised devices by means of interaction with Microsoft Defender from malware-infected machines.
  - Unusual sign-in behaviour could point to an attack if a user logs in at an odd hour or abruptly fails several login attempts.
  - Microsoft crosses login attempts with dark web leaks to find hacked passwords.

- **Risk policies**: When Entra ID finds a compromised user account or high-risk login attempt, risk policies let companies automate replies. These rules assist in reducing security risks without calling for human involvement.

  Key risk policies in Microsoft Entra ID:

  - User risk policy determines the general risk associated with the behaviour of a user. Should Entra ID find an account compromised, it can:
    - Restrict the user from logging in.
    - Before allowing access, reset the password.
    - Verify MFA before we start.
  - The sign-in risk policy is based on login behaviour and finds and reduces real-time authentication threats. Should a dangerous sign-in happen, the Entra ID can:
    - Require MFA automatically to confirm identity.
    - Block access from high-risk areas.
    - Record the event and let managers know.

- **Risk-based policies with Conditional Access**: Dynamic access restrictions depending on detected risk level can be changed by Entra ID. As such:
    - **Low-risk users**: Standard sign-in procedure devoid of further confirmation.
    - **Users under medium risk**: Urged for MFA validation.
    - **High-risk users**: Completely prohibited or mandated credential resetting.

- **Identity governance**: Identity security guarantees that user access is correctly controlled throughout its lifetime, not only about spotting threats. Microsoft Entra ID's identity governance tool enables companies to manage role assignments, enforce compliance, and, over time, eliminate pointless access rights.

  Key features of identity governance:

    - **Access review**: Guarantees that users, guests, and staff just keep the required permissions.
        - Review access rights and role assignments often.
        - Automates contractor and guest user access expiration.
        - Eliminates too old or excessive rights in order to lower security threats.
    - **Entitlement management**: Lists employee, vendor, and outside collaborator self-service access needs.
        - By requesting particular rights, users help to lighten the IT strain.
        - Approvals may be personally checked or automated.
        - Turns off access automatically when no longer required.
    - Automates user access management for new hiring, position changes, and leaving staff members during their lifetime.
        - Guarantees that on day one, new hires have the correct access.
        - Changes rights when users move departments or positions.
        - Immediately eliminates access to stop insider threats for fired staff members.
    - Manages high-privilege accounts in PIM to prevent too liberal admin access.
        - Access sensitive roles JIT.
        - Calls for multi-step clearance for role elevation.
        - Track administrative actions for any security hazards.

Enhancing identity security in Microsoft Entra ID

Organisations should go beyond providing risk detection, risk policies, and identity governance to improve their posture of identity security.

Key strategies for strengthening identity security:

- Turn on user risk policies, including sign-ins. Block automatically high-risk login attempts and demand identity verification for dubious behaviour.
- Review access rights regularly, enforce least privilege access, and automate identity lifecycle management using identity governance to guarantee compliance.
- Track privilege escalations, unauthorised access attempts, and authentication activity constantly in identity logs for abnormalities.
- **Implement passwordless verification**: Windows Hello, FIDO2 security keys, and Microsoft Authenticator can help you reduce password reliance.
- Apply policies for Conditional Access. Control access using behavioural analytics, location, device compliance, and user risk.

Microsoft Entra ID secure application access

Organisations today depend on a mix of cloud-based, on-premises, and third-party applications to keep operations running smoothly. Managing secure access across this ecosystem is challenging, as employees, partners, and guest users access applications from different locations and devices.

This is where Microsoft Entra ID comes in. It provides a consistent, safe method of application access that ensures that users access the correct applications only when needed and without sacrificing security. Entra ID offers capabilities to give access, enforce security standards, and simplify authentication, whether apps are hosted in Azure, on-premise, or as SaaS services.

Organisations may provide a flawless yet safe user experience by using SSO, Conditional Access, and identity protection, therefore preventing cyber risks and guaranteeing compliance with security best standards. Let us explore how Entra ID guarantees application access and the reasons current identity management depends so much on this component.

Securing access to applications with Microsoft Entra ID

Applications are critical components of modern organizations, and ensuring their security involves controlling user access and protecting sensitive data against unauthorized exposure. Microsoft Entra ID provides capabilities to securely manage user access across diverse application environments.

Single sign-on for seamless and secure authentication

Managing multiple credentials across several applications causes user frustration and security issues. Users can use Microsoft Entra ID's SSO to authenticate once and access all assigned applications without re-entering credentials. This increases productivity, streamlines security, and simplifies login.

On-premise legacy systems, custom enterprise apps, and cloud-based SaaS apps can also leverage SSO authentication. It connects with Microsoft 365, Salesforce, Workday, ServiceNow, and hundreds of other cloud services. Entra ID Application Proxy enhances SSO capabilities for on-site applications, allowing safe remote access without exposing internal resources to the internet.

SSO supports several authentication systems like SAML, OAuth, OpenID Connect, and WS-Federation in order to guarantee wide interoperability. To instantly identify and reduce security concerns, IT departments may centrally control access controls, use MFA, and track login activity. Refer to the following figure:

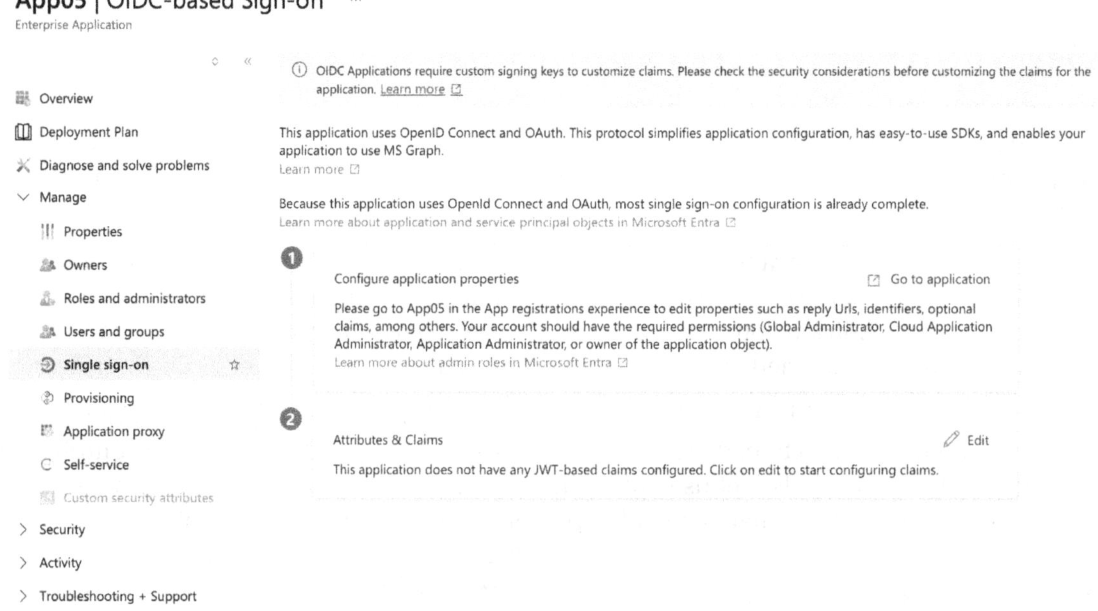

App05 | OIDC-based Sign-on
Enterprise Application
Overview
Deployment Plan
Diagnose and solve problems
Manage
Properties
Owners
Roles and administrators
Users and groups
Single sign-on
Provisioning
Application proxy
Self-service
Custom security attributes
Security
Activity
Troubleshooting + Support
OIDC Applications require custom signing keys to customize claims. Please check the security considerations before customizing the claims for the application. Learn more
This application uses OpenID Connect and OAuth. This protocol simplifies application configuration, has easy-to-use SDKs, and enables your application to use MS Graph.
Learn more
Because this application uses OpenId Connect and OAuth, most single sign-on configuration is already complete.
Learn more about application and service principal objects in Microsoft Entra
1
Configure application properties
Go to application
Please go to App05 in the App registrations experience to edit properties such as reply Urls, identifiers, optional claims, among others. Your account should have the required permissions (Global Administrator, Cloud Application Administrator, Application Administrator, or owner of the application object).
Learn more about admin roles in Microsoft Entra
2
Attributes & Claims
Edit
This application does not have any JWT-based claims configured. Click on edit to start configuring claims.

***Figure 2.10**: SSO for enterprise app*

Conditional Access for intelligent security enforcement

As cyber threats change, organisations must use flexible access control systems instead of set security policies. Microsoft Entra ID's Conditional Access helps companies to set access rules depending on location, device compliance level, and real-time risk analysis.

Unlike traditional security controls, Conditional Access evaluates multiple factors before giving access:

- If a user logs in from an unfamiliar location or an unmanaged device, MFA may be required.
- For high-risk sign-ins, access can be automatically blocked to prevent account compromise.
- Role-based policies can enforce stricter authentication requirements for privileged users.

Custom security rules let organisations balance security with user experience so that authorised users may log in easily while illegal access attempts are blocked.

Conditional Access with advanced controls:

- **Adaptive access policies**: Conditional Access Policies can dynamically adjust authentication requirements based on login and user behaviour.
- **Session monitoring and restrictions**: Organizations can monitor session activity and enforce restrictions to prevent suspicious app usage.
- **Integration with Microsoft Defender for Cloud**: Conditional Access can leverage threat intelligence from Defender for Cloud to detect and respond to identity-based attacks in real-time.

The following figure shows Conditional Access for sample application, **App05**. There are various options that can be configured to secure and protect access to the application as shown:

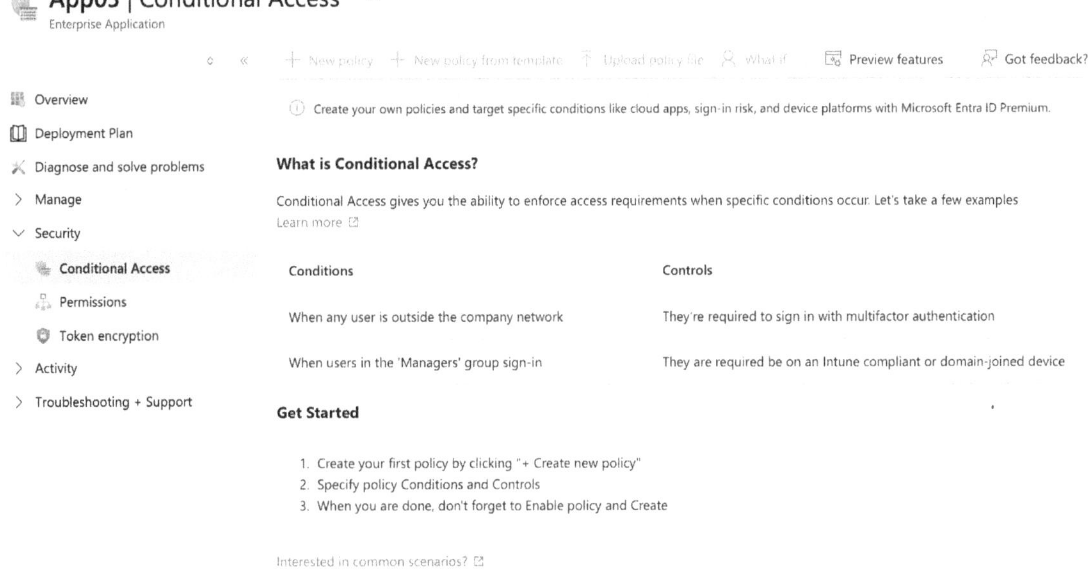

***Figure 2.11**: Conditional Access for apps*

Securing on-premises applications with Azure AD application proxy

Many companies still depend on on-site apps created before the cloud age. Reverse proxies and VPNs are two examples of classic remote access solutions that generate performance bottlenecks, add complexity, and expose security concerns. Modern, cloud-based solution available from Entra ID Application Proxy allows safe remote access to internal apps without exposing them to the internet.

Between Microsoft Entra ID and on-site apps, Application Proxy serves as a link, making sure security requirements are followed before access is permitted.

Advantages of Azure AD application proxy:

- Safe remote access avoids the complexity of conventional VPNs.
- Reduces the attack surfaces by reducing the requirement to open ports.
- It supports modern authentication (SSO, MFA) for legacy apps without needing application modifications.
- Users of on-premise apps can access them exactly as with cloud-based ones.

Application proxy can be configured per app basis as shown in *Figure 2.12*. The configuration shown as follows can also be used in third-party proxy solutions, ensuring the security of the application:

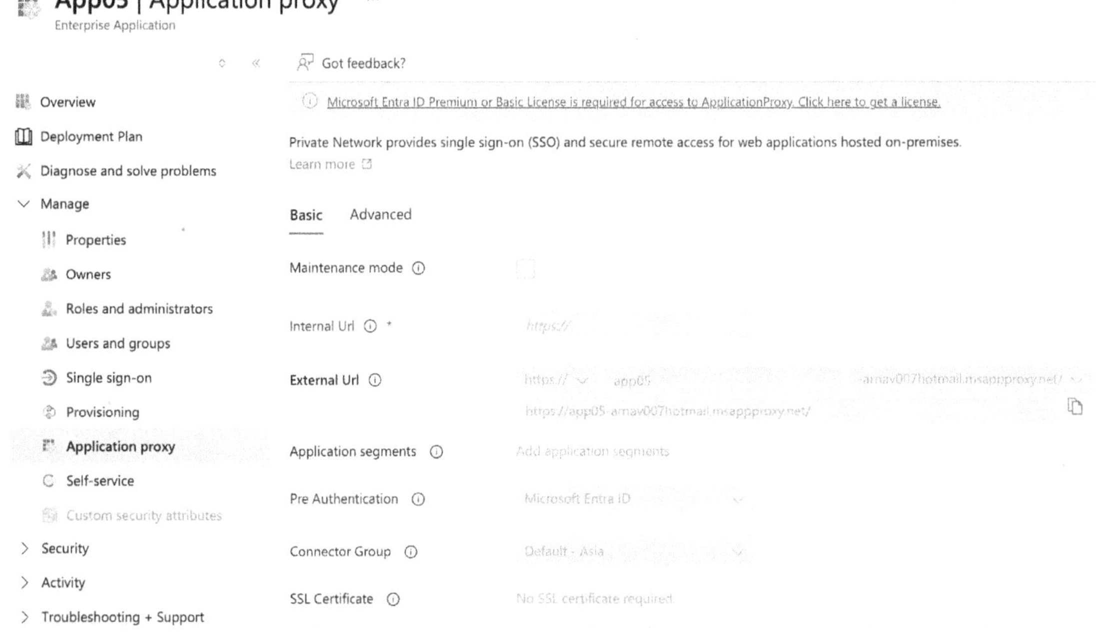

***Figure 2.12**: Application proxy configuration*

Enhancing application security with Microsoft Entra ID

Organisations must enhance application security to guard against unauthorised access, credential leaks, and insider threats, going beyond access control and authentication.

Managed Identity-based secure authentication

Many applications call for access to APIs, databases, and services. Storing passwords, static credentials, or API keys runs security risks. Managed Identities let programmes authenticate without storing secrets, therefore eliminating this risk.

Applications using Managed Identities can safely use Azure services such as SQL database, storage accounts, and Key Vault without requiring manually managed credentials. This simplifies application authentication and eliminates credential leaks' possibility.

Updating applications helps to reduce vulnerabilities

One often used attack path is unpatched apps. Organisations ought to:

- Frequent application of security fixes helps to eradicate discovered weaknesses.
- Track for zero-day vulnerabilities and apply updates right away upon remedies' availability.
- Use an automated fixing system to guarantee ongoing defence.

Session management and monitoring

Policies of session management enable the identification and reduction of attempts at illegal access. Organisations need to:

- Set session times to lower the possibility of session theft.
- Watch ongoing sessions for abnormalities.
- Block inactive user sessions over levels set by policy.

These security policies help companies to keep industry compliance, guard application access, and stop account takeovers.

Risk-based access management and identity protection

Ensuring application access calls for automated risk response systems and real-time threat detection. Microsoft Entra ID identity protection finds compromised accounts and stops illegitimate access by use of AI-powered risk analysis.

If a sign-in request raises concerns, automated remedial procedures can be set off:

- For hacked accounts, instant password reset.
- Blocking from unknown IP addresses.
- Needing extra MFA confirmation for high-risk log-on devices.

Organisations can dynamically apply security measures by combining identity protection with Conditional Access, preventing cyberattacks and reducing disturbance for genuine users.

Ensuring compliance and governance with identity access reviews

Companies have to make sure users have access to the tools they actually need. Access reviews made possible by identity governance in Microsoft Entra ID help to audit and eliminate unwanted rights, therefore lowering the risk of too much access.

Important governance characteristics:

- Reviewing accounts periodically helps to find dormant ones and cancel pointless access.
- Entitlement management will help to simplify approval processes and self-service access requests.
- JIT access for critical apps is enforced by PIM.

These governance instruments enforce a least privilege paradigm for application access and enable companies to follow security rules (GDPR, ISO 27001, NIST).

Conclusion

In this chapter, we evaluated key methods for protecting Microsoft Entra ID IAM systems. Organisations can greatly improve their security posture by comprehending and putting into practice strong authentication procedures, authorisation restrictions, and cutting-edge tools like Secure Score and Conditional Access. Adopting the best practices covered in this chapter ensures regulatory compliance, decreases the possibility of unwanted access, and helps secure identities.

In the next chapter, we will look into Azure Virtual Networks and security. You will learn about how Azure Networking works, its building blocks such as virtual networks, subnets, and IP addressing, and how to secure your network using tools like Network Security Groups, Azure Firewall, and Private Endpoint.

CHAPTER 3
Securing Networks

Introduction

In today's cloud-first landscape, securing networks requires more than just traditional perimeter defenses. In the Zero Trust model, which assumes breach and verifies every request, it is now important in protecting Azure environments. Modern networks face threats such as lateral movement, misconfigurations, and a lack of visibility, making it critical to build in security from the ground up.

A significant example occurred during the 2017 *WannaCry* ransomware outbreak, where poor network segmentation allowed the malware to spread rapidly across unpatched systems within the network architecture. If microsegmentation and strict access controls had been in place, the impact could have been contained significantly.

In this chapter, you will learn skills to master securing Azure network services. Securing virtual networks will be the first topic to ensure we have a secure and protected network topology for our workloads and data to exist within; you will learn about traffic filtering and protection using NSGs/ ASGs, firewall settings for PaaS resources, as well as UDRs for use with NVA's, and finally, Azure Route Server.

Next, you will explore how to secure both public and private access to Azure resources through the use of Azure Bastion, VPNs, ExpressRoute, Azure Virtual WAN, Azure Firewall, Azure Application Gateway, Azure Front Door, WAF, endpoints, and Private Link services, and finally Azure **distributed denial-of-service** (**DDoS**) protection.

Structure

This chapter contains the following topics:

- Overview of virtual networks
- Network segmentation
- Traffic filtering and protection
- Securing private access to Azure resources
- Best practices
- Endpoint security
- Automating TLS certificate rotation with Azure Key Vault

Objectives

By the end of this chapter, readers will gain a deep understanding of securing Azure networks through effective design, segmentation, and traffic control. They will learn how to implement NSGs, ASGs, and Firewalls to enforce security policies. Additionally, they will explore private and public access controls using Azure Bastion, Private Link, Service Endpoints, and WAF. The chapter also covers hybrid connectivity solutions like VPN and ExpressRoute, ensuring secure communication between on-premises and cloud environments. Finally, readers will understand the best practices for monitoring, compliance, and optimizing network security in Azure.

Overview of virtual networks

Azure **Virtual Networks** (**VNets**) are the foundations of Azure Networking. Imagine them as your private network, like the network you might have in your office or home, but way more scalable and secure. VNet lets you run your applications, databases, and virtual machines in a safe and isolated environment. They make sure your resources can all talk to each other without any unwanted traffic getting in.

A good VNet setup is not just about getting connected; it is about having control. You can divide your network into smaller sections, called subnets, and then use resources like NSGs and route tables to decide which resources can communicate and how data moves around. You can add services like Azure Firewall and DDoS protection for even stronger security. So, whether you are building a simple network for one app or a complex hybrid setup that connects to your existing office network, VNet gives you the flexibility and security you need for a reliable cloud network.

Network segmentation

While VNets provide the fundamental networking layer, effective security starts with proper network segmentation. Unsegmented networks can expose resources unnecessarily, increasing security risks. Implementing segmentation with subnets, NSGs, and ASGs helps organizations apply the principle of least privilege at the network level. Let us explore these segmentation methods in detail.

Designing a secure and well-organized Azure environment depends on good network segmentation. Logical segmentation of your VNet will help you to control traffic flow, strengthen security, and increase performance. Subnetting, NSGs, and ASGs are just a few of Azure's built-in tools meant to enable you to achieve this and let you separate tasks, enforce security policies, and simplify access management so that only authorized communication flows between your resources.

The following best practices can help you design a more secure and resilient Azure VNet environment:

- **Subnets**: Azure network segmentation is built from subnets. They enable you to logically break a single VNet into smaller pieces, therefore facilitating the management and security of your infrastructure. You might set up distinct subnets for your web servers, application servers, and databases, for instance, so isolating each level of your operation and yet enable limited communication between them.

  Proper use of the subnets allows you to allocate multiple security policies, control network traffic, and best allocate resources. Additionally, offering private and Service Endpoints, Azure lets resources in a subnet safely use Azure services without exposing them to the internet. Effective subnetting improves the security and efficiency of your cloud environment and helps to lower unneeded traffic.

- **NSGs**: NSGs act as virtual firewalls for your Azure resources, enabling you to filter traffic into and out of subnets or individual virtual machines. They use inbound and outbound rules to determine which traffic is allowed and which should be blocked. This helps prevent unauthorized access and limits exposure to potential threats.

  You could enable an NSG rule, such as allowing HTTPS traffic to a web server but blocking all other inbound requests. Similarly, you can limit outbound traffic from a database subnet to prevent unintentional internet exposure of private information. Applying NSGs at the subnet and **network interface** (**NIC**) level gives you exact control over security policies across your resources.

- **ASGs**: When managing several virtual machines and apps, controlling NSG rules can get complicated. Here is where ASGs find applications. ASGs let you aggregate resources with related roles and apply security policies at the group level, so you replace setting security rules for specific VMs.

For example, if you have several web servers that talk to a backend database, you can arrange all of the web servers in an ASG-WebServers group and specify NSG rules depending on that group. This allows you to apply rules to the group instead of individually configuring them for every virtual machine, thereby simplifying network security management. Large environments where resources are regularly added or removed benefit, especially from ASGs, since they help to preserve consistency in security policies free from human involvement.

Azure's well-organized, secure network can be built from subnets for segmentation, NSGs for traffic control, and ASGs for simpler management. These tools collaborate to increase security, boost performance, and streamline administration, keeping the efficiency, scalability, and protection against threats of your cloud environment.

Network Security Group vs. Application Security Group

To better understand when to use NSG vs. ASG, the following table shows the key differences between the two.

While both play important roles in securing traffic, they operate at different levels and serve distinct purposes within Azure's networking model:

Feature	NSG	ASG
Purpose	Filter inbound/outbound traffic at subnet/NIC level	Group VMs logically for simplified rule management
Scope	Subnet or NIC-based	Used within NSG rules
Configuration	Rule-based (source/destination IPs, ports, protocols)	ASG-based references in NSG rules
Use case	Control access to/from VM/ subnet	Group VMs with similar roles (e.g., web tier)
Scalability	Manual rule updates needed	Automatically includes new members in rules

***Table 3.1**: NSG vs. ASG*

Simple Azure network architecture

To better understand how Azure Networking components come together, let us look at a common architectural pattern used in many enterprise environments in the following figure:

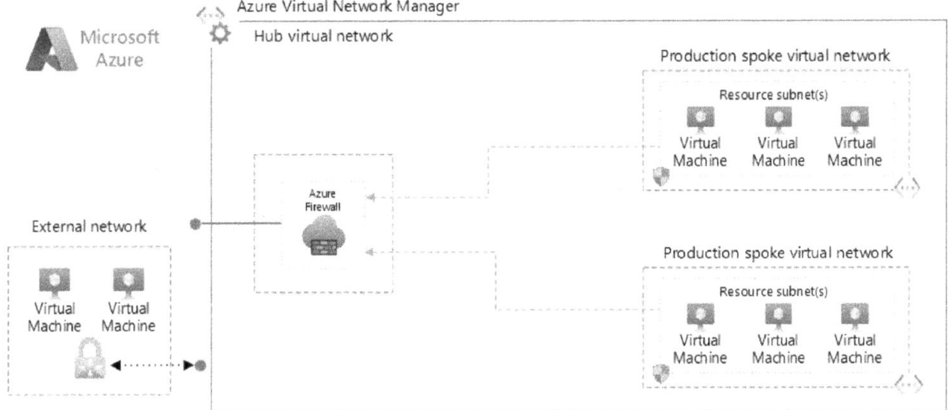

***Figure 3.1**: Simple Azure network architecture*

A hub-spoke network design in Azure is shown in *Figure 3.1*. A central hub virtual network connects to several spoke virtual networks. Organizations often use this design to centralize security controls, make management more manageable, and make the system more scalable.

There is a VNET called **hub** in the middle of the network. It manages security and communication for many virtual networks called **production spoke**. The Azure Firewall that is set up in the hub acts as a secure entrance, inspecting and filtering data before it gets to the workloads in the spoke networks. Traffic from outside networks has to go through Azure Firewall. This makes sure that only authorized traffic can make it through. In the same way, contact between spokes goes through the hub, which adds an extra layer of security.

In each production spoke virtual network, resource subnets hold a group of VMs. This helps divide jobs into groups based on application levels (like web, application, and database layers) or types of environments (like development, testing, and production). NSGs can be used at the subnet level to further restrict access and make sure that only approved data moves between resources.

Though this is not represented on the figure, ASGs can be added to make security control even simpler. Rather than using fixed IP addresses, ASGs enable you to organize virtual machines wisely depending on what they do. Rather than creating several NSG rules for every VM, administrators can create rules depending on ASG memberships. Security policies thus become more scalable and adaptable.

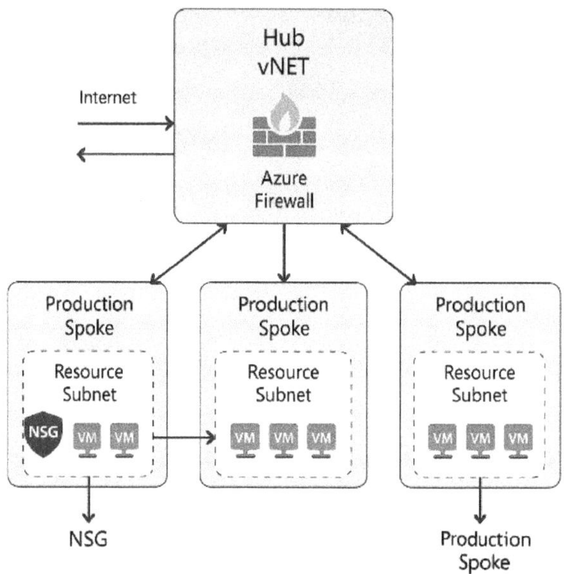

***Figure 3.2**: Hub and spoke topology in Azure*

For example, if you have several web servers on separate spoke networks, you can create an ASG-WebServers group. In this sense, NSG rules allow backend systems and web servers to interact without exchanging IP addresses. More web servers naturally adopt the security guidelines established for the ASG-WebServers group when they are added. This reduces administrative effort and guarantees that security rules remain the same.

Traffic filtering and protection

While segmentation ensures that workloads are logically separated, controlling traffic flows between these segments is equally essential. Traffic filtering mechanisms such as Azure Firewall, **user-defined routes** (**UDRs**), and Route Server provide centralized control to enforce security policies and protect against unauthorized access. Let us examine how these tools work together to enhance network security.

Securing your network in Azure calls for efficient traffic filtering and routing technologies to ensure that just the correct traffic reaches your workloads while preventing or redirecting illegal access. To help enforce security regulations, defend against threats, and maximize network traffic flow, Azure offers many tools, including Azure Firewall, NSGs, UDRs, and Azure Route Server.

Let us explore some of the key tools Azure provides to filter traffic and enforce security policies across your network:

- **Azure Firewall**: Azure Firewall is a fully managed stateful security resource designed to protect Azure networks. Unlike NSGs, which are primarily used for basic traffic filtering, Azure Firewall provides packet inspection, threat intelligence, and deep packet analysis to offer more advanced protection.

One of its main benefits is centralized control, which lets you apply consistent firewall rules or policies to all VNets and traffic coming in or out of Azure. Thereby lowering the risk of cyberattacks, threat intelligence-based filtering's ability to automatically block traffic from identified hostile sources.

For example, if your organization hosts a multi-region web application, you can configure Azure Firewall to allow only HTTPS traffic from trusted IP ranges while blocking any untrusted requests. It can also inspect outbound traffic, ensuring that Azure resources do not connect to malicious destinations—something that NSGs alone cannot do. FQDN filtering allows administrators to create rules based on domain names instead of just IP addresses, making it easier to manage security policies dynamically.

The following figure shows how Azure Firewall works as a centralized security enforcement point within a hub-and-spoke architecture:

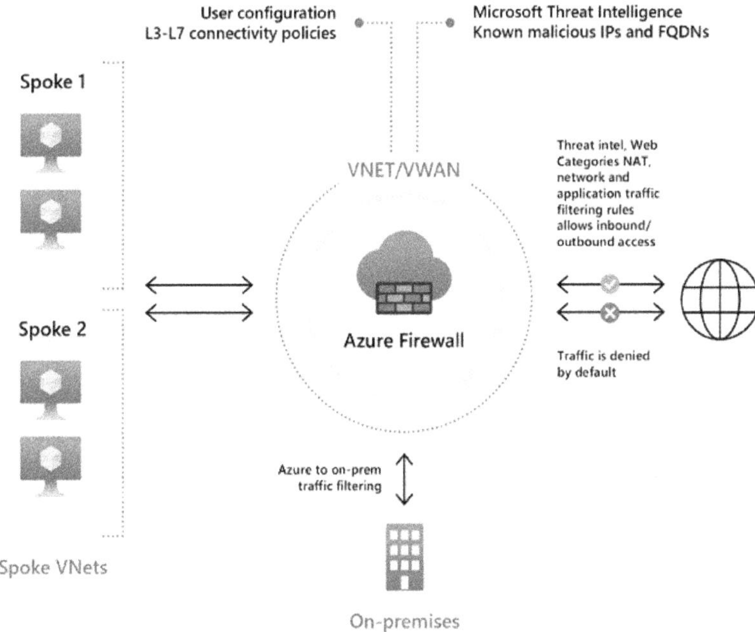

***Figure 3.3**: Microsoft Azure Firewall*

***Reference**: https://learn.microsoft.com/en-us/Azure/firewall/overview*

Azure Firewall is shown in the above diagram as a centralized security enforcement point for on-site networks and VNets housed within a VNET/VWAN. Representing varying workloads, the spoke VNets route traffic across the firewall for inspection and filtering.

The firewall enforces L3-L7 connectivity rules set by the user, therefore granting fine-grained control over network traffic. It also interacts with Microsoft Threat Intelligence to identify and stop traffic from known hostile FQNs and IP addresses.

All traffic is blocked by default. However, NAT, application filtering, and network rules permit approved inbound and outgoing access. Additionally, by classifying web traffic, the firewall lets security teams ban or allow access to particular web categories.

Azure-to-on-premises traffic is filtered for hybrid connectivity, guaranteeing security policy compliance and stopping unwanted access. Using centralized management, threat information, and policy-based control over both cloud and on-site traffic, this arrangement improves security.

- **NSGs**: While Azure Firewall provides centralized protection, NSGs give localized security enforcement at the subnet or NIC level. They provide a more detailed layer of protection by letting you design rules allowing or prohibiting communication depending on source and destination IP addresses, ports, and protocols.

  If you have an internal API service, for instance, that should only be accessed by a certain application deployed in another subnet, you can set an NSG rule allowing just traffic from the IP range of that subnet. This guarantees that the API is segregated from every other workload, therefore stopping illegal access.

  NSGs are lightweight and affordable, unlike Azure Firewall, which makes them perfect for managing east-west (internal) traffic inside a VNet. However, they lack Azure Firewall's sophisticated security features, such as threat intelligence integration and deep packet inspection.

  The following figure shows a NSG and some default rules:

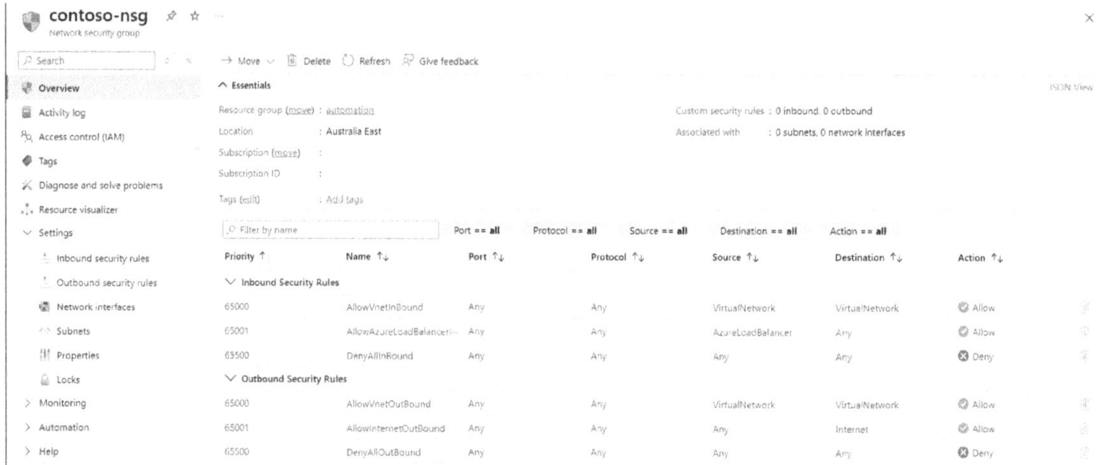

Figure 3.4: NSG

- **UDRs**: The default routing behaviour of Azure automatically controls connections inside a VNet. In many circumstances, you could choose to route traffic through particular security devices, such as **intrusion detection systems** (**IDS**) or firewalls. This is where UDRs become really important.

  UDRs allow you to override Azure's built-in routing decisions, enabling you to force traffic through a **Network Virtual Appliance** (**NVA**) before reaching its final destination.

  For instance, if you are operating a highly regulated environment where all outbound internet traffic must pass through an on-premises firewall, you can create a UDR with a next-hop pointing to a VPN gateway. This ensures that all internet-bound requests are monitored and logged externally before leaving the Azure network.

  UDRs are also rather frequently used for internal service isolation. Using UDRs can help you to guarantee that traffic from a database subnet is solely sent to application servers, therefore preventing external exposure even if that subnet should never interact directly with the internet.

  The following figure shows a sample UDR configuration in Azure, where a custom route directs traffic for the 192.168.0.0/24 address space through the virtual network:

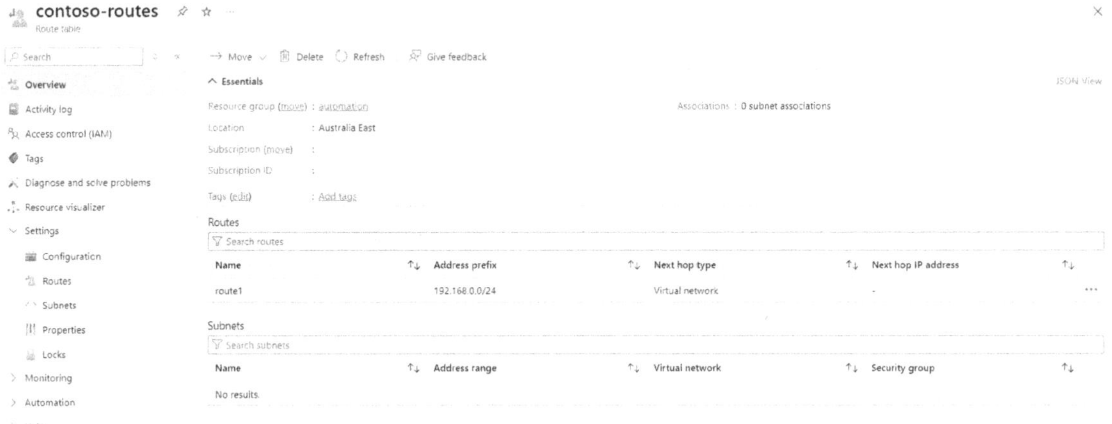

Figure 3.5: Route table

- **Azure Route Server**: It can be hard to connect Azure to a network that is already there, especially when it comes to handling updates to dynamic routing. Azure Route Server makes things easier by using **Border Gateway Protocol** (**BGP**) to make it easy for Azure and external routers to talk to each other.

  Without Route Server, network managers would have to set up static routes manually, which is hard to do in big environments that are always changing. When you set up Route Server, BGP changes happen automatically. This means that any new subnets or resources are immediately recognized and added to routeing decisions, without you having to do anything.

For example, if you use ExpressRoute to connect several branch offices to Azure, Route Server makes sure that any changes to your on-premise network, like adding new subnets or moving workloads, are immediately reflected in every place. Along these lines, hybrid networking is better at growing, staying strong, and being easy to control over time.

The following figure shows how Azure Route Server enables dynamic route exchange between Azure and on-premises networks using BGP, streamlining connectivity and route management:

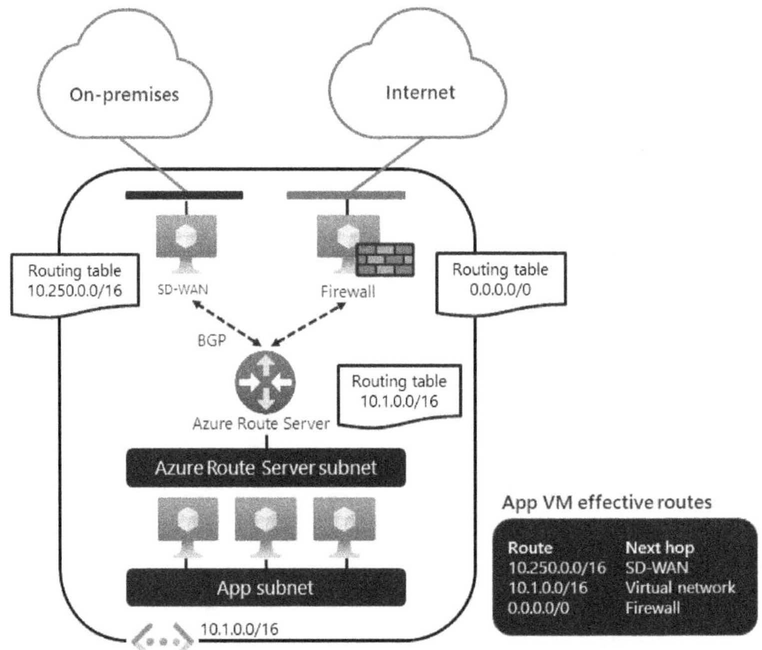

Figure 3.6: *Microsoft Azure Route Server*

Reference: *https://learn.microsoft.com/en-us/Azure/route-server/overview*

In *Figure 3.6*, Azure Route Server uses dynamic routing among on-site networks, the internet, and Azure subnets in the figure above. Through preset routing pathways, the app subnet (10.1.0.0/16) interacts with both on-site (10.250.0.0/16) and the internet (0.0.0.0/0).

In establishing a connection, the SD-WAN device dynamically swaps routes with the Azure Route Server via BGP for on-site connectivity. Traffic headed for the on-site network is guaranteed to pass the SD-WAN equipment via the routing table (10.250.0.0/16).

A firewall filters outgoing requests for internet-bound traffic. Improving security and compliance, the routing table (0.0.0.0/0) guarantees all external traffic is guided through the firewall before reaching the internet.

NSG vs. Azure Firewall

Azure provides multiple tools for managing traffic flow and enforcing security policies, but it is important to know when to use each. While NSGs are lightweight and suitable for internal traffic filtering, Azure Firewall offers advanced protection for more complex scenarios like internet-facing workloads or centralized policy enforcement.

The following table summarizes their key differences to help guide architectural decisions:

Feature	NSG	Azure Firewall
Layer	L3/L4 (Network and Transport)	L3–L7 (Network to Application)
Scope	Subnet or NIC	Centralized for all VNets
Stateful	No (stateless rules)	Yes (stateful packet inspection)
Threat intelligence	Not supported	Built-in Microsoft threat intel filtering
NAT support	No	Yes (SNAT/DNAT)
Logging	NSG flow logs	Full diagnostics, metrics, and alerts
Best use case	East-west VNet traffic filtering	Internet egress/ingress filtering, hybrid routing
Cost	Free	Additional cost (pay-as-you-go)

***Table 3.2**: NSG vs. Azure Firewall*

Best practices for securing Azure Virtual Networks

Here are three key strategies to keep your Azure network secure:

- **Use subnets to isolate workloads by environment or role**: One easy yet effective approach to increase security and speed is to break out your VNet into subnets. Grouping resources depending on their environment—e.g., development, testing, production—or role—e.g., web servers, application servers, databases—helps you to minimize exposure and govern traffic flow.

  For example, a web server in a public-facing subnet shouldn't have direct access to a database in a private subnet. Instead, traffic should be routed through an application layer or a security appliance. Proper subnet segmentation helps contain threats and keeps sensitive workloads isolated.

- **Apply NSGs at both subnet and NIC levels for layered protection**: NSGs are one of the first lines of defense in Azure networking. To maximize security, apply NSGs at both the subnet level and the NIC level.
  - Subnet-level NSGs enforce broad security policies for all resources in that subnet.
  - NIC-level NSGs allow fine-grained control over individual virtual machines or workloads.

Some workloads, for instance, block all inbound traffic at the subnet level but let particular exceptions at the NIC level. While keeping unwelcome traffic out, this layered approach guarantees superior security and flexibility.

- **Regularly review and update firewall and NSG rules**: Security is not a *set it and forget it* task. Over time, your applications and network needs will change, and outdated firewall or NSG rules can create security issues and unnecessary exposure.
  - Schedule periodic audits to remove unused or overly permissive rules.
  - Use Azure Firewall's threat intelligence to automatically block traffic from known malicious sources.
  - Log and monitor network traffic to detect unusual patterns that might indicate security threats.

Securing private access to Azure resources

While traffic filtering mechanisms protect resources from unwanted access, securing private access to Azure services is another critical aspect of network security. Public exposure of resources can increase risks such as DDoS attacks and data exfiltration. Azure provides several options, including Private Link, Service Endpoints, and Azure Bastion, to enable secure access without relying on public IPs. Let us explore these options in detail.

Introduction to private access

A fundamental aspect of cloud security is making sure Azure resources stay unreachable from the public internet. Private access removes the risks related to public IP exposure by letting services interact inside a specified network. Restricted access to private networks helps companies to lower attack surfaces, improve data security, and maintain security policy compliance.

Azure provides several means of enabling private access to resources and maintaining security and isolation. Azure Private Link, Service Endpoints, and Azure Bastion are the main features of private access. While Service Endpoints let VNets securely link to Azure services without using private IPs, Azure Private Link offers private access to Azure services via a private IP. Azure Bastion provides safe RDP/SSH connectivity to virtual machines using the Azure Portal for remote access, therefore avoiding public IP exposure.

Azure offers safe, high-performance ways for companies needing hybrid connections to link on-site networks to Azure. While ExpressRoute provides dedicated, high-bandwidth access to Azure services for increased performance and security, Azure VPN Gateway enables site-to-site and point-to-site VPN connections. Azure Virtual WAN also facilitates large-scale branch-to-Azure communication, hence facilitating the management of worldwide network topologies.

Key features

Azure provides multiple built-in capabilities that allow safe, private access to resources to protect workloads and reduce public internet access exposure. These comprise Azure Private Link, Service Endpoints, and Azure Bastion, each with a different function in maintaining network connectivity inside Azure. Let us explore the options offered by Azure:

- **Azure Private Link**: Azure Private Link is a service that allows you to connect to Azure PaaS services (such as Azure Storage, SQL Database, Key Vault, etc.) or your services using a private IP address. This ensures that the traffic stays within your Azure VNet or the Microsoft backbone and never gets exposed to the public internet.

  Working of Azure Private Link:

  - When you enable Private Link for a service, Azure assigns it a private IP address from your VNet.
  - Your resources (such as virtual machines or applications) can securely access the service through this private IP, preventing any public exposure.
  - The connection happens via a Private Endpoint, which ensures that the data never leaves the Azure backbone network.

  The following figure shows the Azure Private Link Center, which provides a centralized interface for managing Private Endpoint and securely connecting services without exposing them to the public internet:

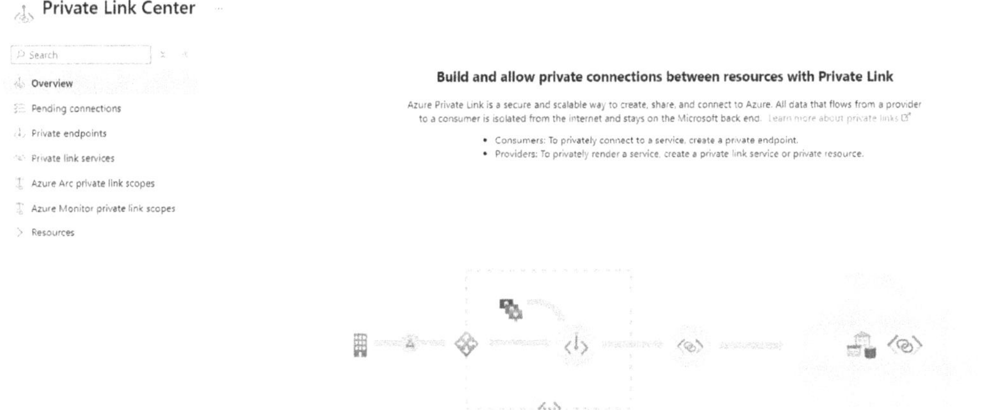

Figure 3.7: Private Link Center

- **Service Endpoints**: Service Endpoints let you access Azure services securely across the Azure backbone network rather than the public internet, therefore extending the identity of your VNet to Azure. Service Endpoints, unlike Private Link, restrict access to particular VNets, therefore enforcing stricter security restrictions rather than assigning a private IP to the resource.

Working of Service Endpoints:

- When you enable a Service Endpoint for a particular Azure service (e.g., Azure Storage, Azure SQL), the traffic from your VNet to that service remains inside the Microsoft Azure backbone, avoiding public internet routing.
- The service itself retains its public IP, but Azure recognizes traffic from your VNet as trusted, allowing access.

The following figure illustrates how Azure Service Endpoints allow secure access to Azure Storage from a virtual network, ensuring traffic remains within the Microsoft backbone and bypasses the public internet:

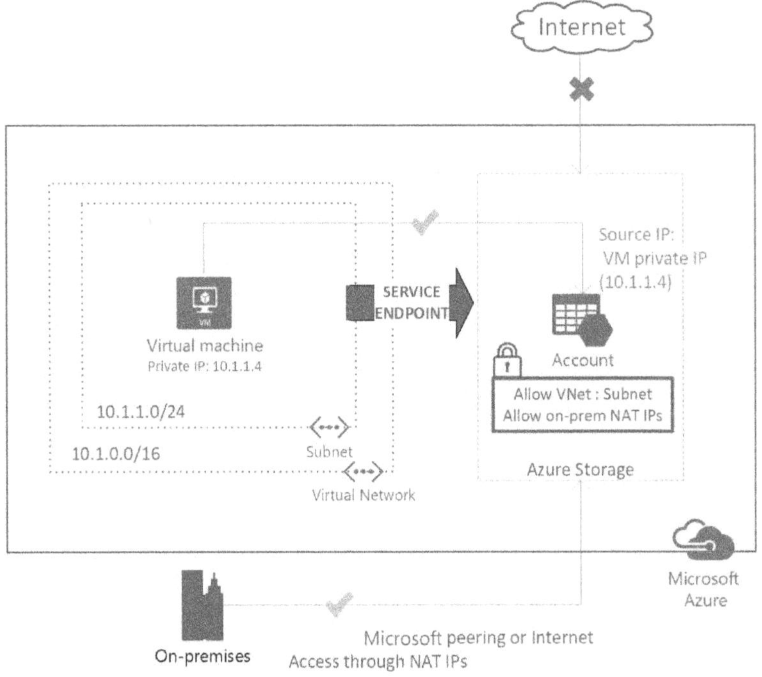

***Figure 3.8:** Microsoft Service Endpoint*

***Reference:** https://learn.microsoft.com/en-us/Azure/virtual-network/virtual-network-service-endpoints-overview*

Figure 3.8, Azure Storage is secured using a Service Endpoint, allowing access only from a specific VNet and on-premises NAT IPs while blocking direct internet access.

A **virtual machine** (**VM**) with private IP 10.1.1.4 sits within the subnet (10.1.1.0/24) inside a VNet (10.1.0.0/16). Instead of exposing Azure Storage to the internet, the VM communicates with Azure Storage via a Service Endpoint, which ensures that traffic remains within Azure's backbone network and does not traverse the public internet.

The storage account is configured with access policies that allow connections only from the designated VNet and permitted NAT IPs from on-premises. Internet-based access is explicitly blocked, enhancing security by preventing unauthorized access.

Microsoft peering or NAT IP-based access allows Azure Storage to be safely reached for on-site connectivity. By enhancing performance, security, and compliance, this method guarantees that data access stays limited to trustworthy networks.

While Service Endpoints help secure service-level access, securing administrative access to virtual machines requires a different approach—this is where Azure Bastion comes in. Let us understand it in more detail:

- **Azure Bastion**: Exposing **Remote Desktop Protocol** (**RDP**) or **Secure Shell** (**SSH**) ports to the internet makes VMs vulnerable to brute-force assaults, resulting in one of the major security dangers in the cloud. Azure Bastion offers safe, web-based access to VMs without exposing them to public IPs, therefore removing this danger.

  Working of Azure Bastion:

  - Instead of assigning a public IP to your VM, Azure Bastion provides a managed jump host that enables RDP/SSH access via the Azure Portal.
  - Users connect to VMs directly from their browser, meaning there's no need to open RDP/SSH ports (3389, 22) to the internet.
  - Since Bastion resides in its own dedicated subnet, traffic flows securely through Azure's private network.

The following figure shows how Azure Bastion enables secure RDP/SSH access to virtual machines directly through the Azure portal without exposing them to the public internet:

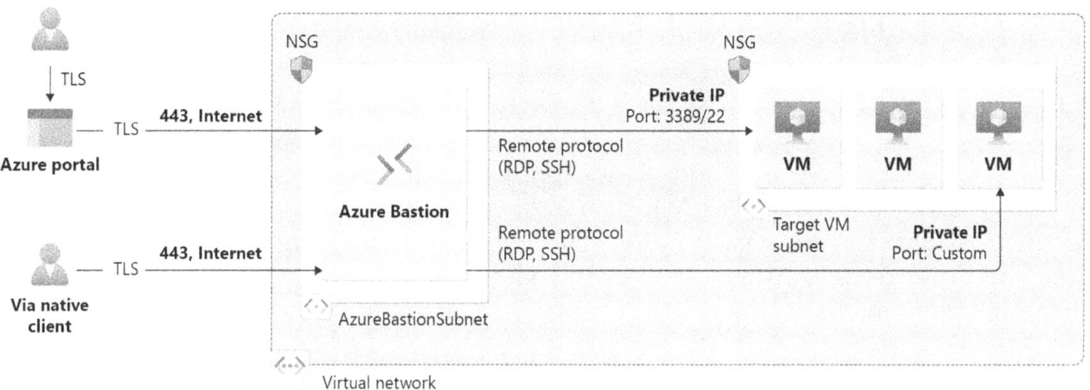

Figure 3.9: *Microsoft Azure Bastion*

Reference: *https://learn.microsoft.com/en-us/Azure/bastion/bastion-overview*

Private Link vs. Service Endpoints comparison table

Here is a comparison of the two services previously discussed:

Feature	Azure Private Link	Azure Service Endpoints
IP assignment	Uses a private IP from your VNet (via Private Endpoint)	No private IP assigned; uses Azure public IPs behind the scenes
Security	Provides true network isolation; traffic never leaves the VNet	Traffic stays on Microsoft backbone but may traverse public IP space internally
Cost	Slightly higher due to data processing and Private Endpoint usage	No extra charge (standard bandwidth billing applies)
DNS behavior	Requires DNS updates or Private DNS Zone to resolve to the private IP	No DNS changes needed; resolves to Azure service's public IP
Hybrid environment impact	Preferred for hybrid scenarios needing end-to-end private routing	Less suitable for on-premises access via VPN/ExpressRoute
Visibility	Appears as a NIC in your VNet	No resource presence in your VNet
RBAC/Control	Enables more granular control via resource-scoped access	Access controlled via VNet and subnet policies only

***Table 3.3**: Private Link vs. Service Endpoint*

Note: **When using Private Link with custom DNS or hybrid environments, be aware of potential DNS resolution conflicts. If the DNS is not properly configured (e.g., without forwarding to Azure's Private DNS Zones), clients may resolve the public IP instead of the private one, breaking connectivity or bypassing isolation.**

Hybrid connectivity

Many organizations use a hybrid cloud approach, which means that their on-premises infrastructure needs to be able to talk to their Azure workloads safely. With hybrid connectivity, on-premises data centers, remote offices, and the cloud can all work together without any problems. This keeps apps and services linked and easy to access without needing to be connected to the internet.

Azure provides several solutions for establishing secure, high-performance, and scalable hybrid connectivity:

- **Azure VPN Gateway**: A flexible VPN solution for securely connecting on-premises networks or remote users to Azure.

- **ExpressRoute**: A dedicated, high-bandwidth private connection between on-premises infrastructure and Azure, bypassing the public internet.
- **Azure Virtual WAN**: A centralized service designed to simplify large-scale branch-to-Azure connectivity.

Hybrid connectivity decision matrix

Azure offers several hybrid connectivity options, each suited to different business and technical requirements. The table below compares VPN Gateway, ExpressRoute, and Azure Virtual WAN based on key factors like bandwidth, latency, cost, and regulatory compliance to help select the right solution.

Here are the deciding features of each option:

Factor	VPN Gateway	ExpressRoute	Azure Virtual WAN
Bandwidth	Up to 10 Gbps (limited by SKU)	Up to 100 Gbps	Aggregated bandwidth via hubs
Latency sensitivity	Moderate to high latency	Very low latency (dedicated line)	Optimized via Microsoft backbone
Cost	Lower cost (internet-based)	Higher (dedicated circuit + provider fees)	Scales with usage; moderate cost
Regulatory needs	Limited support	Strong compliance & SLAs	Supports compliance across geos
Availability zones	Supported	Supported	Global HA with hub redundancy
Hybrid scalability	Manual config per connection	High-capacity, but complex	Designed for large-scale hybrid networks
Best use case	Small/medium hybrid needs, dev/test	Enterprise, finance, regulated workloads	Multi-site, remote workforce, SD-WAN

Table 3.4: *VPN Gateway vs. ExpressRoute vs. Azure Virtual WAN*

Enhancing security with ExpressRoute private access

Azure ExpressRoute supports **private peering**, which allows organizations to access Azure services over a **private connection**, completely bypassing the public internet.

This enhances security by:

- Ensuring **data never leaves the trusted MPLS or enterprise WAN**.
- Enabling direct, private access to services like Azure SQL Database, Storage Accounts, and VMs.

- Providing a consistent and compliant network path is critical for regulated industries.

Pairing ExpressRoute private peering with Private Link further tightens security by allowing resource-level access control via private IPs within your VNet.

Azure VPN Gateway

Azure VPN Gateway is a cloud-based networking service that lets on-premises networks, remote users, and Azure VNets connect to each other safely and securely. It is set up in Azure VNet and works as a gateway appliance. It enables organizations to make secure connections over the internet using VPN protocols like **Internet Protocol Security** (**IPsec**) and **Internet Key Exchange** (**IKE**).

This service is essential for hybrid cloud deployments because it lets organizations connect their on-premises services to Azure without using the public internet.

Types of Azure VPN Gateway connections

Azure VPN Gateway supports multiple types of VPN connectivity to accommodate different needs:

- **Site-to-site (S2S) VPN**:
    - Establishes a permanent, secure connection between an on-premises network (such as a data center or branch office) and an Azure VNet.
    - Uses IPsec/IKE protocols to encrypt traffic over the internet.
    - Requires a VPN device (router or firewall) on the on-premises side to terminate the connection.
- **Point-to-site (P2S) VPN**:
    - Allows individual remote users (such as employees working from home) to securely connect to an Azure VNet.
    - Uses **Secure Sockets Layer** (**SSL**) or IKEv2 protocols for encryption.
    - No need for a VPN device; users can connect via a VPN client on their laptops or mobile devices.
- **VNet-to-VNet VPN**:
    - Enables secure communication between two or more Azure VNets, even if they are in different Azure regions.
    - Useful when separating workloads across different VNets while maintaining private connectivity.

- **ExpressRoute with VPN failover**:
  - o Organizations using Azure ExpressRoute for dedicated private connectivity can configure a VPN Gateway as a backup connection.
  - o If the ExpressRoute connection fails, the VPN Gateway automatically takes over, ensuring continuous connectivity.

How Azure VPN Gateway works

The following steps provide a high-level overview of how the VPN Gateway works in Azure, ensuring security in and out of Azure:

1. **Deployment in Azure**:
   a. A VPN Gateway is created within an Azure VNet, acting as a central connection point.
   b. Azure assigns a public IP address to the gateway for establishing the VPN tunnel.
2. **Connection establishment**:
   a. For site-to-site VPNs, a VPN device on-premises (e.g., Cisco, Palo Alto, Fortinet) is configured to establish an IPsec tunnel to the Azure VPN Gateway.
   b. For point-to-site VPNs, users connect via VPN client software, which securely tunnels traffic through SSL or IKEv2.
   c. For VNet-to-VNet VPNs, Azure automatically manages the encryption and routing between VNets.
3. **Traffic encryption and routing**:
   a. Traffic passing through the VPN Gateway is encrypted using IPsec/IKE protocols before transmission over the public internet.
   b. Azure route tables (UDRs) can be used to control how traffic flows between on-premises, VNets, and remote users.

Benefits of Azure VPN Gateway

The following are the benefits of Azure VPN Gateway:

- **Secure connectivity**: Ensures encrypted communication between on-premises networks, remote users, and Azure workloads, preventing unauthorized access.
- **Cost-effective hybrid networking**: Provides an affordable alternative to ExpressRoute, making it ideal for businesses that need secure hybrid connectivity without a dedicated private circuit.
- **Scalability and redundancy**: Supports Active-Active configurations for high availability and multiple VPN tunnels for scalability.

- **Multi-protocol support**: Works with industry-standard protocols (IPsec/IKEv2, OpenVPN, and SSL) to support a wide range of devices and vendors.
- **Flexibility across different connectivity scenarios**: Supports site-to-site, point-to-site, and VNet-to-VNet VPNs, allowing organizations to adapt to various networking needs.
- **Integration with ExpressRoute for backup connectivity**: Provides failover support for ExpressRoute, ensuring continuous connectivity even if the primary dedicated link goes down.

ExpressRoute

Azure ExpressRoute is a dedicated, private network connection between an on-premises data center, office, or colocation facility and Azure. Unlike a VPN, ExpressRoute provides a direct, secure link via a Microsoft partner network, ensuring higher reliability, lower latency, and better security.

This makes ExpressRoute the preferred solution for enterprises that need fast, private, and mission-critical connectivity to Azure VNets, Microsoft 365, and Dynamics 365.

The following figure shows how Azure ExpressRoute establishes a private, dedicated connection between an on-premises network and Microsoft Azure, bypassing the public internet for enhanced security and performance:

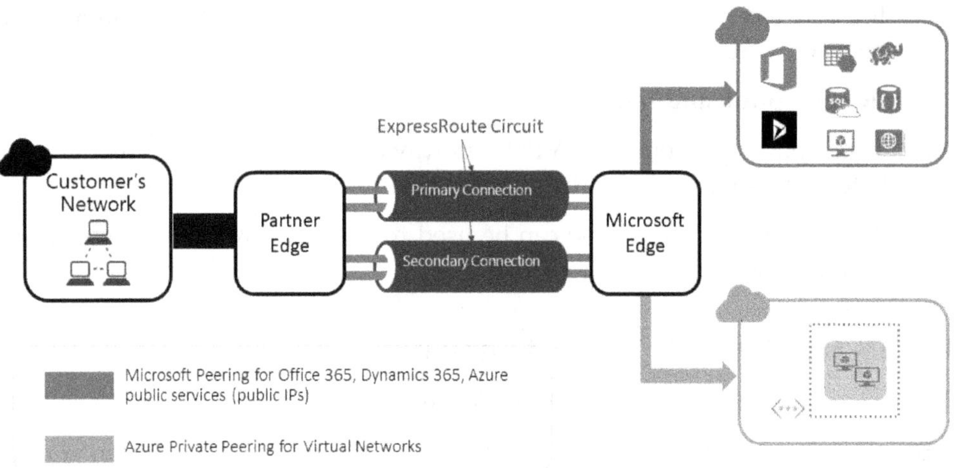

***Figure 3.10**: Microsoft ExpressRoute;*

***Reference**: https://learn.microsoft.com/en-us/Azure/expressroute/expressroute-introduction*

In *Figure 3.10*, Azure ExpressRoute is used to establish a private and dedicated connection between the customer's network and Microsoft Azure, bypassing the public internet for enhanced security, reliability, and performance.

The customer's network connects to Microsoft Edge via a Partner Edge, which provides two redundant connections:

- Primary connection
- Secondary connection

These connections form the ExpressRoute Circuit, ensuring high availability and failover capabilities.

There are two types of peering options:

- **Microsoft peering (Red Path)**: Used for accessing Microsoft public services, such as Office 365, Dynamics 365, and Azure public services (public IPs). This peering allows enterprises to access Microsoft's global services securely without exposing traffic to the public internet.
- **Azure private peering (Blue Path)**: Used for private connections to Azure VNets, enabling secure and high-speed connectivity to Azure VMs, databases, and other resources hosted in private IP spaces.

This setup ensures low-latency, high-performance, and secure hybrid cloud connectivity for enterprises integrating their on-premises infrastructure with Azure.

Types of ExpressRoute circuits

Azure ExpressRoute has three types of circuits, each designed for different networking needs:

- **ExpressRoute standard**:
    - o The default ExpressRoute offering.
    - o Provides private connectivity between an on-premises network and Azure VNets.
    - o Allows communication between an on-premises environment and one Azure region (with the option to add global connectivity).
- **ExpressRoute premium (extended connectivity)**:
    - o Extends the capabilities of ExpressRoute Standard by allowing connections to multiple Azure regions globally using the same circuit.
    - o Supports higher route limits for large-scale enterprise deployments.
    - o Required for scenarios where a single ExpressRoute circuit needs to connect to multiple Azure regions outside the same geo-location (e.g., connecting a circuit in the US to services in Europe or Asia).
- **ExpressRoute Local (lower latency, no egress costs):**
    - o Provides low-latency, high-bandwidth private connectivity to a single Azure region closest to the on-premises location.

- o Unlike Standard and Premium, Local does not support global reach, but it eliminates data transfer (egress) costs, making it cost-efficient for high data transfer workloads.

ExpressRoute connectivity models

Azure ExpressRoute offers different connectivity models, which define how the private connection is established between Azure and the on-premises environment:

- **CloudExchange co-location**:
    - o Connects an on-premises network to Azure via a colocation provider such as Equinix or Megaport.
    - o Suitable for businesses already using colocation data centers to simplify connectivity to Azure.
- **Point-to-point (P2P) connection**:
    - o Establishes a direct Private Link between the customer's on-premises network and Azure using a dedicated ExpressRoute provider.
    - o Ideal for businesses needing secure, high-speed connectivity between Azure and a single data center or office.
- **Any-to-any (IPVPN) connection:**
    - o Extends an existing **Multiprotocol Label Switching** (**MPLS**) network to Azure.
    - o Best for companies with multiple branch offices wanting to integrate Azure as another node in their enterprise WAN.

The following figure showcases the different ExpressRoute connectivity models, highlighting how organizations can establish private connections to Azure through colocation providers, point-to-point links, or existing MPLS networks:

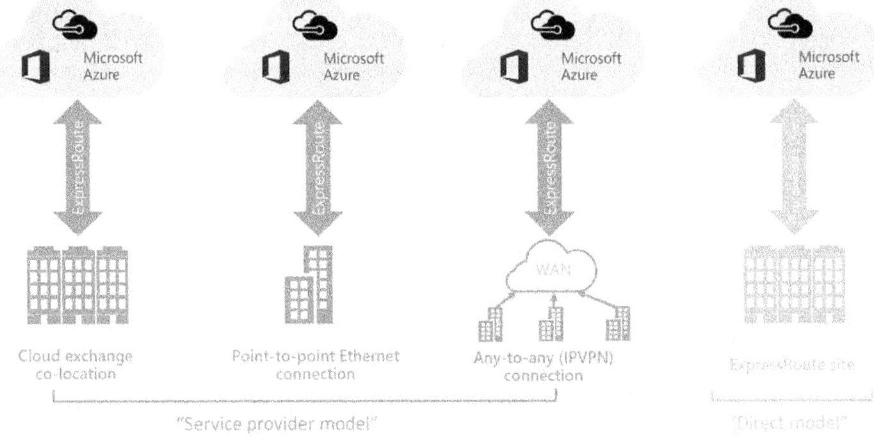

***Figure 3.11**: Microsoft connectivity models*

***Reference**: https://learn.microsoft.com/en-us/Azure/expressroute/expressroute-connectivity-models*

In *Figure 3.11*, different ExpressRoute connectivity models are illustrated, showing how organizations can establish private connections to Microsoft Azure without traversing the public internet. There are two primary models:

- **Service provider model (Orange Arrows)**: This model involves a third-party provider to facilitate connectivity between the customer's network and Azure ExpressRoute:
  - **Cloud exchange co-location:** The customer connects to Azure via a cloud exchange provider, leveraging a shared co-location facility for faster deployment.
  - **Point-to-point Ethernet connection**: A dedicated Layer 2 Ethernet connection is used to directly link the customer's on-premises network to Azure.
  - **Any-to-any (IPVPN) connection**: Customers using a WAN or MPLS-based IPVPN (such as an enterprise WAN) can extend their private network to Azure using ExpressRoute.
- **Direct model (Yellow arrow)**: ExpressRoute direct: This model provides a dedicated, high-capacity connection directly between the customer's network and Azure's backbone, bypassing any intermediaries. It is ideal for enterprises requiring higher bandwidth and lower latency.

  This setup ensures secure, high-performance, and reliable hybrid cloud connectivity, allowing businesses to choose the model that best fits their networking and compliance needs.

Working of ExpressRoute

Following is how ExpressRoute Works:

- **Provisioning the circuit**:
  - The customer partners with an ExpressRoute provider to set up a dedicated circuit between their on-premises network and Microsoft's edge routers.
- **Peering options for traffic routing**:
  - ExpressRoute offers three peering types to handle different types of traffic:
    - **Private peering**: Used to connect Azure VNets to on-premises networks, allowing direct communication between virtual machines and on-premises workloads.
    - **Microsoft peering**: Provides private connectivity to Microsoft cloud services, including Microsoft 365 and Dynamics 365.
    - **Public peering (Deprecated)**: Previously allowed access to Azure services with public IPs, but it has been replaced by Microsoft peering and Private Link.

- **Traffic transmission**:
  - o Data is transmitted over a private circuit, ensuring low latency, high bandwidth, and no internet exposure.
  - o Customers can configure routing policies and apply QoS for optimized performance.

Benefits of Azure ExpressRoute

Following are the benefits of Azure ExpressRoute:

- ExpressRoute establishes a direct, dedicated link to Azure, eliminating internet-related risks. Unlike VPNs, which rely on the public internet.
- Provides bandwidth from 50 Mbps to 100 Gbps, ensuring fast and reliable connectivity for enterprise workloads.
- ExpressRoute circuits have an SLA of 99.95% making it suitable for mission-critical applications.
- ExpressRoute improves latency and throughput when accessing Microsoft 365 and Dynamics 365, especially for large enterprises.
- It allows global reach, enabling businesses to connect multiple Azure regions over the same circuit.
- ExpressRoute can be combined with Azure VPN Gateway as a failover solution, ensuring business continuity if the primary ExpressRoute circuit goes down.

Azure Virtual WAN

Azure **Virtual WAN** (**VWAN**) is a networking service in the cloud that makes it easier and faster for branch offices, online users, on-premises data centres, and Azure to connect with each other. As a central networking hub, it makes it easy for businesses to connect and control many network endpoints.

VWAN is different from standard point-to-point VPN or ExpressRoute connections because it lets organizations use Microsoft's backbone to build a fully meshed global network. This makes the network simpler and faster.

Types of Azure Virtual WAN

Azure VWAN is available in two tiers to accommodate different business needs:

- **Standard VWAN**:
  - o Supports site-to-site VPN, point-to-site VPN (remote users), and ExpressRoute integration.

    - Provides global transit connectivity, meaning traffic can flow between different VNets and branches using the Virtual WAN hub.
    - Integrates with Azure Firewall and third-party security appliances for centralized security enforcement.
- **Basic VWAN**:
    - Offers site-to-site VPN connectivity only, with no support for ExpressRoute, point-to-site VPNs, or global transit.
    - Designed for smaller deployments that only require basic hybrid connectivity to Azure.

Working of Azure Virtual WAN

The following is how Azure VWAN works:

- **Deployment of VWAN hub**:
    - A VWAN hub is created in Azure, acting as a central point of connectivity for all branch offices, remote users, VNets, and on-premises data centers.
    - This hub-and-spoke architecture allows traffic to be efficiently routed through the Azure backbone instead of the public internet.
- **Connecting on-premises and remote users**:
    - **Site-to-site VPN**: Branch offices and on-premises data centers connect securely to the VWAN hub using IPsec/IKE VPN tunnels.
    - **Point-to-site VPN**: Remote users establish SSL or IKEv2 VPN connections to the Virtual WAN hub, allowing secure access to corporate resources.
    - **ExpressRoute**: Enterprises with high-performance private connections can integrate ExpressRoute with Virtual WAN for optimized traffic routing and redundancy.
- **Traffic optimization and security**:
    - Azure Virtual WAN automatically optimizes traffic paths between connected sites, reducing latency and congestion.
    - Integration with Azure Firewall ensures that traffic flowing through the Virtual WAN hub is inspected before reaching its destination.

Benefits of Azure VWAN:

- Routes traffic through Microsoft's global network, ensuring lower latency and higher reliability than traditional internet-based VPNs.

- Works with VPN (site-to-site & point-to-site), ExpressRoute, and SD-WAN solutions, making it flexible for different enterprise needs.
- Integrates with Azure Firewall Manager for secure internet breakout, DDoS protection, and traffic filtering across all connected sites.
- Ideal for enterprises with multiple branch offices looking for a single, scalable networking solution without needing separate VPN appliances for each site.

Best practices

Here are some best practices for securing your workload:

- **Use Azure Private Link instead of public endpoints**: Always prefer Azure Private Link over public endpoints when connecting to Azure PaaS services like Azure Storage, SQL Database, and Key Vault. This ensures that traffic remains within Microsoft's network, reducing external exposures.
- **Restrict public network access**: Disable public access for Azure resources whenever possible. Allow only private connections through Private Link, Service Endpoints, or VPN/ExpressRoute to minimize attack surfaces.
- **Implement Service Endpoints for secure connectivity**: If Private Link is not an option, use Service Endpoints to keep traffic between Azure VNets and services on the Azure backbone network rather than routing through the public internet.
- **Secure remote access with Azure Bastion**: Avoid exposing RDP (3389) and SSH (22) ports to the internet. Use Azure Bastion for browser-based, private remote access to virtual machines without requiring a public IP.
- **Use Private DNS zones for name resolution**: Configure Azure Private DNS Zones to ensure seamless name resolution for Private Endpoint, preventing issues with service connectivity over Private Link.
- **Enforce least privilege access**: Use Azure RBAC to restrict who can configure Private Link, Service Endpoints, and Bastion settings. Limit permissions to only those who absolutely need them.
- **Monitor and audit private access**: Enable Azure Monitor, Microsoft Defender for Cloud, and Azure Policy to track access logs, enforce compliance, and detect unusual activity related to private access.
- **Implement redundancy for high availability**: Deploy multiple Private Link endpoints across availability zones and enable zone redundancy for Azure Bastion to ensure connectivity remains available during failures.
- **Optimise network performance**: Avoid excessive Private Link connections to prevent reaching Azure limits and optimize bandwidth usage. ExpressRoute with Private peering should be used for high-speed, private on-premises connectivity.

- **Regularly review and update security configurations**: Periodically audit Private Link, Service Endpoints, and Bastion settings to remove unused configurations and ensure security policies align with best practices and compliance requirements.

Securing public access to Azure resources

While private access methods ensure that resources remain securely accessible within a controlled network, some workloads must still be exposed to the public internet, such as web applications and APIs. However, public access introduces new security challenges, including DDoS attacks, bot traffic, and unauthorized access attempts. To mitigate these risks, Azure offers security controls such as Azure Application Gateway, Front Door, and WAF. Let us discuss the best ways to protect public-facing resources.

Public Access considerations

Although some Azure resources like web apps, APIs, and **content delivery networks** (**CDNs**) must be publicly accessible, it is essential to apply security controls to guard them against illegal access, cyber threats, and data breaches. Since publicly exposed endpoints are usually the main targets for attackers, it is imperative to implement strong security policies without endangering performance or accessibility.

Organizations have to consider carefully whether and how to provide public access while maintaining compliance, availability, and security. Best practices include limiting exposure, requiring authentication, applying network filtering, and employing Azure-native security services to secure internet-facing apps and services.

Some key security considerations for publicly exposed resources include:

- **Minimizing public exposure**: Make sure that the internet can only see the resources that it needs to see, and limit access whenever you can. For instance, internal apps should stay inside a private network using Azure Private Link and not be open to everyone.
- **Security and authorization**: All apps that are open to the public should need strong security using Entra ID, OAuth, or some other identity solution.
- **Using firewalls and network filtering**: To protect public endpoints from malicious traffic and efforts to get in without permission, use Azure WAF, Azure DDoS Protection, and NSGs.
- **Using secure TLS encryption**: Services that are open to the public should always use HTTPS with TLS 1.2 or higher to protect data in transit.
- **Monitoring and logging access**: Enable Azure Monitor, Microsoft Defender for Cloud, and Azure Sentinel to track and analyze traffic patterns, detect anomalies, and respond to potential threats in real time.

- **DDoS protection**: Large-scale attacks that attempt to overwhelm a public-facing resource should be mitigated using Azure DDoS Protection, which automatically detects and blocks malicious traffic before it reaches your infrastructure.
- **Rate limiting and throttling**: APIs and web applications should implement rate limiting using Azure API Management to prevent abuse and brute-force attacks.

Tools for securing public access

Organizations exposing resources to the public internet need to have strict security policies in place to guard against illegal access, cyber threats, and massive attacks. Azure offers various built-in security measures meant to increase the resilience of public-facing programs and guarantee the best performance and availability.

By filtering hostile traffic, preventing typical online vulnerabilities, and mitigating large-scale DDoS attacks, key resources include Azure Application Gateway, Azure Front Door, online WAF, and Azure DDoS Protection to help defend public endpoints. These services cooperate to offer multilayer security, ensuring that applications remain compatible with contemporary security standards, secured, and responsive.

Azure Application Gateway

Azure Application Gateway is an application layer (7 load balancer) that helps web apps hosted in Azure with intelligent traffic routing, security, and high availability. Application Gateway is different from other load balancers because it works at layer 4, which is the transport layer. It can handle both HTTP and HTTPS traffic and has advanced features like SSL termination, WAF, and URL-based routing.

In addition to ensuring that incoming web requests are routed to the appropriate backend sites, it has security elements that defend against the most typical threats that may be found on the internet. It ensures high speed, safety, and the capacity to expand; it is an ideal choice for web applications that are either public or private, respectively.

How Azure Application Gateway works:

- **Traffic flow and load balancing**: Azure Application Gateway manages how web traffic flows to backend services, ensuring efficient load distribution and intelligent request handling. Unlike basic load balancers that only distribute requests based on server availability, it operates at Layer 7 (Application Layer). It can understand HTTP and HTTPS traffic and make routing decisions based on URLs, headers, and cookies.

  For example, suppose a company hosts multiple applications on a single gateway. In that case, the gateway can route traffic based on the requested URL, like sending requests for **app1.example.com** to one backend and **app2.example.com** to another. It also supports session affinity, which ensures that a returning user connects to the same backend server for a consistent experience. This feature is useful for applications that rely on user sessions, shopping carts, or authentication tokens.

- **SSL termination and offloading**: Encrypting and decrypting SSL/TLS traffic is necessary for security, but it can be a performance killer for backend servers. That is where SSL termination comes in. Instead of making backend servers handle encryption, Application Gateway decrypts incoming HTTPS requests, processes them, and then forwards the requests as HTTP. This frees up computing power on the backend, allowing applications to run more efficiently.

  Some businesses require end-to-end encryption, meaning data remains encrypted even when passing between the gateway and backend servers. Application Gateway supports this, too—it decrypts traffic, applies routing rules, and then re-encrypts it before sending it along. This balances performance and security, keeping data protected without overloading backend resources.

- **WAF protection**: Public-facing web applications are prime targets for cyberattacks, so security is not optional; it is essential. That is why Application Gateway comes with a built-in WAF, designed to detect and block malicious traffic before it reaches your backend servers.

  Think of WAF as a security checkpoint for your application. It scans incoming requests in real-time, looking for SQL injection, **cross-site scripting** (**XSS**), and bot attacks, some of the most common threats that hackers use to exploit vulnerabilities. You can customize WAF policies to allow, block, or monitor specific types of traffic, giving you full control over your security posture. Since the firewall is regularly updated, your applications stay protected without you having to constantly tweak settings.

- **Autoscaling and high availability**: Traffic is not static; it fluctuates. Some days, everything runs smoothly, and then suddenly, there is a surge in visitors, putting stress on your infrastructure. That is where autoscaling comes in. Application Gateway automatically adjusts its capacity based on traffic demands, ensuring your application can handle spikes without any slowness.

  Application Gateway is designed for high availability, meaning it reroutes traffic to healthy instances if something goes wrong. Plus, when deployed across multiple Azure Availability Zones, your application stays up and running even if one data center goes offline. In short, it is built for resilience, reliability, and performance, so you are covered no matter what.

- **Integration with other Azure services**: Application Gateway does not work in isolation; instead, it plays well with other Azure networking and security services to create a fully optimized, secure environment. It integrates with Azure Front Door for global content delivery, Azure Traffic Manager for DNS-based load balancing, and Azure Load Balancer for handling internal traffic distribution.

  This reduces security risks while maintaining seamless communication between services inside Azure.

The following figure demonstrates how Azure Application Gateway routes traffic based on URL paths while providing Layer 7 load balancing and WAF protection for enhanced security:

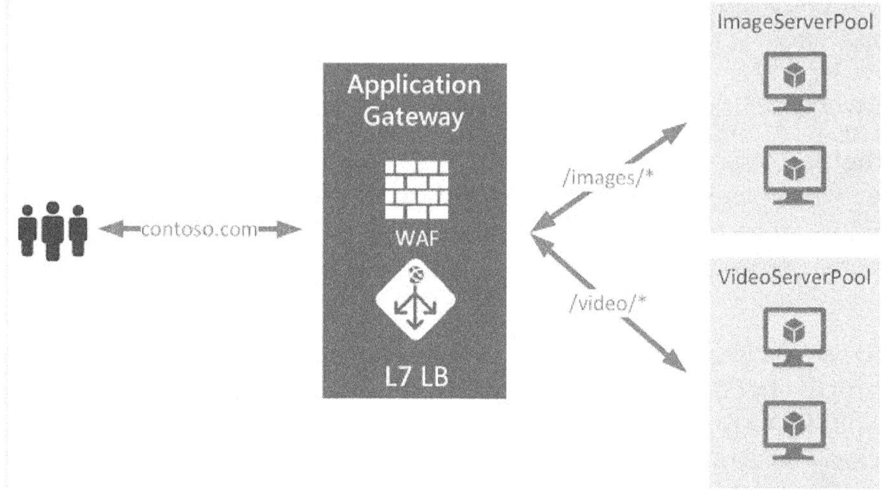

Figure 3.12: *Microsoft App Gateway*

Reference: *https://learn.microsoft.com/en-us/Azure/application-gateway/overview*

In the above figure, Azure Application Gateway is used as an L7 LB and WAF to intelligently route traffic based on URL paths.

Users accessing contoso.com are routed through the Application Gateway, which inspects and directs requests based on predefined rules:

- Requests matching **`/images/*`** are forwarded to the ImageServerPool, which hosts image-related content.
- Requests matching **`/video/*`** are forwarded to the VideoServerPool, which serves video content.

The WAF feature provides protection against common web vulnerabilities, such as SQL injection, XSS, and other OWASP Top 10 threats.

This setup enhances security, scalability, and efficient traffic distribution, ensuring optimized application performance and protection against web-based attacks.

Azure Front Door

In today's digital world, users expect fast, reliable, and secure access to applications, no matter where they are. That's where Azure Front Door comes in. Think of it as your application's global entrance, a cloud-based, scalable CDN and security service that ensures users are always directed to the best-performing, closest, and most secure backend.

Traditional load balancers only work in one area, but Azure Front Door works all over the world, sending traffic to the fastest and healthiest backend in each region. Front Door helps improve the performance, security, and availability of an app without you having to worry about manual configurations or network latency problems. This is true whether the app serves millions of users or just a few.

How Azure Front Door works:

- **Global Traffic Routing and Load Balancing**: Azure Front Door sends user traffic to the backend that is closest and fastest, ensuring the best performance. Front Door works across multiple Azure regions and uses latency-based routing to choose the fastest way. A standard load balancer only moves traffic within one region.

  For example, if you have backend services in *North America*, *Europe*, and *Asia*, a user in *London* would be automatically directed to the European backend rather than one in the U.S. This reduces latency, improves load times, and enhances the overall user experience. If one backend becomes unhealthy or unavailable, Front Door instantly reroutes traffic to another healthy instance, keeping your application online and responsive even during failures.

  Besides that, Front Door offers many types of routing, such as priority-based failover, host header-based routing, and path-based routing. This lets you finetune how different endpoints handle requests and gives you full control over how traffic moves through your app.

- **SSL offloading and secure traffic management**: Web apps need to be encrypted to be safe, but backend servers that handle SSL/TLS termination can slow things down. Azure Front Door offloads SSL processing, which means that it stops HTTPS requests at the edge, decrypts them, and sends them safely to the backend. This lowers the load on your backend computers' CPUs, which makes them faster without lowering their security.

  Azure Front Door also supports TLS pass-through for companies that need end-to-end encryption. This means that encrypted data is safe from the user's browser all the way to the backend server. This makes sure that strict security rules are followed while still using Front Door's speed improvements.

- **DDoS protection and WAF integration**: For public-facing apps, security risks are a big deal, and Azure Front Door protects you against common web attacks right out of the box. It comes with Azure DDoS Protection, which finds and stops large-scale DDoS attacks instantly, so your app can still be used even when an attack is happening.

  Integration of WAF also offers strong security against dangers such as SQL injection, XSS, and malicious bots. You can change the WAF policies to either block, accept, or watch certain types of traffic. This lowers the risk of cyber threats while keeping application performance high.

Because Azure's security services continuously update their threat intelligence, your application remains protected against evolving attack patterns without requiring constant manual rule adjustments.

- **Performance acceleration with caching and compression**: Speed matters, and Azure Front Door optimizes application performance by caching static content closer to users. It acts as a CDN, reducing the need to retrieve the same data from backend servers repeatedly. This significantly improves load times, particularly for users in distant regions.

  Front Door also supports HTTP/2 and gzip compression, which makes sure that data is sent quickly and efficiently while using less bandwidth and speeding up the loading of web pages. These improvements make the experience faster and lag-free for users, especially on apps with a lot of traffic.

- **High availability and automatic failover**: Downtime is not an option for critical applications, and Azure Front Door helps ensure high availability by automatically failing over to healthy backends if an outage occurs. It continuously monitors backend health and redirects traffic in real-time, without user interruption.

  For instance, if your main backend in Europe goes down, users are automatically sent to your backend in North America or Asia. Businesses can keep running even if a server fails or there are problems in another part of the country, thanks to this automatic backup system.

- **Rate limiting and bot protection**: Azure Front Door has built-in rate limiting and bot protection to protect applications against abuse and overload. Its rate limiting rules can throttle excessive requests from a single client IP, helping prevent denial-of-service attempts and credential stuffing attacks at the edge before they reach your application.

  For more advanced protection, Azure Front Door integrates with WAF to block known bad bots, enforce custom match rules, and provide logging. These security signals can be streamed into Microsoft Sentinel, enabling real-time detection, analytics, and automated incident response.

The following figure shows how Azure Front Door securely routes global traffic to the closest and healthiest backend, leveraging integrated WAF and DDoS protection for optimized performance and security:

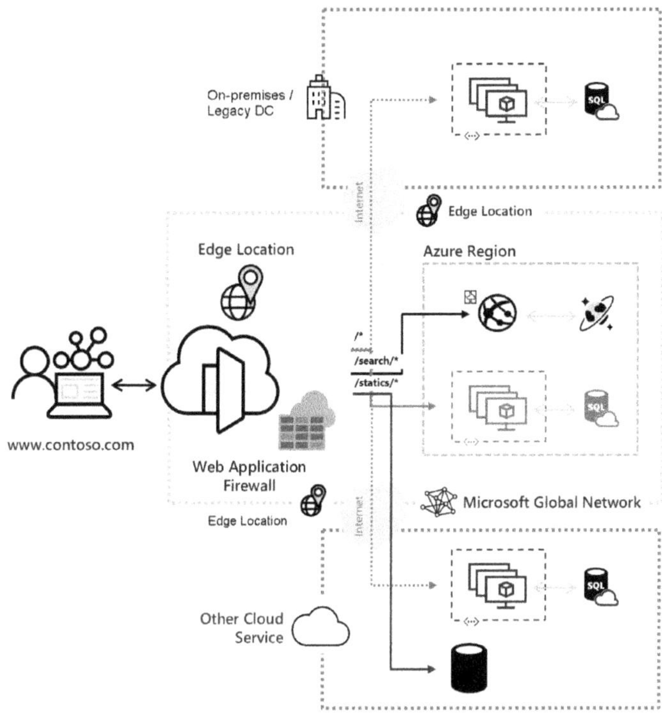

***Figure 3.13**: Microsoft Azure Front Door*

***Reference**: https://learn.microsoft.com/en-us/Azure/frontdoor/front-door-overview*

In *Figure 3.13, Azure WAF* and *Microsoft's Global Network* are used to securely route traffic between users, cloud services, and on-premises resources.

Let us look at the traffic flow:

- Users access the application through **www.contoso.com**, which is protected by an Edge Location with a WAF to filter malicious traffic.
- The WAF routes traffic to different destinations based on request paths:
    - o General traffic (/*) is sent to an Azure Region where application resources, databases, and services reside.
    - o Requests for **`/search/`** and **`/statics/`** are directed through optimized paths within the Microsoft Global Network for efficient content delivery.
- Data may be retrieved from multiple sources, including:
    - o On-premises/legacy data center via a secure connection.
    - o Other cloud services may store external or third-party data.
    - o Azure services, such as databases, storage, and compute resources.

Web Application Firewall

Web apps are always being attacked these days. Whether it's SQL injection, XSS, or bot-driven attacks, hackers are always looking for ways to get into systems and use private data or even take control of the whole thing. We can help with that with WAF.

WAF is a security solution that monitors, filters, and blocks malicious traffic before it gets to backend servers. This keeps web apps safe from common cyber threats. WAF protects HTTP/HTTPS requests, while traditional firewalls protect network-level traffic. This makes WAF important for websites, APIs, and cloud apps that are open to the public.

Azure's WAF is fully integrated with Application Gateway, Azure Front Door, and Azure CDN. This gives you a choice of how to install WAF based on your performance, security, and global reach needs.

Predefined rules and custom policy configurations

Azure WAF comes with out-of-the-box security rules based on the **Open Web Application Security Project** (**OWASP**) Top 10, a global list of the critical security risks for web applications.

These OWASP Top 10 rules help protect against:

- **SQL injection**: Prevents attackers from injecting malicious database queries.
- **XSS**: Stops unauthorized scripts from executing in user sessions.
- **Remote code execution**: Blocks attempts to inject malicious code into an application.
- **Cross-site request forgery (CSRF)**: Prevents unauthorized commands from being executed.
- **HTTP request smuggling**: Detects and blocks requests that try to bypass security controls.

In addition to these predefined protections, organizations can customize WAF rules for specific security requirements. For example, you can:

- Block or allow traffic from specific IP addresses or geo-locations.
- Apply rate limiting to prevent DDoS-like bot traffic from exploiting the backend.
- Create custom rules to detect unique attack patterns targeting your application.
- **Deployment options**: Depending on the architecture of your app, Azure gives you three ways to install WAF:
    - **WAF with Azure Application Gateway**:
        - Best for regional traffic filtering within a specific Azure region.
        - Works in protecting internal applications, backend services, and microservices hosted in Azure VNets.

    - Offers deeper customization, allowing for advanced routing and SSL termination alongside security filtering.
  - **WAF with Azure Front Door**:
    - Ideal for global web applications that need security at the edge.
    - Ensures fast performance and protection by filtering threats before they ever reach an Azure data center.
    - Recommended for deployments in multiple regions and large-scale applications that must protect against DDoS attacks and route data intelligently.
  - **WAF with Azure CDN**:
    - Made for apps that depend on media delivery and cached content a lot.
    - Common web attacks are stopped before information is sent from Azure CDN endpoints.
    - Helps cut down on bandwidth use while keeping security a top concern.

The following figure illustrates how Azure WAF, integrated with Application Gateway, inspects incoming traffic and blocks common web threats before requests reach backend servers:

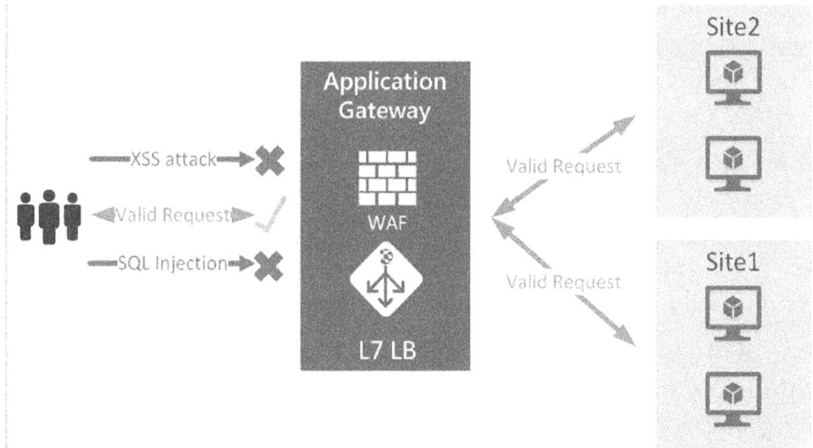

***Figure 3.14**: Microsoft Azure WAF*

***Reference**: https://learn.microsoft.com/en-us/Azure/web-application-firewall/ag/ag-overview*

In *Figure 3.14,* Azure Application Gateway is used as a **Layer 7 Load Balancer** (**L7 LB**) with WAF to filter and distribute traffic securely.

Traffic flow and security features:

- Incoming traffic from users is inspected by the Application Gateway WAF before being forwarded to backend servers.

- The WAF blocks malicious requests, including:
    - o XSS attacks
    - o SQL injection attempts
- Valid requests are allowed and routed to the appropriate backend servers in Site1 and Site2 for further processing.

Azure DDoS protection

In today's digital age, DDoS attacks are among the most common and disruptive cyber threats. These attacks overwhelm web services with enormous amounts of traffic, rendering them slow, unresponsive, or altogether unavailable to legitimate users. Businesses that rely on cloud-based software, e-commerce platforms, or public-facing services cannot afford downtime, so DDoS prevention is critical.

Azure DDoS Protection is a cloud-based security solution for detecting and mitigating DDoS attacks in real-time. It assures that your apps and services are always available and performant, even in the face of large-scale attacks. Azure DDoS Protection protects applications against malicious traffic while allowing genuine queries through.

How Azure DDoS protection works

Traffic analysis and attack detection: Azure DDoS protection monitors network traffic constantly for odd spikes or patterns matching a DDoS assault. Differentiating between attack and legitimate users, the system examines traffic volume, request rates, and packet behaviour.

A typical e-commerce website might have more traffic during a holiday sale, but that is expected. Conversely, a DDoS assault rapidly inundates the site with millions of bogus requests from thousands of IP addresses, therefore rendering legitimate customers unable to browse or make transactions. Azure's artificial intelligence-driven detection engine finds such irregularities and rapidly implements mitigating techniques.

Real-time automated mitigating: Once a possible DDoS assault is discovered, Azure automatically directs harmful traffic away from your systems while letting legal traffic keep on its path. Using adaptive rate limitation, packet inspection, and filtering methods guarantees that attack requests will not interfere with your programs.

Azure DDoS protection responds to threats in seconds and kicks in automatically, therefore eliminating manual involvement. Azure's solution is completely automated, therefore lowering downtime and maintaining application availability free from delays, unlike conventional DDoS mitigating services requiring human inspection.

Two tiers of Azure DDoS protection

Azure offers two levels of DDoS protection, depending on the security needs of your organization:

- **DDoS protection basic**:
    - o It is enabled by default for all Azure services, providing basic network-level protection against common volumetric attacks.
    - o It protects the Azure infrastructure but does not offer detailed reporting or controls for specific resources.
- **DDoS protection standard**:
    - o Provides enterprise-grade security with AI-driven attack detection and automatic mitigation.
    - o Offers detailed traffic analytics, logging, and attack forensics, allowing businesses to analyze and understand attempted attacks.
    - o Includes cost protection, meaning Microsoft will credit back costs associated with extra scaling caused by a DDoS attack.
    - o Ideal for organizations running mission-critical applications, online services, APIs, and large-scale web platforms.

Endpoint security

A key part of cloud security is protecting endpoints that are open to the public. This keeps services and apps accessible, resilient, and safe from cyber threats. Unprotected endpoints put businesses at risk of issues like data theft, service interruptions, and unauthorized access. This is why it is important to set up strong security controls for encryption, traffic management, and domains.

Azure has a number of built-in security features that protect endpoints. These include Azure Traffic Manager, Azure DNS, and Custom DNS, which resolve domain names securely, and SSL/TLS Certificates, which require protected communication. These tools help keep resources open to the public, safe, available, and running at their best, lowering the risk of data breaches and hacks.

Azure Traffic Manager

Designed for DNS-based traffic routeing, Azure Traffic Manager directs users to the geographically closest or best-performing endpoint. Traffic Manager uses clever distribution of requests instead of depending just on a single server or data centre, therefore enhancing performance, availability, and resilience.

Azure Traffic Manager guarantees that customers always connect to the most responsive and healthiest backend, hence lowering latency and downtime for companies running worldwide applications, multi-region deployments, or services with high availability needs.

By always directing consumers to healthy, safe, and available backend services, Azure Traffic Manager is essential in safeguarding public-facing endpoints. Although its main use is worldwide traffic distribution, it also improves endpoint security by eliminating downtime, enforcing geographical limitations, and reducing some attack risks.

How Traffic Manager boosts endpoint security

Let us understand, in the following, how traffic manager boosts endpoint security:

- **Protecting against service disruptions and failures**: Among the biggest risks to public-facing endpoints are service interruptions from cyberattacks, system failures, and network disruptions. When an attack or unplanned disturbance renders an endpoint unreachable, Traffic Manager automatically switches users to a backup or failover instance to avoid service interruptions.

  For instance, Traffic Manager can automatically reroute traffic to a safe backup instance in Europe or Asia should a cyberattack strike a web application in North America, causing performance problems or downtime, therefore maintaining business continuity and lessening the impact of the assault.

- **Geo-based traffic routing for security and compliance**: Traffic Manager lets companies limit access to particular endpoints depending on geographical location, therefore providing security to stop unwanted access from high-risk areas. Especially helpful for this is:

  - Regulatory compliance is making sure sensitive information stays inside allowed areas (GDPR compliance for European users).
  - Stopping traffic from untrusted sources helps to prevent access from areas known to be highly cyberactive.
  - Managing internal or partner access means guiding trusted partners or users to assigned safe endpoints.

  For instance, a financial institution managing sensitive transactions could wish to block all outside approved country requests, therefore stopping illegal customers from using their services.

- **Reducing exposure to attackers with failover routing**: Attacks, including DDoS, brute force efforts, and API misuse, can compromise endpoints exposed to the internet. Traffic Manager can be set to fail over to a secondary, more secure environment should an assailant overrun a main service.

  For a continuous attack on a public API, for example, Traffic Manager can:

  - Reroute traffic to a backup environment with additional security measures (e.g., a secondary API with tougher rate limitation).
  - For only trusted users, move traffic to an internal VPN-protected variation of the service.

This reduces an assailant's capacity to overwhelm or take advantage of the system, therefore lessening the effect of their attacks.

- **Masking backend infrastructure and preventing direct attacks**: Direct targeting of an application's IP address rather than working across its domain is a frequent attack tactic. Traffic Manager routes traffic at the DNS level. Hence, attackers cannot immediately view or engage with backend infrastructure.
  - Without Traffic Manager, for instance, an assailant can search public IP addresses and try brute-force attacks right on servers.
  - Backend IP addresses stay concealed using Traffic Manager, therefore lowering the attack surface and increasing the difficulty for attackers to directly breach a system.

Azure Firewall, WAF, and Private Link, taken together, greatly enhance endpoint security.

Custom DNS and Azure DNS

Although security usually ignores DNS, it is absolutely vital for protecting internal networks, cloud apps, and services. Inappropriate or insecure DNS can lead to data theft, traffic interception, and service disruptions that find their way into businesses. Attackers can change DNS settings to send guests to phony websites, disrupt services with DNS-based DDoS attacks, or perhaps completely take over domain names.

Two solutions from Azure help to reduce these risks: Custom DNS allows businesses to control over private domain resolution inside their Azure VNets, while Azure DNS securely hosts public domain records. These services maintain DNS traffic safe, reliable, and free from outside attacks.

How Azure DNS enhances endpoint security

Azure DNS is a fully managed domain name service designed for security and performance. Unlike traditional DNS providers that can be vulnerable to attacks or downtime, Azure DNS operates on Microsoft's global infrastructure, offering built-in security, high availability, and low-latency resolution.

Tight interaction with Azure security technologies is one of the main benefits of Azure DNS. Ensuring that only authorized users may perform DNS updates, it supports RBAC, MFA, and Azure Security Centre monitoring. Common strategies used by cybercriminals, DNS hijacking, spoofing, or unauthorized changes, which greatly increase the danger, are therefore drastically lowered.

Since Azure DNS is natively integrated with Azure DDoS Protection, it can help mitigate large-scale attacks that attempt to flood DNS servers with malicious queries. This means organizations do not have to worry about DNS-based service disruptions; Azure's infrastructure automatically detects and mitigates these threats in real-time. Here are the types of attacks on DNS and how Azure DNS helps for each:

- **Preventing DNS hijacking**: A significant security risk, DNS hijacking is the manipulation of DNS records by attackers, rerouting users to phishing websites, fake login pages, or dangerous downloads. Stealing credentials, data breaches, and financial fraud can all follow from this.

  By keeping DNS records within Azure, organizations significantly reduce the risk of hijacking attempts. Azure's security model ensures that all DNS changes are logged, monitored, and protected against unauthorized access. Since DNS settings are managed within Microsoft's highly secure environment, attackers can't easily modify records or take control of domain settings.

  For example, if an attacker gains access to a compromised third-party DNS provider, they could redirect a banking website's domain to a phishing site, tricking users into entering their credentials. With Azure DNS's built-in security controls, such an attack would be far more difficult to execute, as strong authentication and access policies protect against unauthorized DNS changes.

- **Restricting external DNS exposure with Custom DNS**: It is not only necessary for businesses that run internal apps, databases, and cloud services to make DNS information public, but it is also a security risk. In this case, Custom DNS comes in handy.

  Businesses do not have to use public DNS servers to handle private name resolution; they can use Custom DNS within Azure VNets. This keeps outside threats from seeing secret resources and makes sure that applications can safely talk to each other within a private network.

  One of the best things about Custom DNS is that it stops DNS leaks, which happen when queries from inside a domain get sent to public DNS servers by mistake. Attackers often use DNS monitoring to learn more about a company's infrastructure. But with Custom DNS, these internal searches stay within Azure, which makes it much harder for cybercriminals to do reconnaissance.

  Custom DNS also works well with hybrid cloud setups, which lets companies connect their DNS servers on-premises with workloads that run in Azure. This keeps domain resolution safe and uniform across both cloud and on-premise networks, keeping private services from being seen by the public internet.

- **Ensuring secure DNS communication with encryption**: DNS traffic may be intercepted across an unprotected network, even with robust access restrictions. **Man-in-the-middle** (**MITM**) attacks let attackers control DNS responses, therefore guiding users to phony websites or changing traffic flows.

Through encrypted DNS searches and integration with safe transit systems, Azure helps reduce these dangers. This guarantees safe transmission of all DNS resolution queries, therefore preventing unwanted access or manipulation.

Organizations can implement TLS security standards for Azure-hosted web apps and APIs to provide extra protection, requiring **DNS over HTTPS** (**DoH**) or **DNS over TLS** (**DoT**). DNS interception, data leaks, and domain spoofing efforts are among the security risks these policies aid against.

- **Support for encrypted DNS (DoH/DoT)**: While Azure DNS does not yet natively support DoH or DoT, users can enhance endpoint protection by forwarding DNS requests through custom resolvers or proxies.

  For example, use Azure DNS Private Resolver in combination with Azure Firewall DNS Proxy or external DNS forwarders to enable encrypted name resolution for hybrid and regulated environments.

- **Enhancing availability and performance with Azure DNS**: Azure DNS is designed not only for security but also for reliability and low latency. Sending users to the closest accessible server allows Azure DNS to guarantee low-latency name resolution. This is not the case with traditional DNS providers, whose services could suffer from latency or may go down. This makes websites and apps far faster, particularly for businesses serving clients all around the globe.

  Azure DNS offers automatic failover for mission-critical applications when used in conjunction with Azure Traffic Manager. If a primary endpoint is attacked or goes down, Azure may automatically divert traffic to a backup instance, providing continuous availability.

  For instance, if a company's main online application is hosted in the *United States* but goes down, Azure DNS can instantly transfer customers to a backup server in *Europe* or *Asia*. This reduces downtime and keeps systems functioning smoothly, even in the case of cyberattacks or unanticipated outages.

Certificates

Securing communication between users, apps, and cloud services is absolutely crucial in today's digital environment. Inappropriate encryption allows attackers to compromise authentication systems, intercept private information, and carry MITM attacks. SSL/TLS certificates are among the best means to guard cloud resources and guarantee data integrity.

Azure offers a number of choices for handling certificates that guarantee applications and endpoints follow industry security guidelines, enforce safe connections, and stop illegal access. Certificates are essential for maintaining cloud environments safe, whether they are used for the security of a public website, an internal API, or an authentication system.

How certificates enhance security in Azure

Certificates serve two primary purposes in cloud security:

- **Encrypting data in transit**: Ensures that all communication between clients, servers, and APIs is encrypted, preventing interception or tampering.
- **Authenticating identities**: Validates that users, applications, and services are communicating with trusted endpoints, reducing the risk of impersonation attacks.

In Azure, SSL/TLS certificates are used across various services, including Azure Web Apps, Virtual Machines, Application Gateway, Azure Front Door, and API Management. Organizations can enforce encryption policies by using certificates while ensuring that only authenticated connections are allowed.

Managing certificates in Azure

Azure ensures that apps are compliant and safe by offering several ways to handle SSL/TLS certificates. By automatically creating, storing, and renewing certificates, administrators help to lower the security risk resulting from expired or incorrectly configured certificates.

Azure Key Vault for secure certificate storage

Certificates, encryption keys, and secrets can all be securely stored in Azure Key Vault. Organizations can safely save and access certificates from Key Vault instead of keeping them on local servers or virtual machines, therefore guaranteeing that:

- Private keys are never exposed to unauthorized users.
- Automated certificate renewal prevents downtime caused by expired certificates.
- Access controls and logging help monitor and restrict who can manage certificates.

By using Azure Key Vault, businesses eliminate manual certificate handling errors, reducing the risk of misconfigurations and security vulnerabilities.

Automating TLS certificate rotation with Azure Key Vault

To reduce operational risk and eliminate downtime from expired TLS certificates, Azure supports automated certificate rotation across several services:

- **Azure Application Gateway** (v2 SKU) integrates with **Azure Key Vault**, automatically syncing new versions of certificates without manual redeployment.

- **Azure Front Door** (**Standard/Premium**) provides **Azure-managed certificates** that renew automatically for custom domains.
- **Azure App Service** supports certificate rotation via **Key Vault references** in App Settings or via **App Service Managed Certificates**.

Best practices

By applying these best practices, organizations can significantly reduce attack surfaces, enhance network visibility, and ensure compliance with security standards. Network security is not a one-time effort but an ongoing process that requires continuous monitoring and proactive risk management. Let us summarize the key takeaways from this chapter:

- **Enable WAF on Application Gateway or Front Door for web applications**: Protect web applications from common threats like SQL injection, XSS, and bot attacks by enabling WAF on Azure Application Gateway or Azure Front Door. WAF provides real-time threat detection and mitigation for internet-facing applications.
- Azure DDoS Protection Standard helps protect important applications from broad DDoS assaults. This prevents users from being able to access the service amid traffic surges brought on by cyberattacks.
- Always require HTTPS (SSL/TLS) encryption to keep data safe whilst it is being transmitted and stop MITM threats. Create Web Apps, Azure Front Door, and Azure Application Gateway needing TLS 1.2 or above. This will render useless old or poor encryption techniques.
- Azure Front Door secures traffic routing with built-in DDoS protection, WAF integration, and SSL lifting. This makes sure that content is delivered securely and quickly across the world.
- Limit public access to only the tools that they need. RBAC and Azure AD authentication can be used to make sure that only certain people can handle and set up services that are open to the public.
- For remote access, Private Link for PaaS services, and application gateway to restrict who may view what, use Azure Bastion instead. Do not assign public IP addresses to virtual machines if it is truly not required.
- By using Azure API Management to set rate limits and throttling on public APIs, you can stop brute-force attacks.
- To stop DNS hijacking or incorrect configurations, make sure that public DNS records are handled correctly. To safely manage domain resolution, use Azure DNS with proper rules.

Conclusion

Securing networks in Azure is a critical aspect of cloud architecture, ensuring that workloads, applications, and data remain protected from unauthorized access and cyber threats. This chapter covered key concepts, including network segmentation, traffic filtering, and private/public access security, demonstrating how tools like NSGs, ASGs, Azure Firewall, and Route Server can strengthen security postures.

Additionally, we explored private access mechanisms such as Azure Private Link, Service Endpoints, and Bastion to minimize internet exposure while ensuring secure connectivity. Application Gateway, Front Door, and WAF provide advanced protection against threats like DDoS attacks, malicious traffic, and unauthorized access to public-facing resources. Hybrid networking solutions like VPN Gateway and ExpressRoute enable secure, high-performance communication between on-premises and Azure environments.

By applying best practices, such as least privilege access, regular firewall rule audits, and encryption enforcement, organizations can build resilient, scalable, and well-protected network architectures in Azure. As cloud security continues to evolve, continuous monitoring, compliance adherence, and proactive threat detection will be key to maintaining a good security posture in an ever-changing digital landscape.

In the next chapter, we will look into securing compute resources in Azure. You will learn how to protect virtual machines, containerized workloads, and App Services using security best practices, endpoint protection, and runtime controls.

CHAPTER 4
Securing Compute

Introduction

In this chapter, you will learn skills to master securing Azure compute services. Topics covered will include securing IaaS compute Services such as virtual machines, then you will look at PaaS services such as Azure Container services, including the **Azure Kubernetes Service** (**AKS**), **Azure Container Instances** (**ACI**), **Azure Container Apps** (**ACA**), as well as **Azure Container Registry** (**ACR**). Finally, you will look at securing Azure Serverless services such as Azure Logic Apps and Azure Functions and securing Azure API Management.

Structure

This chapter contains the following topics:

- Securing Azure Virtual Machines
- Securing Azure Container Services
- Securing Azure App Service
- Securing Azure Serverless
- Securing Azure API Management

Objectives

By the end of this chapter, readers will gain a comprehensive understanding of securing Azure compute resources across IaaS, PaaS, and serverless environments. They will learn how to protect virtual machines, containers, and serverless applications using best practices for encryption, access controls, and network security. The chapter also covers securing APIs with **Azure API Management** (**APIM**) to prevent unauthorized access and mitigate API-related threats. Additionally, readers will explore monitoring and threat detection strategies using Azure Monitor, Microsoft Defender for Cloud, and Azure Sentinel to respond to security risks proactively.

Securing Azure Virtual Machines

Foundational components of IaaS on the Azure cloud platform are Azure VMs. They allow users to use and oversee virtualized computing resources, offering a degree of control and customization like that of on-premises servers. Using the worldwide reach and dependability of Microsoft's Azure data centers, this capability lets organizations move current workloads, create new applications, and dynamically extend their infrastructure. Azure VMs meet a broad spectrum of demands, from running sophisticated business applications to hosting development and testing environments.

However, along with this adaptability comes the need for strong security. For PaaS or SaaS, the cloud provider manages most of the underlying infrastructure security, but for IaaS, a significant security load is on the customer. This covers maintaining the operating system, applications, network layouts, and data kept within the virtual machines. Maintaining the integrity of your cloud architecture and protecting private data mostly depends on your knowledge and the use of reasonable security measures for Azure VMs. This section will go over the key components of safeguarding Azure VMs, thereby giving you the information and tools needed to lower possible risks and strengthen your security posture.

Overview of Azure Virtual Machines

The fundamental building blocks of IaaS within Microsoft Azure are Azure VMs. They effectively let you have virtual servers in the cloud by offering a very flexible and customizable computing environment. This gives you direct control over the operating system, applications, and configurations, enabling you to customize your environment to fit certain job requirements.

Imagine needing a Linux distribution for a web server, a Windows Server to operate a legacy application, or even a specialist data science environment—that is where Azure Virtual helps. With a wide range of operating systems, sizes, and configurations, you can be sure you have the correct tools for your requirements. This adaptability also covers your VMs' management, including the need to start, pause, resize, and delete them to offer dynamic scalability and cost control.

Beyond simple computation, Azure VMs connect effortlessly with other Azure products so you may create strong and sophisticated cloud solutions. For secure communication, Azure Virtual Network can be coupled with VMs; Azure Storage provides permanent data storage; and Azure SQL database manages relational data. From basic web apps to sophisticated business systems, Azure VMs are a great tool for distributing and controlling varied workloads.

Remember, though, that this degree of control comes with responsibility. Unlike managed services, when Microsoft manages most of the underlying infrastructure, you are in charge of maintaining and securing your VMs. This covers operating system patching, firewall configuration, and access control management. The key security issues for Azure VMs will be discussed in the following parts so that you can use the tools and knowledge to secure your virtual infrastructure.

Key security features for Azure VMs

When running virtual machines in Azure, security is a top priority. Whether it is protecting private information, preventing cyberattacks, or controlling access, the correct measures can significantly improve security. Let us go over some of the main security measures meant to protect your virtual machines:

- **Disc encryption**: Maintaining data security is absolutely vital, and disc encryption is among the strongest strategies available. This guarantees that even in cases of access to a virtual machine's disc, the data cannot be read. Azure uses BitLocker for Windows VMs and DM-Crypt for Linux, then offers **Azure Disc Encryption** (**ADE**) for whole disc encryption. **Server-side encryption** (**SSE**) with Azure Managed Discs is another choice that automatically encrypts data without your end needing any setup.

  Azure helps organizations requiring more control handle encryption keys themselves using **customer-managed keys** (**CMK**) kept in Azure Key Vault. For companies with rigorous compliance needs, this is especially helpful. Encryption guarantees that your data stays locked up and unreadable even if someone has access to your storage.

- **Endpoint protection**: Cyberattacks and malware can affect virtual machines as much as physical ones. That is where Microsoft Defender for Servers comes to the rescue.. This security tool constantly watches VMs for odd behaviors, such as attempts at illegal access or suspicious software, and alerts you to any hazards. To keep your VMs safe, it can also suggest changes and scan security patches.

  Your VMs should have an antivirus or antimalware program installed alongside Defender. Microsoft has a built-in solution, but you can also employ other security tools or applications for further security. Regular scans and real-time monitoring help lower the danger of a security breach by removing harmful software before it can cause damage.

- **Access management**: Leaving **Remote Desktop Protocol** (**RDP**) or **Secure Shell** (**SSH**) open all the time is one of the main risks, and organizations usually do that. When searching the internet for open ports, hackers may try to access your system through brute-force attacks, should they come upon any. Azure provides JIT VM access to help to stop this, therefore guaranteeing that VMs are just accessible when required.

JIT turned on grants access for a limited period only to authorized users. Unless someone asks explicitly for access, RDP and SSH ports stay closed down rather than open. Even then, IP address, role-based restrictions, and time constraints might restrict access, drastically lowering the attack surface. Admin may thus still control their VMs without letting hackers walk right through the doors

- **Update management**: Though it is often disregarded, maintaining current VMs is one of the easiest methods to avoid security flaws. Regular patching is crucial since hackers usually use out-of-date apps with unacknowledged flaws. With automation update management, which analyses your VMs for missing updates and runs them automatically, Azure streamlines this procedure.

  The best thing is scheduling updates to run at designated times, guaranteeing they will not disturb business operations. Azure also offers a compliance dashboard where one may find which VMs require care and which are entirely patched. Automating updates guarantees that your VMs remain safe against the most recent threats and helps you save yourself from the work involved in hand fixing.

- **Secure networking**: Leaving a VM online vulnerable is like leaving your front door wide open. Azure offers NSGs, which function as a firewall by letting only authorized traffic reach your VMs, lowering this risk. For instance, you might implement rules in an NSG to prevent all other connections if you want some IP addresses to access your virtual machine.

  Azure Bastion is a managed service that allows you to securely connect to VMs without exposing them to the internet. Bastion lets access through the Azure portal instead of leveraging public IPs for RDP or SSH, removing the need to open dangerous inbound ports. Businesses might also use Azure or a WAF to screen harmful traffic for further security. These best practices can help you significantly lower the possibility of an assailant gaining illegal access to your VMs.

Best practices for securing virtual machines

Securing virtual machines is about adopting best practices that reduce risk and safeguard your workloads, not just providing security features. The following guidelines will help you ensure your systems remain safe, whether you run a large-scale environment or a small number of VMs:

- **Use Managed Identities for secure access**: While hardcoding passwords or keys in scripts is a security catastrophe just waiting to happen, managing credentials for VMs can be a nuisance. Azure Managed Identities give VMs a flawless and safe way to access Azure services without storing secrets, instead of manually managing authentication.

Every VM with system-assigned Managed Identities has a distinct identity in Microsoft Entra ID, which lets it authenticate straight with databases, Azure Key Vault, Storage Accounts, etc. There is no risk of inadvertent exposure since no credentials are kept in configuration or code files. User-assigned Managed Identities can be distributed over several VMs for more flexibility, guaranteeing better security and simpler identity administration.

- **Apply least privilege access with RBAC**: Giving users greater access than required is a typical security flaw. Due to the PoLP, every user, service, or application only has the minimal rights needed to do its job. Azure's RBAC makes implementation simple.

  Custom roles with unique permissions catered to each user's tasks are better than assigning generic contributor or owner roles. A developer who merely wants to restart a virtual machine, for instance, should not be able to delete it. Reviewing access rights often and eliminating unwanted access helps stop unauthorized changes and lessens the effect of possible security lapses.

- **Regularly back up VM data with Azure Backup**: Accidents happen—cyberattacks, system failures, human mistakes, etc., regardless of how effectively you secure your VMs. Having a strong backup plan is, therefore, essential. Azure Backup can automatically create regular backups of your VMs, guaranteeing rapid recovery should something go wrong.

  With incremental backups, only the changes since the last backup are stored, lowering backup times and storage expenses. Keeping copies of your backups across several Azure sites allows **geo-redundant storage** (**GRS**) to provide another layer of safety. Enable soft delete, which keeps backups for an additional 14 days even after deletion, thus preventing accidental or malicious deletions and strengthening your backup strategy.

- **Keep your VM OS and software updated**: One of the easiest ways attackers could take advantage of systems is unpatched software. Frequent updates guarantee that security flaws are resolved before they can be turned against you. Azure offers automation update management, which automatically applies updates depending on a schedule that fits your organization, thereby maintaining both Windows and Linux VMs up to date.

  Patching for critical workloads must be done with little interruption. Azure Hotpatching for Windows Server VMs guarantees constant availability while remaining safe by enabling upgrades to be implemented without the system restarting.

- **Restrict VM Access with JIT and Azure Bastion**: Leaving RDP or SSH ports accessible 24/7 runs a security risk—attackers are always looking for vulnerable endpoints. JIT access locks down these ports and opens them only as needed. This means an attacker searching for open ports won't find any unless specifically approved for a limited period.

Use Azure Bastion, a completely managed solution that enables managers to safely access VMs without revealing public IP addresses for even better security. You do not need to bother with VPN setups or jump server management since connections are created using the Azure interface.

- **Enable NSGs and private networking**: Private networking VMs and NSGs should never be freely accessible to the internet. Acting as a firewall, allowing or denying traffic depending on your defined rules, NSGs can be used. A best practice is to block everything else by default and let only the traffic you require.

  For delicate workloads, keep VM traffic inside an Azure VNet and avoid exposing services to the public Internet. By enabling VMs to securely link themselves to Azure services without passing over public IPs, Private Endpoint help lower the risk of data leakage.

- **Monitor and respond to security threats**: Security calls for constant monitoring; it is not only about arranging once-forgotten events. Real-time security insights from Microsoft Defender for Cloud identify dangers, including brute-force assaults, dubious scripts, and unapproved changes.

  Configuring Azure Monitor and Log Analytics tracks activity across your virtual machines. Creating warnings for odd behavior, such as failed login attempts or high CPU use from unidentified processes, allows you to react fast before an assailant finds a footing.

- **Protect VM disks with encryption**: Disc encryption guarantees that the data will not be accessible even if someone gains control of a virtual machine's disc. For managed discs, Azure provides SSE and automatic data encryption. **Customer-managed keys** (**CMK**) in Azure Key Vault allow you to have complete control over encryption and decryption for additional protection.

Azure Virtual Machines baseline architecture

Figure 4.1 is a reference architecture for Azure VMs, representing a scalable and high availability framework with Azure **Virtual Machine Scale Sets** (**VMSS**) incorporated along with load balancing and security networking components. This structure aims at resilience, security, and performance optimization for applications operating on Azure.

At the front of this architecture stand the users who enter the system via an Application Gateway integrated with a WAF. The WAF processes all the incoming traffic scans and shields it from web vulnerabilities, including SQL injection and XSS. The Application Gateway is zone-redundant, meaning it is deployed across multiple Azure Availability Zones, ensuring high availability and fault tolerance. In addition, Azure Key Vault is used to manage and store sensitive information, such as API keys, passwords, and certificates, while maintaining zone resilience for reliability.

The central computing layer contains frontend and backend VMSS. The frontend VMSS comprises virtual machines (SKU A) distributed in three different availability zones, thus providing distributed and highly available processing power. Traffic flow is internally managed by an internal load balancer (zone-redundant), which routes requests from frontend to backend services effectively. It is worth noting that the backend VMSS contains virtual machines (SKU B) distributed across zones, ensuring back-end processes, such as databases or API services, are constantly running and adapting to the load well.

The components concerning the network are of paramount importance when it comes to isolating and managing the connection between resources. Private Endpoint are employed to provide transport to services without exposure to the public internet. Subnets logically separate workloads, while NSGs implement security policies by managing ingress and egress traffic to both the 'subnet' and 'network interface' levels. This organization, to some extent, resolves the issues of security and the reduction of the attack surface.

On the outer edge of the network, an Azure Load Balancer (zone-redundant and public) is planted at the perimeter for the distribution of external traffic. It efficiently performs the distribution of the incoming requests across the available front-end VMs and consequently ensures optimal resource utilization and fault tolerance. With workload-supporting resources such as Azure Bastion, Azure Log Analytics, and Azure Application Insights, administrators can manage virtual machines safely, observe the system's performance, and provide feedback, which greatly helps develop a healthier and more secure environment. Refer to the following figure:

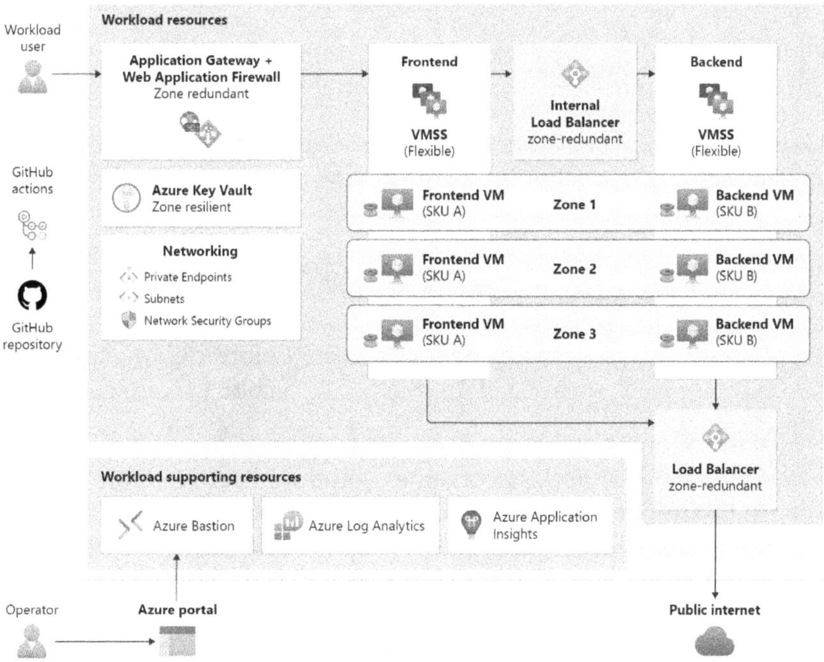

***Figure 4.1**: Baseline architecture for VMs*

***Source**: https://learn.microsoft.com/en-us/Azure/architecture/virtual-machines/baseline*

Securing Azure Container Services

As containerized apps become more popular, it is vital to ensure Azure's container services are safe from threats like supply chain attacks, unauthorized access, and incorrect settings. Azure has many container services, each one used for a different purpose and needing different protection measures.

Overview of container services

To address these risks, Azure provides multiple container services, each tailored for different workloads and security needs. Let us examine these services and how to keep them safe in more detail:

- **AKS**: Designed as a completely managed Kubernetes platform, AKS streamlines container orchestration, hence facilitating deployment, management, and scaling of containerized applications. Kubernetes clusters, however, manage critical workloads, thus, the security of them is absolutely important.

  Let us look at how to secure AKS:

  - **RBAC**: Enforcing Kubernetes RBAC combined with Microsoft Entra ID will help to guarantee that only authorized users can access and change cluster resources. This limits access depending on responsibilities instead of granting all-permission.
  - **Policies regarding network security**: Limit traffic between pods and stop illegal cluster communication using Azure Network Policies or Calico rules.
  - **Azure defender for Kubernetes**: This offers real-time threat detection and flags dubious behavior, including cryptojacking or unauthorized privilege escalation.
  - **Make use of private clusters**: AKS nodes by default interact over the public internet. Private clusters guarantee that the control plane can be accessed only through Private Endpoint.
  - **Implement image security best practices**: Before deploying them using ACR) security features (described in the ACR section), scan container images for vulnerabilities.

- **ACI**: Designed as a serverless container solution, ACI lets you run containers free from control of underlying infrastructure. For light-weight, on-demand projects, this is a fantastic option, but the security of it depends on access control and networking.

  Let us look at how to secure ACI:

  - **Managed Identities**: Use Managed Identities to authenticate securely with other Azure services rather than inserting credentials inside containers.

   - **Public access**: ACI containers by default can be publicly visible. Put them within a VNet and substitute Private Endpoint for public IPs to enhance security.
   - **Limit privileged containers**: Steer clear of running containers with root access since attackers may use them to seize environmental control.
   - **Monitoring**: Track container utilization, identify anomalies, and guarantee that security policies are followed by means of Azure Monitor and Azure Policy.

- **Azure Container Apps (ACA)**: Offering built-in scalability, service discovery, and networking, ACA is meant for microservices and event-driven apps. Unlike AKS, the ACA isolates Kubernetes's complexity, yet still offers the ability to run several containers together with some freedom.

  Here are some ways to secure ACA:
   - **Authentication**: Using Microsoft Entra ID, OAuth, or OpenID Connect, enable authentication to guarantee only legitimate users and services connect with your application.
   - **Secrets and credentials**: Store secrets in environment variables. Never hardcode your application's credentials. Instead, run safely by storing and retrieving secrets with Azure Key Vault.
   - **Networking**: Use **Distributed Application Runtime** (**Dapr**) and VNet integration to keep internal container communication private and hence reduce needless exposure.
   - **Turn on TLS for APIs**: Use **Transport Layer Security** (**TLS**) to encrypt all correspondence, therefore safeguarding data in route.

- **ACR**: Private container image storage and management are housed in ACR. Since ACR is the provider of containerized apps, maintaining its security is crucial to stop supply chain attacks.

  Here are some ways to secure ACR:
   - **Defender for Containers**: Use Microsoft Defender for Containers to scan container images for flaws before they are turned on. This helps spot security issues.
   - **Private access**: Steer clear of publicizing your register. Rather, control access to trustworthy networks using VNet integration and Private Endpoint.
   - **Trusted images**: Turn on Content Trust to guarantee that the registry pulls just signed, certified container images. This helps stop images that have been altered with or unauthorized from executing throughout your system.
   - **Tagging**: Use immutable tags to avoid inadvertent image changes rather than the most recent tag, which can cause discrepancies.

Best practices

Setting up infrastructure is not enough to keep containerized processes safe in Azure. Policies must also be enforced, and vulnerabilities must be constantly scanned for. If you follow these best practices, your container deployments will be safer from security risks and will run more smoothly and in line with regulations:

- **Use Azure Policy to enforce compliance standards for AKS**: Managing security in Kubernetes can get hard very quickly, especially in big environments with lots of clusters and teams. By automating governance and making sure that all AKS deployments follow set security configurations, Azure Policy helps maintain compliance.

  Enhancing security with Azure Policy:

  - Azure Policy lets admins implement rules, like blocking public IP addresses, limiting privileged containers, and requiring RBAC for cluster authentication.
  - You can check to see if groups meet industry standards such as **Centre for Internet Security** (**CIS**) benchmarks, NIST, or ISO 27001, and make sure they do. If a cluster does not follow the rules, Azure Policy can either show problems or fix them on its own.
  - You can stop devs from deploying services that are not allowed, like load balancers, storage accounts, or networking parts that do not meet security standards.

- **Implement image scanning to detect vulnerabilities**: Container images are what make deployments possible, but images that are not secure can pose real security risks. Attackers often get into containerized apps by using pictures that are out of date or not set up correctly.

  Some best practices for image security:

  - Before putting container images into AKS or other Azure services, check them with Microsoft Defender for Containers or third-party tools such as Trivy, Clair, or Aqua Security. You can use these tools to find known security holes, old libraries, and other issues.
  - Turn on **Azure Content Trust** (**ACT**) to make sure that only signed images are downloaded and used. This will stop any images that are not authorized or have been tampered with from working in your environment.
  - The container image is less likely to be vulnerable if it is smaller. Alpine Linux-based images are a great example of a base image that is both light and focused on security.
  - It is important to keep images up to date. To get rid of old dependencies, automate the process by rebuilding images whenever security changes are released.

- **Use Azure Monitor to track cluster performance and security events**: Prevention is not the only part of security; you also need to be able to find problems and fix them. Azure Monitor helps monitor performance measures and security events across all AKS clusters. This lets teams spot odd behavior, fix problems, and boost performance.

  Key benefits of Azure Monitor for AKS security are:

  - When you connect Azure Monitor to Microsoft Defender for Containers, you can get real-time alerts about security risks like containers being accessed without permission, privileges being raised, or strange traffic patterns.
  - Azure Monitor gives teams real-time information on the performance of the CPU, memory, and nodes, which helps them make the best use of the cluster's resources and avoid slowdowns.
  - You can use Azure Log Analytics to get detailed logs from Kubernetes audit logs, container logs, and system activity. This will help you figure out who is trying to get in without permission and why authentication attempts fail.
  - Set up Azure Monitor alerts to let security teams know about possible threats, like multiple failed login attempts, sudden increases in resource use, or changes to how Kubernetes is configured.

- **Enforce least privilege access for Kubernetes workloads**: RBAC in Kubernetes lets you fine-tune who can access what, but if you set up rights incorrectly, it can pose a security risk.

  RBAC best practices for AKS:

  - Do not give users who do not need it cluster-wide admin access. Instead, to control access, give roles that are specific to the namespace.
  - Kubernetes service accounts should only have the rights they need. Do not use the basic service account that has too many rights.
  - Instead of using Kubernetes-native authentication, connect AKS to Microsoft Entra ID to handle identities centrally and enforce **multi-factor authentication (MFA)**.

- **Secure Kubernetes network traffic with private networking**: Kubernetes pods and services can talk to each other easily within the cluster by default, which could be bad for security. It is important to manage the flow of traffic and let only trusted links through.

  Best practices for network security in AKS:

  - Turn off public IP access to the Kubernetes API service and use Private Clusters.
  - Set up network rules at the pod level to stop workloads from talking to each other without permission. For instance, you can stop cross-namespace activity that is not needed.

- Keep DDoS attacks and SQL injection attempts from getting into the cluster through its entry points.
- Locking down network access makes sure that only authorized traffic moves into and out of your AKS environment. This lowers the risk of data leaks and people getting in without permission.

- **Secure container runtime and host nodes**: It is just as essential to protect the nodes below as it is to protect the cluster itself because containers share the same host system.

  Some key security measures are:

  - Use Azure Security Benchmark and set make worker nodes' OS settings as per requirements.
  - You can enforce runtime security rules by using Linux security modules like Seccomp and AppArmor to limit the system calls that containers can make.
  - Turn on Microsoft Defender for Servers on AKS nodes to look for possible threats like rootkits or unauthorized power escalations.
  - Attackers cannot get out of containers and take control of the systems below if host-level security is in place.

Baseline architecture for an Azure Kubernetes Service Cluster

The diagram below is an AKS baseline architecture that shows a secure and scalable networking model using a hub-and-spoke topology, private networking, and monitoring functions. The design provides secure access, optimal performance, and high observability for Kubernetes workloads in Azure.

The AKS cluster is the central part of the architecture, which is set inside a spoke virtual network. The spoke is a properly isolated environment being deployed with multiple subnet resources to enhance security and traffic separation. The cluster nodes subnet is the hosting site of the AKS cluster, which is built with both system node pools and user node pools. The user node pool includes a Traefik ingress controller and workload containers, thus establishing that external requests are properly routed to applications running within the cluster. For the ingress traffic, an ingress resources subnet is set with an internal load balancer for efficient traffic distribution in the cluster.

The Azure Application Gateway is deployed in a dedicated subnet within the spoke network to manage external requests from the internet. The Application Gateway ensures secure application delivery and **secure socket layer** (**SSL**) termination, thus improving security and scalability. Also, the Private Link endpoints subnet allows secure connectivity to Azure Key Vault and Azure Container Registry, which means that secrets, certificates, and container images are securely accessed without bringing them to the public internet.

The hub virtual network is a key player in the operation of the previously mentioned network and is responsible for interconnecting on-premises networks and remote offices (spokes) through virtual network peering. The hub comprises an Azure Firewall subnet for outgoing traffic security, an Azure Bastion subnet for virtual machines' secure management access, and a Gateway subnet that bridges the connection to on-premises environments via VPN or ExpressRoute. The spoke virtual network where the AKS cluster is located uses resources in the hub network while remaining entirely isolated.

Monitoring is a priority in this architecture, and this is achieved with the Azure Monitor workspace, which integrates metrics, logging, and monitoring tools like Managed Prometheus. This helps organizations track performance, diagnose issues, and thus efficiently optimize workloads. This architecture mitigates risks, ensures compliance, and follows the best practices for securing Kubernetes workloads in Azure through the use of **NSGs** and private networking.

Following is the baseline architecture for AKS that shows various components securely connected with each other:

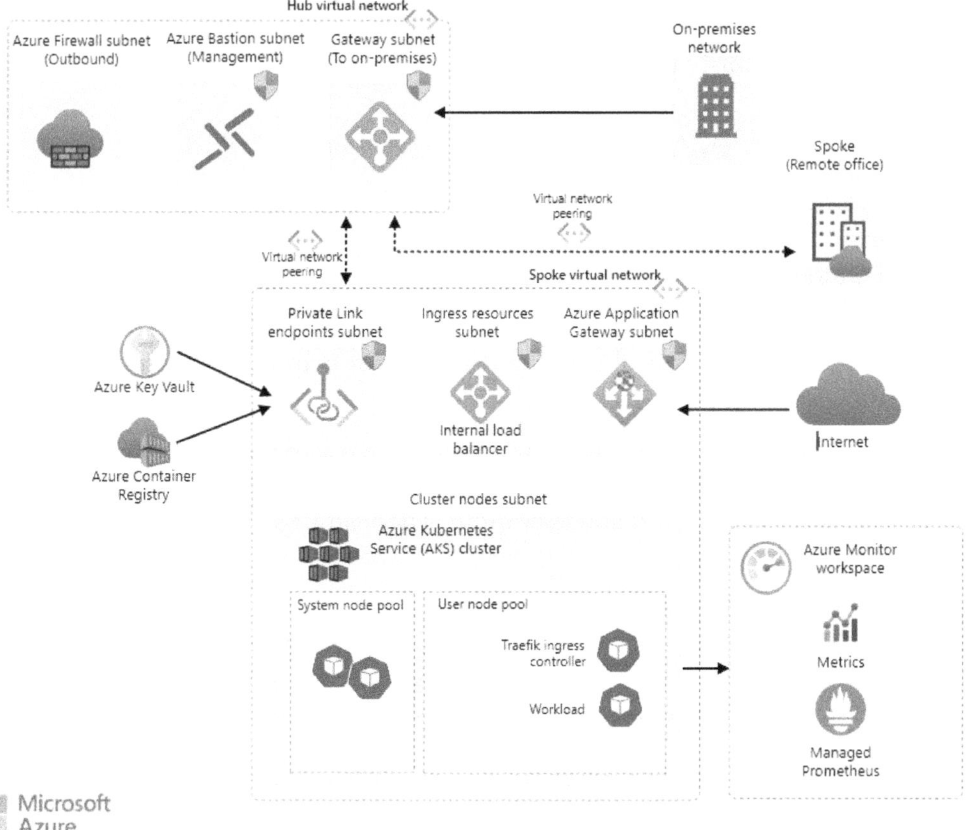

Figure 4.2: Baseline architecture of AKS

Source: *https://learn.microsoft.com/en-us/Azure/architecture/reference-architectures/containers/aks/baseline-aks*

Securing Azure App Service

While deploying web apps, APIs, or mobile backends to the cloud presents excellent agility, it also brings great responsibility, that is, security. An effective PaaS is Azure App Service, which simplifies deployment and lets developers concentrate on creating features instead of infrastructure. This ease does not release us from our essential requirement for strong security. Imagine deploying an application without appropriate security, as building a house with open windows and unguarded doors. It attracts unwelcome attention.

Overview of Azure App Service

With support for a vast range of programming languages from .NET, Node.js, and Java to Python, the Azure App Service boasts outstanding capabilities. It saves valuable development time by handling the complexity of scalability and monitoring. Still, it makes it a perfect target for hackers. These public-facing applications expose their users to an ongoing stream of possible hazards. Some issues, like DDoS attacks, illegal access attempts, and sensitive data exfiltration, are real-world challenges that can compromise operations and ruin reputations. Thus, using the best security policies is a necessity.

Key security features of Azure App Service

It is not enough to write secure code for cloud apps; you also need to use the platform's built-in security features to keep data safe, control who can access it, and reduce threats. The Azure App Service offers several security features to protect web apps, APIs, and mobile backends from hackers, data breaches, and people who aren't supposed to be there.

Here are some of the most critical security features that help make applications running on Azure App Service safer:

- **HTTPS enforcement**: To keep data safe while it is being sent, you must ensure all traffic uses HTTPS. If HTTPS is not used, attackers could steal private data like login credentials, API requests, and user input. These attacks are called **man-in-the-middle (MITM)**.

  To enforce HTTPS in Azure App Service, enable the **HTTPS Only** setting to redirect all HTTP requests to secure HTTPS. Ensure your app supports **TLS 1.2 or higher** to avoid vulnerabilities in older versions. For custom domains, **install an SSL/TLS certificate** from a trusted CA or use Azure's free managed certificate.

- **Authentication and authorization**: It is not enough to protect data in an application; you also need to control who can view it. Authentication and authorization are very important for keeping Azure App Service apps safe.

Best practices for authentication and authorization:

- o **Integrate with Microsoft Entra ID**: Instead of relying on custom authentication mechanisms, use Microsoft Entra ID to enforce SSO, MFA, and conditional access policies.
- o **Enable Azure App Service authentication**: This built-in feature allows authentication with Microsoft Entra ID, *Google*, *Facebook*, *Twitter*, and other OAuth/OpenID providers without modifying the application code.
- o **Use RBAC**: Restrict access to Azure resources by assigning RBAC roles to users and service principals, ensuring they only have the necessary permissions.
- o **Disable anonymous access**: Make sure that sensitive applications and APIs need to be authenticated in order to keep unauthorized people from accessing data or Private Endpoint.

- **Networking**: Even a well-secured application can be compromised if network access is too open. To minimize risk, restrict public access, and limit network exposure using Azure networking features.

  Best practices for network security in App Service:

  - o **Use VNet integration**: Deploy Azure App Service in a VNet to restrict access to internal resources, such as databases and APIs, ensuring traffic does not flow over the public internet.
  - o **Enable Private Endpoint**: Instead of exposing your app to the public, use Azure Private Link to create Private Endpoint, allowing only internal network traffic to reach your App Service.
  - o **Restrict IP access**: Use Access Restrictions in App Service settings to define an allowlist of trusted IP addresses or subnets, blocking all other connections.
  - o **Protect APIs with Azure APIM**: Use APIM to implement rate limits, authentication, and security controls if your application exposes APIs in order to stop misuse.

- **Data encryption**: Securing an application also means ensuring that data remains protected, both when stored (at rest) and transmitted (in transit).

  Best practices for data encryption in App Service:

  - o **Enable Always Encrypted for application data**: Use Always Encrypted to safeguard private information such as credit card numbers, passwords, and personal information if your application communicates with Azure SQL Database or Cosmos DB.
  - o **Store secrets securely in Azure Key Vault**: Instead of storing API keys, database credentials, or secrets in application code, use Azure Key Vault to manage secure storage and retrieval of sensitive configuration data.

    - **Ensure Azure Storage encryption**: If your App Service integrates with Azure Blob Storage or Azure Files, enable **Storage Service Encryption** (**SSE**) to encrypt stored files automatically.
    - **Use Managed Identity for secure authentication**: To allow the application to securely authenticate with Azure services without disclosing credentials, enable Managed Identity instead of placing connection strings in configuration files.

- **Secure configuration and environment hardening:** Applications may be vulnerable to unauthorized access and vulnerabilities due to misconfigured Azure App Service settings. Common security threats can be avoided by making sure setups are secure.

  Best practices for securing configurations:

    - **Disable unused features**: If not required, disable FTP access, remote debugging, and App Service extensions, as these can be exploited by attackers.
    - **Set up Content Security Policies (CSP)**: By establishing stringent CSP headers to restrict which scripts and resources can be loaded, you can defend your web application against XSS assaults.
    - **Enforce HTTP security headers**: Enable essential security headers like:
        - **Strict-Transport-Security (HSTS)**: Forces browsers to connect using HTTPS.
        - **X-Content-Type-Options**: Prevents MIME-sniffing attacks.
        - **X-Frame-Options**: Protects against clickjacking attacks.
    - **Enable Azure Defender for App Service**: This feature detects and alerts against threats, such as malicious code injection, suspicious traffic, and SQL injection attempts.

- **Backup and disaster recovery**: Disasters can occur even with robust security measures, whether as a result of system failures, unintended deletions, or cyberattacks. If necessary, you can promptly restore services if you have a strong backup and disaster recovery plan.

  Best practices for backups and recovery:

    - **Enable automated backups**: Use Azure Backup service or App Service Backup to schedule automatic daily or weekly backups of application code and databases.
    - **Enable geo-redundant storage (GRS)**: Store backups in a secondary Azure region to ensure resilience in case of regional failures.
    - **Test disaster recovery plans**: Test disaster recovery scenarios regularly to make sure backups can be restored effectively and quickly.

- **Continuous monitoring and threat detection**: Continuous monitoring is necessary to identify and address possible risks before they cause harm; security is not something that can be put up once.

  Best practices for security monitoring are:

  - **Use Azure Monitor and Log Analytics**: Track performance metrics, security logs, and failed login attempts to detect anomalies.
  - **Enable Microsoft Defender for App Service**: Get real-time threat detection for SQL injection attempts, web shell attacks, and suspicious file uploads.
  - **Set up Azure Defender alerts**: Configure alerts for unusual activities, such as:
    - Repeated failed authentication attempts (potential brute-force attack).
    - Sudden traffic spikes from unknown locations.
    - Unauthorized modifications to App Service settings.
  - **Use Azure Sentinel for advanced security analytics**: Security teams may more effectively investigate and address attacks with the support of Azure Sentinel's SIEM capabilities.
- **Secure DevOps and CI/CD pipelines**: Ensuring safe software delivery is essential to preventing supply chain assaults when delivering apps using CI/CD pipelines.

  Best practices for secure app deployment:

  - **Use Azure DevOps or GitHub actions with secure credentials**: Store secrets in Azure Key Vault instead of hard-coding them in pipelines.
  - **Enable code scanning for vulnerabilities**: Use tools like Microsoft Defender for DevOps or Snyk to detect security flaws in application code before deployment.
  - **Implement infrastructure as code (IaC) security**: If using Terraform, **Azure Resource Manager** (**ARM**) templates, or Bicep, scan configurations for security misconfigurations before deploying resources.
  - **Enforce deployment approvals**: Before implementing significant modifications in production environments, manual approvals are necessary.

Securing Azure Serverless

Serverless computing has become a powerful tool for building scalable and reasonably priced applications as organizations choose cloud-native architectures. Azure Functions and Logic Apps let developers focus on building business apps instead of running servers, scaling, or maintaining infrastructure. Though they offer many security advantages, serverless systems do have certain risks that come along with them.

Overview of serverless security

Serverless services like Azure Functions and Logic Apps hide the infrastructure underneath, so interfaces, access controls, and configuration security are critical. Since serverless apps connect to many different services like APIs and databases, attackers may try to break in without permission by using configuration mistakes, unprotected endpoints, or too-open permissions. Due to the fact that serverless apps are temporary, real-time monitoring and logging are also necessary to spot any suspicious activity.

Enterprises must ensure security in Azure Serverless workloads by means of a Zero Trust approach, strong authentication, least-privilege access, and continuous monitoring of API interactions and data flows. The following sections look at essential security aspects and advise procedures to help shield serverless applications against constantly shifting risks.

Key security features

To keep workloads safe from hackers and possible data breaches, Azure Serverless apps need to be authenticated, the network needs to be protected, and secrets need to be managed. Here are some key security features for Azure Functions and Logic Apps that keep them safe in a highly integrated, cloud-native environment:

- **Azure Functions**: Through Azure Functions, developers can manage event-driven programming in a fully controlled setting. Given that such systems often cater to HTTP queries, storage activities, and message queues, their operations need to be secure.

  Here are some key ways to secure functions:

  - Use function-level authentication to limit access to just authorized users and services. This guarantees security policy compliance and helps to stop anonymous execution.
  - To protect Azure Functions access to services like Azure Storage, Event hubs, and SQL databases without revealing credentials, do not insert connection strings or API keys. Instead, use Managed Identities.

- **Logic Apps**: By linking APIs, SaaS apps, and Azure services, Azure Logic Apps help automate processes. Protecting Logic Apps is essential because these processes deal with private data and run automated tasks.

  Here are some key ways to secure Logic Apps:

  - Restrict Logic App access to specific IP addresses and virtual networks, ensuring that only trusted sources can trigger or modify workflows. This prevents unauthorized executions from public endpoints.
  - Azure Key Vault is a safe place to store API keys, connection strings, and passwords instead of putting them directly in workflow definitions. This lowers the chance that secrets will be leaked and makes it easier to follow best practices for security.

Best practices for securing serverless applications

Beyond built-in security features, implementing best practices helps reinforce security, reduce attack surfaces, and ensure compliance in serverless environments. Proper security measures can protect Azure Functions and Logic Apps from unauthorized access, misconfigurations, and potential cyber threats:

- **Enable logging and diagnostics for serverless workloads**: Visibility into serverless execution is critical for detecting security threats and operational issues. Use Azure Monitor, Application Insights, and Log Analytics to track function executions, detect anomalies, and analyze security threats in real-time. Setting up alerts for unusual API calls, failed authentication attempts, or excessive function invocations helps detect potential bot attacks, API abuse, or unauthorized access attempts early. Regularly reviewing logs ensures compliance and helps teams quickly respond to incidents before they escalate.
- **Apply strict RBAC policies**: Adopting the PoLP is important to avoid unauthorized access to serverless applications. Assign RBAC roles carefully only to users, service principals, and applications so they can perform their functions with the permissions they need. Do not use broad contributor or owner roles; instead, find ways of creating custom roles that are related to particular roles. It is recommended to check on the permissions occasionally and disable any access that is not required to avoid privilege escalation attacks.
- **Secure connections between serverless services and data sources**: Serverless applications connect to databases, storage accounts, and external APIs; hence, there is a need to secure the connectivity. The only way to ensure that communication is internal and does not escape to the public internet is by using Private Endpoint and VNet integration. Also, enable firewall rules and network security policies to only allow access to approved services and regions. Data in transit is encrypted using TLS 1.2 or higher to prevent man-in-the-middle attacks and secure communication.
- **Enforce Zero Trust security and authentication controls**: Implementing a Zero Trust model will authenticate and authorize every request before executing it. Enforce strong authentication mechanisms like MFA and conditional access policies for serverless applications using Microsoft Entra ID. Disable public access by default and only allow authenticated requests to Azure Functions and Logic Apps to avoid unauthorized executions.
- **Protect API endpoints and input validation**: Serverless applications typically involve the consumption or exposure of APIs that interface with external resources or consumers, and therefore are susceptible to injection attacks and abuses. Secure API endpoints using APIM to enforce rate limits, authentication, and IP filtering. Avoid SQL injection, XSS, and command injection attacks through input validation. In addition, learn from API usage patterns to identify unusually high traffic, like a DDoS attack or unauthorized access attempt.

- **Harden networking security for serverless workloads**: By default, serverless services in Azure are accessible over the internet, which increases the risk. To mitigate this risk, use Private Link and VNet integration to allow access only to internal traffic. NSGs and firewall rules should be used to allow communication only between trusted resources. Outbound and inbound traffic should be restricted according to security policies to prevent attack vectors as much as possible.
- **Secure secrets and credentials with Azure Key Vault**: Hardcoding of API keys, database connection strings, or access credentials within the serverless applications is a major security concern. Instead, all sensitive secrets should be stored in Azure Key Vault, which offers secure access management, auto rotation, and encryption. Azure Functions and Logic Apps should be able to access Key Vault without embedding credentials in configuration files, which is done through Managed Identities. Strict access policies and secret usage tracking contribute to greater security.
- **Monitor and detect threats with advanced security tools**: As serverless job tasks are incredibly dynamic, monitoring in real-time and threat detection are mostly required. Turn on Microsoft Defender for Cloud to find any abnormalities, including function invocations, API abuse, or privilege escalation that are totally out of the ordinary. Manage security information and events with Azure Sentinel (SIEM) to bring together security incidents, examine attack patterns, and apply automated measures. The configuration of security alerts will help to spot potential threats and take prompt measures to reduce them.
- **Implement automated backups and disaster recovery**: Even with strong security measures in place, unexpected failures, data corruption, or security incidents can occur. Enable Azure Backup or App Service Backup to schedule automatic backups of function code, workflow definitions, and configuration settings. Use GRS to keep secondary backups in a different Azure region, ensuring business continuity in case of a regional outage. Regularly test recovery procedures to confirm that backups can be restored quickly and efficiently.

Securing Azure API Management

The API's are the foundation of modern architecture and are used to facilitate data sharing between internal services, third-party applications, and external consumers. Despite this, unsecured APIs can serve as a primary entry point for attackers, thus exposing confidential information, boosting the attack surface, and making systems susceptible to unauthorized access, injection flaws, and API misuse.

Securing and utilizing an API with APIM is the best solution. Organizational entities can protect overrides on the back end or transformation through security by means of effective policies, authentication mechanisms, and monitoring tools and APIs, thus achieve both resilience against evolving threats and high performance and compliance.

Overview of API Management

APIs are the bridges you connect between applications, services, and external users to establish communication, integration, and automation. APIs are very much like doorways into the APIM cloud. They put it all in a unified approach for organizations to publish, protect, trace, and analyze APIs in the Azure environment and across other environments, respecting the policies on governance, security, and performance.

Through the APIM gateway, APIM allows organizations to impose authentication, access control, rate limits, and security policies, thus diminishing the risk of becoming exposed to common attacks. Additionally, the integrated analytics and monitoring tools relay information on the API usage statistics, suspicious activities, and performance trends.

If API settings are not correct, they can expose users to risks like stealing authorizations, DDoS attacks, and data breaches. To balance the risks above, the organization must have strong control over security, limit unjust access, and continuously monitor the API traffic.

Key security features of Azure API Management

API protection encompasses more than mere identity verification; it also involves authorizations and requires network restrictions, data protection, and monitoring that continue without interruption to thwart unauthorized access, API breaches, and data leakages. Azure APIM consists of bulk security features that are instrumental in organization protection, adaptation, and control of APIs. Following are the key security features that help strengthen API security in Azure API Management:

- **Authentication**: Authentication is the foremost defense line against unauthorized API access. Without a proper authentication mechanism, ill-intentioned individuals can take advantage of APIs to access confidential information or manipulate services.

  Here are some ways to authenticate API's:

  - **Integrate APIs with OAuth 2.0 and OpenID Connect**: Using the authentication methods of OAuth 2.0 and OpenID Connect allows for the safe and token-based authentication of the API. This eliminates the need for the client to implement the logic of access token management.
  - **Enforce Microsoft Entra ID authentication**: Restrict API access to only authenticated users and applications by integrating with Microsoft Entra ID, thus ensuring secure and centralized identity management.
  - **Enable API keys and certificates for extra security**: The implementation of API keys, client certificates, or **mutual TLS (mTLS)** offers an additional phase of authentication control to the API consumption.
  - **Block anonymous access**: Make authentication mandatory for all the API endpoints to avoid the invocation of APIs by uninvited users.

- **Rate limiting controls**: The absence of appropriate provisions for rate limiting can lead to an API being bombarded with an abnormal number of requests. This can, in turn, lead to a deterioration in performance, API downtime, or DDoS attacks.

  The following are key practices to rate limit controls:

  - **Setting up request quotas and throttling**: It is possible to prevent API excessive calls by defining the API usage quotas each user, application, or subscription can have. Additionally, throttling is used to limit requests per second, thereby making it compatible with APIs and legitimate users.
  - **Usage of Azure API Management policies to control traffic**: Use IP-based rate limiting, per-client quotas, and burst limits to control traffic spikes and ensure network functioning.
  - **Block automated attacks with request limits**: One of the ways to counter automated bot attacks is to restrict the number of API requests from unknown sources or untrusted applications.
  - **Enforce subscription-based package access:** API consumers must always step on the subscription of API plans, which, in this way, only lets approved applications access while controlled API consumption is still maintained.

- **Network security**: APIs should always be covered by additional protection not only by internet security. The restrictive API network security policies put in place prevent unauthorized access and data leaks.

  Following practices can be used to secure API's from a networking perspective:

  - **Use VNet integration to restrict API access**: Introduce the APIM in Azure VNet to limit API access to trusted networks and private environments.
  - **Enable Private Link for secure API connections**: Azure Private Link ensures that APIs communicate securely over Private Endpoint, preventing exposure to the public internet.
  - **Apply IP filtering and firewall rules**: API access can be restricted only to the approved IP ranges or particular Azure services that are allowed to call APIs.
  - **Deploy WAF for API protection**: Employ Azure Application Gateway or Azure Front Door with WAF to block SQL injection, XSS, and many other API risks.

- **Adherence to data protection**: APIs handle highly confidential data, which is why encryption and secure communication are very important to prevent the occurrence of man-in-the-middle attacks, data leaks, or unauthorized access.

  Here are some ways to ensure data security when using API's:

  - **Encrypt API traffic using TLS 1.2 or higher**: Make sure that every API call is made over TLS 1.2 or 1.3, promoting security for the data in transit.

  - **Enable response encryption for sensitive data**: If APIs return **personally identifiable information (PII)** or financial data, implement response encryption to protect sensitive payloads.
  - **Use Azure Key Vault for secrets management**: Store API keys, tokens, and client credentials securely in Azure Key Vault, avoiding hardcoded secrets in applications.
  - **Mask sensitive data in API responses**: Use Azure API Management policies to redact or mask sensitive fields in API responses, ensuring that only authorized consumers see confidential data.

- **API monitoring and threat detection**: Even the most secure APIs can be accessed without permission, causing security failures and performance issues. Hence, constant monitoring is required.

  API's can be monitored using the following practices:

  - **Enable Azure Monitor and Log Analytics for API insights**: Go into the API statistics to API traffic, and see failed authentication tries along with other facts gathered by Azure Monitor and Log, including data on unusual request patterns.
  - **Detect threats with Microsoft Defender for APIs**: The Microsoft Defender for APIs is the instrument part of Microsoft Defender for Cloud. It is precisely that which gives you, as the customer, real-time threat detection and a reference to identify API attacks, data exfiltration attempts, and other malicious acts.
  - **Set up alerts for unusual API traffic**: The benefits of alert systems are more than just one thing. By making a list of alerts for unusual traffic activity, too many requests, unauthorized API calls, or DDoS offenses, you will be able to understand the security dangers earlier as well as possible.
  - **Use Azure Sentinel for API security analytics:** Besides the correlation of the API logs, Azure Sentinel (SIEM) may serve in the assessment of vulnerabilities and include additional features to carry out automated security incident responses through the integration with Logic App.

- **API gateway security**: Azure API Management is a service for all API traffic; therefore, it is crucial to have it properly secured as a gateway to prevent direct attacks on backend services.

  API Gateways can be used to secure API's in the following ways:

  - **Do not let direct access to backend APIs**: You need to ensure that only the API Gateway (Azure APIM) is allowed to communicate with backend services, therefore preventing direct disclosure of application logic and databases.
  - **Request validation and input sanitization**: Implement policies of APIM to validate and sanitize the inputs of the users to prevent injection attacks and malformed requests from reaching the backend services.

- o **Cross-origin resource sharing (CORS) should be enabled only in a safe manner**: Set the CORS settings to accept only trusted origins, thus preventing unauthorized web applications from accessing APIs.
- o **Utilize mTLS for API client authentication**: The requirement for Users of API is to be presented with a trusted client certificate by the API consumers to ensure that only approved clients can communicate with the API.

Best practices for securing Azure API Management

Apart from the built-in security features, following best practices helps strengthen security, prevent misconfigurations, and improve visibility into API usage and potential threats:

- **Use API policies to enforce security standards**: Azure API Management provides a policy engine to control API behavior at various levels (global, product, or API-specific). Use API policies to:
  - o Filter incoming requests based on IP ranges or geolocation.
  - o Enforce rate limiting and throttling to prevent API abuse.
  - o Sanitize user inputs to block SQL injection and XSS attacks.
  - o Modify request and response headers to enhance API security (e.g., enforce HSTS, CSP, and CORS policies).
- **Regularly audit and monitor API activity with Azure Monitor**: Continuous logging and monitoring are critical for detecting suspicious API activity and ensuring compliance with security best practices.

  Here are some best practices:
  - o Enable API logging using Azure Monitor, Log Analytics, and Application Insights to capture API traffic, latency, and error rates.
  - o Set up alerts for high request volumes, repeated failed authentications, or unusual data access patterns.
  - o Use Microsoft Defender for APIs (part of Microsoft Defender for Cloud) to detect malicious API behavior, data exfiltration attempts, and brute-force attacks.
  - o Automate threat response by integrating Azure Sentinel with APIM.
- **Secure API keys and tokens in Azure Key Vault**: Keys, tokens, and passwords that are used to access APIs should never be hardcoded in apps or kept in configuration files, but we have some workarounds for those.

  Following are the ways to secure API keys and tokens:
  - o Store all API secrets in Azure Key Vault, ensuring encrypted storage with strict access policies.

- o Use Managed Identities to eliminate the need for hardcoded secrets in API integrations.
- o Rotate API keys and tokens regularly to minimize the risk of unauthorized access.
- o Restrict API key access based on user roles and applications, ensuring that only authorized entities can retrieve sensitive credentials.

- **Restrict API Access with network security controls**: APIs should not be publicly exposed unless necessary. Implementing network security best practices reduces the risk of data exposure and API abuse.

  Following best practices can be used from a networking perspective:

  - o Enable Azure Private Link to keep API traffic internal and restrict access to approved private networks.
  - o Use VNet integration to prevent direct internet exposure.
  - o Configure NSGs to allow access only from trusted sources.
  - o Deploy Azure WAF with Azure Front Door or Application Gateway to block DDoS attacks, bot traffic, and common API exploits.

- **Implement Zero Trust security for API access**: Adopting a Zero Trust model ensures that every API request is authenticated, authorized, and validated before being processed.

  Here are some best practices for API access:

  - o Require strong authentication for all API consumers using Microsoft Entra ID OAuth 2.0, or mTLS.
  - o Enforce least privilege access by granting the minimal API permissions to users, applications, and integrations.
  - o Use conditional access policies to block API requests from untrusted locations, unmanaged devices, or high-risk IPs.
  - o Disable anonymous API access and require token-based authentication for all endpoints.

- **Protect sensitive data with API response filtering**: APIs often handle sensitive customer, financial, or PII making data protection a top priority.

  The following are some ways to protect your data:

  - o Mask or redact sensitive data in API responses before returning them to clients.
  - o Encrypt sensitive fields in API payloads using Azure API Management policies.
  - o Apply role-based access to API responses, allowing only authorized users to view specific data.
  - o Prevent excessive data exposure by enforcing field-level access control for API consumers.

- **Enforce API gateway security to protect backend services**: APIs should never expose backend services directly. Instead, Azure API Management should act as a secure API gateway, preventing direct client access to backend applications.

  An API gateway can be used to secure API's in the following ways:

  - Use the API gateway pattern to add an extra security layer between consumers and backend services.
  - Block direct access to backend APIs by ensuring that only the API Gateway (Azure APIM) can communicate with backend services.
  - Validate and sanitize all incoming API requests to prevent malicious payloads from reaching backend systems.
  - Enable request and response transformation to strip unnecessary headers or modify API calls before forwarding them to the backend.
- **Enable automated API security testing and compliance checks**: Regular security testing ensures APIs meet compliance requirements and detect vulnerabilities early.

  Following are some ways to secure API's based on regulatory needs:

  - Perform API security testing using tools like OWASP ZAP, Burp Suite, or Microsoft Defender for APIs to detect misconfigurations and security flaws.
  - Validate API compliance with industry standards like GDPR, HIPAA, and ISO 27001 by setting up Azure Policy and Compliance Center.
  - Automate API security reviews with Azure DevOps pipelines, ensuring security checks are performed before deploying new API versions.
  - Regularly audit API permissions and configurations to identify and remove unused or overly permissive access settings.

Baseline architecture for APIM

Figure 4.3 is a representation of Azure API Management and Kubernetes architecture, and it interconnects web applications, APIs, and databases with security and scalability best practices. The architecture is implemented for both external and internal API access, which are secured by APIM, Application Gateway, and WAF that ensure DDoS protection, private networking, and controlled access to backend resources.

At the entry point, clients interact with APIs online, where external and internal APIs are accessible via specific domain names. The **Application Gateway** (**AG**), accompanied by a WAF, provides secure ingress points of control by filtering and inspecting traffic before forwarding it to the proper backend services. The DDoS Protection service is integrated into the network to mitigate volumetric attacks and increase security against distributed denial-of-service attacks.

The APIM service is launched in a dedicated APIM subnet, thus serving as a centralized platform for exposing, managing, and securing APIs. The service also includes policy-based

API control, authentication, and analytics to ensure that clients interact with the backend services only after proper authorization. The integration with APIM is done with several services, such as the **App Service Environment** (**ASE**), **Kubernetes Service** (**AKS**), and **SQL managed instances** (**SQL MI**).

Inside the ASE subnet, the Linux-based App Service is managed to host web applications in a fully isolated and managed environment, thus providing extra security and performance benefits to the web workloads. The AKS is in a separate aks-subnet, and it manages containerized applications and microservices that need to scale and orchestrate. API calls sent through APIM might access these services via private networking instead of public exposure.

For data storage and processing, the SQL MI service is effectively installed in its own sqldmi-subnet with entirely privately connected high-availability and low-latency relational database features offered. With the APIM and AKS services being the only entities capable of making secure traffic to SQL MI, this guarantees that the right information remains outside the world of the Azure VNet.

For security reasons, the architecture comprises a sinkpool (dead-end) route, which locks out unauthorized destinations altogether. This helps to block API requests made inadvertently or routing traffic wrong. On the other hand, DDoS protection is a powerful network security tool providing resilience against massive cyberattacks.

Following figure is the reference architecture as discussed before:

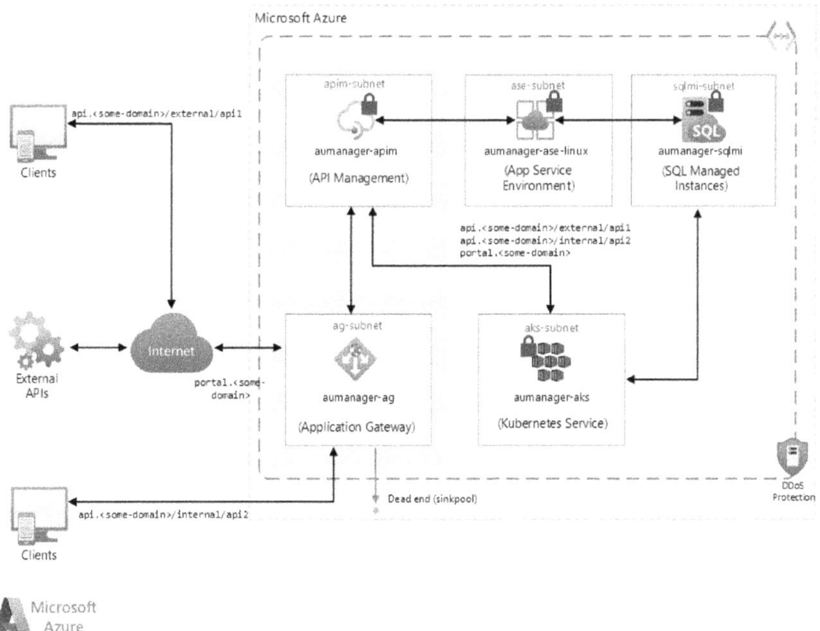

***Figure 4.3**: APIM architecture*

***Source**: https://learn.microsoft.com/en-us/Azure/architecture/web-apps/api-management/architectures/protect-apis*

Conclusion

Securing compute resources in Azure is fundamental to protecting workloads from cyber threats, unauthorized access, and data breaches. This chapter covered key IaaS, PaaS, and serverless security strategies, highlighting best practices for Azure VMs, Containers, App Services, Serverless Functions, and API Management.

Organizations can significantly enhance VM security by leveraging disk encryption, RBAC, network segmentation, and JIT access. Container security is strengthened through image scanning, role-based access control, and private networking, ensuring compliance and protection against supply chain attacks. Securing Azure App Service, API Management, and serverless workloads requires access control, encryption, and continuous monitoring to minimize exposure.

Organizations should implement Zero Trust principles, enforce compliance policies, and regularly audit security configurations to maintain a strong security posture. Security is an ongoing process, and proactive monitoring with Microsoft Defender for Cloud and Azure Sentinel will help detect and mitigate threats before they impact.

In the next chapter, we will look into securing the data. *Chapter 5, Securing Data,* gets into protecting Azure Storage and databases, implementing encryption, access controls, and advanced data security techniques like masking and auditing. Whether you are protecting files, blobs, or SQL data, the upcoming chapter will help you with best practices to ensure your data remains secure at rest and in transit.

Join our Discord space

Join our Discord workspace for latest updates, offers, tech happenings around the world, new releases, and sessions with the authors:

https://discord.bpbonline.com

Chapter 5
Securing Data

Introduction

In this chapter, you will learn skills to master securing Azure Storage and data services. You will learn topics like storage access control, data protection, and encryption, as well as securing database services for Azure SQL Database and Azure SQL Managed Instance. You will explore database authentication, auditing, data masking, and conclude with encryption.

Structure

This chapter contains the following topics:

- Access control for storage services
- Data protection for storage services
- Encryption for storage services
- Security of database services

Objectives

By the end of this chapter, readers will be able to understand the procedures for securing data on Azure through access control, encryption, auditing, and disaster recovery strategies. They will acquire the skills of restricting unauthenticated access by Microsoft Entra ID and

RBAC, protecting the data with **transparent data encryption** (TDE) and Always Encrypted, monitoring the threats with **advanced threat protection** (ATP) and auditing, and ensuring high availability through geo-replication and backups. Following these best practices will help organizations protect sensitive information, identify security issues, and comply with Azure environments.

Access control for storage services

Access control to storage services is the essential and initial element of data security in the cloud. Azure offers several ways to ensure that only users and applications permitted by the administrators can communicate with the storage resources. A specific and complete access control strategy is the best solution to reduce the risks of the issues above. Organizations have to balance the permissions they give users with the actual users' demands for operating the services without being impacted.

Overview of storage access control

Azure Storage account offers various ways to secure and protect storage components, i.e., objects, containers, files, etc. The mechanisms ensure that only required users have relevant access to the resources.

Utilizing Azure's identity and access management features allows organizations to implement the least privilege access strategy and be flexible in their business requirements.

Azure Storage's main governing access controls are Microsoft Entra ID, RBAC, and **shared access signatures** (SAS). By allowing users to employ basic or suggested roles, the Microsoft Entra ID helps administrators maintain the degree of security based on the requirements of users and services. RBAC also provides uniform access control administration, therefore augmenting the straightforward approach of controlling rights across storage systems.

In cases where there is a need to limit access to temporary environments or external services, a SAS is a robust mechanism where time-limited permissions are granted to users or external applications that are needed. Azure Storage supports the direct **access control list** (ACLs) option to manage file and directory permissions in Azure Files and Azure Data Lake Storage.

Access control methods for storage

The most significant consideration for protecting Azure Storage services is to use the right access control methods. Access control systems in Azure are designed to meet various security needs and usage scenarios. These methods can make storage resources accessible only to authorized users while still providing a means for legitimate users and applications to interact with the data correctly.

Here are the primary access control methods that are available in Azure Storage:

- **RBAC**: Azure RBAC is primarily a security feature that gives users, groups, and service principals specified permissions to perform tasks with the predefined or custom roles assigned by the administrator. RBAC works at the subscription, resource group, and storage account levels, thus providing a granular approach to the storage resources access and what actions can be performed.

  In contrast to other methods, through RBAC, the access is handled by Microsoft Entra ID identities, meaning that the permissions are applied dynamically, considering the roles of the users. The platform has predefined roles, such as Storage Blob Data Reader (to read-only access to Blob Storage), Storage Blob Data Contributor (read/write access), and Storage Account Contributor (full storage account management). The ability to create custom roles with specific permissions for security policy is provided in addition to built-in roles. By using a hierarchical structure of the authorization of the resources with RBAC, organizations can regulate the least privileged access in the system, and the risks associated with over-provisioning permissions can be reduced.

- **Shared access signatures (SAS)**: The method is entirely different from other ways and is not susceptible to account key exposure. SAS primarily allows sharing access to resources without endangering account keys. SAS tokens enable users/apps to access storage services (Blobs, Queues, Tables, and Files) with particular permissions for a specified time. Therefore, resource access is possible with this method when temporary/peripheral access is required, for example, when an external user or a third-party app has to be given access.

  There are different types of SAS tokens, including Service SAS (grants access to specific resources like a blob or queue), Account SAS (provides access at the storage account level), and User Delegation SAS (leverages Microsoft Entra ID authentication). To enhance security, SAS tokens should always be generated with limited permissions and short expiration times. Besides this, organizations can manage SAS permissions from one central place by using stored access policies, reducing the risk of token misuse.

- **Microsoft Entra ID Integration**: The joining of Microsoft Entra ID makes it possible for organizations to continue using identity-based access control with Azure Storage. Contrary to the traditional keys of storage accounts or using the SAS tokens, Microsoft Cloud Entra ID allows authentication to take place through Managed Identities, service principals, and user accounts. The key point of this methodology is the absence of the need to store or distribute the access keys, thus addressing the credential leak risk issues.

  With Microsoft Entra ID, access to storage services can be governed through RBAC and **conditional access** (**CA**) policies. Organizations can enforce **multi-factor authentication** (**MFA**), network restrictions, and sign-in risk policies to further improve security. Furthermore, on-premise Active Directory integration is supported by Microsoft Entra ID authentication for Azure Files, thus enabling Windows systems to access File Shares securely with Kerberos authentication and NTFS permissions.

Managing access policies for storage services

Securing Azure Storage accounts and ensuring compliance with security best standards depend on good access policy management. Azure lowers the risks linked to issues such as unauthorized access, data breaches, and noncompliance with the SDLC phases by using different access limits and data protection mechanisms.

Among the implementation examples, three methods for managing access policies in Azure Storage are as follows:

- **Storage account keys**: Azure Storage accounts are designed to accommodate two primary and secondary access keys. The keys provide complete administrative authority over the account. The keys then grant complete access to all storage services, including file, table, queue, and Blob Storage. It is risky to use these keys to overlay access because anyone having them can fully modify the storage account.

  To minimize security risks, best practices recommend avoiding direct use of storage account keys. Organizations should instead use SAS to provide limited permissions for a specific time. Azure Key Vault can be used to store and manage storage account keys securely by reducing exposure, and Azure Storage supports key rotation, allowing administrators to regenerate keys periodically to enhance security. Forcing the key to limit direct access to storage account keys and using other authentication tools like Microsoft Entra ID can lead to a stronger security culture among organizations.

- **Immutable Blob Storage**: Immutable Blob Storage has been recently designed for compliance and data integrity. It verifies the timelessness of the Azure Blob Storage data that cannot be changed or deleted for a certain amount of time. This option is vital for organizations with specific requirements that must be followed according to the regulations, for instance, finance, healthcare, and legal businesses that must adhere to data retention and tamper-proof storage guidelines.

  Azure immutability can be configured in two ways:

  - **Time-based retention**: The data is locked without modification for a specific time period; in this way, regulations such as SEC 17a-4, FINRA, and HIPAA are enforced.

  - **Legal hold**: Until the legal investigations or reviews are completed, no changes or deletions of anything can be made.

  Immutable storage aims to prevent people from accidentally or maliciously removing or modifying the data, so it is a good choice for critical logs, backup data files, and compliance records. Organizations may try to add **write once, read many (WORM)** policies that specify that data can be altered only once, thus providing a vital line of defence against ransomware and threats from the inside.

- **Access tiers**: Azure Storage has introduced the concept of access tiers to optimize data storage expenses while keeping them available based on usage patterns. In categorizing data, for example, based on accessibility, organizations could optimize their storage costs. The access tiers available are:
  - o **Hot tier**: For the data that needs to be frequently used, it provides a low-latency, high-performance level of access, but at a more significant storage price.
  - o **Cool tier**: For the data that will not be accessed frequently, the storage cost is less, but the retrieval charge is a little bit higher.
  - o **Archive tier**: This is the option of retaining rarely accessed data; thereby, the storage becomes the cheapest, but the retrieval times are higher.

  Access tiers make it possible for organizations to have intelligent management of their storage costs because that way, files that are usually accessed often are always available, while those in the archive mostly stay secure and are not at the expense of the budget. Lifecycle management policies can be applied to initiate the automatic transition of data from one tier to another, depending on how frequently it has been accessed. Thus, optimization of storage efficiency can be optimized. In addition, moving data from the Archive Tier back requires rehydration, which is helpful for regulatory requirements, backups, and long-term retention.

Best practices for securing Azure Storage access

Utilizing robust security measures is crucial for Azure Storage to protect against unauthorized access, data breaches, and compliance drift. The following recommended practices not only maintain data security but also operational efficiency.

Here are security recommendations to help users limit access and protect their data in Azure Storage:

- **Use Microsoft Entra ID-based authentication instead of shared keys**: The safest method of allowing access to Azure Storage is using Microsoft Entra ID-based authentication. Unlike shared account keys, which are the only way to enable entire access and endanger security if given to the wrong people, Microsoft Entra ID authentication is used for identity-based access control, meaning that the storage resources can be accessed only by users and apps that have been authorized.

  Here are some ways in which Microsoft Entra ID can be used:
  - o **RBAC integration**: Assign RBAC roles, e.g., Storage Blob Data Reader and Storage Account Contributor, to enforce least privilege access.
  - o **User delegation SAS**: Generate user delegation SAS instead of the standard SAS tokens, allowing temporary access on an identity basis.

  - o **Managed Identities**: Deploy Managed Identities for Azure resources to allow the services access to storage accounts without managing the credentials.

- **Enable Azure Storage Firewalls and Private Endpoint to deny access**: Denying network access is a key part of protecting Azure Storage. By default, Azure Storage is primarily accessed over the public internet, making it vulnerable to unwanted access.

  The following steps should be taken to manage this risk:

  1. **Allow Azure Storage Firewalls**: Configure the storage account firewall to allow traffic from trusted IPs, VNets, or specific Azure services.
  2. **Private Endpoint use**: Integrate Azure Private Link to ensure that storage traffic flows over a private network connection, eliminating public internet exposure.
  3. **Public access disable**: Disable anonymous public access to storage accounts from the beginning to avoid unauthorized data exposure.
  4. **Cross-tenant access restriction**: Make use of the Conditional Access policies in Microsoft Entra ID that prohibit providing authentication from unmanaged tenants.

- **Regularly conducting access policy reviews and updates**: Security measures should not remain unchanged; they must be periodically tracked and changed to keep up with the dynamically evolving security needs.

  Some of the practices include:

  - o **Perform regular access audits**: Use Azure Monitor, Defender for Cloud, and Storage Analytics for access pattern tracking and anomaly detection.
  - o **Rotate access keys on schedule**: If the account keys are in circulation, rotate and use Azure Key Vault to make sure they are safely secured.
  - o **Monitor SAS token usage periodically**: Shorten the expiration period of SAS and use management policies.
  - o **Enforce RBAC reviews**: Review RBAC assignments at scheduled times to ensure that only authorized personnel can access them.

- **Activate advanced threat protection for storage**: Microsoft Entra ID ATP for storage accounts is a real-time observer of security threats and is helpful in detection and prevention. It is also an alerting system for suspicious behaviours that are reported, such as:

  - o Unusual access patterns that indicate potential data exfiltration.
  - o Unauthorized anonymous access attempts.
  - o Malicious activity, such as ransomware attacks targeting storage resources.

- **Implement encryption for data at rest and in transit**: Encryption protects data and prevents unauthorized users from reading stored information. Some of the recommendations are:
  - o **Storage service encryption (SSE) enable**: Secure data at rest with Microsoft-managed or **customer-managed keys** (**CMK**) in the Azure Key Vault.
  - o **Transport Layer Security (TLS 1.2+) use**: Encrypt data by allowing secure HTTPS/TLS connections to storage accounts.
  - o **Double encryption for sensitive data implementation**: Using both SSE and CSE for additional protection.
- **Use soft delete and versioning to protect against data loss**: Data loss can be caused by unintentional deletion or malware attacks. The key solutions include:
  - o **Blobs and files soft delete**: Keep the deleted data for a configurable time, recovering it if necessary.
  - o **Blob versioning**: Keep previous blob versions to recover the data in case of unintended changes or overwrites.
  - o **Point-in-time restore (PITR) for Azure Storage**: Recover storage accounts to a previous state based on a predefined timestamp.

Data protection for storage services

Data security is as crucial in cloud systems as access control is. Organizations should take the required actions to keep attacked, changed, and deleted files on their storage resources safe from either access by hackers or by accident. Azure uses strict protection mechanisms to guarantee the data stays undamaged, secure, and available to authorized users.

Introduction to data protection

Azure also has various tools and configurations to help organizations minimize data loss, corruption, and unauthorized changes. These capabilities ensure that stored data remains resilient, recoverable, and secure against accidental deletions and external attacks.

In Azure Storage, data protection strategies are:

- Redundancy and backup solutions to prevent data loss in case of failures.
- Data encryption is one of the mechanisms that ensures data confidentiality.
- Control access measures to prevent unauthorized changes.
- Versioning and immutability policies to safeguard data integrity.
- Disaster recovery and backup procedures to restore lost or overwritten data.

Key features

Through its built-in features, Azure Storage ensures that stored data is protected from unintentional deletions, corruption, or malicious modifications. These capabilities improve data resilience, recovery, and compliance by allowing organizations to restore necessary information when required.

The following are the three fundamental features that are central to securing Azure Storage data:

- **Soft Delete**: The Soft Delete feature prevents accidental or malicious deletions from permanently deleting the data. With it turned on, deleted blobs and Azure Files are retained for a period defined by the user, allowing their retrieval if needed.
    - **How it works**: Azure does not fully delete a blob or file but sets the soft delete attribute, which retains a shadow copy for the retention period (up to 365 days).
    - **Use case**: Protects critical data from inadvertent deletions, ransomware attacks, or misconfiguration of apps. For example, it helps recover accidentally deleted security logs needed for investigations, restores user files deleted by mistake, and protects data targeted by ransomware attacks.
    - **Recovery process**: During the retention period, the restored blobs or files do not need additional backup solutions.

  The organization can easily enable Soft Delete, and through this, the lost data can be recovered in no time; thus, the downtime and operational risks are reduced. It is highly recommended for use with business-critical applications, log storage, and user-generated data.

- **Snapshots**: Azure Snapshots is a feature enabling users to make point-in-time copies of blobs or files, which are read-only, thus giving a simple and efficient solution to data backup. In contrast to standard backups, snapshots are part of the same storage account, so they are immediately accessible for recovery.
    - **How it works**: Snapshots take a picture of the state of a blob or file at one particular point in time. The snapshot can restore the previous version if the original data is modified or deleted.
    - **Use case**: Handy for those cases where there are frequent changes, such as databases, app setups, and shared file storage.
    - **Cost efficiency**: Snapshots save the changes (incremental data) rather than duplicating complete files, which means less storage space is used.

  For their prompt and easy usage, it is preferable that the snapshots used in short-term versioning quickly go back to their original state in case of corrupted data or unintended modifications.

- **Azure Backup**: Azure Backup is a fully managed **backup as a service** (**BaaS**) solution that is specially designed to cater to long-term retention and disaster recovery. It efficiently backs up storage data and creates a robust system against data loss, hardware failures, and cyber-attacks.
  - **How it works**: Azure Backup will automatically take and retain backups of Azure File Shares, Managed Disks, SQL Databases, and more, depending on predetermined schedules.
  - **Use case**: Best suited to **business continuity planning** (**BCP**), regulatory compliance, and ransomware protection.
  - **Key features**:
    - **Policy-based backup management**: Allows the retention policy definition for daily, weekly, monthly, or yearly backups.
    - **Incremental backups**: Optimization of disk space through the backup of only new or modified files instead of duplicating full backups.
    - **Geo-redundant storage (GRS)**: Backing up across numerous Azure regions for disaster recovery.
    - **Multi-layered security**: Prevent unauthorized changes using immutable vaults and soft-delete backups.

Using Azure Backup avoids the need for manual backup scripts and complies with industry standards. Thus, it becomes a significant part of the successful deployment of the cloud storage strategy.

Governance and data classification

Governance and data classification are key components in protecting customer data, ensuring that sensitive information is properly managed, monitored, and controlled, to rule out any chances of accidental or intentional external access. Azure features a collection of **data loss prevention** (DLP) frameworks that help organizations implement security protocols, spot unauthorized activities, and classify data.

Here are three key methods to upgrade the protection and governance of Azure Storage.

- **Azure Policy**: Azure Policy allows enterprises to enforce security measures and compliance demands across Azure resources, including storage services. Through custom policies, only administrators can limit access to unauthorized data uploads, and proper handling of sensitive information can be ensured.
  - **How it works**: Azure Policy examines the storage configurations in real-time and applies compliance rules to receive either prevention or logging of policy violations.

  - **Use case**: Discourage users from uploading unencrypted files, PII, or regulated financial data.
  - **Example policies**:
    - **Block public access**: Prevent storage accounts from being publicly accessible.
    - **Enforce encryption**: Ensure all data stored in blobs is encrypted using CMK.
    - **Restrict locations**: Limit data storage to specific Azure regions to comply with data sovereignty laws.
- **Storage monitoring**: The constant monitoring of storage activities is essential in tracing anomalies that could probably lead to data breaches, unauthorized access, or insider threats. Azure offers Azure Monitor and Azure Storage Analytics to supervise and log storage operations.
  - **How it works**: Azure Monitor collects metrics and logs from storage accounts, while Defender for Cloud provides security recommendations.
  - **Use case**: Detect large-scale data transfers, suspicious access attempts, and policy violations.
  - **Key monitoring tools**:
    - **Azure Storage Logs**: Track read/write/delete operations on blobs and files.
    - **Activity Logs**: Monitor administrative actions, such as role assignments and key rotations.
    - **Azure Sentinel**: Use threat intelligence and AI-driven alerts to identify security incidents.
- **Tagging**: Proper classification of storage resources is essential for better governance, cost management, and security enforcement. Azure Tags are a conventional way to tag storage accounts according to their purpose, sensitivity, and ownership.
  - **How it works**: Tags are key-value pairs that help categorize storage resources for better tracking.
  - **Use case**: Identify storage accounts containing sensitive data and apply automated security policies accordingly.
  - **Example tagging strategies**:
    - **Environment (Prod, Dev, Test)**: Helps enforce different security policies based on the environment.
    - **Data sensitivity (Confidential, Public, Restricted)**: Ensures appropriate access controls are applied.

- **Compliance (GDPR and HIPAA)**: Marks storage accounts that require specific audit and security settings.

Best practices

Organizations must build effective data protection strategies in Azure Storage to stop data loss, unauthorized access, and security breaches. Their only option should be a multi-layer security model, which should embrace access control, encryption, monitoring, and recovery mechanisms to guarantee compliance and security of their storage resources.

The following are the best practices for securing storage services:

- **Enable Soft Delete for blobs and files**: Soft Delete plays a protective role by configuring against accidental deletions and malicious modifications, and thus retaining deleted data for a selectable retention period. As a result of this configuration, blobs and deleted files are not permanently erased but instead are kept in a recoverable state for up to 365 days. This feature allows corporations to restore the necessary information without any additional backups. Soft Delete is one of the best measures to be implemented in multi-user environments where the accidental deletion of a file is routine, or in situations where cyber threats, such as ransomware attacks, attempt to remove important files. Activating this option allows organizations to enhance their data resilience and reduce the risk of data loss.

- **Regularly create and test backups**: An effective backup strategy is critical to business continuity and lost data mitigation. The solution for Azure is to use Azure Backup to automate the backup process and keep it geo-redundant, ensuring availability even in case of regional outages. Snapshots also offer a point-in-time recovery option if a quick rollback is needed because of data corruption or accidental modifications. However, just having a backup is not the answer—the regular testing of backup recovery processes is critical to verifying data integrity and accessibility. Organizations without backup testing might find their backups incomplete or corrupted, which can cause issues during disaster recovery.

- **Monitor access logs for unauthorized data changes**: The monitoring of storage access acts as an early warning for troublesome issues so that they can act swiftly before they escalate to security incidents. Azure provides Storage Logging and Azure Monitor in the same way to track data access, modification events, and potentially malicious behaviors. Organizations should set up alerts in real time to detect unauthorized access, abnormal data transfers, or failed authentication attacks that could indicate a brute-force attack. Integrating Azure Sentinel into storage monitoring adds AI-driven anomaly detection, which helps security teams investigate and remove threats proactively. Businesses prevent data leaks and unauthorized modifications by continuously checking the logs and monitoring storage activity before they face the consequences.

- **Use encryption for data at rest and in transit**: Encryption is your friend during unauthorized access attempts, and data will still be unreadable to the attackers. Azure provides SSE, which encrypts the data automatically and stores it in blobs, files, tables, and queues. This is done using either Microsoft or CMK stored in the Azure Key Vault. Organizations can implement double encryption for sensitive data that needs an extra layer of security by using both server and client-side keys. Also, it is essential to talk about data in transit that must be secured by TLS 1.2 or higher, as eavesdropping and interception are possible during data transfers. Enforcing the encryption policies will make them more secure and keep the regulations like GDPR, HIPAA, and ISO 27001 intact.

- **Restrict public access and use Private Endpoint**: Deploy storage accounts on the public internet, and you ride the security risk rollercoaster, with big chances of being hacked or having data breaches. Organizations that cannot avoid it should first turn off public access to storage accounts and use them only if there is a real need. Azure Storage Firewalls give organizations the option of allowing access from trusted IP addresses and VNets to the private network. Besides, they can leverage Azure Private Link to provide a storage service that can be accessed via only private network connections; therefore, no public exposure is made. By only allowing the internet connection for internal networks, organizations reduce their attack surfaces and prevent unauthorized data from being exposed.

- **Implement RBAC and least privilege access**: Providing proper access control is critical in storage security, thus keeping unauthorized actions at bay. Instead of solely using secret storage account keys, which can allow unlimited access, organizations should use Microsoft Entra ID authentication for identity-based access control. RBAC can be used to limit permissions, which ensures that users, groups, and applications have access only to what is necessary. The setting in predefined roles like Storage Blob Data Reader (for read-only access) and Storage Account Contributor (for storage mgmt) prevents excessive privileges. However, it is important to regularly audit the role assignments and remove unnecessary access, which will minimize everyone's privilege escalation and attacks. For momentary access, the organizations should choose User Delegation SAS over the traditional one to achieve more security, as it is integrated with Microsoft Entra ID.

- **Enable immutable storage for regulatory compliance**: As regulatory and compliance needs demand it, the organizations managing sensitive or legally secured data should use immutable storage in Azure Blob Storage. The feature prevents data from being locked or deleted for a specific period, thus it becomes the perfect candidate for compliance industries such as finance, healthcare, and legal. Organizations can set time-based retention policies that will automatically enforce data retention rules and prevent accidental or malicious deletions. On top of that, enacting legal hold policies will ensure that the data is maintained for the audits and investigations until authorization for a specific removal is given.

Encryption for storage services

Data encryption is a major security measure that guarantees confidentiality, integrity, and compliance for Azure-stored data. Whether data is at rest, in transit, or being processed, Azure supplies various encryption options to guard against unauthorized access and data breaches. Strong encryption techniques are the only way to ensure that sensitive information will be invisible to adversaries, even when the storage accounts are attacked.

Overview of encryption

Encryption in Azure Storage comes with automatic and configurable security controls to protect data from unauthorized access. All data at rest is encrypted by Azure by default, and additional encryption options are available for customers who need higher security. Organizations can select the most suitable option between Microsoft-managed, customer-managed, or client-side encryption, depending on their security and compliance requirements.

Azure's encryption framework guarantees that:

- **Confidentiality**: It is impossible for an unauthorized person to access stored data
- **Data integrity**: It is impossible to tamper with the data by encrypting it before storage.
- **Compliance**: Meets regulatory requirements like GDPR, HIPAA, and ISO 27001.

Through the execution of a thorough and all-embracing encryption plan, businesses can justify their data security, regulatory compliance, and risk mitigation through the same.

Encryption methods

Azure provides various encryption mechanisms to save data across various storage services. Through these methods, data is preserved in an encrypted state during storage, in transit, and before being uploaded to storage:

- **SSE**: It automatically encrypts data before storing it in Azure Storage and decrypts it when accessed. This ensures that data at rest is always encrypted without requiring additional user configuration. Azure provides three different server-side encryption options:
    - **Microsoft-managed keys (SSE with PMK)**: Azure encrypts all storage data by default using Microsoft-managed keys, eliminating the need for manual configuration. This option provides seamless encryption with minimal management overhead.
    - **Customer-managed keys (SSE with CMK)**: Organizations with strict compliance or security policies can manage their own encryption keys using Azure Key Vault. This allows greater control over key rotation, access permissions, and encryption lifecycle management.

  - **Customer-provided keys (SSE with CPK)**: For businesses requiring full control over encryption keys, Azure allows customers to provide their own encryption keys for each data transaction. This option benefits organizations that store highly sensitive data requiring external key management and security audits.

- **Client-side encryption**: Client-side encryption provides an additional security layer by encrypting data before uploading it to Azure Storage. In this method, the encryption process occurs on the client application before the data is sent to Azure. Only authorized users with the correct decryption keys can read the data.

  How it works:

  - The data is encrypted using encryption libraries such as Azure Storage SDK, .NET, or Java-based encryption APIs.
  - The customer manages encryption keys using Azure Key Vault or an external key management system.
  - Encrypted data is stored in Azure, ensuring that even if unauthorized users access it, they cannot decrypt it.

- **Encryption in transit**: Encrypting data in transit ensures that information remains protected while being transferred between storage services, applications, and users. Azure enforces TLS to secure all communications.

  Some recommended security controls are:

  - Enforce HTTPS (TLS 1.2 or higher) for all connections to Azure Storage.
  - Use Azure Private Link to ensure that storage traffic remains on private networks instead of the public internet.
  - Disable legacy TLS versions (TLS 1.0 and 1.1) to prevent security vulnerabilities.
  - Implement VPN or ExpressRoute to securely transfer sensitive data to and from Azure storage.

Encryption methods comparison

The following table summarises Azure's encryption options, outlining who manages the keys, their best use cases, benefits, and key considerations to help you choose the right approach for your data security needs:

Encryption type	Key managed by	Use case	Benefits	Risks/considerations
SSE-PMK	Microsoft	Default encryption for general data protection	Zero management overhead	Less control over key rotation and access policies

Encryption type	Key managed by	Use case	Benefits	Risks/considerations
SSE-CMK	Customer via Azure Key Vault	Compliance requirements needing a customer-managed lifecycle	Full control over key rotation, revocation, and permissions	Requires Key Vault management and cost
SSE-CPK	Customer (provided per request)	Highly sensitive data needing external key management	Maximum control, no storage of keys in Azure	High operational complexity; key must be available for each transaction; loss of key = permanent data loss
Client-side encryption	Customer before upload	Encryption before data enters Azure	Complete ownership of the encryption process	Application changes needed; must securely manage encryption and decryption keys
Encryption in transit	N/A (TLS enforced)	All data transfers	Protects data from interception	Must enforce TLS 1.2+; does not encrypt data at rest

***Table 5.1**: Comparing various encryption options*

Key management

Correctly managing the keys is the most important part of encryption security. Azure is the choice of organizations that focus on automating the management and security of their encryption keys in a central manner.

Here are three ways to properly manage keys:

- **Azure Key Vault**: Azure Key Vault is a secure cloud-based key management system that allows organizations to store, manage, and control the encryption keys that are used to encrypt Azure Storage data.

  Benefits of Azure Key Vault:

  - Securely stores encryption keys, secrets, and certificates.
  - Enforces access control using Azure RBAC and Azure Policies.
  - Supports **hardware security modules** (**HSMs**) for enhanced encryption security.

- **Key rotation**: Regular key rotation is a critical security practice that prevents the attacker from using compromised encryption keys. Azure Key Vault is the platform that allows organizations to:

  - o Automate the key rotation.
  - o Restrict the key access according to the ACL.
  - o Create new keys without affecting existing operations.

- **Audit logs**: Monitor key usage for compliance and anomaly detection. Managing the encryption key usage by tracking is crucial for the detection of security attacks. Azure offers businesses tools for audit logging and monitoring, as well as the means to comply with encryption standards.

  Audit logs can be leveraged by following the resources to ensure security and reduce risk:

  - o Azure Monitor tracks all events concerning the access of encryption keys.
  - o Defender for Cloud detects suspicious activities related to the key being used.
  - o Azure Policy enforces compliance with the encryption of all storage accounts.

Best practices

Implementing encryption alone is not enough to secure data; businesses have to strictly adhere to the protocols to avoid security breaches like mismanaging encryption keys, conducting unsecured data transmission, and having difficulty monitoring key usage. By following these protocols, they can avoid unauthorized access, comply with the security regulations, and ultimately preserve the integrity of data kept in Azure.

To make it easier for you to encrypt your data on Azure Storage, here are some key best practices:

- **Use Azure Key Vault for encryption key management**: Having to manually manage encryption keys can be an overwhelming ordeal and carry serious security threats, such as accidental key exposure or cases of wrongful access. Azure Key Vault is a secure, centralized solution that ensures encryption keys are stored and managed safely, preventing any unauthorized access or misuse. Instead of hard-coding keys in the application code or storing them in configuration files, organizations should utilize Key Vault to operate key access, force key rotation, and track usage logs.

  With the use of CMK coupled with Key Vault, organizations get the upper hand in managing encryption policies that dictate access through RBAC. This makes it impossible for unauthorized personnel or applications to use encryption keys to decrypt sensitive data. The additional key rotation that is done automatically will also help the organization replace the keys at risk of being compromised. HSMs are also supported by Key Vault, giving organizations another level of security as the encryption keys are stored in hardware that is resistant to tampering.

- **Require HTTPS for safe data transmission**: Encryption is not only about saving data at rest; it also involves protecting data in transit against possibly being intercepted or tampered with. The primary way of achieving this is to enforce HTTPS (TLS 1.2 or higher) for all connections to Azure Storage. TLS ensures that the data transferred between clients, applications, and storage services is all securely encrypted. Thus, hackers cannot intercept any sensitive information.

The setup of Azure Storage accounts must only permit secure HTTPS connections while disabling HTTP to eliminate possible vulnerabilities. Organizations need to ensure that storage traffic remains on private networks by using Azure Private Link, besides ensuring that no storage traffic goes to the public internet. Thus, they can prevent **man-in-the-middle** (**MITM**) attacks by encrypting the whole transmission and asking for only secure communication channels.

- **Activate encryption for both managed and unmanaged disks**: By default, Azure applies SSE to managed disks, which ensures that **virtual machine** (**VM**) disks are encrypted automatically. Yet, organizations that go for unmanaged disks must first enable encryption before averting unauthorized data access in Azure VMs.

  Encryption of unmanaged disks can be done by using **Azure Disk Encryption** (**ADE**), which makes use of BitLocker (for Windows) and DM-Crypt (for Linux) to protect data while at rest. Organizations should also think of the best place to store the encryption keys for the disks in Azure Key Vault as opposed to embedding them in VM configurations. The benefit of disk types encryption is that the data will still be incomprehensible without the corresponding decryption key if a disk is copied or extracted at any point.

- **Limit the use of encryption keys only to certain users and services**: Encryption keys are very precious properties that urge the strictest controls against misuse. When such keys are accessed by unfriendly individuals, decrypting the encrypted data, thus exposing it can happen. Organizations are advised to apply least privilege access policies through Azure RBAC to cut down on risk. Thus, only authorized users and applications with adequate permission will be able to access or change the encryption keys.

  Moreover, isolating encryption keys by their sensitivity level also consolidates security by applying separate Key Vault instances for different workloads. An example would be very sensitive data handled by a dedicated Key Vault, which has stricter access controls and allows only a handful of administrators and security personnel to manage the encryption keys. Also, regular audits will help check and revoke irrelevant key permissions, thus preventing privilege creep and unauthorized access.

- **Keep track of encryption key usages and identify anomalies**: Monitoring encryption key usage is critical in identifying suspected security breaches, unauthorized access attempts, or deviations from set policies. Azure provides tools such as Azure Monitor, Key Vault logging, and Defender for Cloud that give organizations the power to track encryption key access and issue alerts if they spot anything suspicious.

As an illustration, if a specific encryption key was accessed from an unfamiliar location or outside the normal hours, it could indicate a compromised account or an insider threat. Real-time alerts should be configured to notify security teams of any anomalous key access behaviour. The utilization of Azure Sentinel facilitates the business in the application of AI-driven threat detection, wherein key usage patterns are correlated with different security events, thus improving the overall threat visibility.

Monthly audit logs must also be kept and reported, which will also guarantee compliance and that key access records are available for forensic analysis and security reviews. Continuing to monitor encryption key usage will equip organizations with the skills to notice the threats earlier and thus protect sensitive data in a proactive way.

Security of database services

Any organization with a cloud-based database service should give data protection the utmost priority. Enterprise-level security is the only way to protect Azure from unauthorized access to databases, data breaches, and compliance risks. By using authentication controls, encryption mechanisms, and real-time auditing, organizations avail it as a secure option to ensure that the data is confidential, intact, and available.

Overview of Azure database security

Azure SQL Database and Azure SQL Managed Instance are the cloud's secure storage environments for managing relational data. This database service has self-security features such as authentication, encryption, firewall protection, vulnerability assessments, and auditing to support the organization's efficient establishment of data protection policies.

The Azure database security is structured into four main principles:

- **Authentication and access control**: Allowing only authorized users and applications to access the database is a top priority.
- **Data protection**: Data are encrypted when they are stored, being transferred, and when they are being worked on in order to make sure they are not accessed by anyone without authority.
- **Threat detection and auditing**: The ability to detect unusual behaviours and keep a record of all operations done on the database.
- **Network security**: The mechanism by which the database is accessed solely through trusted IPs, VNets, and Private Endpoint.

Authentication and access control

One major part of Azure database security is database access control. Databases are always subject to loss of access to them or even unauthorized access, brute-force attacks, as well as insider threats, when they lack the proper type of authentication and access control mechanisms.

Azure SQL Database and Azure SQL Managed Instance have provisions for multiple security measures that can be used to authenticate users, enforce the principle of least privilege access, and restrict the connectivity of the database.

Typically, authentication and access control in Azure databases are carried out through three main mechanisms: Microsoft Entra ID integration, firewall rules, and the SQL authentication policies:

- **Microsoft Entra ID integrated**: The integration of Microsoft Entra ID with Azure SQL databases allows organizations to be able to handle their users' identity and authentication policies from one point. In traditional SQL authentication, the token is introduced instead of entering a password, and SSO with Microsoft Entra ID, as well as MFA, and conditional access policies are available, which improve security and handle most password-related risks.

  Unlike Microsoft Entra ID, which does not need a password, traditional SQL authentication demands user accounts through password identifiers. This risk is removed by Microsoft Entra ID, which uses token-based authentication and is protected by strong identity policies.

  Let us see how to implement it:

  - Set Microsoft Entra ID authentication as active in the Azure SQL Database settings.
  - Use Azure SQL built-in roles (e.g., SQL Server Administrator, Database Reader, or Contributor) to grant RBAC permissions.
  - All privileged users are required to have MFA.
  - Using Managed Identities allows Azure services (such as VMs or applications) to access databases securely without saving any credentials.

- **Firewall rules**: By default, Azure SQL databases are accessible only to allowed networks, making firewall configuration a key security measure. Blocking unauthenticated connections and only permitting ones from trusted IP addresses or virtual networks are the main tasks of firewall rules, i.e., they act as a first line of defence for that particular purpose.

  In the absence of firewall restrictions, the database could be a potential target for brute-force attacks, unauthorized logins, and data breaches.

  The implementation process is as follows:

  - Create server-level firewall rules to allow the database to be accessed only from an approved IP range (e.g., corporate office networks, VPNs).
  - Use database firewall rules for user access control at a granular level.
  - Activate VNet service endpoints to deny database access to any resource outside of a private network.

   - Link Azure SQL Database to on-premises environments using Private Link, which offers security as it does not expose the database to the public internet.

- **SQL authentication**: While Microsoft Entra ID authentication is recommended, some legacy applications still rely on SQL authentication using the username and password credentials. On these occasions, it is necessary to enhance the policies on the strength of dues to fight the threats from credentialing.

  The use of weak passwords or first-time accounts with default credentials significantly increases the chances that various hacking techniques, such as SQL injection, credential stuffing, or brute-force attacks, are successfully employed.

  How to implement:

   - Disable the **system administrator** (**SA**) account from logging on and set up customizable administrator accounts that have unique usernames.
   - Enforce that strong passwords of at least 16 characters be used, including uppercase and lowercase letters, numbers, and special symbols.
   - Ensure standardized password rotation so that SQL authentication credentials are changed on a regular basis.
   - Utilize Azure Key Vault to safely store and manage database credentials while not hardcoding them in the respective applications.
   - Introduce failover login restrictions to identify and block unnecessary failed login attempts.

Auditing and monitoring

A proactive approach to auditing and monitoring is essential for ensuring the security and performance of databases. Azure SQL Database and Azure SQL Managed Instance are equipped with features enabling user activity tracking, potential threat detection, and database performance analysis. These tools allow organizations to maintain compliance, identify anomalies, and respond very quickly to security incidents. Without proper monitoring, unauthorized access and malicious activities may remain undetected, eventually leading to data breaches and operational interruptions.

Here are some key techniques for auditing and monitoring:

- **Azure SQL Auditing**: The Azure SQL Auditing approach strongly contributes to the database security level because it records detailed logs about database operations, including login attempts, data changes, and permission shifts. Those audit logs serve as the basis that organizations use for enforcing compliance, as they contain the full history of all database interactions. For example, the administrators can notice activities like privilege escalation and unauthorized schema modifications, and, as a result, they can quickly detect and inquire about suspicious actions.

The first step to accomplishing high security is to enable auditing at both the server and database levels. The audit logs can be stored in Azure Blob Storage or sent to Azure Monitor or Event hubs, thus allowing for centralized analysis and integration with security tools. Aside from that, reviewing audit reports regularly helps identify unusual access patterns and probable policy violations. Audit log retention policies ensure that the logs needed for regulatory compliance are kept while preventing excessive storage consumption.

- **Advanced threat protection**: The database security is completely enhanced with the addition of ATP, as it provides real-time detection of potentially dangerous doings. ATP does this activity by machine learning algorithms, which analyze the patterns in the data management accessibility to identify threats like SQL injection attempts, brute-force login attacks, and data exfiltration. The system sends alerts when it detects any suspicious or unusual behaviour, giving the security teams time to act before a breach happens.

  The configuration of ATP in Defender for Cloud will benefit the organization by improving its ability to detect high-risk database operations in real time. These alerts can be set to result in automated actions, such as a query block action or an IP address restriction from a suspicious source. ATP could be combined with Azure Sentinel to facilitate the correlation of advanced threats, and thus, security units will be able to follow the patterns of attacks across various resources. A recurring review of ATP alerts and implementing security policies based on the detected threats is the best guarantee for the dynamic evolution of database safeguarding.

- **Azure Monitor**: The security of databases should not be limited to identifying unauthorized access, but should also involve tracking performance metrics that can affect the smooth and reliable operation. Azure Monitor is at the forefront of database performance and security data collection, analysis, and visualization. Using this tool, the database administrators can observe metrics such as execution time for queries, resource spend, and anomalies in access, which, in turn, will help them find performance bottlenecks and attacks.

  Organizations should enable Log Analytics to collect database telemetry data to get the full benefits of Azure Monitor. Custom alerts can be configured to notify administrators of issues such as excessive CPU usage, long-running queries, or abnormal connection attempts. The Azure Workbooks can be utilized to visualize the **key performance indicators** (**KPIs**) that will provide a friendly interface for the health status of the database. The correlation of security events with performance logs will make it possible for security teams to discover slow, ongoing attack signs, for example, a sudden increase in the number of failed logins or a gradual rise in the resource consumption caused by unauthorized data extraction.

- **SQL Server audit logs**: Ensuring compliance and investigating security incidents: When using SQL Server on Azure VMs, enabling SQL Server audit logs is essential for tracking user activities and maintaining compliance. These logs provide a detailed relationship of all data transactions and explicitly mention any access to the system, such as role assignments and scheme changes. Analyzing these logs, the administrators will have a very easy time detecting any unauthorized changes, and thus they will be able to take corrective measures in time and hence act responsibly for any data integrity issues.

Audit logs should be well secured and should be in a centralized location, for instance, in Azure Storage or Event hubs, thus ensuring long retention and easy access to forensics. The integration of SQL Server audit logs with Azure Monitor allows security teams to see anomalies in real time. The use of SQL Profiler by administrators makes it possible to dive deep into the tracking of the database, and the results are very valuable as they uncover any potential security threats that need handling and prevent any future breaches.

Data protection techniques

Data protection in databases is an important and essential part of security that keeps sensitive information secure from being accessed without authorization, both internally and externally. Both Azure SQL Database and Azure SQL Managed Instance have a variety of data protection methods to protect data that is not in the air, in transit, and during processing. The preceding techniques ensure the automatic encryption of data, the masking of unauthorized users, and the secure storage of data and compliance with security regulations such as GDPR, HIPAA, and PCI-DSS.

Here are some key techniques for protecting data:

- **Transparent data encryption (TDE)**: It is a standalone encryption scheme that indirectly allows data at rest to be automatically encrypted through the encryption of databases, backups, and transaction logs. TDE ensures that the data will remain safe without the need for any separate decryption keys, even if the database files are under attack.

  TDE works by storage-level encryption, so it encrypts all the databases on the storage level. Therefore, the applications and users do not have to modify their queries or database connections. The encryption and decryption processes take place in real time without impacting the performance. The default setting for TDE uses Microsoft-managed encryption keys, but for organizations that have more strict security requirements, it is possible to spend CMK stored in Azure Key Vault. This way, organizations can fully delegate encryption management, providing rotation, access policies, and audit tracking.

  The enabling of TDE will allow organizations to completely mask by encrypting sensitive database files, backups, and transaction logs from being exposed or stolen. This technique is crucial in the context of regulatory requirements because it guarantees that database data is not always clear.

- **Dynamic data masking (DDM)**: DDM is a technique that is used in real time to obfuscate any sensitive information in the query results for non-privileged users that should not be seeing it. DDM, as opposed to encryption, does not affect the data on the storage level, but it gives administrators the right to configure who sees what data (full values and masked results), thus minimizing the risk of unintended PV106004.re embedding978-3-030-37491-8.pdf 6 exposure.

  By implementing DDM, organizations can set up masking rules for columns with sensitive information like credit card numbers, social security numbers, or addresses. The possibilities of masking can be partial, full, or random. Partial masking, xxxxxxxx-****-2345, shows just a part of the value, for example, the last four digits of a credit card number. In full masking, the original number is totally replaced with generic placeholders (e.g., XXXXXX). Random masking replaces numbers with random but allowable values in order to carry forward values required for format checks.

  Only specific personnel with permission can remove the masks and see the exact data. With the implementation of DDM, an organization can prevent insider threats, minimize exposure to data that is not adequately protected, and comply with privacy laws without changing data that has been stored permanently.

- **Always Encrypted**: Always Encrypted is a form of client-side encryption designed to protect sensitive data in transit and maintain data at rest. Hence, even if a database administrator wants to, they cannot see the plaintext data. Unlike TDE, it treats an entire database as one unit. Always Encrypted encrypts specific columns (like personal identifiable information, financial data) before storing them.

  In the case of Always Encrypted, encryption and decryption occur at the level of the client's application and use encryption keys stored outside of the database, normally in Azure Key Vault. Hence, even if hackers access the database, they are not able to read the sensitive data without the client-side decryption keys.

  Always Encrypted offers two modes of encryption:

  - **Deterministic encryption**: The same encrypted value is used for identical plaintext values, thus permitting indexing and filtering operations to work on encrypted columns.

  - **Randomized encryption**: It is for the same value to be treated differently on different occasions, making the value more secure but preventing searching or filtering on encrypted columns.

- **Row-level security (RLS)**: It is a mechanism that allows or denies the user accessing certain rows in a table relevant to their identity or role. The technique seems especially helpful in multi-tenant applications where no user can see or access data that is not about them.

  By using RLS, an organization can define security policies for row-based filtering and predicate logic. This means that different users querying the same table only get the rows of the table that they are allowed to view. In contrast to the usual access control mechanisms, RLS works directly on the database, thus ensuring the correctness of rules in every use.

The RLS implementations in the organization may lead to minimizing the risk of data leakage, enabling strict access control policies, and strengthening the security of the database itself, all without any modification of application logic.

- **Backup encryption**: Database backups are often the target of cyber-attacks, as they contain entire copies of production data. Backup encryption prevents unauthorized access to database backups, even in cases where they get stolen or accessed improperly.

  Azure SQL Database automatically encrypts using TDE on the backup side. Moreover, an additional layer of security is added with a backup encryption option that uses CMK, which are stored so that only the authorized user can decrypt the backup files. This method stops data exfiltration attacks where hackers try to steal the backups of the database to get sensitive information.

Best practices for securing Azure database services

Ensuring Azure databases' security, availability, and resilience requires a proactive approach to encryption, threat detection, and disaster recovery planning. Adopting the best practice will help secure sensitive data from cyber threats and increase compliance with the industry's regulations, like GDPR, HIPAA, and ISO 27001.

The following are the key security measures that, when added, will strengthen the database protection, threat monitoring, and high availability in Azure SQL Database and Azure SQL Managed Instance:

- **Encrypt all databases with Enable TDE**: TDE is the core security feature that makes sure that all the database files, backups, and transaction logs are automatically encrypted at rest. TDE is the one needed to encrypt stored data. TDE is the one preventing unauthorized access to the data, even if an attacker gains access to the underlying database files or the backups.

  TDE is carried out by default in Azure SQL Database and managed instances, so organizations should check whether encryption is still active and consider using CMK in Azure Key Vault for better control. The CMKs allow organizations to rotate, revoke, and audit the encryption keys, by which they ensure compliance with the data security policies. In the case of either an on-premises one or a SQL Server one on Azure VMs, TDE must be manually configured to protect against data theft or accidental data exposure.

- **ATP**: Use ATP to monitor and reduce security threats: ATP adds database security monitoring by employing the AI-driven threat detection, which, to identify SQL injection, attempts brute-force attacks, and abnormal user behaviors. Attackers could misuse bugs not noticed by the software, leading, for instance, to data breaches, privilege escalation, and unwanted alterations.

Enabling ATP in the Defender for Cloud alerts organizations as they witness suspicious activities. Security teams can analyze the threat intelligence reports, the number of failed logins, and unusual SQL query patterns to track the root of potential compromises before they expand. Additionally, the integration of ATP with Azure Sentinel allows for the central aggregation of security events so that incident response is faster and shape mitigation automated.

- **Implement geo-replication for high availability and disaster recovery**: Ensuring business continuity and data availability in case of hardware malfunctions or regional outages is one of the conditions required to be met. Geo-replication allows organizations to synchronize the databases over one or more Azure regions; that is to say, a secondary database would be present all the time in case of failures due to this process.

  By configuring active geo-replication in Azure SQL Database, organizations can operate up to four readable secondary replicas in different regions. If a particular area suffers from downtime, the failover operation would be automatic, benefiting the applications with minimal downtime. For Azure SQL Managed Instance, organizations can use auto-failover groups to provide a global deployment with seamless failover.

  Geo-replication is particularly important in **disaster recovery planning** (**DRP**) because it allows critical applications to continue working even though regional failures are threatened. Organizations ought to test the failover procedure regularly to ensure that secondary databases can be promoted without data loss in real-world cases.

- **Enforce least privilege access control and role-based permissions**: One of the most considerable security threats in the environmental database is the overwhelming number of user permissions. Granting broad database access increases the risk of insider threats, privilege abuse, and data leaks. The establishment of RBAC not only ensures that users and apps have access only to the data they need.

  Organizations should only use Microsoft Entra ID, which is a secure database authentication method instead of SQL Authentication that comes with shared credentials. Database roles like db_datareader, db_datawriter, and db_owner can be assigned to different users only to ensure that those roles can perform only authorized actions. Security teams should conduct regular access reviews and revoke unused or excessive permissions to prevent privilege escalation attacks.

- **Secure data in transit with connections (TLS 1.2 or higher)**: Transferring data securely with encryption is as important as the data being secured at rest. Encryption stands as a shield against attackers who would intercept the database traffic and gain sensitive information. The default setting of Azure SQL Database requests that all connections use TLS encryption, but organizations are expected to enforce TLS 1.2 or higher for compliance with the security standards.

Security teams should disable outdated TLS versions (TLS 1.0 and 1.1), which pose a risk of MITM attacks. The use of Azure Private Link for database access ensures that database traffic is not routed over the public internet, which is a significant security advantage.

- **Enable database auditing and retain logs for compliance**: Establishing an audit log of database activities is the most significant step in detecting security breaches, tracking user actions, and ensuring regulatory requirements. Azure SQL Auditing traces the query executions, schema modifications, login attempts, and access control changes.

  Organizations should store the audit logs in Azure Storage, Log Analytics, or Event hubs, where long-term retention and centralized analysis will be facilitated. Security analysts are supposed to routinely assess audit logs to perceive anomalies like unexpected data access or privilege escalation incidents. SQL Server audit logs for databases running on Azure VMs also furnish additional forensic insights that can be used for incident response and compliance reporting.

- **Perform regular backups and validate backup Integrity**: A regular database backup is a must for disaster recovery as well as protection of data integrity. The point-in-time automatic backups for Azure SQL Database allow organizations to revert databases to an earlier state where data has been corrupted or accidentally deleted.

  The security teams should routinely practice backup restoration procedures to ascertain that backup data is complete, uncorrupted, and fully recoverable. The use of GRS, which will store critical data copies in multiple Azure regions, will ensure the recovery from regional failures.

  On top of that, organizations can encrypt database backups with CMK to keep away unauthorized access to the backup data.

- **Use Always Encrypted for sensitive data**: Always Encrypted should be implemented in databases dealing with the most sensitive information, such as PII or financial records, to ensure that the sensitive columns are client-side encrypted. In contrast to TDE, which encrypts the entire database, Always Encrypted guarantees that specific fields are set to encrypted even if the database administrators query them.

  Storing encryption keys outside the database (for instance, in Azure Key Vault) can help organizations enforce strict data access policies, allowing only the authorized applications to decrypt sensitive data. The approach of this kind is the additional layer that the sensitive records are getting, thus they are protected even in a scenario where the database servers are breached.

Comparing security capabilities

The following table highlights key differences in security capabilities between Azure SQL Database and SQL Managed Instance to help you choose the right service for your organizational needs:

Security feature	Azure SQL Database	Azure SQL Managed Instance
Authentication	Supports SQL authentication, Entra ID authentication, and Managed Identities	Supports SQL authentication, Entra ID authentication, and Managed Identities
Network security	Public endpoint with firewall rules, Private Link support	Private endpoint within VNet (full isolation), supports Private Link
Encryption at rest	TDE with Microsoft-managed or customer-managed keys	TDE with Microsoft-managed or customer-managed keys
Encryption in transit	TLS is enforced for all connections	TLS is enforced for all connections
Advanced threat protection	Supported	Supported
Auditing and vulnerability assessment	Supported; integrated with Log Analytics and Event hub	Supported; integrated with Log Analytics and Event hub
Data masking	Dynamic data masking is supported	Dynamic data masking is supported
Instance-level security configurations	Limited (managed by Microsoft)	Greater control over instance-level security configurations, similar to on-prem SQL Server
Compliance certifications	Broad compliance coverage (PCI DSS, HIPAA, ISO, etc.)	Broad compliance coverage (PCI DSS, HIPAA, ISO, etc.)

Table 5.2: Comparing security for Azure SQL and Managed Instance

Conclusion

Securing data in the cloud is a challenge that requires a combination of encryption, access control, monitoring, and disaster recovery strategies. Azure provides a robust security framework and tools to protect storage and database services from unauthorized access, data loss, and cyber threats.

Access control is the first line of defense. Integrating Microsoft Entra ID and configuring firewalls helps restrict access to authorized users and applications, reducing risks from insiders and external actors.

Data encryption protects confidentiality and integrity. Organizations can use TDE, Storage Service Encryption, and Always Encrypted for sensitive records. Azure Key Vault allows the use of customer-managed keys to enforce regulatory compliance and maintain control.

Auditing and monitoring tools like Azure SQL Auditing, advanced threat protection, and Azure Monitor are important for identifying threats. Alerts help security teams respond quickly.

DLP further improves protection. Features like soft delete, dynamic data masking, row-level security, and encrypted backups minimize the impact of cyber breaches.

Securing Azure storage and databases is an ongoing process. By implementing layered controls, such as access management, encryption, monitoring, and DLP, organizations can reduce risk, ensure compliance, and build a resilient data infrastructure in the cloud.

In the next chapter, we will explore how to enforce security across your cloud environment using frameworks like CAF and WAF, along with tools like Azure Policy, Blueprints, and Purview.

CHAPTER 6
Security Governance

Introduction

In this chapter, you will learn skills to master securing Azure resources and operations through governance approaches. You will cover aspects such as the Cloud Adoption Framework and Well-Architected Framework, comparing both of these, as well as Microsoft Purview Data Governance, Azure management groups, and Azure Blueprints. Next, you will cover security governance tooling such as Azure Resource Graph, Azure Policy, and Azure Key Vault.

Structure

This chapter contains the following topics:

- Cloud Adoption Framework
- Well-Architected Framework
- Microsoft Purview data governance
- Azure management groups
- Azure management groups sample architecture
- Azure Blueprints
- Azure Landing Zones

- Azure Resource Graph
- Azure Policy
- Azure Key Vault
- Azure Locks

Objectives

The focal area of this chapter is Microsoft Azure governance frameworks and the corresponding tools that are available for managing security, automation, and compliance of cloud environments. The readers will discover how to execute the **Cloud Adoption Framework** (**CAF**) and the **Well-Architected Framework** (**WAF**) as a means to journal business goals alongside cloud governance methods.

The chapter also discusses governance tools such as the Azure management groups, Azure Blueprints, and Azure Policy, which help with the implementation of security, compliance, and operational efficiency by organizations. As a result of an introductory understanding of the Azure Resource Graph, Azure Key Vault, and Azure Locks, the readers will be able to secure sensitive information, oversee large-scale resources, and avoid changing configurations for guests and accidents.

By the end of this chapter, readers will expand their knowledge to implement excellent life governance, asset security, and management in the Azure environment, so they benefit from the compliance and operational stability they ensure.

Cloud Adoption Framework

Microsoft CAF supports the organization's journey to the cloud. A CAF is a set of recommendations that provides different strategies to organize, migrate, and manage your cloud space with complete security, compliance, and operational excellence. Thus, with it, organizations can develop a well-governed cloud infrastructure that would scale along with their digital transformation.

Overview of CAF

The Microsoft CAF provides a structured framework to design, secure, and manage Azure environments aligned with business goals using well-defined cloud strategies. Cloud strategies must align with the business goals; this is the central principle for helping enterprises with digital transformation. CAF supplies the best or proper practices, tools, and instructions to every organization at any stage of its cloud journey.

CAF Governance Model

The CAF Governance Model is a must-have for organizations moving to the cloud, ensuring that security, compliance, cost, and operational efficiency are preserved. Effective governance is a good way for businesses to set out definite policies, handle risks, and reduce the amount of cloud resources; thereby, cloud strategy improvement is attained.

The model can be summarized around the following points:

- **Policy and compliance**: Policy and compliance are crucial areas of cloud governance, as they ensure that any deployed resources meet the organization's and regulatory standards. Organizations must create policies outlining security controls, access permissions, and operational procedures.

  Here is how this can be achieved:

  - Azure Policy is important in implementing governance since it allows administrators to set and enforce compliance rules for various resources.
  - Azure Blueprints assists organizations in uniforming best practices by offering ready-to-use templates for automatically setting security, networking, and access management parameters.
  - Compliance monitoring is a continuous process, and the presence of tools such as Microsoft Defender for Cloud for auditing environments, issuing alerts about compliance violations, and verifying timely remediation actions makes a whole lot of difference.
  - Formulating and enforcing applicable policies to meet both organizational and regulatory requirements.
  - Harnessing Azure Policy for automation and oversight of compliance rules across the cloud infrastructure.
  - Using Azure Blueprints to implement and secure best practices across varied environments consistently.

- **Identity baseline**: Identity management is the most basic and essential step in cloud governance, as it decides who can access the resources and what actions they can perform. The clearly articulated identity baseline reduces security risks and strictly implements the least privilege principle.

  Here are some ways to create a baseline:

  - Entra ID enables centralized identity and access management, providing secure authentication and authorization mechanisms.
  - RBAC ensures that users, groups, and applications only have the permissions necessary for their tasks, reducing the risk of unauthorized access.

- MFA adds an extra layer of security by requiring multiple verification steps before granting access.
- PIM allows for JIT access, ensuring administrative privileges are granted only when needed and are automatically revoked after use, preventing persistent elevated access rights.
- Establish identity and access management standards to secure Azure resources.
- Utilize Entra ID for RBAC and MFA.
- Ensure that there is the least privileged access using PIM.

- **Cost management**: Cloud spending will stay within the budget with the intervention of effective cost management and risk, and then the resources can be deployed more effectively. Cloud resources can be costly without governance, which could happen because of inefficient resource allocation, underutilized services, etc.

  Here are some ways to save on consumption costs:

  - Azure cost management and billing help organizations track cloud expenses, analyze spending trends, and identify cost-saving opportunities.
  - Organizations can set budgets and spending alerts to prevent unexpected cost overruns and ensure financial accountability.
  - **Reserved instances** (**RI**) and savings plans provide discounted pricing for long-term cloud commitments, reducing operational costs.
  - Azure advisor provides cost recommendations, identifying underutilized resources that can be downsized or deallocated to optimize spending.
  - Implementing tagging strategies for resources helps track expenses by departments, projects, or applications, allowing businesses to allocate costs effectively.
  - Optimize resource utilization and costs through monitoring and governance.
  - Utilize Azure cost management and billing to track and analyze cloud expenditures. Set budgets and alerts to prevent cost overruns.

- **Monitoring and reporting**: The main factors for cloud environments' security, health, and performance are ongoing monitoring and reporting. An important point is that an organization's wide-ranging monitoring plan is discovering problems early, mitigating risks, and ensuring its activities align with the regulations.

  Here are some tools and techniques for monitoring and reporting:

  - Azure Monitor provides real-time insights into the performance and health of cloud resources, enabling organizations to detect and resolve issues before they impact operations.

- o Log Analytics collects and analyzes telemetry data across services, offering deep visibility into security threats, performance bottlenecks, and operational trends.
- o Microsoft Defender for Cloud continuously assesses security configurations, detecting vulnerabilities and potential threats while recommending remediation actions.
- o Microsoft Sentinel enhances security monitoring by offering a cloud-native SIEM solution that aggregates logs, detects anomalies, and helps with incident response.
- o Service Health alerts notify administrators about potential service disruptions, ensuring proactive responses to maintain business continuity.
- o Enable visibility into system performance, security, and compliance.
- o Use Azure Monitor for real-time insights into workloads.

Best practices for CAF

To ensure successful cloud adoption using the CAF, organizations should adopt best practices across governance, security, and operational efficiency. This helps standardize cloud adoption processes, reduce risks, and streamline cloud operations with business objectives. The achievements of businesses with secure and well-managed cloud infrastructures can be realized by using automated tools, incorporating governance in development workflows, and optimizing cloud environments.

Here are all the tools and techniques that are helpful in CAF execution:

- **Azure Policy is used to manage compliance through automation**: Manage the enormous scope of resources in Azure by simply planning and implementing policies across Azure resources.
- **Embed CAF into the DevOps lifecycle for continuous governance**: Utilize Microsoft Azure DevOps or GitHub Actions to incorporate security and compliance inspections into CI/CD pipelines.
- **Governance goals should be aligned with business priorities**: Ensure that the rules set for governance align with the business needs, thus promoting operational efficiency and risk mitigation.
- **Use Azure Landing Zones**: Achieve uniformity in cloud environments by using pre-set security, networking, and identity settings.
- **Conduct a Well-Architected Framework evaluation**: Periodic workload assessments and optimizations through Microsoft's Well-Architected Framework result in better security, performance, and cost-efficiency features.

CAF sample architecture

The CAF architecture (link at the end of this section) from Microsoft provides a methodical way to create and manage an enterprise Azure infrastructure using Microsoft's CAF. It covers fundamental pillars like identity management, networking, security, and subscription organization.

Microsoft Entra ID is linked at the top with Active Directory Domain Services to enable identity federation and apply RBAC. Management groups arrange multiple Azure subscriptions, guaranteeing consistent policy implementation and oversight.

Each of the several Landing Zones in the design reflects a particular environment, such as sandbox, connectivity, and application hosting. These Landing Zones build a well-architected cloud foundation, including virtual networks, DNS, firewalls, and security controls.

Furthermore, underlined in the following figure are platform services that improve operational efficiency: DevOps, automation, and monitoring. Emphasizing Azure governance capabilities such as Azure Policy, Blueprints, and management groups, it guarantees security and compliance all over the corporate cloud environment:

CAF architecture:

https://learn.microsoft.com/en-us/Azure/cloud-adoption-framework/ready/landing-zone/

Well-Architected Framework

The WAF primarily focuses on assisting enterprises in constructing cloud solutions that effectively meet their business and technical objectives. This framework acts as a pathway through which enterprises can ensure their workloads are secured, running at high performance, and consuming less cost. The WAF is a well-defined instrument for architects to analyze, detect weaknesses, and apply best practices corresponding to the recommended Microsoft cloud governance and operations standards.

Overview of WAF

Organizations must use the CAF Governance model to keep security, compliance, cost control, and operating efficiency high when moving to the cloud. When organizations follow the governance framework, it helps them set clear rules, deal with risks effectively, and use cloud resources well, which supports their cloud strategy.

The framework is made up of five primary parts:

- **Cost optimization**: The cost optimization process for cloud services is cost-effective, so it can help an organization make the most of its money and cut down on wasteful spending. With Azure cost management, businesses can look at their spending, set goals, and make good use of their resources. Some ways to lower costs without affecting speed are to use reserved instances, autoscaling, and rightsizing the resources.

- **Operational excellence**: Completing ordinary operations is all about decreasing the processes and improving the cloud service via automating and continuous growth. Instruments, such as Azure DevOps and Azure Monitor, which accompany the organization, help automate the deployment of the devices, implement CI/CD pipelines, and provide preemptive solutions to problems. When using the IaC approach with Terraform or Bicep, the organizations can, in both cases, manage the infrastructure more efficiently and consistently.
- **Performance efficiency**: Performance efficiency is about creating highly available, scalable cloud solutions with better performance. Organizations can take advantage of the built-in functionality of Autoscale, load balancing, and caching for the best performance and help manage the peak load. Initial performance tests and design assessments will help ensure that workloads are efficient and responsive.
- **Reliability**: Reliability is also an important measure to protect business loss. It implies deploying systems that can withstand downtime and disasters and ensuring the system's availability. Using Azure Site Recovery and Availability Zones, businesses can secure data loss by implementing Azure Backup and recover from failures quickly. A further measure to strengthen reliability is the implementation of redundancy and failover strategies.
- **Security**: Security is a key factor that preserves the integrity of the cloud resources, data, and applications while being attacked. The organization can reinforce its security via Zero Trust principles, Azure Defender, and Microsoft Sentinel for threat detection and response. RBAC, MFA, and encryption help secure access and protect sensitive data.

Comparing CAF and WAF

CAF and WAF are two essential frameworks in cloud technologies that facilitate their practical use and management in organizations. Their common aspect, which is offering directions to the organizations towards best practices, is the only reason they share some similarities. In reality, they are different from each other and, hence, focus on various aspects of the cloud adoption process.

CAF focuses on strategic governance and organizational alignment. It presents a broad strategic view of the cloud adoption process and guarantees that the cloud initiatives are aligned with the business goals and objectives of the organization. It highlights governance, security, and compliance issues and assists businesses in designing policies and controlling risks.

CAF helps in planning cloud adoption, cost structure optimization, and ensuring long-term operational success. Azure Policy, Azure Blueprints (depreciated soon), template spec, Deployment Stacks, and Microsoft Purview are some of the tools that support the enforcement of CAF governance rules.

WAF focuses on technical implementation and operational excellence. The key focus of WAF is the technical and architectural best practices that need to be followed to create secure, efficient, and high-performing cloud workloads.

It offers a framework for evaluating workloads in terms of five pillars: Cost optimization, operational excellence, performance efficiency, reliability, and security.

WAF is a hands-on and more technical tool that is a roadmap for organizations on how to design scalable, resilient, and cost-efficient cloud solutions.

Best practices for WAF

As a best practices implementation, the WAF makes sure that organizations have built and kept up safe, efficient, and resilient cloud workloads. Businesses can make the most of their Azure while still following best practices for security and industry standards by using these methods.

Here are some best practices:

- **Regularly assess workloads using the Azure Well-Architected Review tool**:
    - The Azure Well-Architected Review tool can be used to carry out periodic reviews so that areas for improvement in cloud workloads can be identified.
    - Properly utilize the data analyzed by Azure Advisor to contribute to performance enhancement, cost savings, and security strengthening.
    - Ensure workloads are compatible with the five WAF pillars: cost optimization, operational excellence, performance efficiency, reliability, and security.
- **Prioritize security and reliability for mission-critical applications**:
    - Employ a defence-in-depth approach using encryption, RBAC, and identity management with Microsoft Defender for Cloud.
    - Utilize Azure Backup with Site Recovery as the channel for promoting site availability and disaster recovery.
    - Effectively use Microsoft Sentinel to monitor security threats daily by integrating AI-driven threat intelligence.
- **Automate governance and compliance procedures**:
    - Use Azure Policy and Azure Blueprints to fulfill compliance and security best practices.
    - Automate infrastructure deployment through tools such as Terraform, Bicep, or ARM templates that use IaC.
    - Install a system for automated security monitoring with the use of Azure Monitor and Log Analytics.

- **Increase cost efficiency through intelligent resource management**:
    - o Use auto-scaling and reserved instances to mitigate the undesired expenditure.
    - o Azure cost management is the ideal tool to monitor your spending and set up budget alerts.
    - o Implement resource tagging policies for tracking resources and for chargeback allocation.
- **Integrate DevOps with continuous value addition**:
    - o With the utilization of Azure DevOps and GitHub Actions, deployment automation is achieved, and security is incorporated into CI/CD pipelines.
    - o Adopt IaC to eliminate the time consumption and ensure deployment is done in the same way every time.
    - o Keep cloud infrastructures updated constantly with WAF reports and new business needs.

WAF review tool

You can assess your workload by using the core pillars to identify and prioritize opportunities for improving the posture of your workload.

This is the homepage for the WAF assessment, which can be used to validate the state of the architecture:

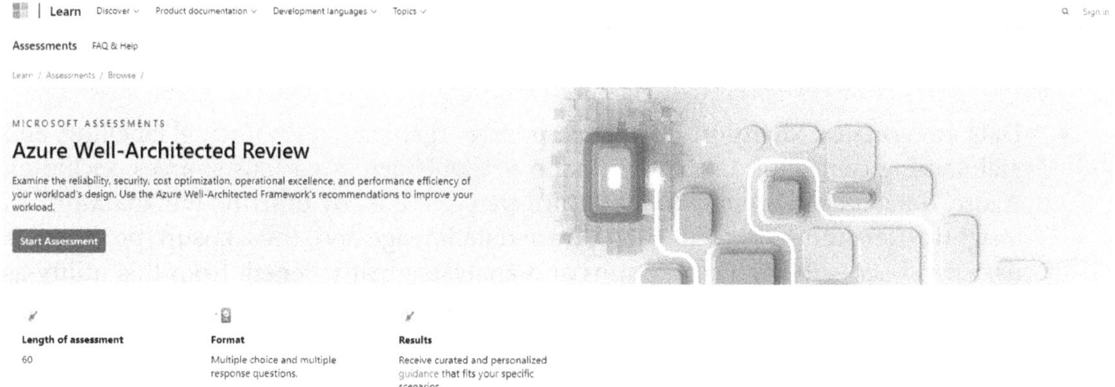

***Figure 6.1**: WAF homepage*

***Reference**: https://learn.microsoft.com/en-us/assessments/Azure-architecture-review/*

Microsoft Purview data governance

The Microsoft Purview unified data governance solution helps businesses control, protect, and learn from their data sources in the best way possible. For compliance, security, and operational efficiency, companies need to make sure they have the right governance for the huge amounts of data they create across on-premises, cloud, and hybrid environments. Microsoft Purview has all the tools you need to catalogue, organize, and handle data. This lets businesses get the most out of their data while also making sure they follow the rules set by regulators.

Overview of Microsoft Purview

Microsoft Purview is a platform for data control, risk management, and compliance. It lets businesses set up data monitoring, security, and lifecycle management, and it makes sure that the right people can still access the data. Purview makes it easier to classify data, control access, and apply policies across many different data sources by using automation and AI-driven insights.

Key features

Microsoft Purview is a one-stop solution with a full array of tools for data governance and compliance, and it provides deep insight into organizational data. Employing automation and artificial intelligence functionality, Purview becomes a more powerful assistant in the data management process and helps ensure security and regulatory compliance. These capabilities help organizations in finding, classifying, protecting, and tracking data in their cloud and local data centres; hence, they have become a must-have component for contemporary data governance.

Here are the key features:

- **Data governance**: Microsoft Purview supports organizations in tracing, labelling, and maintaining control of data that is made available across various sources, including Azure, databases in on-premise and third-party clouds. By utilizing metadata-driven insights, users can search, filter, and trace data lineage and, thus, ensure proper data usage and accessibility. Data admins and analysts greatly benefit from this utility as they can quickly find the relevant data while maintaining data security standards.
- **Policy governance**: One of the significant issues for organizations is observing regulations, especially for those organizations that handle personal or sensitive information. Microsoft Purview, pre-integrated with GDPR, HIPAA, and ISO 27001 assessments, lets businesses define and enforce data protection, access, and retention policies. This built-in security solution works with Microsoft Defender for Cloud and Microsoft Sentinel; thus, the organization can improve its security posture by identifying these threats.

- **Tracking data flow**: It is crucial to the organization's transparency to understand how to track data. Microsoft Purview provides comprehensive data line tracking through which users can illustrate how data is exchanged between systems and causes transformations. This feature, in particular, is helpful in data governance, auditing, and impact analysis since the data integrity and security are preserved during the whole data lifecycle.
- **Security and access based on roles**: Microsoft Purview allows enterprises to apply RBAC and data-sensitive protection directives across their data estate. By detailing the permissions and access rules, organizations can ensure that only the identified people can access confidential information. Integration with Azure Entra ID benefits identity and access management when data governance is concerned.
- **Data categorization and risk labels**: Microsoft Purview applies the intelligence functions that automatically focus on classification modelling to the labelling modes such as PII, financial data, and healthcare records. These labels support organizations in their expedition for security and simultaneously help them follow retention and compliance policies on all data types, whether structured or unstructured.
- **Data lifecycle and settings management**: Ensuring data applicability and keeping data retention policies as prescribed is significant for making regulatory compliance possible. Microsoft Purview empowers organizations to set and automate data retention and archival policies, ensuring that the data is kept or deleted based on relevant compliance requirements like GDPR, HIPAA, or ISO 27001.
- **Integration with Microsoft 365 and other data sources**: Microsoft Purview has embedded Microsoft 365 applications such as SharePoint, OneDrive, and Exchange that extend the line of data governance and compliance policy application to productivity tools. Additionally, it can work with off-the-shelf data sources like Google Cloud Storage, AWS S3, and SQL databases that run on-premise, thus making platform-wide governance possible.
- **Growth in analysis and insights**: Users can use the dashboard's built-in and analytic customizations to track data usage, compliance adherence, and security risks. Microsoft Purview is integrated with Power BI and Azure Synapse Analytics, through which organizations get relevant real-time information on how the data is stored, shared, and used during their operations.

Best practices for Purview

The way to maximize the advantages of Microsoft Purview is for enterprises to apply practices that make their data safer, more secure, and more compliant.

With these best practices, you can be sure that the data you collect, and store will always be well organized, protected from unauthorized access, and compliant with the requirements through adherence to the company and government rules:

- **Define a clear data governance strategy**: A successful Microsoft Purview implementation relies on a well-defined data governance scheme. Organizations must ensure that all users know data ownership, responsibility, and regulation, and everyone is under the same rules. Recognizing the roles of data owners, managers, and users facilitates appropriately tracking and managing data assets. For instance, companies should label this information and define terms such as confidential, restricted, and public to demonstrate the different levels of security.
- **Automate data discovery and classification**: Identifying and classifying data manually among the numerous data sets acquired by a company is a cumbersome and error-inclined task. Organizations should take advantage of the automated scanning features of Microsoft Purview to discover and classify both structured and unstructured data located in Azure, on-premises, and in multi-cloud environments. Deploying AI-driven sensitivity labelling automatically detects and tags PII, financial data, and healthcare records. Automation in data classification brings uniformity in governance, which helps organizations meet regulations like GDPR, HIPAA, and ISO 27001.
- **Implement RBAC and least privilege access**: Data security is not only a primary feature of data governance, but a complete failure can lead to massive losses due to unauthorized user access to sensitive data. Organizations must implement RBAC by establishing roles and permissions that will work at different levels within Microsoft Purview. Implementing the PoLP guarantees that a user has access only to the data directly related to their jobs, thereby reducing unauthorized access and data breaches. Joining Microsoft Entra ID with Microsoft Purview gives additional strength to identity and access management while also enhancing compliance and security controls.
- **Enable data lineage tracking for transparency and compliance**: For security, compliance, and transparency, knowing how data flows between systems and applications is key. Microsoft Purview keeps a history of data that enables organizations to visualize data movements, transformations, and dependencies on other data. This helps data teams to detect bugs, trace changes, and ensure compliance with the regulations as imposed. Organizations should carry out daily checks of the data lineage reports to catch unusual activities, prevent unauthorized modifications, and enhance data auditing.
- **Establish data retention and lifecycle policies**: Monitoring data management and lifecycles is needed to meet the challenge of cost, security, and legal compliance. Organizations must establish Microsoft Purview's retention policies, which will result in data being archived, deleted, or retained automatically in compliance with business needs and legal obligations. The inputting of rules for the erasure of data helps with properly disposing of old and useless data, which not only cuts down on storage costs but also decreases the risk of security. In addition, businesses ought to reassess and modify their retention policies regularly to keep up with the changes in compliance regulations.

- **Integrate Microsoft Purview with security and compliance tools**: The ultimate data control strategy is grouping Microsoft Purview security and compliance tools, such as Microsoft Defender for Cloud, Microsoft Sentinel, and Azure Policy. This consolidation is the key to efficient surveillance of data protection, closure of security gaps, and fulfilling the regulations. Utilizing real-time notification systems and security intelligence enables firms to observe and avert potential breaches aimed at confidential data.
- **Optimize data governance with advanced analytics and reporting**: With the in-built dashboards and reporting mechanisms available in Microsoft Purview, organizations can track their data utilization, security level, and compliance in real-time. Organizations that make use of Power BI from Microsoft and Azure Synapse Analytics in conjunction with Microsoft Purview can create the reporting and analytical tools that fit their specific control demands. Reading reports on data governance consistently allows organizations to prevent compliance risks, security holes, and inefficient data management.
- **Continuously monitor and improve data governance policies**: Data governance is not a one-time thing. Organizations should frequently check and improve their governance rules. Regular auditing, security, and compliance checks ensure that data governance practices align with dynamic legal standards and the company's goals. To nurture a culture of data governance awareness, organizations need to push their IT, security, and compliance teams to work together.

Purview sample architecture

Figure 6.2 provides an overall idea of how Microsoft Purview operates inside an Azure subscription to assist with managing and governing data.

The core has Microsoft Purview, which establishes itself in a separate resource group and serves as a data governance tool that scans, classifies, and organizes data from various sources. For example, it connects to Azure data sources such as SQL databases, Data Factory, and Blob Storage through Azure Integration Runtime, a data movement and metadata scanning tool.

The following figure shows an option for the event hub in a separate user resource group, which can be utilized for real-time data ingestion. The ingestion storage account is the dedicated storage account that temporarily holds the data during data processing.

This way, the general setup allows organizations to efficiently keep track of, secure, and manage their data while ensuring everything is in control of compliance and governance needs.

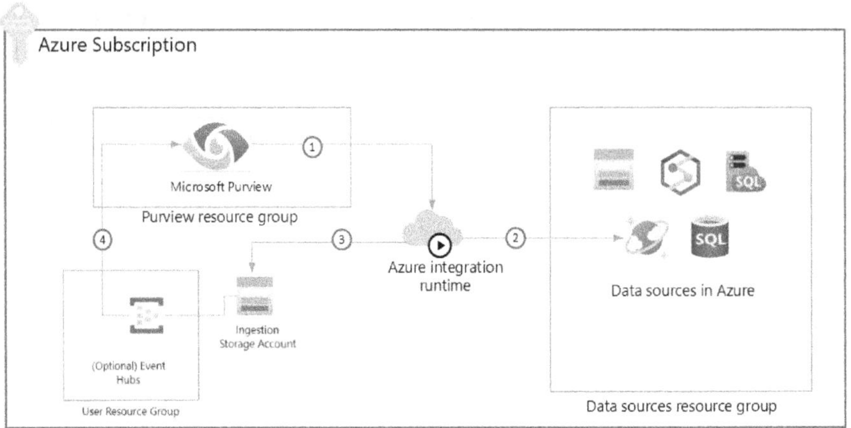

***Figure 6.2**: Purview architecture*

***Reference**: https://learn.microsoft.com/en-us/purview/legacy/concept-best-practices-network*

Azure management groups

Managing Azure subscriptions is critical for organizations as they grow their cloud footprint. The Azure management groups are the solution to this problem as they offer a way for the structuring of subscriptions, centralized management, governance, and policy setting. By logically grouping subscriptions, organizations can guarantee that security, compliance, and resource management, which are the bases of policy development, are the same across the entire cloud.

Overview of management groups

The Azure management groups are the tools for organizations to create a hierarchical structure that would ease subscription management at a maximal scale. As a consequence, the management groups do not require the application of governance policies at the subscription level, allowing administrators to implement Azure Policies, RBAC, and compliance regulations consistently over several subscriptions in an organized manner. This guarantees the fulfillment of the requirements through uniform governance and a reduction in administration efforts through implementing the same across all the cloud resources.

Key features

Azure management groups present a lot of benefits, especially for businesses that operate multiple subscriptions:

- **Tree structure for simple governance**: Management groups allow organizations to design a tree-like hierarchy representing their business structure. This allows centralized governance and easier enforcement of policies at the higher levels that propagate automatically down to all child subscriptions.

- **Consistent policy and security enforcement**: Organizations can consistently set security baselines, compliance rules, and operational standards across all subscriptions by assigning Azure Policies to the management group level. Critical security configurations like data encryption, network security settings, and access controls are uniformly applied.
- **RBAC at scale**: Instead of handling permissions at the single subscription or resource group level, management group-level roles can be assigned RBAC roles. This process makes user and resource access management easy, guaranteeing that administrators, developers, and security teams have the correct permissions across subscriptions without having to configure them many times.
- **Improved cost management and resource visibility**: Organizations can keep track of costs and resource usage better by setting up subscriptions based on business units, projects, or environments (for example, production, development, and testing). This process provides the finance and operations teams with an overview of the spending, thus allowing them to allocate budgets and optimize cloud investment more efficiently.
- **Scalability and flexibility**: With the support of up to 10,000 management groups per organization, Azure management groups can form the basis of scalable governance frameworks without any complexity. The flexibility allows new subscriptions to be added to the existing structure without disruption.

Best practices for management group

For organizations to gain the most from using Azure management groups, they have to use the following guidelines:

- **Create a logical hierarchy of subscriptions**: Organizations should create a hierarchy of management groups that aligns with their business units, departments, or cloud environments. A popular approach is to divide subscriptions by function, for instance, production, development, and testing, which ensures clear governance boundaries.
- **Enforce policies and security controls at the root stage**: With the help of Azure Policies and security baselines at the root management group level, organizations ensure that they have the same compliance policies for all subscriptions. This process is valuable in identifying misconfigurations and security vulnerabilities observed at lower levels.
- **RBAC for efficient permission management**: Using RBAC roles at the management group level offers centralized access control, making it easier to avoid the need to configure permissions for subscriptions or resource groups manually.
- **Cost tracking and budgeting techniques**: Organizations should also use Azure cost management to check on their spending patterns and help with cloud budgeting across numerous subscriptions, trying to avoid greed. Management groups can be further improved by assigning financial accountability for cost allocation and forecasting.

- **Automation with the help of Azure Blueprints (deprecated and replaced by template specs and deployment stacks) and policy assignments**: The integration of Azure Blueprints with organizational resource deployment, security, and compliance policies is the automation of policy assignments achieved by governing at scale while minimizing the operational overhead.

Azure management groups sample architecture

The image gives a simplified understanding of the management group and subscription organization in Azure, demonstrating that the resources are being arranged within a tenant root group.

The tenant root group at the topmost position represents the primary management level, dealing with all the Azure subscriptions in the organization. Under it, the organization is structured into management groups that are responsible for the execution of governance, security, and policies across several subscriptions.

The structure comprises some significant management groups, such as:

- **Platform**: The identity, management, and connectivity subscriptions are under this group.
- **Landing Zones**: These are the environments, like SAP, Corp, and Online, included in the group, to which applications and workloads are deployed.
- **Decommissioned**: This group is for the old or unused subscriptions.
- **Sandbox**: This one is for isolated environments for testing, with both single and multiple sandbox subscriptions available.

Each management group sorts its associated subscriptions, providing facilities to apply the policies, permissions, and controls efficiently. The architecture leads to better governance, compliance, and operational efficiency for the extensive use of Azure services. Refer to the following figure:

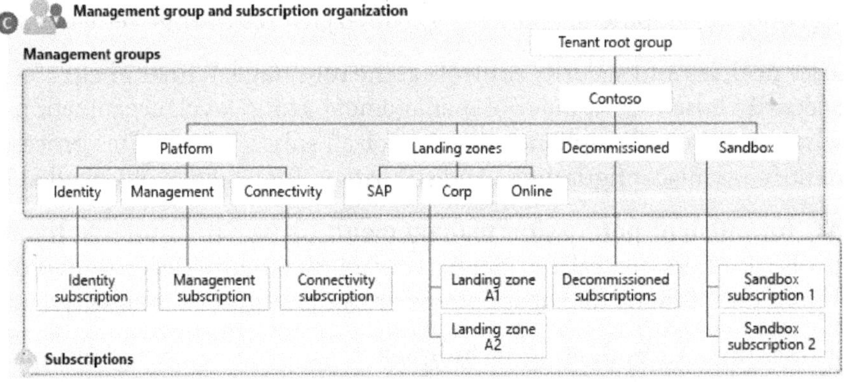

***Figure 6.3**: Azure management groups*

***Reference**: https://learn.microsoft.com/en-us/Azure/governance/management-groups/overview*

Azure Blueprints

Scaling Azure environments in organizations has made it difficult to maintain operating rules, security, and resource settings uniformly across several subscriptions. Azure Blueprints form a pre-structured technique for deploying and managing cloud environments, thus letting organizations continually define, standardize, automate, and provision Azure resources, policies, and security configurations.

Overview of Azure Blueprints

Azure Blueprints allow organizations to automate infrastructure deployment and maintain compliance with security, operational, and regulatory requirements. In contrast to autonomous ARM templates that target only infrastructure provisioning, Azure Blueprints extend themselves by incorporating policies, role assignments, and resource groups into a single deployable package. This is why it becomes much more manageable for enterprises to apply the same standards to various environments without requiring manual configurations.

Key features

Azure Blueprints is an instrument of power that is a large-scale resource to simplify the deployment, policy enforcement, and governance of the Azure environment.

These characteristics allow organizations to create, deploy, and manage cloud environments in a standardized way while ensuring security and regulatory norms are met across several subscriptions:

- **Consistent and repeatable deployments**: Azure Blueprints makes it easy for organizations to create and manage the same environments across their subscriptions. When creating a development, testing, or production environment, the Blueprints consistently apply all configurations, policies, and access controls.
- **Policy-driven governance**: Organizations can directly integrate related Azure Policy definitions into their environment; hence, they can ensure security and compliance from the start. For instance, a Blueprint can establish network security baselines, enforce encryption for development, and restrict resource deployments to specific Azure regions.
- **RBAC integration**: Blueprints enable organizations to specify roles and permissions, ensuring the right teams have the required permissions from when resources are deployed.
- **Simplified subscription management**: Organizations handling several Azure subscriptions can utilize Azure Blueprints to ensure that every new subscription automatically inherits all resource configurations, security, and compliance. This, in turn, eliminates human provisioning mistakes and, thus, hastens cloud adoption at a larger scale.

- **Versioning and change management**: Azure Blueprints has a version control feature that allows organizations to look out for changes, updates, and rollbacks to the Blueprint definitions. Thus, the security policies, role assignments, or infrastructure configurations will be modified systematically without any adverse effect on the present environment.

Best practices for Blueprints

Organizations should follow the recommended practices to improve governance, security, and automation across their entire cloud environment.

These practices include resource provisioning, compliance enforcement, and security policies that are consistent and scalable:

- **Create standardized Blueprints for different environments**: The correct way is to develop a separate Blueprint for the development, testing, and production environment, which will ensure that each of the environments conforms with the security and governance policies appropriate for its workload.
- **Azure Policies and security controls inclusion**: Including Azure Policy definitions within Blueprints guarantees a uniform standard for security, compliance, and operational standards. For example, enforcing MFA for privileged access or restricting public IP address assignments.
- **Automate resource provisioning with ARM templates**: ARM templates can be integrated into Azure Blueprints for the deployment automation of VMs, databases, storage, and networking configurations. This will not only economize the time of the infrastructure provisioning process but also help keep the governance controls in place.
- **Use versioning to manage updates**: With version control of Blueprints, organizations can make planned changes to their environment without breaking anything. This ensures that security patches, policy changes, or infrastructure modifications are delivered in an organized way.
- **Assign Blueprints at the management group level**: Instead of applying Blueprints at the subscription level, organizations should assign Blueprints at the management group level; thus, they can ensure governance policies across multiple inherited subscriptions automatically.

Azure Blueprint sample

Figure 6.4 shows the Azure Blueprints interface, where a Blueprint is being created to define and enforce resource deployment standards across an Azure subscription.

In the Artifacts tab, different elements are added to the Blueprint, like:

- **Role assignment**: A user group or application is assigned the Contributor role, ensuring the right level of access.
- **Policy assignment**: A policy is applied to enforce tagging rules for resource groups to maintain compliance.
- **Resource group**: A specific resource group is defined to organize Azure resources.
- **Azure Resource Manager (ARM) template**: A Storage Account is deployed using an ARM template to automate infrastructure setup.

This Blueprint provides a structured way to standardize, automate, and enforce governance in Azure environments, ensuring consistent deployment of resources. Refer to the following figure:

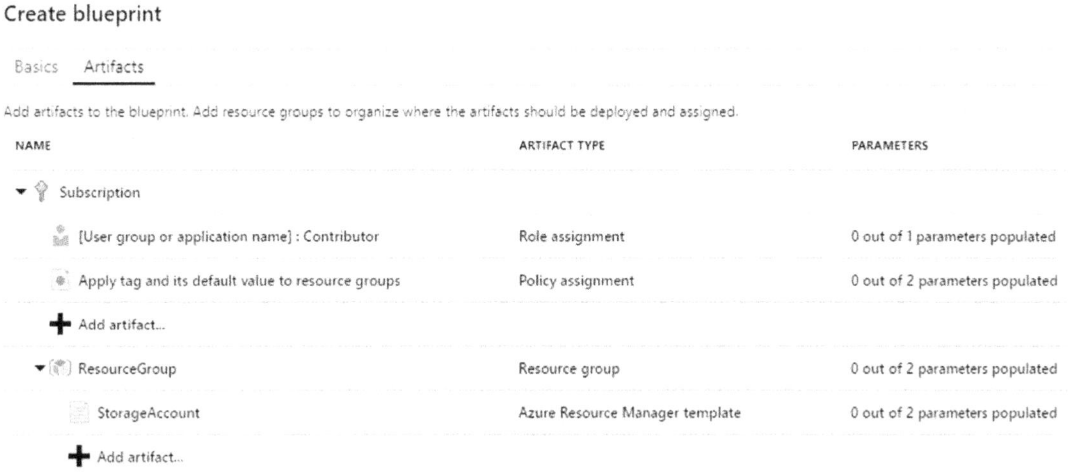

Create blueprint

Basics Artifacts

Add artifacts to the blueprint. Add resource groups to organize where the artifacts should be deployed and assigned.

NAME	ARTIFACT TYPE	PARAMETERS
Subscription		
[User group or application name] : Contributor	Role assignment	0 out of 1 parameters populated
Apply tag and its default value to resource groups	Policy assignment	0 out of 2 parameters populated
+ Add artifact...		
ResourceGroup	Resource group	0 out of 2 parameters populated
StorageAccount	Azure Resource Manager template	0 out of 2 parameters populated
+ Add artifact...		

***Figure 6.4**: Azure Blueprint*

Azure Landing Zones

The Azure cloud adoption journey requires the collaboration of organizations with a determined effort to be structured and well-architected to support secure, scalable, and compliant workloads. Azure Landing Zones provides organizations with ready-to-use tools that guarantee adherence to best practices, security controls, and governance standards before deploying workloads. This approach uses cloud services faster by eliminating the complexity and providing the same standard across different environments.

Overview of Landing Zones

Azure Landing Zones are pre-provisioned environments designed according to Microsoft CAF to host cloud workloads securely and consistently. They are pre-configured and offer the Microsoft CAF as a guideline. The Landing Zones have networking, identity, governance, security, and operational policies showing that deployments follow enterprise-grade best practices. Landing Zones facilitate the onboarding of cloud technologies for organizations that are moving to the Azure cloud for the first time or those growing their cloud presence and help maintain compliance. Landing Zones are also helpful for exiting workloads to streamline the operations, maturity, and security.

Key features

Azure Landing Zones are templates for cloud resource provisioning that comply with security, governance, and operational best practices in a scalable and repeatable manner.

These capabilities help organizations deploy workloads effectively while preserving the same conditions across many subscriptions:

- **Pre-build controls for security and compliance**: Azure Landing Zones include a built-in set of security baselines, compliance policies, and governance controls that provide workloads with the necessary conditions for regulatory compliance, such as GDPR, HIPAA, and ISO 27001. Organizations can enforce access control, encryption, and logging policies from the beginning.
- **Identity and access management (IAM) integration**: Through the integration of Entra ID, Landing Zones assist organizations in centralizing identity management and enforcing RBAC across cloud environments. This ensures that users and applications follow the least privilege principle, reducing security risks.
- **Networking and connectivity**: Azure Landing Zones also represent a precise placement in networking, connecting enterprises with their Vnet, subnets, Azure firewall, and ExpressRoute so that cloud resources are deployed using a secure and optimized network configuration. These settings permit the attainment of hybrid cloud conditions across local data centres.
- **Scalability and standardization**: Landing Zones are capable of supporting both small and large deployments, which makes them suitable for startups, midsized organizations, and big organizations. Using the available functions, organizations can deploy standardized resource configurations and governance models across multiple subscriptions.
- **Automation and IaC**: Azure Landing Zones have features supporting automated installations by using IaC tools like Terraform, Bicep, and ARM templates. Organizations can deploy and manage repeatable, scalable cloud environments without straying from the governance standards.

Best practices for Landing Zones

By implementing excellent practices that will increase security, governance, and scalability, organizations can take full advantage of Azure Landing Zones, apart from the fact that end users will experience workloads deployed consistently and operated efficiently.

Here are some best practices when deploying a Landing Zone:

- **Choose the right Landing Zone model**: For organizations, the best choice for the Landing Zone model is to align it with the business needs and cloud adoption strategy. Microsoft provides enterprise-scale, small-scale, and industry-specific Landing Zones, which allow businesses to customize their cloud architecture according to specific needs.
- **Implement governance and security from the start**: Governance should be the first element considered in site security before going to deployment, which will guarantee that all of the upcoming workloads will inherit the monitor, security, and compliance rules. It takes advantage of Azure Policy and Microsoft Defender for Cloud for continuous security compliance.
- **Automate deployments with IaC**: Organizations are encouraged to use Terraform, Bicep, or ARM templates to automate the deployment of Landing Zones. This will improve the environment's consistency, eliminate manual errors, and speed up the installation.
- **Optimize networking and connectivity**: The most essential part of a secure workload is having the correct network segmentation and hybrid connectivity. Azure Virtual WAN, ExpressRoute, and Azure Firewall are the perfect options to link the on-premises with Azure securely.
- **Continuously monitor and improve Landing Zones**: Organizations must regularly review and improve Landing Zones to meet changing security, performance, and compliance requirements. They can utilize Azure Monitor, Log Analytics, and Azure cost management to check how resources were used, identify performance bottlenecks, and discover cost inefficiencies.

Azure Landing Zone Architecture

In *Figure 6.5* an Azure application Landing Zone architecture developed for deploying cloud-based applications spanning multiple Azure regions, with the key features of being scalable and secure. It combines global, regional, and on-premises hardware, and this service is offered on Azure.com through strong governance, security, and networking.

At the global level, apart from the Azure Front Door with WAF (for routing and security), Azure Container Registry, Azure Cosmos DB, and Azure Log Analytics provide centralized monitoring, security, and content distribution. Users access applications via the internet, with routing managed globally.

Multiple deployments exist in regional deployments, each containing a container orchestration service (like AKS) with a Private Link, API, background processing, and health services, and supporting packages of Azure Key Vault, Azure Event hubs, and Checkpoint Storage control security and data flow issues.

Networking is set up through a connectivity subscription, where hub VNets lie in various geographic areas connected via VNet peering. These hubs incorporate security features, such as Azure Firewall, ExpressRoute, and VPN, ensuring a secure hybrid connection to the on-prem digital systems.

Also, the architecture has management and monitoring components like self-hosted build agents, Jump Boxes, Azure Bastion, and Azure Log Analytics, which offer safe operational access and visibility throughout the environment. The architecture is thus a scalable, resilient, and well-governed cloud deployment.

Following is the Azure Landing Zone Architecture representing various resources linked with each other:

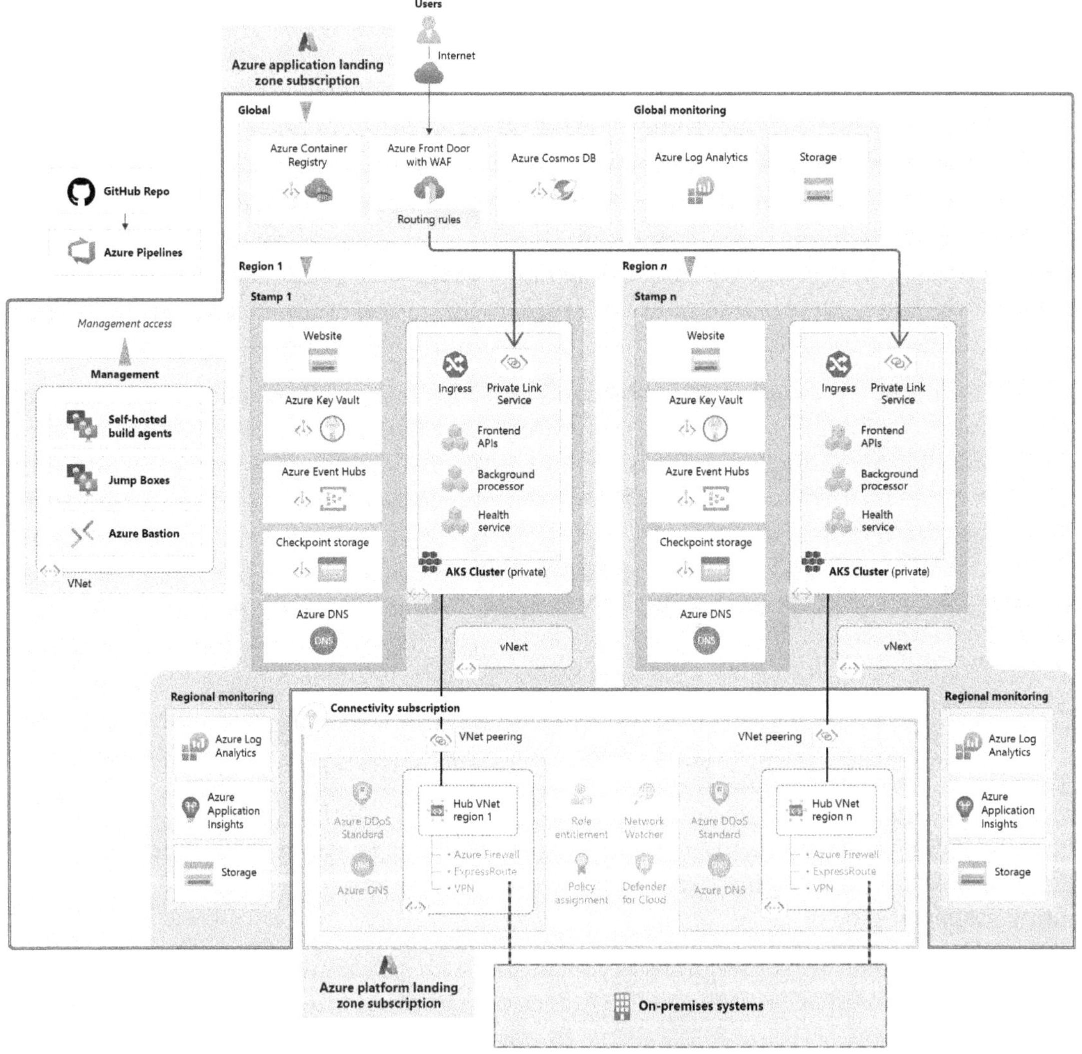

Figure 6.5: Azure Landing Zones

***Reference**: https://learn.microsoft.com/en-us/Azure/architecture/reference-architectures/containers/aks-mission-critical/mission-critical-landing-zone*

Azure Resource Graph

Cross-subscription cloud resource management and analysis can be complex, especially in complex environments. Azure Resource Graph is an effective and advanced service that enables organizations to use highly sophisticated query capabilities to scale, manage, and glean insights from their Azure resources more efficiently. Organizations can benefit from the real-time resource visibility implemented with Azure Resource Graph by improving governance, security, and cost optimization.

Overview of Resource Graph

Azure Resource Graph is a query service with exceptional performance that elevates Azure resources exploration using a real-time **Kusto Query Language** (**KQL**) based interface. Compared with traditional ARM queries, which are slower and have reduced in scope options, the Azure Resource Graph is faster and more complex, and it is expected to be more scalable with cloud sizes of these proportions. This allows enterprises to track the changes in resources, ensure compliance with the governance policies, and monitor compliance efficiently.

Key features of Resource Graph

Azure Resource Graph is a valuable tool that helps to discover, govern, and apply operational efficiencies in the Azure ecosystem through its capabilities.

These features enable organizations to filter and analyze resources at their convenience:

- **Fast and efficient querying**: Azure Resource Graph allows organizations to query all their resources across the hundreds of subscriptions they hold, all at lightning speed. This facility is tailored to quickly process huge queries and is very suitable for inventory control, governance, and reporting.
- **Intelligent filtering and data analysis**: With KQL, organizations can create custom queries that filter, aggregate, and group resource data based on specific tags, locations, types, or configurations. Users can quickly discover misconfigured resources, track configuration changes, or analyze trends across their Azure environment.
- **Continuous resource inventory and compliance**: Azure Resource Graph ensures that organizations have the latest and most complete inventory of all their resources in Azure. This means they can also easily view the resources from other subscriptions. It helps the admin to detect non-compliant resources, implement governance, and improve resource allocation.
- **Resource change monitoring and history analysis**: This allows users to track resource changes over time and analyze configuration drift, security deviations, and unexpected modifications. With the help of Azure Change History, teams can go back to the desired states quickly.

- **With Azure Monitor and security tools**: Azure Resource Graph is integrated fully with Azure Monitor, Azure Policy, Microsoft Defender for Cloud, and Azure cost management, which provides enhanced security monitoring, compliance tracking, and cost analysis. These measures ensure that businesses can carry out maximum active management of risks and constantly improve cloud trading.

Best practices for Resource Graph

The application of Azure Resource Graph is the key to best practices that significantly increase query performance, governance, and security monitoring.

At the same time, the overall resource management will be more efficient:

- **Centralize and fine-tune queries for performance**: It is a must for organizations to optimize their KQL queries so that they run efficiently on big datasets. The correct filtering, aggregation, and indexing of cavity solicitation time, thus, uh, either, or, both of the above.
- **Resource Graph for compliance and policy oversight**: Azure Resource Graph should be coupled with Azure Policy to promptly detect non-compliant resources, enforce security standards, and track policy violations. Preemptive governance ensures a company that queries are regularly executed to detect misconfigured resources.
- **Utilize tags and metadata for better resource organization**: Organizations can effectively query and manage resources by implementing a consistent tagging strategy across subscriptions, resource groups, and workloads. Tags make tracking costs, analyzing security, and gaining operational insights easier.
- **Azure Monitor should be autonomous reporting and alerts**: Managing the costs, raising security issues, and tracking the changes in resources should be done on a real-time basis by implementing the automation of custom dashboards and alerts using Azure Monitor and Log Analytics.
- **Security and cost management solutions integration**: Employing Azure Resource Graph with Microsoft Defender for Cloud and Azure cost management allows organizations to pinpoint security issues, make cloud expenses more efficient, and continuously apply best practices.

Azure Resource Graph homepage

The following figure displays the **Azure Resource Graph Explorer**, a tool used for efficiently querying and analyzing resources across an Azure environment:

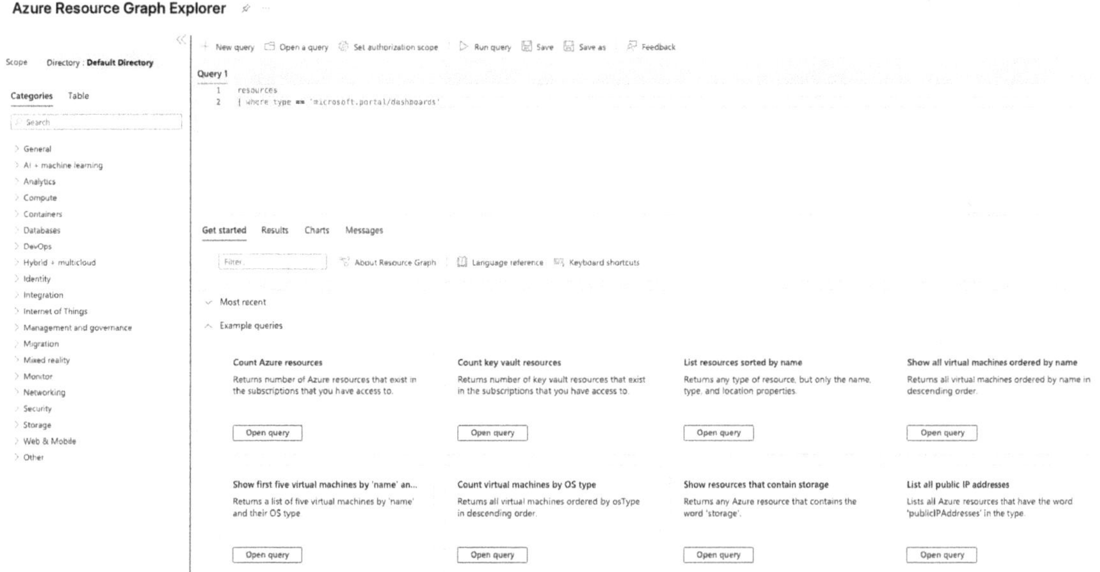

***Figure 6.6**: Azure Resource Graph Explorer homepage*

Azure Policy

For large-scale enterprises, it is critical to maintain compliance, security, and governance throughout cloud settings. Azure Policy is a built-in Azure service that organizations can utilize to impose organizational standards, audit assets, and automatically remediate configurations that are not compliant. Organizations can maintain best practices, abide by security measures, and meet regulatory requirements by setting up custom or built-in policies and governance rules.

Overview of Azure Policy

Azure Policy is a governance service enabling organizations to set and impose resource deployment and management rules. It assists in auditing pre-existing resources, preventing configuration errors, and automating the drift of the configurations. Unlike RBAC, Azure Policy ensures that the resources are correctly set and compliant with security and compliance policies.

Key features

Azure Policy helps with compliance and governance, facilitating the monitoring, enforcement, and configuration remediation of all Azure resources in an organization.

With these characteristics, the organization can assure security, cost, and operational consistent practices:

- **Policy definition and high-demand enforcement**: The approaches organizations take depend on the specifics of their policies. Not only is it possible, but organizations can also use custom policies to enforce compliance across Azure resources. Restrictions on the availability of specific VM sizes, enforcing encryption on storage accounts, or requiring tagging for cost tracking are all viable policies.
- **Continuous compliance check**: Azure Policy is vigilant, as it constantly monitors resources and audits them to identify non-compliance. Organizations can generate compliance reports to show that resources violate governance standards, making security controls much more enforceable.
- **Auto-fixing of non-compliant items**: Azure Policy can make things easier by correcting the issues of resource states from the policy definitions. For instance, Azure Policy can turn on encryption automatically without manual operation if a storage account is missing encryption.
- **Policy assignments and management of scope**: Policies may be assigned at different levels, such as management groups, subscriptions, resource groups, and individual resources. This feature thus enables organizations to implement governance policies across their cloud ecosystem in a uniform manner.
- **Collaboration with Azure security and compliance tools**: Azure Policy merges with Microsoft Defender for Cloud, Azure Monitor, and Azure cost management. These applications provide user security insights, compliance tracking, and cost control issues. This has enabled customers to identify and mitigate risks in real time.

Best practices for Azure Policy

To ensure effective Azure Policy implementation, organizations have to follow the best practices that, besides raising compliance enforcement, enhance security governance and operational efficiency:

- **Define and assign policies based on business requirements**: Organizations should create policy definitions tailored to their specific needs for security, cost management, and operations. Assigning policies at the management group level means all subscriptions will automatically inherit governance rules.
- **Use Policy initiatives for grouped enforcement**: Organizations should use the Azure Policy initiative instead of applying single policies. In this way, they can combine several policies for the complete governance of the system. For instance, a security initiative can comprise policies related to encryption settings, public IP blocking, and MFA assurance.
- **Automate compliance remediation**: Azure Policy makes it possible to embed the remediation tasks within such rules, thus allowing automatic correction of non-compliant resources. This lessens the need for human interference and guarantees ongoing security compliance.

- **Monitor compliance with Azure Policy insights**: Organizations should use Azure Policy Insights to track the trends in compliance, generate audit reports, and find the policy violations that appear repeatedly. The integration with Azure Monitor and Log Analytics provides real-time insight into policy compliance.
- **Regularly review and update policies**: The periodical review and subsequent policy updates are necessary since the governance needs are conditional. Thus, organizations should ensure they periodically examine and reissue the policies in light of the revelation of new security threats, regulatory standards, and supply chain needs. Ensuring updates through versioning and change tracking safeguards against disrupting existing workloads.

Azure Policy homepage

The following screenshot shows the Azure Policy dashboard, which manages compliance and governance across an Azure environment by enforcing rules on resources:

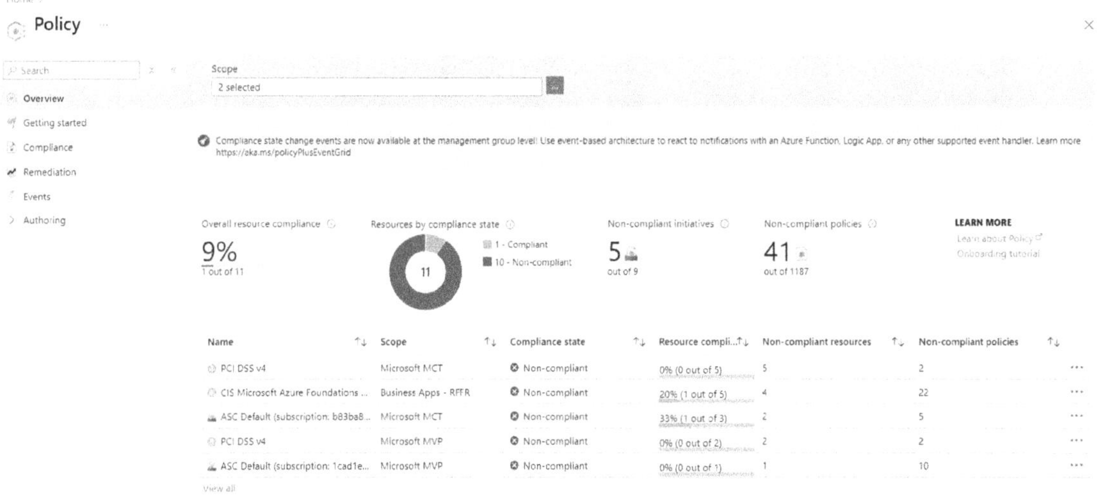

Figure 6.7: Azure Policy homepage

Azure Key Vault

With the expansion of cloud environments, it becomes crucial for businesses to have a safe and centralized storage and management system for sensitive information like secrets, encryption keys, and certificates. Azure Key Vault is a security-as-a-service run by a managed system. It is a solution that helps secure the cryptographic keys and secrets used in cloud applications and workloads. The use of Azure Key Vault not only provides strong encryption, access control, and auditing capabilities but also helps with data protection and compliance while at the same time reducing security risks.

Overview of Key Vault

The purpose of Azure Key Vault is to assist organizations in the secure management of access to secrets, cryptographic keys, and certificates. It creates a single, centralized location for managing sensitive information, ensuring that no secrets are embedded into the application code or exposed in configuration files. The integration with Entra ID further strengthens the tight control over access, wherein Azure Key Vault implements RBAC to the fullest, providing only the allowed users and applications the rights to retrieve or change secrets.

Key features

Azure Key Vault is a stable, scalable, high-performance resource for sensitive information.

Hence, organizations can use it to add secrets, enforce compliance, and ease the process of key and secret management.

The following are key features of Azure Key Vault:

- **Secure storage of secrets**: Azure Key Vault provides a platform for organizations to securely store and manage their application secrets, such as API keys, passwords, database connection strings, and authentication tokens. By keeping secrets out of application code, the Azure Key Vault minimizes the risk of unintentional access to them.
- **Centralized management of encryption keys**: Organizations can produce, preserve, and administer cryptographic keys involved in data encryption and digital signing. Azure Key Vault permits using software-based keys and HSM-protected keys, thus ensuring compliance with top encryption standards.
- **Automated certificate management**: Azure Key Vault offers easier lifecycle management of SSL/TLS certificates, including automatic renewal and rotation. The public CA integration guarantees that applications can use the valid certificates immediately without manual intervention.
- **Access control and role-based permissions**: Key Vault is integrated with Entra ID, so it imposes restricted access control, ensuring that only approved users, applications, or Managed Identities can get secrets or keys. Organizations can fully integrate the Zero Trust security model by using RBAC and Managed Identities.
- **Auditing and monitoring**: Azure Key Vault can capture all access requests and changes, thus providing information for organizations to check on the use of keys and detect unauthorized entry attempts. Organizations can benefit from increased threat detection and compliance monitoring by integrating Azure Monitor, Azure Sentinel, and Microsoft Defender for Cloud.

Best practices for Key Vault

Organizations should adhere to the best practices when deploying Azure Key Vault to achieve the highest possible security, compliance, and operational efficiency.

Following these suggestions guarantees that the secrets, keys, and certificates are secured and managed efficiently:

- **Secure all sensitive data on Azure Key Vault**: Organizations should refrain from hard-coding secrets in application code or storing them in environment variables and configuration files. To prevent unauthorized access, the best practice is to safely keep all sensitive information in Azure Key Vault, such as API keys, passwords, and connection strings.
- **Use RBAC for the least privilege principle**: Permissions must be restricted using Azure RBAC and Managed Identities, thus allowing only those users and applications who require access to the secrets or keys. Applying the PoLP principle little by little decreases the number of security threats.
- **Keep Key Vault access logs and monitor**: Organizations should make Azure Key Vault logging active and integrate it with Azure Monitor and Microsoft Defender for the Cloud. It ensures that all access requests and changes made to the logs, audits, and potential threats are analyzed.
- **Secret and certificate renewing the automated way**: Organizations are advised to implement the Azure Key Vault built-in expiration alerts and automated renew features to avoid credential shrinkage and expired certificates.
- **Firmware security modules (HSM) for compression and masking the data**: In cases where operations with higher-standard cryptography are required, organizations should utilize HSM-backed mechanics in the Azure Key Vault Managed HSM. This is a non-tamperable access and makes available encryption keys that are FIPS 140-2 Level 3 certified and thus are subjected to a high level of security.

Azure Key Vault sample

The following screenshot displays the Azure Key Vault overview page for a vault named **samplekeyvaultau**. Azure Key Vault is a secure service that manages keys, secrets, and certificates for applications and services:

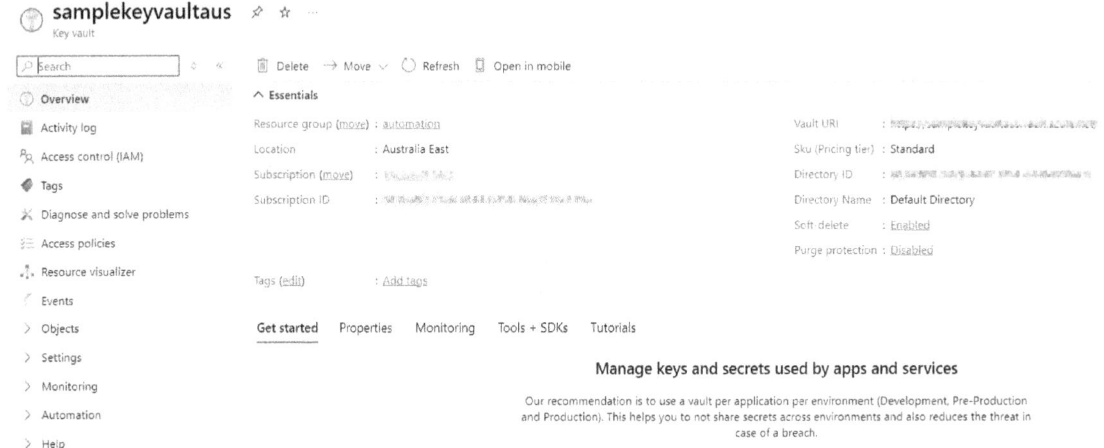

***Figure 6.8:** Sample Azure Key Vault*

Azure Locks

In cloud environments, the accidental deletion or modification of critical resources can lead to downtime, data loss, and security risks. Azure Locks have added protection that can prevent the deletion or modification of Azure resources, resource groups, or subscriptions either mistakenly or without authorization. Organizations can ensure the security of the mission-critical resources by applying lock policies, as they will enforce governance and secure the resources.

Overview of Azure Locks

Azure Locks are a line of defence against modifying or deleting resources in Azure subscriptions. While RBAC limits the number of people who can make changes. Azure Locks are a complete inhibitor for actions at the resource, resource group, or subscription level, regardless of the user's full administrative permissions.

Azure Locks play an important role in the organization's operational stability by limiting the governance rules and thereby averting accidental misconfigurations, which may lead to security vulnerabilities or service interruptions.

Key features

Locks provided by Azure represent a minimalistic yet effective method for the added protection of the Azure resources from unintended changes. These features contribute to cloud environments' operational integrity, security, and compliance among different organizations.

There are two lock levels for different use cases:

- **Read-only lock**: Modifications are blocked, while viewing resources is permitted. Production workloads can be secured this way while monitoring and troubleshooting are still allowed.
- **Delete lock**: Resource deletion is blocked but allows configuration changes. Thus, essential virtual machines, databases, and storage accounts can not be unintentionally deleted.
- **Applies at multiple hierarchy levels**: Three lock levels are available to organizations, providing protection at different scopes.

  Here are the levels where locks can be applied:

  - **Subscription level**: All resources within the subscription are affected.
  - **Resource group level**: All resources within a certain group are locked.
  - **Individual-resource level**: A specific VM, database, storage account, or any other Azure resource is secured.
- **Overrides RBAC permissions**: Locked resources can be modified or deleted even by users who have Owner or Contributor roles if the lock is removed explicitly. This imposes stricter governance enforcement over and above the RBAC policies.
- **Prevents accidental service disruptions**: The significance of Azure Locks is maximized in areas that present high risks, like production deployments, where a single accidental deletion could lead to downtime, loss of data, and breach of security.
- **Automation and IaC support**: Cross-protection of resources as part of deployment pipelines is done by the automation of Azure Locks management via the Azure Portal, Azure CLI, PowerShell, ARM templates, and Terraform.

Best practices for Azure Locks

Efficient management of Azure Locks can be carried out by a set of best practices deliberated by organizations to ensure proper security and resource handling while preventing disruptions, like the following:

- **Utilize locks in production and critical workloads**: Organizations must enforce Delete locks on relevant production environments, security resources (like Key Vaults), and mission-critical applications to ensure that no one accidentally removes them. To avoid unintended modifications, Read-Only Locks should be used on static networks.
- **Use locks together with RBAC and Azure Policy**: Azure locks must be one layer of the multi-layered governance approach alongside RBAC and Azure Policy to ensure that only authorized changes happen. RBAC prevents some users from changing resources, while locks even prevent authorized users from making any accidental changes.

- **Place locks at the appropriate level**: It is essential for an organization to evaluate and identify where to install locks.
    - o Use subscription-level locks for broad governance enforcement across multiple teams.
    - o Use resource group-level locks for departmental or application-specific resources.
    - o Use individual resource locks for highly sensitive assets like databases, storage accounts, and security tools (e.g., Azure Key Vault).
- **Regularly check and update locks**: As the business and operational dynamics shift, organizations are advised to periodically check on the locked resources to determine whether they adapt to the governance policies. Deleting unnecessary locks will not only help avoid operational blockers but also ensure that security is intact.
- **Automate Lock management in deployment pipelines**: Organizations using IaC are encouraged to integrate Azure Locks into ARM templates, Terraform, and Bicep scripts to make the automated resource protection feature part of their cloud governance strategy.

Azure Resource Lock sample

The following figure shows the **Locks** section within the automation resource group in Azure. Resource locks help prevent accidental modifications or deletions of critical Azure resources.

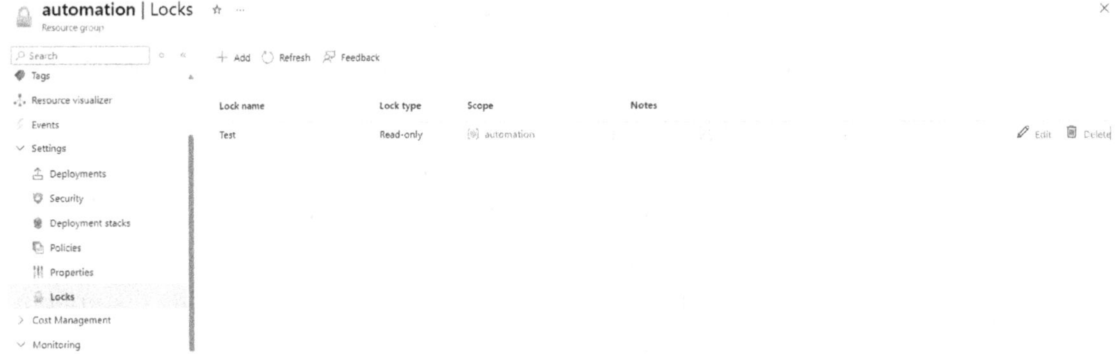

***Figure 6.9**: Sample lock on a resource group level*

Conclusion

Governance serves as the foundation for securing, managing, and optimizing Azure environments. In this chapter, we explored governance frameworks such as the CAF and the WAF. It also covers tools like Azure management groups, Azure Blueprints, and Azure Landing Zones that help organizations to enforce consistent policies, deploy secure environments, and manage multiple subscriptions.

We also covered how Azure Resource Graph enhances visibility into resource configurations, while Azure Policy enables organizations to enforce compliance automatically. Azure Key Vault was discussed as a component in managing secrets and encryption keys securely. These governance tools are essential not only for operational efficiency but also for reducing risk, maintaining compliance, and enabling secure scalability in the cloud.

In the next chapter, we will focus on security posture management, learning how to assess, monitor, and continuously improve the security health of Azure environments. It introduces tools like Azure Advisor and Microsoft Defender for Cloud, exploring how to use Secure Score, compliance tracking, external attack surface management, and hybrid/multi-cloud monitoring to build a robust security posture.

CHAPTER 7
Security Posture

Introduction

In this chapter, you will learn skills to master securing Azure resources and operations through security posture management. Azure Advisor will be explored, as well as Cloud Security Posture Management using Microsoft Defender for Cloud. Topics covered will include the Secure Score, Inventory, and External Attack Surface Management capabilities, security frameworks compliance, and adding industry and regulatory standards, and custom initiatives. In addition, hybrid and multi-cloud environment connectivity will be explored.

Structure

This chapter contains the following topics:

- Azure Advisor
- Microsoft Defender for Cloud
- Implementing CSPM with Microsoft Defender for Cloud

Objectives

By the end of this chapter, readers will be able to evaluate and improve the security posture of their Azure environments using Azure Advisor and Microsoft Defender for Cloud. They will understand how to use **Cloud Security Posture Management** (**CSPM**) to improve Secure Score, monitor security risks, and enhance visibility with Inventory and **External Attack Surface Management** (**EASM**). Additionally, readers will learn how to align security with industry compliance frameworks and implement custom security initiatives to meet organizational requirements.

The primary intention of this chapter is to familiarize readers with extending security posture management not only to Azure but also to hybrid and multi-cloud environments, which will ensure a common and proactive security approach. These lessons will teach them to observe vulnerabilities, make security settings, and thus augment cloud resilience to changing threats.

Azure Advisor

The cloud is highly sophisticated in securing and optimizing, as the required tasks involve continuous management and proactive improvements. Organizations seek ways to assess their cloud environment and acquire valuable tips for improving security, performance, cost, operational excellence, and reliability. Azure Advisor is a cloud management tool that offers organizations actionable insights. This solution provides customized recommendations, leveraging Azure's current state and established best practices.

Overview of Azure Advisor

Azure Advisor is a personalized AI cloud advisor that provides customized notifications and recommendations for different categories requiring manual intervention, such as security, performance, cost, and reliability. After the cloud analyst reviews the resource settings and application use patterns, Azure Advisor spots inefficiencies, risks, and improvement areas, thus allowing for a better cloud investment.

It is also a tool that systematically analyzes Azure resources in an organization and generates the necessary prioritized recommendations based on the established Microsoft best practices. The Advisor has helped businesses address vulnerabilities and strengthen security, reduce the costs of using inefficient resources, and increase reliability by mitigating the potential of failures by maximizing workload performance. Azure Advisor is one of the principal resources in the Azure cloud, which keeps organizations well-informed and improves the overall cloud posture.

The following figure shows the Azure **Advisor** homepage:

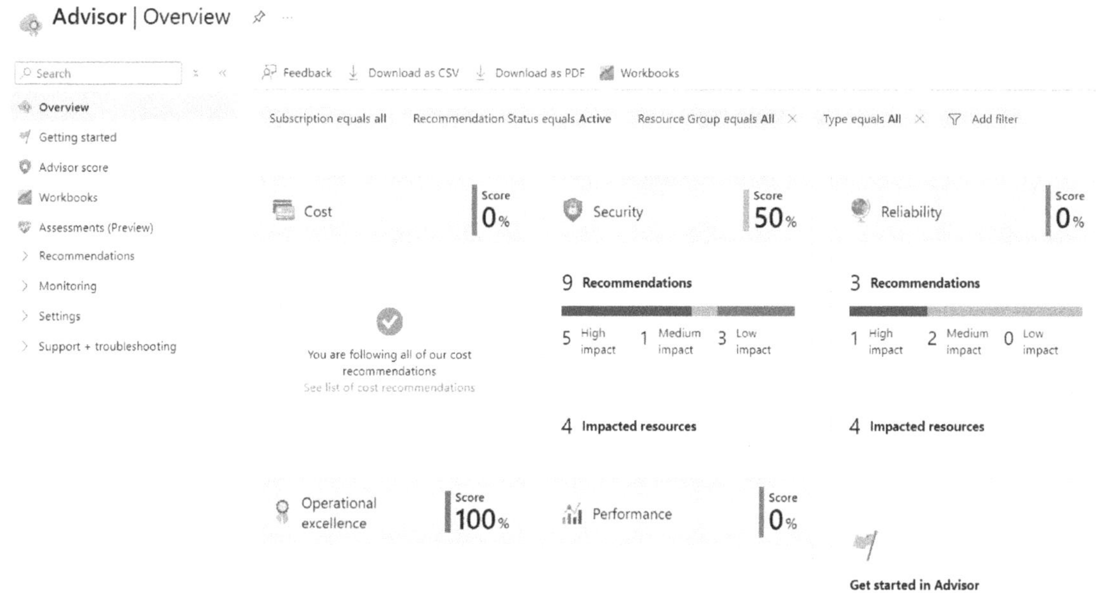

Figure 7.1: Azure Advisor homepage

The Azure Advisor overview dashboard shown in the image above is a tool that provides an overview, plus insights and recommendations for optimizing an Azure environment across various categories. The dashboard measures the resource by analyzing it against five separate indices: Cost, security, reliability, operational excellence, and performance.

In this instance, the cost and reliability scores are 0%, indicating no active recommendations or unaddressed issues in those areas. The security score is 50%, suggesting there are unresolved security recommendations. The operational excellence score is 100%, meaning all best practices in this category are followed, while the performance score is not displayed. The dashboard also underlines three recommendations, one being high-impact and four impacting resources. Users can explore these recommendations further to improve their Azure environment.

Key features of Azure Advisor

Cloud security is enhanced with Azure Advisor as it gives actionable insights and easy-to-follow recommendations. Taking a proactive role, Azure Advisor helps enterprises identify possible risks and remove them to prevent complicated situations. Therefore, it keeps them secure.

These are the characteristics that make Azure Advisor a must-have tool for security oversight:

- **Security recommendations**: Azure Advisor scans your environment, finds vulnerabilities, misconfigurations, and security gaps, and adds suggestions. Azure Advisor can also recommend security measures such as enabling MFA, securing network access, and strengthening identity management controls to reduce the risks.

The following figure shows security recommendations in Azure **Advisor**:

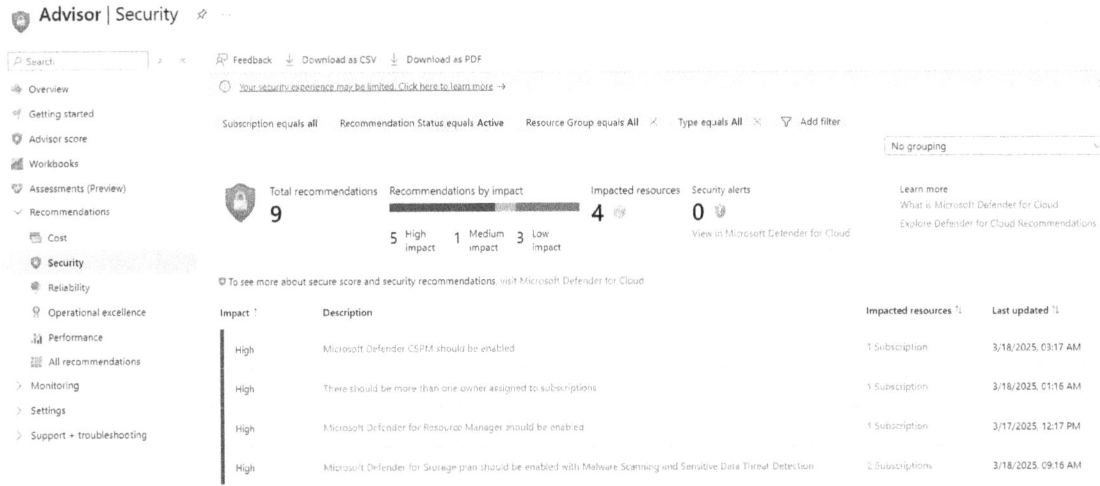

Figure 7.2: Security recommendations in Azure Advisor

- **Integration with Secure Score**: Microsoft Defender for Cloud Secure Score is an advanced system that integrates Microsoft Azure Advisor. It empowers organizations to focus on their security posture based on assessing the potential risk. In this way, the organizations can follow the Azure Advisor's instructions and, at the same time, improve their Secure Score.

The following figure shows the **Advisor score**:

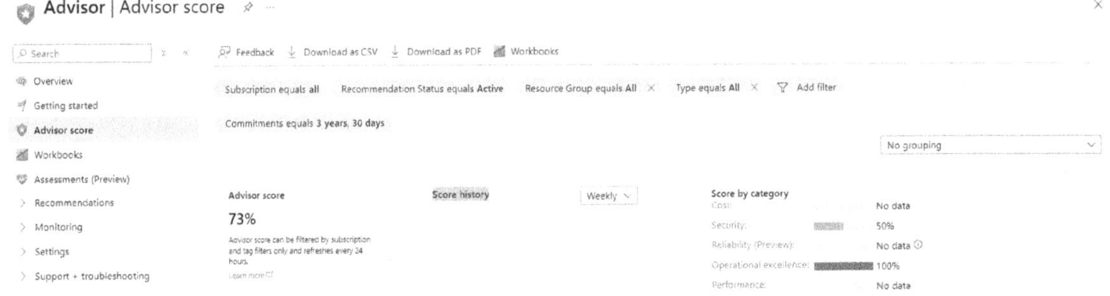

Figure 7.3: Secure Score in Azure Advisor

- **Actionable insights**: Azure Advisor highlights the issues and directly gives users instructions and links to fix security risks. So, the customers could execute the recommendations fast, which, in turn, would reduce the time consumed to enhance the security settings.

A sample actionable item is shown in the following figure:

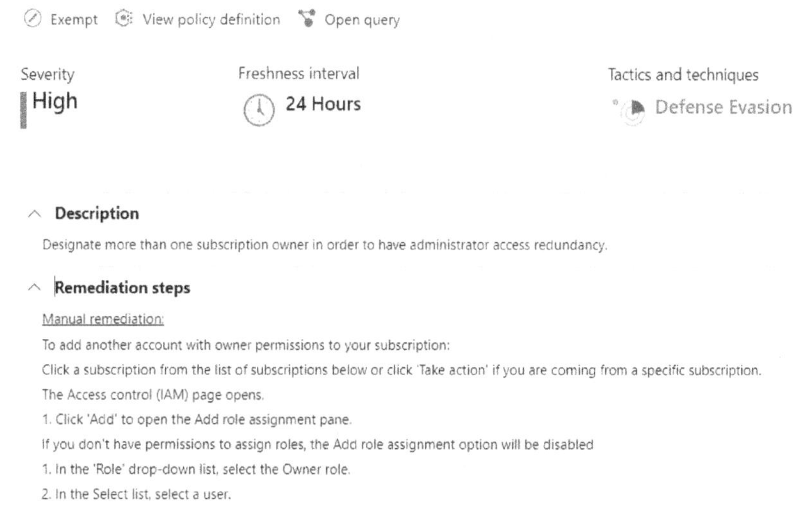

There should be more than one owner assigned to subscriptions
Exempt
View policy definition
Open query
Severity
High
Freshness interval
24 Hours
Tactics and techniques
Defense Evasion
Description
Designate more than one subscription owner in order to have administrator access redundancy.
Remediation steps
Manual remediation:
To add another account with owner permissions to your subscription:
Click a subscription from the list of subscriptions below or click 'Take action' if you are coming from a specific subscription.
The Access control (IAM) page opens.
1. Click 'Add' to open the Add role assignment pane.
If you don't have permissions to assign roles, the Add role assignment option will be disabled
1. In the 'Role' drop-down list, select the Owner role.
2. In the Select list, select a user.

***Figure 7.4**: Actionable item*

- **Proactive monitoring**: The continuous analysis of Azure resources, workloads, and configurations makes Advisor one of the fastest ways to get real-time insights on the change frequency and possible risks. Thus, companies can operate effectively by removing potential threats that can negatively influence business processes.
- **Customizable recommendations**: Customers can choose which recommendations to implement based on their unique business needs, industry compliance requirements, and risk appetites. This way, focusing on the most relevant security actions becomes possible while suggestions that are not applicable are ignored.
- **Multi-category optimization**: Along with security being the top priority, Azure Advisor also ensures that organizations maintain a well-architected and optimized cloud environment by balancing performance, reliability, and cost efficiency without compromising security.

Using Azure Advisor effectively

To get the most out of Azure Advisor, it is suggested that organizations follow a tactical approach to its best. Organizations can proactively create security measures, improve performance, lower costs, and boost reliability by adding Azure Advisor to their security and cloud management processes.

The key practices that ensure the proper use of Azure Advisor, in the case of keeping a secure environment and an optimized Azure ecosystem, are as follows:

- **Regular assessments**: Security risks and optimization opportunities vary as cloud environments develop. Regular transformations of Azure Advisor's recommendations, revising on a schedule, should be the organization's target to continue improving. Automating the execution of periodic assessments helps to discover new risks earlier and to take measures before they reach critical levels.
- **Custom reports**: Azure Advisor offers a feature that enables users to create personalized reports for security posture, cost optimizations, and performance enhancements. These reports are tools to check progress, set priorities for the needed actions, and help align security with business objectives. Cybersecurity organizations can also utilize these reports to prove their compliance with security frameworks and regulatory standards.
- **Integration with governance tools**: Best practices in security risk should be enforced uniformly. Integrating Azure Advisor with Azure Policy and Azure Blueprints is the way to go. Application and enforcement, thus, reduce manual oversight and ensure compliance, as the means mentioned above will be adequately implemented in all cloud settings.
- **Prioritizing high-impact recommendations**: Not all the recommendations are urgent or impactful in the same way. Organizations should first consider suggestions that focus on vulnerabilities, namely identity protection, mandatory encryption, and network security hardening, before the ones relating to performance and cost-saving. Secure Score integration is a vital resource that can be used to rate the issues by vulnerability levels.
- **Automating remediation**: In the cases where it is practical, organizations are recommended to leverage Azure Automation, Logic Apps, or Azure Functions to be the hands of the machines to carry out the fixes at scale. Consequently, treating the risks becomes less time-consuming, and manual tasks are saved.
- **Efficient team collaboration**: The joint effort between the security and cloud management teams has given good results in terms of accepting and implementing Azure Advisor's suggestions based on their analysis and decision-making skills. The outcomes can be recorded through Azure DevOps, Microsoft Teams, or a centralized security dashboard, dealing with efficiency and accountability.
- **Hybrid and multi-cloud visibility**: Organizations' hybrid and multi-cloud systems occur due to mixing their own and other cloud assets. Azure Advisor statistics can be related to the other CSPM tools that the user owns to maintain the services at the level the vendor demands. Thus, security tends to be kept beyond Azure, which protects both the on-premises and the cloud workloads.

Best practices of Azure Advisor

The main prerequisite for Azure Advisor is adopting good practices, and the organization must use cloud optimization and best practices for security compliance.

By discovering these techniques, security will be maintained proactively, cloud governance will be fair, and operational efficiency will be high:

- **Regularly review Advisor security recommendations**: Cloud settings continually change, and vulnerabilities can emerge. To keep this from happening, businesses should think of periodical maintenance to check Azure Advisor's recommendations on security, applying corrections wherever necessary. The maintenance of the cloud is like the regular checking of the computer for viruses and bugs. Continuous monitoring is the process that does these things; it stops new problems from forming and causing disruptions to progress.
- **Prioritize high-impact actions aligned with Secure Score**: Not all safety recommendations weigh the same. Organizations should focus on critical issues that render the Secure Score highly vulnerable, such as fixing identity gaps, encryption, and injected code. These fixes must be prioritized over not-so-serious ones.
- **Use automation to implement recommendations where feasible**: By utilizing Azure Automation, Logic Apps, or Policy Initiatives to remediate the faults automatically, the organizations can annihilate manual work and, hence, also secure the policies impartially. Automating security fixes, such as enabling MFA, enforcing JIT access, or blocking public access to storage, helps minimize human error and speeds up implementation.
- **Integrate Advisor Insights with Azure Policy and Defender for Cloud**: Compliance and best practices in security should be built into the governance agents. Azure Policy allows institutions to automatically manifest the Advisor's recommendations, thus providing compliance across all the subscriptions. Besides, the concatenation with Microsoft Defender for Cloud can provide an additional visible compliance posture and attack management surface.
- **Monitor and optimize security posture continuously**: Protection is a permanent concern, not an intermittent duty. Businesses should note the improvements in the long run, look at the points of the Secure Score, and change the security settings as needed. Using custom dashboards in Azure Monitor, you can get the actual position of your security state alterations in real time.
- **Collaborate across teams for faster remediation**: Security is a co-shared duty of the IT, security, and compliance body. Organizations should ensure inter-team collaboration by bringing Azure Advisor's insights into forms in Microsoft Teams, Azure DevOps, or ticketing systems like ServiceNow that integrate.

Microsoft Defender for Cloud

The key to maintaining a strong security posture in the Cloud is through continuous assessments, preventive evaluation of risks, and following industry security standards. Organizations venturing into multi-cloud and hybrid cloud infrastructure across Azure need a centralized security posture management solution to track vulnerabilities, detect misconfigurations, and enforce compliance. Microsoft Defender for Cloud provides a CSPM solution that helps organizations increase their security, reduce risks, and adhere to compliance requirements in their cloud environments.

Overview of Microsoft Defender for Cloud

Microsoft Defender for Cloud is a security solution with a unified system that includes CSPM functionalities to strengthen organizations' security in Azure. Defender for Cloud offers customers visibility into security risk into executing compliance guidelines, and logic to act accordingly on the cloud workloads that must be manipulated protectively.

Defender for Cloud is a unique kind of cloud protection that hands over human tasks and problems to AI. In addition to its ability to identify potential threats, it moves a step further by proactively performing a search for possible misconfigurations, security vulnerabilities, and compliance deficiencies. In this way, enterprises are able to remove the risk of unsecured cloud environments quickly, which is possible even if they do not see it before.

One of the key features of Defender for Cloud is the hybrid and multi-cloud management, which allows security teams to monitor not only Azure but also AWS and Google Cloud. This product can work with various security frameworks and compliance standards, giving organizations a single view of cloud security risks. Additionally, the common usage of Azure Policy and Secure Score with the product offers prioritized improvement of security measures and automatic fixes, which create a more efficient and scalable security management process.

The following image shows the Microsoft Defender for Cloud Overview dashboard, displaying security posture and assessments across two Azure subscriptions. It highlights 27 assessed resources, zero critical recommendations, zero attack paths, and a 50% Secure Score for Azure. The left panel includes security-related options like **Recommendations**, **Attack path analysis**, **Security alerts**, and **Cloud Security Explorer**.

Microsoft Defender for Cloud homepage is shown as follows:

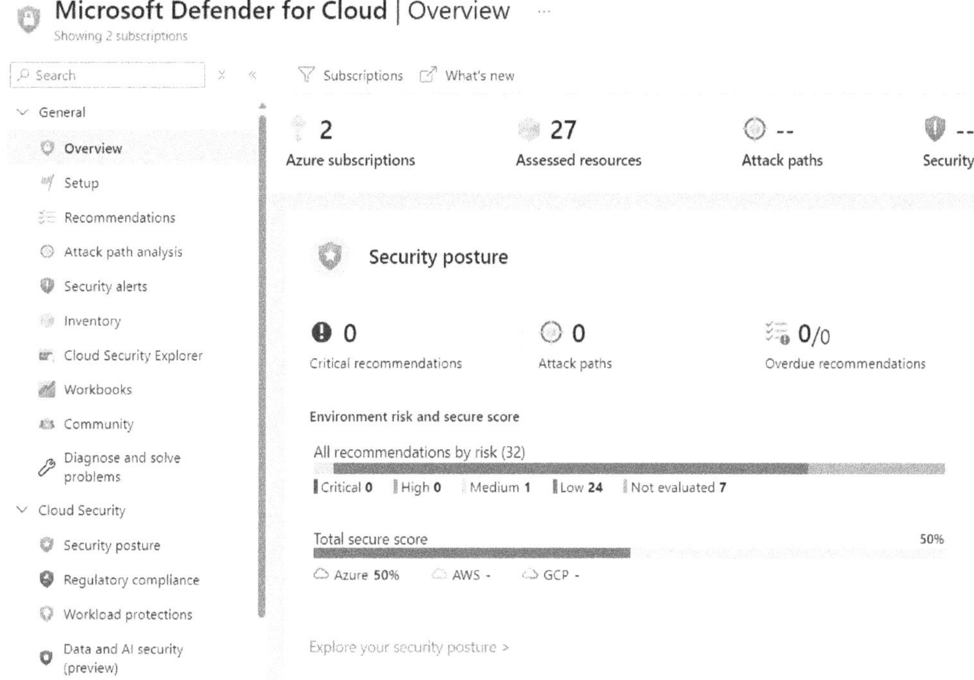

Figure 7.5: Defender for Cloud

The **Microsoft Defender for Cloud** dashboard, like the one illustrated in the preceding image, is over the view, delivering security insights and suggestions for Azure subscriptions. It is shown on the dashboard that the number of the assessed Azure subscriptions is 2, and that of the resources is 27. The security posture section presents the total security score as 50%, which means there is still a need for improvement in the environment's security.

Recommendations are classified in the environmental risk assessment based on their severity, where critical and high-risk recommendations are absent, one medium-risk recommendation is there, and there are 24 low-risk recommendations. Moreover, seven recommendations are yet to be evaluated. The lack of significant problems is good; however, dealing with both medium and low-level recommendations could further improve security.

The dashboard also confirms zero attack paths and zero overdue recommendations, meaning no immediate threats have been identified, and all required security actions are current. The platform primarily evaluates Azure security, as indicated by the 50% Secure Score for Azure.

At the same time, no data is displayed for AWS or GCP, suggesting those environments are either not assessed or not configured.

Users can explore detailed recommendations under the Security posture section for further improvement to identify and mitigate potential vulnerabilities. Proactively addressing low- and medium-risk findings will enhance the overall security score and reduce the risk of possible future security threats.

Key features of Microsoft Defender for Cloud

CSPM is a strong choice for Microsoft Defender for Cloud, which offers a complete approach to sustaining security, risk assessment, and compliance monitoring for organizations' cloud environments.

The key features listed in the following section help to improve safety, remove threats, and ensure adherence to the regulations in Azure, hybrid, and multi-cloud infrastructures.

Secure Score

The following points highlight the scope and function of Secure Score:

- A metric that reflects and measures the security state of the Azure environment of the organization.
- Delivers recommendations for improving security in order of priority based on risk severity and impact, thus really assisting organizations in focusing on the most critical vulnerabilities in the first place.
- Logs the improvements in security measures over time; this way, teams get a chance to measure their progress and keep a proactive security mode.
- It makes it possible for organizations to measure their security stance against the set standards of best practices.

  The following figure portrays Secure Score:

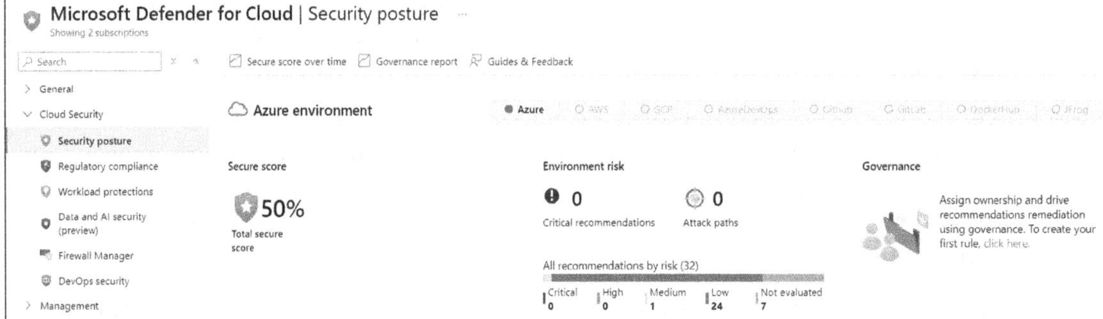

Figure 7.6: Secure Score

Inventory management

The following points highlight the scope and functions of inventory management:

- The system automatically identifies and classifies all Azure resources, providing total visibility into cloud assets.

- It finds unmanaged, misconfigured, or non-compliant assets, alleviating the problem of security blind spots.
- It offers an interactive inventory dashboard that allows security teams to evaluate and handle security risks quickly and efficiently.

The following figure displays **Inventory** in Defender for Cloud:

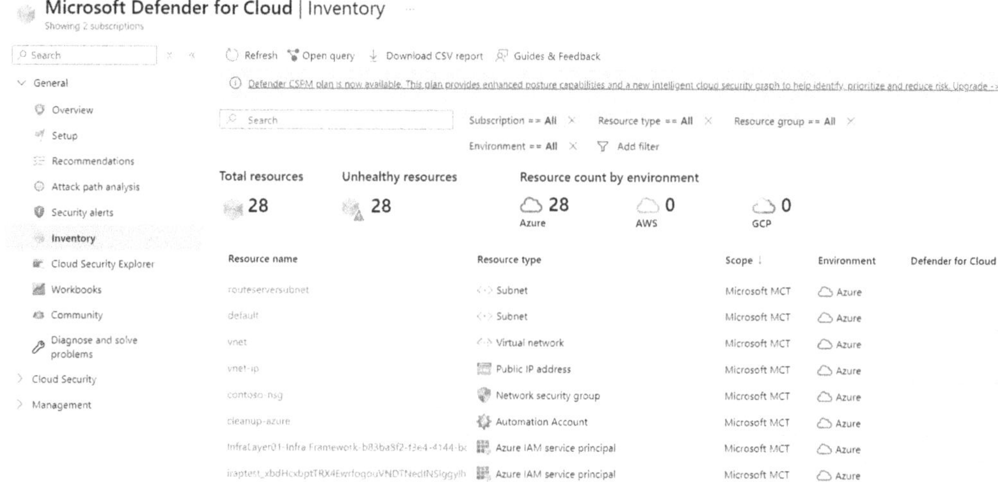

Figure 7.7: Inventory of environment

External Attack Surface Management

The following points highlight the scope and functions of EASM:

- Assesses the exposure of public-facing assets, helping security teams understand how an attacker might exploit misconfigured resources.
- Identifies vulnerabilities in internet-facing applications, storage accounts, virtual machines, and APIs.
- Provides actionable remediation steps to reduce risks, such as enforcing network access restrictions, enabling encryption, or reducing open ports.

The following figure depicts **Attack Path Analysis**:

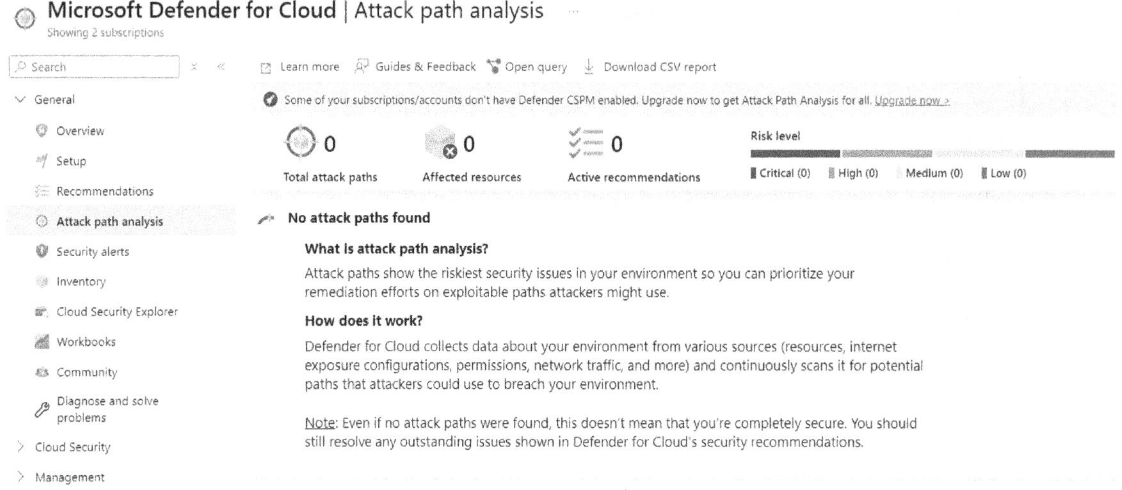

Figure 7.8: Attack surface status

Compliance monitoring

The following points highlight the scope and function of compliance monitoring:

- Manages compliance of cloud security with different industry standards like GDPR, HIPAA, ISO 27001, NIST, and PCI DSS.
- Helps with the mapping of security recommendations to the organization's compliance requirements to ensure adherence to legal and regulatory standards.
- It helps create non-standard compliance initiatives that allow businesses to go further and implement an organization-specific security framework.
- Offers compliance score tracking, which, in turn, assists the security teams in providing solid proof to auditors and regulatory agencies for their compliance.

The following figure depicts the compliance status:

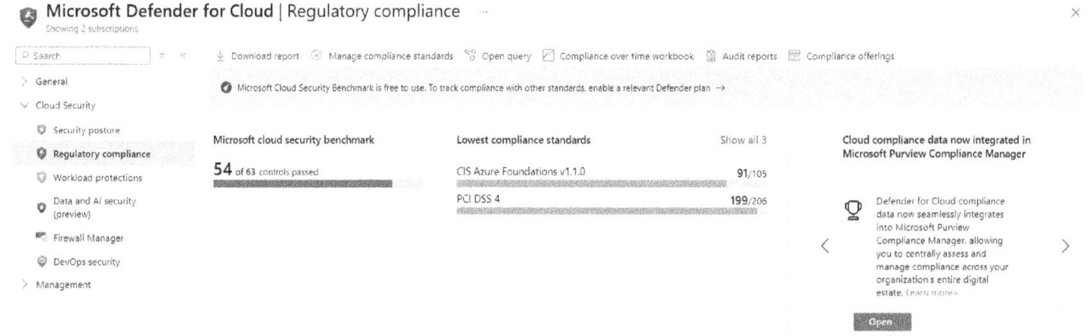

Figure 7.9: Regulatory compliance

Hybrid and multi-cloud support

The following points highlight the scope and functions of hybrid and multi-cloud support:

- Extends security posture management beyond Azure to AWS, Google Cloud, and on-premises environments.
- Ensures consistent security policies across different cloud providers, preventing misconfigurations in multi-cloud architectures.
- Integrates with third-party security tools and SIEM platforms, allowing organizations to centralize security monitoring across multiple infrastructures.
- The solution provides support for agentless scanning and integration with cloud-native security tools, thus simplifying the process of managing hybrid environments.

The following figure depicts multi-cloud connectors:

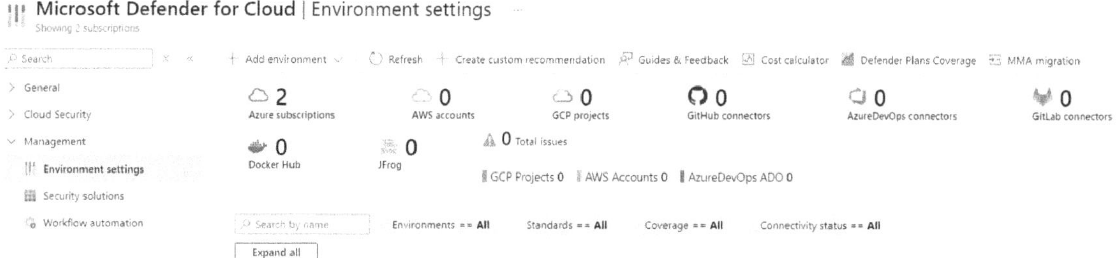

***Figure 7.10**: Multi-environment connections*

Agentless and agent-based scanning

Defender for Cloud supports both agent-based and agentless scanning, giving organizations flexibility in how they monitor their cloud resources. Agentless scanning is ideal for quick visibility into workloads without deployment overhead, while agent-based scanning allows for deep, continuous assessments and integration with other Defender plans (e.g., Defender for Servers, Containers).

Threat detection and alerts

Defender for Cloud uses advanced analytics and threat intelligence to detect anomalies, malicious behaviors, and known attack patterns. These are surfaced through real-time alerts with severity levels, helping security teams to respond quickly and effectively.

Recommendations Engine

The built-in Recommendations Engine prioritizes security misconfigurations and vulnerabilities based on severity and impact. Recommendations can be filtered by resource type, control category, or compliance domain, enabling organizations to focus on the most critical areas first.

Implementing CSPM with Microsoft Defender for Cloud

Integrating CSPM with Microsoft Defender for Cloud is a multi-step process that helps with continuous monitoring and automation of security practices. Organizations should take full advantage of Defender for Cloud's integrated functionalities to improve security and ensure compliance, and proactively apply additional risk-mitigating measures across Azure, hybrid, and multi-cloud configurations.

The following are key steps to successfully implement CSPM with Microsoft Defender for Cloud:

1. **Enable Secure Score**:
    a. Use Secure Score as a baseline metric to assess and monitor the security posture of your cloud environment.
    b. Regularly review and act on prioritized security recommendations to reduce risks.
    c. Set security benchmarks and track progress over time to ensure continuous improvement.
    d. Align Secure Score improvements with regulatory compliance and corporate security policies to meet business objectives.
2. **Automate remediation**:
    a. Using Logic Apps and Azure Policy, one can incorporate security recommendations and automatically rectify frequently encountered misconfigurations.
    b. Utilize the automated rules to deploy JIT VM access, require encryption, and limit public network exposure.
    c. Set up and use Azure Automation for patching, set security configurations, and resolve security issues.
    d. Trim down on manual efforts by following the use of remediation playbooks for a speedy response to threats.
3. **Custom compliance initiatives**:
    a. Define custom compliance initiatives customized to industry regulations such as GDPR, HIPAA, ISO 27001, and NIST.

   b. Map security controls to organizational compliance frameworks and ensure continuous monitoring.

   c. Use Defender for Cloud's built-in regulatory compliance dashboard to track adherence and detect deviations.

   d. Implement custom policies and alerts for organization-specific security and governance requirements.

4. **Integration with SIEM solutions**:

   a. Leverage Microsoft Sentinel, a cloud-native SIEM solution, to collect, analyze, and correlate security data from Defender for Cloud.

   b. Set up real-time security alerts and enable automated incident response through **Security Orchestration, Automation, and Response** (**SOAR**) playbooks.

   c. Integrate log data from multi-cloud and hybrid environments into Sentinel to gain unified security insights.

   d. Use threat intelligence capabilities in Sentinel to detect, investigate, and respond to security threats proactively.

5. **Monitor and optimize security posture continuously**:

   a. Conduct regular security assessments to ensure security recommendations and compliance initiatives are followed.

   b. Utilize Microsoft Defender Threat Intelligence to stay ahead of emerging threats and vulnerabilities.

   c. Implement RBAC to manage security permissions and restrict unnecessary privileges.

   d. Enable auditing and logging with Azure Monitor and Azure Activity Logs to track changes and detect anomalies.

6. **Enhanced visibility with Azure Resource Graph**: For large-scale environments spanning multiple subscriptions, Azure Resource Graph enables efficient querying of compliance, resource state, and security posture data. Security teams can use KQL to:

   a. Identify non-compliant resources across environments.

   b. Track Secure Score trends and recommendation status.

   c. Correlate policy assignments with actual resource compliance.

   d. Build custom dashboards for governance and audit reporting.

CSPM best practices with Microsoft Defender for Cloud

To effectively use Microsoft Defender for Cloud's CSPM capabilities, organizations should adopt best practices that ensure continuous security monitoring, proactive risk mitigation, and compliance enforcement.

Implementing these practices will help maintain a strong, scalable, well-governed cloud security posture across Azure, hybrid, and multi-cloud environments.

- **Continuously monitor and update the Secure Score**:
  - Regularly assess Secure Score recommendations to identify and remediate security risks.
  - Establish security benchmarks and track progress over time to measure improvements.
  - Automate security enforcement using Azure Policy to maintain a consistently high Secure Score.
  - Use RBAC as a foundational model to assign least-privilege access according to job roles, and regularly audit role assignments to eliminate unused or overly broad permissions.
- **Use inventory tools to identify unprotected or misconfigured resources**:
  - Leverage Microsoft Defender for Cloud's Inventory feature to maintain real-time visibility of all Azure assets.
  - Detect and classify unmanaged, unprotected, or misconfigured resources, ensuring they meet security best practices.
  - Automate resource tagging and categorization to improve governance and security tracking.
  - Perform frequent security audits to identify and mitigate shadow IT risks.
- **Regularly review and update compliance initiatives**:
  - Ensure compliance with industry regulations such as GDPR, HIPAA, ISO 27001, NIST, and PCI DSS by mapping security controls to organizational policies.
  - Regularly update custom compliance initiatives to align with evolving business and regulatory requirements.
  - Utilize Defender for Cloud's compliance dashboard to monitor regulatory adherence and detect real-time deviations.
  - Conduct internal security assessments and compliance audits to ensure continuous enforcement.

- **Extend security monitoring to hybrid and multi-cloud environments for consistent protection**:
    - Integrate AWS, Google Cloud, and on-premises infrastructure with Microsoft Defender for Cloud to maintain a unified security posture.
    - Use Microsoft Sentinel to centralize security event monitoring across multi-cloud and hybrid infrastructures.
    - Deploy agent-based or agentless scanning to detect misconfigurations and vulnerabilities beyond Azure.
    - Establish automated security workflows using Azure Automation, Logic Apps, or SOAR tools to standardize platform incident response.
    - Use Azure Arc for hybrid/on-prem servers and CSPM connectors for AWS/GCP to ensure consistent posture management across all environments.
- **Automate security recommendations and remediations**:
    - Implement Azure Policy and Remediation Playbooks to enforce best practices automatically.
    - Use Azure Logic Apps or Power Automate to resolve common security misconfigurations with minimal manual effort.
    - Enable JIT access for virtual machines to minimize the risk of unauthorized access.
    - Apply network segmentation and firewall rules dynamically based on risk assessment from Defender for Cloud.

Conclusion

This chapter illustrated how Azure Advisor and Microsoft Defender for Cloud's CSPM capabilities help organizations constantly evaluate, adjust, and enhance net security. Companies can use Secure Score, compliance monitoring, inventory management, and external attack surface assessments to list the weak points, improve security first, and later consider the attack as a part of a defense strategy.

The deployment of CSPM effectively needs to be fully integrated with monitoring the system, automation, and governance frameworks. To do this, organizations have to embed the best practices in place, which consist of continuously tracking the Secure Score, shutting down vulnerabilities with automated solutions, acting on policy, and running security monitoring on top of the hybrid and multi-cloud environments. Using Microsoft Sentinel, Azure Policy, and automation tools, organizations can decentralize security management, reduce misconfigurations, and make the cloud environment resilient.

By adopting the strategies outlined in this chapter, organizations can establish a strong, scalable, and continuously improving security posture, ensuring their cloud environments remain secure, compliant, and resilient against evolving threats.

In the next chapter, we will be looking at workload protection, which will cover the workload protection services capabilities of Microsoft Defender for Cloud. The workload protections will cover servers, storage, and other components of Azure.

CHAPTER 8
Workload Protection

Introduction

In this chapter, you will learn skills to master securing Azure resources and operations through workload protection. Topics will include the workload protection services capabilities of Microsoft Defender for Cloud, including exploring Microsoft Defender for Servers, Storage, Databases, Containers, App Service, Key Vault, Resource Manager, and DNS.

Structure

This chapter contains the following topics:

- Microsoft Defender for Cloud CWPP services
- Microsoft Defender for Servers
- Microsoft Defender for Storage
- Microsoft Defender for Databases
- Overview of Defender for Databases
- Microsoft Defender for Containers
- Microsoft Defender for App Service
- Microsoft Defender for Key Vault

- Microsoft Defender for Resource Manager
- Microsoft Defender for DNS

Objective

In this chapter, you will discover the opportunities to secure Azure products and operations through workload protection by utilizing Microsoft Defender for Cloud. When organizations migrate workloads to the cloud, it is essential to implement strong security measures for computing, storage, databases, and application services. This chapter will equip you with the knowledge to leverage **cloud workload protection platform** (**CWPP**) services available in Microsoft Defender for Cloud, which you can utilize for proactive threat detection, vulnerability management, and implementation of security best practices across different Azure resources.

By the end of this chapter, you will be able to configure and optimize Microsoft Defender for Servers, Storage, Databases, Containers, App Service, Key Vault, Resource Manager, and DNS. You will learn how these security solutions provide advanced threat protection, anomaly detection, and compliance monitoring to safeguard workloads against cyber threats. Whether you are an architect, security engineer, or administrator, mastering these workload protection capabilities will help you build a more resilient and secure cloud environment.

Microsoft Defender for Cloud CWPP services

Microsoft Defender for Cloud's CWPP services provide a strong security framework to protect cloud workloads across environments, including Azure, hybrid, and multi-cloud deployments. With more and more organizations shifting workloads to the cloud, they are challenged with new security issues like misconfigurations, exposed endpoints, and evolving cyber threats. Standard security techniques developed for on-premises conditions are insufficient in cloud systems, where the workload is subject to dynamic changes and distributed across multiple platforms.

The main goal of Microsoft Defender for Cloud's CWPP services is to protect the cloud and services that work with the Azure platform. The platform makes sure that weaknesses are found and fixed before they become an issue. It also finds threats in real time and manages compliance. By using threat intelligence, behavior analytics, and automatic responses, CWPP is the first step towards maintaining the organization's defenses and lowering attack areas, which protects applications from cyberattacks.

Defender for Cloud homepage

The following figure displays Defender for Cloud portal with details on resources and subscriptions attached to it:

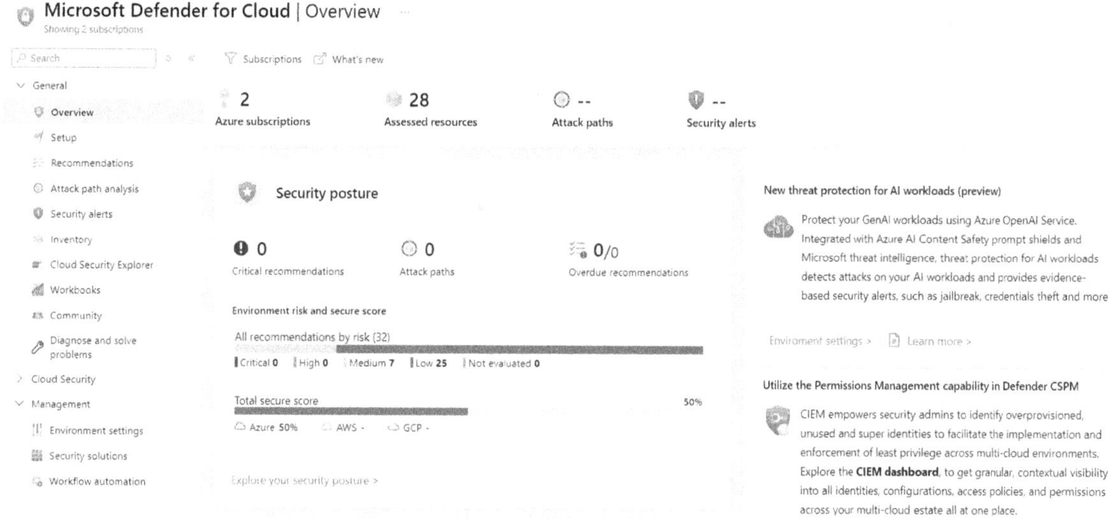

***Figure 8.1:** Defender for Cloud homepage*

Overview of CWPP

Microsoft Defender for Cloud's CWPP services help address security issues, and with a large number of cloud workloads, you must secure against various risks. The CWPP solution differs from the security tools commonly used in traditional environments. Instead, it is specifically designed for cloud and hybrid ecosystems. Hence, security teams can efficiently observe and secure workloads.

Key features of CWPP

The Microsoft Defender for Cloud CWPP is a useful solution that addresses evolving threats in the cloud. It features an automated cloud protection system that continuously checks and protects your cloud-based resources, making security management proactive, threat response automated, and compliance adherence easy to achieve.

The following are the features that have made CWPP an indispensable part of cloud security:

- **Threat detection**: Modern threat intelligence, machine learning, and behavioral analytics are used by CWPP to instantly detect and eliminate security risks on cloud workloads. It may identify anomalous activity, attempts at illegal access, and security breaches, providing immediate notifications to the security teams. The collaboration with Microsoft Threat Intelligence provides more information on attack patterns and **indicators of compromise** (**IoCs**), resulting in improved visibility of overall threats.
- **Vulnerability management**: The services provided by Defender for Cloud's CWPP are enriched by a built-in vulnerability scanner that scans workloads. It identifies misconfiguration, outdated applications, and security vulnerabilities in virtual

machines, containers, and databases. Security teams covering potential breaches receive pre-emptive guidance on the necessary actions to be taken, ensuring that these vulnerabilities will not be exploited by the time the risk is reduced.

- **Compliance monitoring**: Workload security requires adherence to regulatory frameworks and industry norms. CWPP routinely evaluates workloads to suggest best practices like PCI-DSS, NIST, CIS, and ISO 27001. Organizations can meet their governance standards by being accountable and adhering to appropriate security baselines using automated compliance evaluations.
- **Security posture management**: Defender for Cloud provides recommendations and fixing guidelines to improve cloud security. With an aggregated security score, this tool highlights the need to correct poor setups and provides recommended practices to ensure workload security. Security teams can aggressively follow policies to stop attacks on the cloud.
- **Automated response and remediation**: To deliver prompt incident response, CWPP integrates with Microsoft Sentinel and additional security automation solutions. Security teams set up automated operations that will be executed, such as blocking malicious IP addresses, isolating infected workloads, or setting out notifications for further investigation. This reduces occurrences that would have otherwise been harmful while optimizing the effectiveness of security procedures.
- **Hybrid and multi-cloud protection**: Microsoft Defender for Cloud offers workload protection for hybrid and multi-cloud setups in addition to Azure security. Defender's security features may be integrated with AWS, Google Cloud, and on-premises infrastructure to provide users with consistent protection across all platforms.
- **Container and Kubernetes security**: Defender for Cloud includes integrated protection for Kubernetes clusters and containerized applications in response to the increasing use of containerized workloads. It functions by scanning the network, images, and runtime threat detection to prevent container-focused attacks.
- **File integrity monitoring (FIM)**: FIM in CWPP is one of its primary characteristics, as it can detect unauthorized changes to critical system files, configurations, and registry settings. This also prevents viruses from entering, fixes, and protects against data attack activities.
- **DNS security and network protection**: Defender for Cloud continuously checks network bonds to cloud workloads, detecting traffic from unauthorized locations and attacks, such as lateral movement. DNS Defender is responsible for detecting domain-based threats, including phishing and malware **command and control** (**C2**) traffic. It is also responsible for the DNS tunnelling process, C2 traffic, and DNS tunnelling attempts.
- **Zero Trust integration**: Microsoft Defender for Cloud walks the talk to Zero Trust principles by implementing least-privilege access controls and verifying workloads

continuously. The integration of Entra ID, Conditional Access policies, and JIT VM access positively affects the identity security for workloads that depend on it.

Benefits of cloud workload protection platform

Organizations need a complete security solution that offers ongoing protection for their workloads as cloud environments get more complicated. Microsoft Defender for Cloud's CWPP provides an extensive way of protecting cloud-based resources, guaranteeing that businesses can function safely while lowering risks.

The primary advantages of CWPP and its enhancements to cloud security operations are outlined in the following list:

- **Enhanced visibility across workloads**: The inability to view distributed workloads is one of the biggest challenges in cloud security. A centralized security dashboard from CWPP provides users with up-to-date information on security risks, weaknesses, and compliance status for databases, applications, virtual machines, and containers. Because of end-to-end visibility, security teams can promptly detect and eliminate potential threats before attackers can exploit them. Better threat identification and response are also made possible by the rich insights into workload behavior that security alerts and analytics offer.
- **Centralized management for multi-cloud and hybrid environments**: Organizations frequently manage workloads across several cloud platforms, such as Azure, AWS, and Google Cloud, in addition to on-premises infrastructure. The CWPP in Microsoft Defender for Cloud simplifies security operations by providing a single view for workload monitoring and protection across all cloud and hybrid environments. Regardless of where their workloads are distributed, organizations guarantee that security policies are constantly followed by implementing integrated policies, compliance tracking, and automated security recommendations.
- **Automated responses to detected threats**: When addressing security incidents, speed is crucial, and manual involvement can cause mitigation actions to be delayed. Organizations can react to risks instantly because of the automation integrated into CWPP.

  Defender for cloud can initiate automated remedial activities, such as the following, when a security event is detected:

  - Isolating compromised workloads to prevent lateral movement of threats.
  - Blocking malicious IP addresses or network traffic to stop active attacks.
  - Triggering security playbooks for incident response through Microsoft Sentinel integration.
  - Applying patches or configuration changes automatically to remediate vulnerabilities.

These automated responses reduce the time to attack, limit damage, and enable security teams to focus on higher-priority tasks rather than manually addressing every security alert.

- **Improved compliance and governance**: Organizations in regulated sectors have to follow industry standards such as PCI-DSS, CIS, NIST, and ISO 27001. CWPP routinely assesses workloads against compliance criteria and provides comprehensive reports and security advice to help businesses maintain compliance. Automated compliance monitoring reduces the risk of security breaches and noncompliance, ensuring that security rules are consistently followed.
- **Reduced security complexity and cost**: Multiple security systems are typically needed to manage security across workloads, which increases complexity and cost. CWPP eliminates the need for external security tools by integrating workload protection into a comprehensive security solution. Organizations can enhance protection while streamlining security operations and reducing costs by leveraging built-in integration with other Microsoft security solutions, such as Defender for Endpoint, Azure Policy, and Microsoft Sentinel.
- **Proactive threat prevention and risk reduction**: CWPP takes a proactive approach to security rather than merely responding to attacks. Organizations can identify security flaws and address them before they are exploited by using automated risk assessments, security recommendations, and continuous monitoring. Microsoft Defender for Cloud always maintains a strong security posture by detecting and preventing attacks with AI-driven threat intelligence.

Microsoft Defender for Servers

As more people utilize the cloud, organizations must ensure that server workloads are secure in Azure, on-premises, and multi-cloud environments. It is not always easy for traditional server security solutions to identify new threats and simultaneously protect all your distributed systems. Microsoft Defender for Servers offers comprehensive security tracking, advanced threat protection, and vulnerability management to safeguard both VMs and physical servers against emerging cyber threats.

Overview of Defender for Servers

VMs and physical servers operating in Azure, on-premises data centres, and multi-cloud environments like AWS and Google Cloud are protected by the Microsoft Defender for Servers security suite. Constant monitoring, real-time threat detection, vulnerability management, and regulatory compliance assist businesses in maintaining the security of their server workloads.

Defender for servers can protect servers either with or without agents, thus offering you more options for configuring them. The system employs **Microsoft Defender for Endpoint** (**MDE**) to offer advanced **endpoint detection and response** (**EDR**) capabilities. These functions avow the prompt identification of security threats and their rectification. It also connects with

Microsoft Sentinel, which has SIEM tools and automated threat response to improve incident management.

Defender for Servers can protect your servers with or without agents, providing you with more options for setting it up. The system utilizes MDE to provide advanced EDR capabilities. These features ensure that security threats are quickly identified and addressed. It also integrates with Microsoft Sentinel, which enables the use of SIEM tools and automated threat response to better manage incidents.

Microsoft Defender Vulnerability Management, which automatically checks security flaws and unpatched software, is another feature of Defender for Servers. This helps organizations to identify obsolete software, compliance issues, and inadequate security settings. In addition, it allows JIT VM access, which requires specific permission and makes it more difficult for users to remotely access vital servers. This reduces the possibility of illegal access and brute-force attacks.

Since it offers security capabilities that extend beyond Azure, defend against attacks, verify file integrity, and integrates with other security solutions, the Defender for Servers Plan 2 is suitable for enterprises that utilize hybrid and multi-cloud environments. For organizations that want to apply the same security guidelines to both on-premises and cloud infrastructures, this makes it a versatile choice.

Enabling and configuring Defender for Servers

Defender for Servers can be enabled from **Settings** inside the Defender for Cloud portal, as portrayed in *Figure 8.2*:

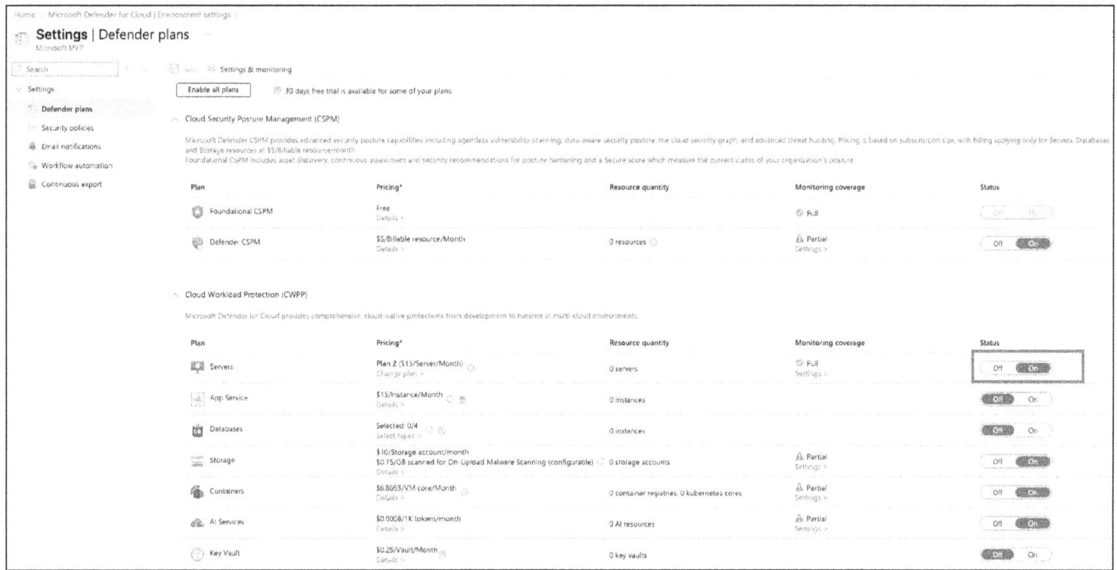

Figure 8.2: Enabling Defender Plans

The plan can be changed as per the following figure after the Defender is enabled:

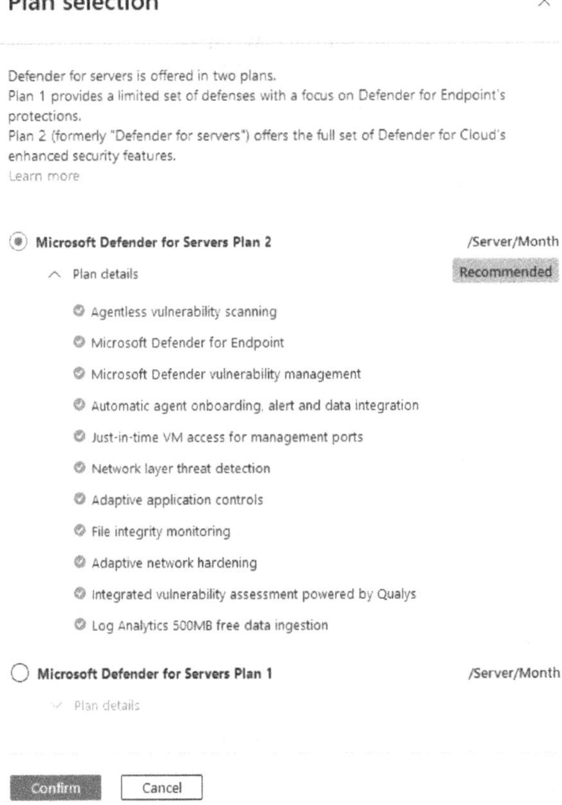

***Figure 8.3**: Plan selection for Servers*

Key features of Defender for Servers

Microsoft Defender for Servers offers numerous security features designed to protect VMs and physical servers from sophisticated threats. This system utilizes Microsoft Defender for Cloud to ensure that Azure, hybrid, and multi-cloud environments are continuously monitored, threats are identified before they occur, and security management is automated.

The following are some of the key features of Defender for Servers:

- **EDR**: Defender for Servers integrates with MDE to provide EDR. Using this, it is possible to detect APTs, suspicious activities, and malicious threats to the application. EDR, being the system's brain, takes information from AI and behavior analytics mechanisms to detect fileless working methods, unknown vulnerabilities, and ransomware attacks during operation. Security teams receive the full lifecycle of the attack, forensic data, and recommendations for automatic remediation to manage risks effectively.

- **FIM**: It is a utility that allows organizations to detect unauthorized modifications to their system files, data, registry keys, and application settings. This ability assists organizations in finding potential insider threats, malware infestations, and unauthorized changes made to critical files. FIM provides security teams with immediate alerts and audit trails showing who made the changes, when, and what was changed. Therefore, this kind of adherence to industry rules and security procedures is ensured.
- **Integration with Microsoft Defender for Endpoint**: Defender for Servers and Microsoft Defender for Endpoint work together seamlessly, protecting you from threats in real time and reducing the number of attack surfaces. This integration enables the automation of threat hunting, endpoint behavioral analysis, and the isolation of systems that have been compromised. It also connects threat data, which lets security teams look into server threats in the bigger picture of the attack surface.
- **JIT VM access**: When Defender for Servers is used, the JIT VM access is enabled. This lowers the chance of brute-force attacks and unauthorized remote access. JIT access limits access to RDP and SSH by only letting approved users, specific IP addresses, and limited time windows join. This makes credential-based attacks and unauthorized server entry much less likely.
- **Vulnerability management and security recommendations**: With its built-in vulnerability assessment tools, Defender for Servers continuously checks VMs and physical servers for outdated software, incorrect settings, and security vulnerabilities. Priority-based security suggestions are sent to organizations to fix vulnerabilities before attackers can use them. This feature works with Microsoft Defender Vulnerability Management to offer risk-based patch management and automated remediation.
- **Adaptive application controls**: Defender for Server features adaptive application controls that support this. This is a capability that helps businesses create whitelists of the software that are only allowed to run on specific or key machines. The block list includes unapproved apps that may be harmful, preventing the system from launching malicious software, installing unauthorized applications, and executing unidentified scripts.
- **Threat analytics and AI-driven security insights**: Defender for Servers uses machine learning algorithms to give security analytics that help managers stay ahead of current and emerging attack patterns. Microsoft's advanced threat intelligence and analytics help targeted clients understand cyber attackers' behavior and tactics. With the ability to see the future, security teams can take action before a failure occurs due to a cyberattack.
- **Network security and lateral movement detection**: The Defender for Servers performs a network traffic scan to detect anomalies in the behavior of the assets being inspected, track down connections, and find lateral mobility indicators within the organization's landscape. It spots such compromised credentials, the intrusion of an

elevated privileged user, and communications that should not happen. In this way, security specialists can obviate the threat of persistence by attackers.

- **Integration with Microsoft Sentinel**: Defender for Servers works with Microsoft Sentinel to provide SIEM and SOAR features. This integration allows companies to centralize security monitoring, connect threat intelligence, and automate incident reaction workflows. This makes security operations more efficient.
- **Security baselines and compliance enforcement**: Industry security standards, such as CIS, NIST, and ISO 27001, are checked in real-time against server configurations by Defender for Servers. It offers automatic compliance reporting, security posture assessments, and recommendations to ensure servers are safe and compliant with regulations.

Best practices of Defender for Servers

To use all the benefits of Microsoft Defender for Servers, organizations must follow the industry best practices for monitoring, configuration, and threat response. These practices involve the protection of both VMs and physical servers against web-based attacks, improper settings, and hacking through the application of the preceding protections.

Key best practices for setting up and maintaining Defender for Servers are described in the following list:

- **Enable Defender for Servers across all workloads**: Ensure all the servers and virtual machines in Azure, on-premises, and multi-cloud configurations have Defender for Servers enabled. This can be achieved by implementing threat detection and security monitoring across all workloads to cover almost everything, which would help reduce the blind spots in security operations.
- **Leverage MDE integration**: Defender for Servers offers enhanced EDR capabilities by integrating with MDE. If this integration is enabled, security teams will receive automatic threat remediation for compromised systems, forensic insights, and real-time alarms.
- **Implement JIT VM access**: Limit access to essential servers via SSH and RDP by allowing JIT virtual machine access. With JIT, only authorized users are granted access for a brief period, lowering the danger of brute-force attacks, credential stuffing, and unauthorized remote access.
- **Enable FIM**: To identify unauthorized modifications to system files, registry keys, and configuration settings, set up **FIM**. This helps security teams identify insider threats, malware infections, and unauthorized changes to critical resources.
- **Regularly perform vulnerability assessments**: Utilize the integrated vulnerability assessment tools in Defender for Servers to check for unprotected endpoints, unpatched applications, and security configuration errors. Frequent vulnerability scans help companies identify and fix security flaws before hackers can exploit them.

- **Apply adaptive application controls**: Set up adaptive application restrictions to prevent unauthorized software execution and whitelist authorized applications. This protects secured servers against ransomware attacks, malware infections, and unauthorized script execution.
- **Monitor and respond to threats using Microsoft Sentinel**: Automate incident response, correlate security events, centralize threat monitoring, and integrate Defender for Servers with Microsoft Sentinel. Sentinel enhances comprehensive security operations by offering SOAR and SIEM capabilities.
- Implement network security best practices, such as the following:
    - o Control the flow of inbound and outbound network traffic to servers by leveraging Azure Firewall, **Network Security Groups** (**NSGs**), and Private Endpoint.
    - o Enable threat detection for DNS traffic to track and block harmful connections to domains.
    - o Implement micro-segmentation to separate workloads and limit the movement in the horizontal direction in case of a security incident.
- **Enforce security baselines and compliance policies**: To ensure workloads adhere to CIS, NIST, ISO 27001, PCI-DSS, and other security frameworks, use Defender for Servers' compliance assessments. Automate the enforcement of security baselines to correct configuration errors and ensure compliance.
- Configure automated remediation playbooks to respond to security incidents, for example:
    - o Automatically isolate a compromised server if Defender detects an active attack.
    - o Block suspicious IP addresses or disable user accounts showing anomalous activity.
    - o Enforce patching policies to apply security updates to vulnerable servers automatically.

Microsoft Defender for Storage

Since data is the most important asset of an organization, it is a top target for cyberthreats such as viruses, theft, and unauthorized access. As more businesses rely on cloud storage solutions for flexibility and scalability, it is essential to ensure that Azure Storage services are secure. To keep data in Azure Blob Storage, Azure Files, and Azure Data Lake safe, Microsoft Defender for Storage checks for threats, identifies anomalies, and enforces security policies in real-time.

Defender for Storage assists organizations in detecting and fixing security flaws, making sure users follow data access guidelines, and spotting harmful activity, including ransomware attacks, illegal access attempts, and data breaches. Integrating with Microsoft Defender for Cloud offers automatic attack response, security insights, and ongoing monitoring.

Overview of Defender for Storage

Defender for Storage is a cloud-native security product designed to defend Azure storage accounts from attacks.

It provides complex security mechanisms to protect data in:

- **Azure Blob Storage**: Used for unstructured data storage, including logs, backups, and application files.
- **Azure Files**: A managed file share service that supports SMB and NFS protocols for cloud-based file storage.
- **Azure Data Lake Storage**: Optimized for big data analytics and large-scale data processing.

Common threats targeting storage include exposed public endpoints, misuse of **shared access signatures** (**SAS**), and malicious file uploads leading to ransomware. A misconfigured container with anonymous read access can lead to unauthorized data exposure.

This security solution monitors storage activity for anomalies, suspicious access patterns, malware injection attempts, and misconfigurations. It analyzes logs, detects potential data breaches, and alerts security teams to take necessary actions.

Defender for Storage also connects with Microsoft Sentinel, including SIEM and SOAR features, to improve storage security monitoring and automate incident response processes. By using AI-driven threat intelligence to spot malicious file uploads, unauthorized changes, and unusual access patterns, organizations can safeguard data and uphold security standards.

Enabling Defender for Storage

Defender for Storage can be enabled from **Settings** inside the Defender for Cloud portal, as portrayed in the following figure:

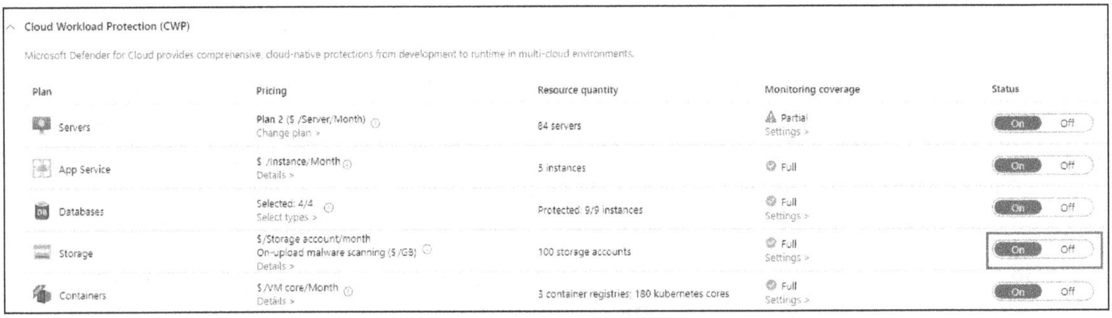

Cloud Workload Protection (CWP)

Microsoft Defender for Cloud provides comprehensive, cloud-native protections from development to runtime in multi-cloud environments.

Plan	Pricing	Resource quantity	Monitoring coverage	Status
Servers	Plan 2 ($ /Server/Month) Change plan >	84 servers	Partial Settings >	On Off
App Service	$ /Instance/Month Details >	5 instances	Full	On Off
Databases	Selected: 4/4 Select types >	Protected: 9/9 instances	Full Settings >	On Off
Storage	$/Storage account/month On-upload malware scanning ($ /GB) Details >	100 storage accounts	Full Settings >	On Off
Containers	$/VM core/Month Details >	3 container registries; 180 kubernetes cores	Full Settings >	On Off

Figure 8.4: Enabling Defender for Storage

Key features of Defender for Storage

Microsoft Defender for Storage is a comprehensive and upscale security monitoring option exclusively for Cloud storage in Azure Blob Storage, Azure Files, and Azure Data Lake. Microsoft Defender for Storage is only available for cloud storage in Azure Blob Storage, Azure Files, and Azure Data Lake. The technology is powerful enough to help organizations recognize, stop, and deal with threats that are expressly directed at cloud storage systems. Defender for Storage shields your data from malware attacks, data breaches, and unauthorized access with AI-driven threat intelligence, anomaly detection, and access control rules.

The following are the key features of Defender for Storage:

- **Malware scanning**: Defender for Storage checks files in Azure Files and Azure Blob Storage using state-of-the-art malware detection technology. By identifying and blocking malicious file uploads, ransomware payloads, and malware-infected documents, the system prevents cloud storage from being an entry point for the spread of malware. Security teams can react swiftly since real-time alerts instantly inform them of security risks.

- **Threat detection and anomaly monitoring**: Defender for Storage continuously scans storage access patterns to identify unusual behavior, unauthorized access attempts, and potential data exfiltration. Through telemetry utilization from storage operations, it detects uncharacteristic I/O operations, unidentified IP address throttling, and brute-force attacks on storage IDs. Detection of these anomalies helps companies to avoid insider threats, data breaches, and wrong use of credentials.

- **Access controls and least privilege enforcement**: Defender for Storage is strict on permissions, incorporating a fine-grained access control measure that restricts access, modification, or even deletion of files on Azure only. An organization can use the RBAC mechanism, authentication through Entra ID, and Private Endpoint to avoid unwanted access to data.

- **Integration with Microsoft Sentinel**: Defender for Storage can be integrated with Microsoft Sentinel; this lets the security teams balance threats related to Storage with security events. This promotion to a higher level of SIEM and SOAR functionality, tremendously advances incident response workflows. For illustration, Sentinel can activate procedures such as blocking malicious IP addresses or revoking access rights to Storage that has been compromised.

- **Data exfiltration prevention**: One major issue with cloud storage is data exfiltration, which occurs when hackers do unauthorized tasks and, as a result, move sensitive data outside the company. Defender for Storage, for example, checks and identifies unauthorized API requests, unexpected access from unreliable sources, and large data downloads that could lead to unnoticed efforts at data theft.

- **Protection against ransomware attacks**: Ransomware attackers often encrypt or delete data in cloud storage to demand ransom. Defender for Storage has the power to detect early signs of ransomware activity, such as mass modification or deletion of storage accounts. It has a feature to trigger alerts and includes appropriate countermeasures, which can be implemented in a very short time, allowing companies to get back to normal before they incur major losses.
- **Security posture recommendations and compliance monitoring**: Defender for Storage continuously scans storage security settings and provides security recommendations aligned with CIS, NIST, ISO 27001, and PCI-DSS standards. It identifies the incorrect access controls, public exposure risks, and poor encryption settings, ensuring storage accounts use best security practices.
- **Encryption and data protection monitoring**: Storage data security is mainly concerned with data being well-secured both at rest and in transit. The Defender for Storage serves the purpose of monitoring encryption settings and notifying you in cases where there are unencrypted storage accounts or if the TLS configuration is weak. Also, it ensures the Azure Key Vault is being used for key management, thus acting as a reminder for the encryption best practices that help protect sensitive data.
- **Protection against insider threats**: Defender for Storage helps identify internal security threats, such as users with unauthorized access to sensitive files, excessive permission changes, or irregular access patterns. Organizations can determine insider threats before they cause data loss or other breaches through behavioral analytics and anomaly detection.

Best practices of Defender for Storage

Organizations should use best practices while establishing Microsoft Defender for Storage to guarantee optimum security and compliance for data kept in Azure Blob Storage, Azure Files, and Azure Data Lake. These recommended practices protect private information from cyberattacks, help reduce attack surface area and stop unwanted access.

Following these security guidelines will improve cloud storage and protect data:

- **Enable soft delete**: Data loss can happen due to intentional or unintentional file deletions. For Azure Blobs, Azure Files, and Azure Data Lake Storage, soft delete enables organizations to retrieve deleted data within a configurable retention period of up to 365 days. This helps restore files affected by accidental or unauthorized deletions and stops ongoing data loss.

  Blob soft delete should be enabled to allow recovery of accidentally deleted blob objects. Similarly, enabling soft delete for Azure File shares protects against unintended deletions, ensuring critical files can be restored when needed. Additionally, turning on versioning and change feed provides a mechanism to track changes over time and restore previous versions of objects, helping maintain data integrity and historical records.

- **Use Private Endpoint to restrict access**: Organizations should set Private Endpoint for their storage accounts to reduce public internet exposure. Private Endpoint provide secure, internal-only communication by linking storage accounts to a private IP address inside an Azure VNet. This ensures that data flows via private connections rather than the public internet.

  To secure access to Azure Storage accounts, several network-level controls should be implemented. Public network access should be restricted by setting the **Public Network Access** option to **Disabled**, effectively blocking any inbound traffic from the public internet. For secure, internal connectivity, Azure Private Link should be used to create Private Endpoint, ensuring that access to the storage account is routed through the corporate network. Additionally, applying NSGs and configuring firewall rules allows for more granular control, enabling access restrictions based on specific IP ranges and virtual networks.

- **Encrypt data at rest and in transit**: Encryption helps protect sensitive data from unauthorized access and tampering. Defender for Storage supports encryption at multiple levels, ensuring data is protected both at rest and during transmission.

  To ensure data is protected both at rest and in transit, Azure Storage security features should be properly configured. **Server-side encryption** (**SSE**) should be enabled using either Microsoft-managed keys or **customer-managed keys** (**CMKs**) stored in Azure Key Vault, providing control over encryption policies and compliance. For data in transit, it is important to use **Transport Layer Security** (**TLS**) 1.2 or higher to encrypt communications between clients and the storage account. Enforcing the Secure Transfer Required setting ensures that only secure HTTPS connections are allowed, blocking any unencrypted HTTP access to the storage account.

- **Implement RBAC and least privilege access**: Unauthorized changes or data disclosure might result from poorly set permissions. Azure RBAC guarantees that users and applications have minimal access.

  To improve access control and minimize risk in Azure Storage, the PoLP should be applied to ensure users and services have only the permissions necessary for their tasks. Azure RBAC roles with wide permissions should be assigned directly to the specific resources where needed, rather than at higher scopes such as the storage account or container level. Privileged access should be closely monitored and managed using Entra ID PIM, which enables tracking of elevated roles and validation of access rights over time.

- **Enable advanced threat protection for Storage: Microsoft** Defender for Storage provides real-time threat detection against malware uploads, unauthorized access, and anomaly-based threats.

To enhance threat detection and response for Azure Storage, Defender for Storage should be enabled to identify suspicious data access patterns, potential malware activity, and data exfiltration attempts. Integrating with Microsoft Sentinel allows these alerts to be correlated with broader security incidents across the organization, providing a unified view of threats. Configuring automated playbooks can help respond quickly to incidents by isolating suspicious activities, revoking access tokens, or triggering targeted security alerts, thereby reducing response times and minimizing potential damage.

- **Restrict access using SAS with expiry dates**: SAS provides Azure Storage temporary, scoped access. If exposed, however, poorly set SAS tokens create security concerns.

  To securely manage access through SAS, it is important to apply strict controls. Setting an expiration date on SAS tokens ensures they remain valid only for a limited time, reducing the risk of long-term exposure. Whenever possible, SAS rights should be limited to read-only access to minimize the potential impact of misuse. Restricting SAS token access to trusted networks through the Azure Storage Firewall helps prevent unauthorized access from unapproved locations.

- **Enable immutable storage**: Immutable storage stops data modification by keeping objects unchangeable for a designated retention time. This supports regulatory compliance and ransomware.

  To support regulatory compliance and data governance, time-based retention policies should be enabled to lock data for a specified period, ensuring it cannot be modified or deleted until the retention period expires. Legal hold policies should be established to prevent data deletion during legal investigations or audits, preserving critical information regardless of existing retention settings.

- **Use Azure Monitor and storage logs**: Monitoring storage activity provides visibility into suspicious behavior and potential risks.

  To maintain visibility and proactively detect potential threats in Azure Storage, it is essential to enable Azure Monitor logs and Azure Storage diagnostics to track access patterns and usage behaviors. Defender for Cloud and Microsoft Sentinel can be used to monitor high-risk events such as unexpected bulk data transfers or access from unusual geographic locations. Setting up custom security alerts for failed access attempts, anonymous requests, or multiple access attempts from different regions allows for early detection of suspicious activity and faster incident response.

- **Implement data loss prevention and Conditional Access policies**: Preventing data leaks is critical for protecting sensitive information stored in Azure.

  To protect sensitive information stored in Azure, Microsoft Purview DLP policies should be implemented to detect and block the transfer of confidential data. CA policies in Entra ID should be configured to enforce MFA for users accessing storage resources, adding an extra layer of security. Data loss policies can be used to classify and label sensitive storage objects, helping to prevent unauthorized access or sharing by enforcing appropriate restrictions based on data sensitivity.

- **Regularly audit and rotate storage access keys**: Storage access keys provide full control over a storage account and must be protected from unauthorized use.

  To minimize security risks in Azure Storage, access keys should be rotated regularly to reduce the potential impact of compromised credentials. Azure Key Vault should be used to securely store and manage encryption keys, ensuring centralized control and compliance with security standards. Whenever possible, Account Key authentication should be disabled in favor of Entra ID based access, which provides more granular control, auditing capabilities, and integration with identity governance policies.

Microsoft Defender for Databases

Databases often hold private and important information for a business, and they are often the target of hacking, threats from inside the business, and unauthorized access. As businesses move to cloud-native architectures, they need to protect cloud-hosted databases to keep data security, privacy, and compliance. Microsoft Defender for Databases has advanced security features that can be used to monitor, find, and fix threats to Azure-based databases. It helps businesses improve their security across multiple database sources, follow the regulations, and keep data safe on their own.

This solution provides behavioral analytics, vulnerability assessments, intelligent threat detection, and compliance tracking for managed database services through integration with Microsoft Defender for Cloud. Workloads for **platform as a service** (**PaaS**) and **infrastructure as a service** (**IaaS**) databases are supported, assisting businesses in guaranteeing data security without compromising performance or availability.

Overview of Defender for Databases

To protect different Azure database services from internal and external threats, Defender for Databases is a cloud-native intelligent threat protection solution.

It offers advanced analytics and security monitoring for a variety of databases:

- Azure SQL Database (single databases, elastic pools, and managed instances)
- Azure Cosmos DB
- Azure SQL on VMs
- PostgreSQL and MySQL (flexible servers)
- Other IaaS-hosted databases via the Defender for Servers integration

This service continuously monitors database activity to identify unusual access patterns, SQL injection attempts, permission escalations, and brute-force login attacks. Through vulnerability assessments, it also finds exposure risks, unpatched engines, too many rights, and wrong configurations.

Defender provides a single view of database security for Databases, and it has seamless integration with Azure-native tools like Microsoft Sentinel, Azure Monitor, and Azure Policy. This integration also makes alerting, incident response, and compliance enforcement easy. It ensures that database threats are identified early and dealt with promptly by utilizing Microsoft threat intelligence and built-in machine learning, assisting organizations in safeguarding their data.

Enabling Defender for Databases

Defender for Databases can be enabled from **Settings** inside the Defender for Cloud portal, as shown in the following figure:

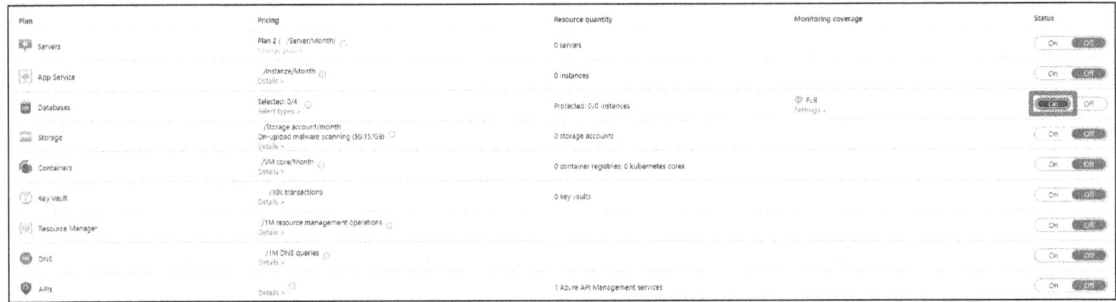

Figure 8.5: Enabling Defender for Databases

Key features of Defender for Databases

Microsoft Defender for Databases is a modern and smart way to handle and deal with the security of cloud databases against external attacks, insider threats, and misconfigurations. It is an intelligent and extensible service that provides threat monitoring, detection, and continuous database security posture monitoring.

The following are the key features that contribute to data security across Azure database services:

- **Advanced threat protection**: Defender for Databases is capable of real-time detection of threats like SQL injection attacks, brute-force login attempts, data exfiltration, anomalous access behavior, and privilege escalations. The use of machine learning algorithms and Microsoft Threat Intelligence represents a significant part of the process through accessing patterns, query behavior, and login anomalies. It is the best way to know if there are any potential breaches. In the case of identifying suspicious activities, it sends out alerts containing complete information necessary for a rapid investigation and response.

- **Vulnerability assessments**: The primary work of this feature is to perform scans of vulnerabilities to detect misconfigurations, outdated database engines, weak authentication settings, open network exposure, and various other security risks. Defender for Databases assists organizations in resolving these vulnerabilities by supplying prioritized remediation recommendations. The recommendations come with stepwise instructions, thus allowing organizations to address the problems effectively and be sure that the issues will not be exploited before the resolution. It supports both platform-managed and self-hosted (IaaS) databases, which makes it easier to ensure a consistent security baseline across different workloads.

  For example, Defender for Databases flagged a PostgreSQL server allowing root login over the public internet. The recommendation advised disabling public access and enforcing network rules via NSG and Private Link.

- **Data security insights**: Defender for Databases illustrates the security conditions of all protected databases via the authority granted by the Microsoft Defender for Cloud dashboard. Security guidance tailored to each resource involves actionable suggestions on reinforcing access controls, setting encryption keys, and auditing configurations. These insights allow security teams to monitor compliance posture, reduce attack surfaces, and apply the best practices aligned with security standards like CIS, NIST, and GDPR.

- **Continuous activity monitoring**: Monitoring is an important part of the overall security of the system, and this fact is reflected in the Defender tool, which keeps track of the database activities, such as login patterns, schema modifications, and query execution, to find any unusual or unauthorized access. The creation of audit trails is the basis for security reporting for compliance, and they also help find possible insider threats, such as data leakage attempts or the excessive use of privileges.

- **Integration with Microsoft Sentinel and Azure Monitor**: Security reports from Defender for Databases can be sent straight to Microsoft Sentinel. After that, Sentinel's correlation engine will identify threats and automatically handle related events. Integration with Azure Monitor is also guaranteed, which lets you keep an eye on specific telemetry, set up your own alerting rules, and see how the database's health and security are doing.

- **Support for multi-cloud and hybrid workloads**: Organizations can protect their SQL Server databases on-premises, in Azure VMs, on AWS, and in GCP settings with Defender for Servers. This makes sure that the level of security is flawless, no matter where the information is located.

- **Minimal performance overhead**: Defender for Databases has been planned as a lightweight Virtual Agent-free service that operates for platform-managed databases, thus ensuring the security monitoring does not interfere with performance and availability. IaaS-hosted databases utilize existing agents from Defender for Servers, which, in turn, reduces the amount of extra software or other burdens.

- **Compliance readiness and reporting**: The initiative provides organizations with the tools necessary for successful data security management by offering built-in compliance assessments, exhaustive reports that highlight compliance gaps, and suggestions for improvements. Such quality audits are commodities for ISO 27001, HIPAA, PCI-DSS, and several other frameworks.

Best practices of Defender for Databases

Implementing best security practices while using Microsoft Defender for databases is the easiest way to keep cloud-hosted databases safe and secure while maintaining regulatory compliance. Such measures can reduce the chances of data breaches, and, in addition, organizations also gain an advantage in maintaining a strong security posture, limiting exposure, and securing information across all environments in Azure SQL Database, Cosmos DB, and other managed and self-hosted database services.

The following are some of the best practices:

- **Enable transparent data encryption (TDE)**: TDE is one way to help protect data at rest by encrypting the database, related backups, and transaction logs without application changes. Activating TDE guarantees the continuing degradation of storage media and that the data cannot be decrypted using keys other than the appropriate decryption keys. For CMK, use Azure Key Vault if you want more control over encryption key management.

- **Regularly review and implement vulnerability assessment recommendations**: Vulnerability assessments are indispensable and primary reinforcing tasks. Defender for Databases conducts scans and gives top recommendations to repair such vulnerabilities as high privileges, weak authentication, hidden endpoints, and outdated database engines. Review these monthly and resolve the reported problems to maintain a hardened and compliant database configuration.

  To maintain continuous security coverage, vulnerability assessments should be scheduled on a weekly or monthly basis, ensuring regular identification of potential risks. Designating specific owners to track and remediate high-risk findings helps ensure timely resolution and accountability. Integrating these with Microsoft Sentinel or existing ticketing systems streamlines incident tracking and remediation workflows, improving overall response efficiency and reducing the window of exposure.

- **Use dynamic data masking (DDM) to protect sensitive information**: DDM ensures that sensitive data is not visible to non-privileged users but is automatically masked in query results. For example, in this case, they might look undisguised, but in the case of unauthorized viewers, the credit card number may read as XXXX-XXXX-XXXX-1234. You need to use DDM to protect PII, financial documents, and health records without changing how your database stores information.

To protect sensitive data in Azure, you can apply either predefined or custom rules depending on the criticality of the information. Columns containing PII, such as Social Security Numbers, email addresses, or account numbers, should be masked to prevent unauthorized exposure. Access to unmasked data must be restricted to only those users and roles that are explicitly authorized, ensuring compliance with privacy and security policies.

- **Implement RBAC and least privilege**: Apply the principle of least privilege to limit access to database resources. Use Azure RBAC, SQL roles, and custom permissions to guarantee that users and applications directly access only what is necessary for their tasks.

  To maintain strong security in Azure environments, avoid using shared or highly privileged accounts, as they pose risks and lack accountability. Regularly auditing user access and promptly revoking unnecessary permissions helps enforce the principle of least privilege and reduces potential attack surfaces. Entra ID should serve as the centralized identity and access management solution, providing secure authentication, role-based access control, and comprehensive auditing capabilities.

- **Enable advanced threat protection alerts**: The module for advanced threat detection that Defender for Databases offers can monitor you to be aware of, for instance, SQL injections, suspicious login attempts, data exfiltration, and abnormal behavior.

  To ensure a timely response to security events, set up email notifications and forward alerts to Microsoft Sentinel or another SIEM solution for centralized monitoring. For high-severity alerts, clearly defined incident response procedures are important to guide effective actions. Automating playbooks for repetitive detections helps streamline remediation efforts, reduce manual workload, and improve response consistency.

- **Enable auditing and retain logs for compliance**: Auditing offers insight into the database activities such as user logins, updates of permissions, changes to schema, and data read/writes. Ensure you enable auditing and keep logs for compliance, forensic, and anomaly detection.

  To ensure proper logging and compliance, logs should be stored in a secure, immutable storage location such as Azure Storage or Log Analytics to prevent tampering. Microsoft Purview can be used to enhance data governance and provide advanced auditing capabilities across stored logs. It is also important to implement log retention policies aligned with regulatory or organizational compliance requirements, such as retaining logs for 90 days, one year, or longer as needed.

- **Use Private Endpoint and firewalls to restrict access**: To eliminate unwanted traffic, security configurations like Private Endpoint, firewall rules, and virtual network service endpoints can be used. This will help you be sure that only the verified networks or applications are allowed to connect to your database.

  To strengthen network security for Azure resources, public network access should be disabled unless absolutely necessary, minimizing exposure to external threats. Access should be limited to specific IP ranges or trusted VNets to enforce controlled connectivity. NSGs and Azure Firewall should be used to implement additional network segmentation and perform deep traffic inspection, ensuring only authorized traffic can reach the resources.

- **Patch and update database engines regularly**: Using outdated database engines might lead to an increased risk of vulnerabilities to exploit. As such, make sure you frequently patch all self-hosted databases (IaaS) and on-premises SQL servers.

  Staying current with Microsoft security advisories is essential to remain informed about emerging threats and vulnerabilities. To maintain a secure environment, automate patching in test systems first and validate updates thoroughly before deploying them to production. For SQL Servers running on virtual machines, Azure Update Management can be leveraged to streamline the patching process, ensuring timely and consistent updates across the environment.

- **Encrypt data in transit using TLS**: Ensure all your database connections are approved to use TLS to avoid spying and man-in-the-middle attacks. Forcing the applications and databases to encrypt communications requires TLS 1.2 or higher.

- **Classify and label sensitive data**: Use Microsoft Purview or the features of built-in SQL classification to identify, label, and classify sensitive data. It helps apply access controls, audit access to classified data and generates compliance reports.

Microsoft Defender for Containers

The attack surface grows as more companies use containerized workloads because of their scalability and agility. This creates new security issues concerning runtime threats, image vulnerabilities, and container orchestration. Traditional security methods frequently fall short when it comes to visibility and control over transient container environments. Microsoft Defender for Containers protects containerized workloads operating on AKS, **Azure Container Instances** (**ACI**), and even hybrid and multi-cloud Kubernetes setups.

Defender for Containers helps organizations build, deploy, and manage containers securely from development to production with capabilities ranging from image scanning, cluster hardening, threat detection, and runtime protection. Integrated with Microsoft Defender for Cloud, it provides security insights and policy recommendations, helping teams enforce best practices and respond to risks quickly across containerized environments.

Overview of Defender for Containers

Defender for Containers, designed to secure the entire container lifecycle, protects self-hosted Kubernetes clusters, AKS, and ACI. It works closely with Kubernetes and enables both agent-based and agentless methods to monitor cluster configurations, network traffic, node behaviors, and container runtime activity.

Key coverage includes the following:

- **AKS Clusters**: Defender provides full-stack security for managed Kubernetes clusters, covering both the control plane and worker nodes.
- **ACI**: Lightweight containers in ACI are monitored for anomalous behavior and potential threats.
- **On-premises or multi-cloud Kubernetes**: With Azure Arc-enabled Kubernetes support, Defender extends protection to non-Azure environments, ensuring a consistent security posture.

Enabling Defender for Containers

Defender for Containers can be enabled from **Settings** inside the Defender for Cloud portal, as shown in *Figure 8.6*:

Onboard environments

Select subscriptions | Select plans | Review and generate

Plan	List price	Billable resources	Status
Servers	Plan 2 ($15 Server/Month)	0	On
App service	$15 Instance/Month	0	On
SQL Databases	$15 Server/Month	0	On
SQL servers on machines	$15 Server/Month	0	On
Open-source relational databases	$15 Server/Month	0	On
Azure Cosmos DB	$0.0012 per 100RU/s per hour	0	On
Storage	$10 Storage account/Month	0	On
Containers	$6.8693 VM core/Month	0	On
AI workloads	Free (preview)	0	On
Key vault	$0.25 Vault/Month	0	On

***Figure 8.6**: Enabling Defender for Containers*

Key features of Defender for Containers

Microsoft Defender for Containers is a cutting-edge security solution designed for the cloud and is primarily for containerized environments. It safeguards the entire lifecycle of containers, starting from image creation and cluster configuration to runtime protection, thus guaranteeing the containers used in AKS, ACI, and self-hosted or multi-cloud Kubernetes clusters are unassailable against the ever-evolving threats.

The following are the key features of Defender for Containers:

- **Image vulnerability scanning**: Defender for Containers works with ACR and other registries to check container images for known vulnerabilities such as out-of-date packages, incorrect settings, and unsafe components. This solution assists in the shift security left approach by identifying risks upstream in the CI/CD pipeline, thus diminishing the opportunities for insecure workloads being deployed to production.

- **Kubernetes cluster hardening recommendations**: The solution checks the configuration of all AKS and Kubernetes clusters with regard to best practices as put forward by the industry and the CIS benchmarks. It makes the cluster more secure by RBAC-based recommendations, public exposure limiting, and securing the control plane access.

- **Runtime threat detection**: Defender for Containers monitors container behavior in real-time, detecting signs of compromise like unexpected process executions, access to sensitive files, or attempts to escape container boundaries. It uses behavioral analytics and threat intelligence to reveal fileless malware and zero-day attacks.

- **Network traffic monitoring**: The solution inspects east-west (pod-to-pod) and north-south (external) traffic all the time, thus aiding in the detection of unusual communication patterns, potential command-and-control traffic, and lateral movement in the cluster. Integration with Microsoft Defender for Cloud improves the visibility of network risks across workloads.

- **RBAC and identity monitoring**: The Defender scans the Kubernetes RBAC configurations that can identify over-privileged users, insecure bindings, or service accounts misused. This lowers the risk of identity-based attacks or privilege escalation inside the cluster.

- **Agent-based and agentless deployment options**: Organizations have the liberty to select between agent-based (Defender agent installed on nodes) for deep monitoring or agentless options for faster deployment and simplified management, offering flexibility based on operational requirements and compliance needs.

- **Multi-cloud and hybrid Kubernetes protection**: By the utilization of Azure Arc-enabled Kubernetes, Defender for Containers allows the security to include the on-cloud as well as on-premises, AWS, and Google Cloud Kubernetes clusters, maintaining the same level and quality of protection in different environments, whether they are hybrid or multi-cloud.

- **Integration with DevOps workflows**: Having the integration with Azure DevOps, GitHub Actions, and third-party CI/CD tools, Defender allows security scanning of the container images at their build stage; hence, vulnerable containers will not be promoted to production environments.
- **Integration with Microsoft Sentinel**: Defender for Containers, besides sending alerts, also sends logs to Microsoft Sentinel by correlating them for hazardous threats, incident investigations, and automated responses. Security teams can also prepare custom-built analytics rules and playbooks to enhance container threat hunting.
- **Compliance and posture management**: The solution also examines the container and Kubernetes configuration metrics in order to follow the applicable laws and policies, besides providing insights on expired terms, actionable tasks needed to be carried out, and Plans for compliance reporting.

Best practices of Defender for Containers

To get the most out of Microsoft Defender for Containers' security features, businesses should follow best practices that make sure their Kubernetes and containerized processes are better protected, monitored, and in line with regulations.

The listed practices help keep the container process safe, from building to running, by using controls that stop problems before they happen, keeping an eye on things constantly, and following the rules:

- **Azure Policy to enforce Kubernetes security standards**: Use Azure Policy to audit and enforce security best practices across AKS clusters. Azure Policy can validate configurations like disabling privileged containers, restricting public exposure, and enforcing RBAC controls. This helps maintain cluster hygiene and compliance with internal or external security standards such as CIS benchmarks.

  To enforce governance and security in Azure Kubernetes environments, use built-in policy initiatives like Kubernetes cluster baseline standards to apply recommended configurations by default. For organization-specific needs, custom policies can be deployed to address unique compliance or operational requirements. Depending on the enforcement strategy, these policies can be configured in audit mode to monitor compliance or in deny mode to block non-compliant deployments outright.

- **Regularly scan container images in ACR**: You can connect Defender for Containers to Azure Container Registry to check container images for vulnerabilities immediately when pushed or at regular intervals. This keeps unsafe images from getting into production and lets devs fix problems early in the process.

  To maintain a secure container deployment pipeline, ensure that all ACR sources are configured for vulnerability scanning. By implementing pipeline gates, deployments can be halted if images contain high or critical security vulnerabilities, preventing insecure code from reaching production. Integrating vulnerability scanning as a mandatory step in the CI/CD process helps identify and address security issues early in the development lifecycle, reinforcing DevSecOps best practices.

- **Enable network policies to control traffic between pods**: Implement Kubernetes network policies to limit communication between pods to only what is necessary. This reduces the risk of lateral movement in case a pod is compromised and helps segregate workloads by environment, tier, or sensitivity.

  To enforce secure communication within Kubernetes environments, use namespaces and labels to clearly define and manage traffic rules between workloads. Applying Zero Trust networking principles ensures tight control over network flows. Monitoring pod-to-pod communication patterns with Defender for Containers network analytics provides visibility into unexpected behaviors, helping to detect and respond to potential threats effectively.

- **Enforce RBAC**: Limit access within Kubernetes using RBAC rules to ensure users and service accounts operate with the least privilege. Regularly audit roles, bindings, and permissions to prevent privilege escalation or misused identities.

  To maintain strong access controls in Kubernetes clusters, avoid using cluster-wide roles unless absolutely necessary, as they grant broad permissions that can increase security risk. Integrating Entra ID enables centralized identity management and enforces consistent access policies across environments. Regular audits of role bindings should be conducted using Defender for Containers' identity insights, ensuring that permissions are appropriate and aligned with the principle of least privilege.

- **Enable runtime threat detection**: Make sure runtime monitoring is enabled to detect abnormal behaviors, such as unexpected process executions, anomalous network connections, or attempts to access host-level resources. Defender for Containers uses behavioral analysis and threat intelligence to alert you to real-time container-based attacks.

  To maintain a proactive security posture, it is important to investigate and respond to alerts without delay, minimizing potential damage from security incidents. Integrating with Microsoft Sentinel enables automated incident response and provides comprehensive SIEM capabilities, allowing for efficient detection, correlation, and remediation of threats across the environment.

- **Harden AKS node pools and base images**: Keep AKS node pools updated with the latest security patches and ensure container base images are hardened and minimal to reduce attack surfaces.

  To enhance the security of containerized workloads in (AKS), avoid running containers as root or privileged users, as this reduces the attack surface and limits potential damage from compromised containers. Use distroless images or minimal base images like Alpine Linux to reduce vulnerabilities and keep container footprints lightweight. Enabling auto-upgrade for AKS node pools helps ensure that the cluster infrastructure stays up to date with the latest security patches and performance improvements.

- **Secure CI/CD pipelines**: Protect your DevOps workflows by securing your CI/CD pipelines, where containers are built and deployed. To secure the software supply chain in containerized environments, implement secure credentials management using services like Azure Key Vault to protect secrets and sensitive data. Incorporate scanning steps into CI/CD pipelines, such as static code analysis and container image scanning, to detect vulnerabilities early in the development process. Enforce the use of signed and verified images through content trust to ensure only trusted artifacts are deployed, mitigating the risk of tampered or malicious components entering production.
- **Limit container capabilities**: Define and restrict Linux capabilities in container specs to limit what containers can do. Removing unneeded privileges helps reduce the blast radius of potential exploits.

  To reduce security risks in Kubernetes workloads, avoid assigning the **`CAP_SYS_ADMIN`** capability to containers unless it is necessary, as it grants broad system-level privileges that can be exploited. Instead, use **Pod Security Admission** (**PSA**) to enforce privilege boundaries by defining and applying security standards across pods, ensuring workloads adhere to least-privilege and compliance requirements.
- **Regularly review Defender for Containers alerts and recommendations**: Monitor and act on alerts generated by Defender for Containers. Use the Microsoft Defender for Cloud dashboard to identify trends, threat patterns, and misconfigurations.

  To maintain a strong security posture, prioritize high-severity findings identified by Defender for Containers to address the most critical risks first. Follow Defender's guided remediation recommendations to resolve issues efficiently and in alignment with best practices. For streamlined response and accountability, integrate these findings with your organization's incident management systems to ensure proper tracking, assignment, and closure of security issues.
- **Use immutable infrastructure principles**: Deploy containers as immutable artifacts—rather than patching or modifying them in production, replace them with updated versions built through a secure and tested pipeline.

Microsoft Defender for App Service

Attacks like SQL injection, XSS, remote code execution, and privilege escalation are common on web apps. Strong application-level security is becoming more critical as businesses put more business-critical apps in the cloud. Microsoft Defender for App Service is a cloud-native security solution that keeps web apps hosted on Azure App Service safe from threats by constantly watching, finding threats, and giving security advice that can be used.

This service, which is integrated with Microsoft Defender for Cloud, assists enterprises in identifying vulnerabilities, spotting malicious activities, and defending against threats that target platform dependencies, environment parameters, and app code. It supports a variety of web frameworks and languages, including .NET, Java, Python, PHP, and Node.js, that are frequently used in App Services. Organizations that require automated attack responses and visibility into application-layer vulnerabilities without compromising app availability or performance will find Defender for App Service especially helpful.

Overview of Defender for App Service

Defender for App Service helps in the security of web applications, APIs, and mobile backends built on Linux and Windows, delivered on Azure App Service. It continuously monitors the underlying infrastructure and application behavior to scan unusual activity, and exploitation attempts that target the file system, network connections, and application runtime.

Key threats detected by Defender for App Service are as follows:

- Remote code execution attempts
- Unexpected file changes or uploads
- Web shell deployments
- Behavior consistent with C2 activity
- Attacks on vulnerable third-party packages or dependencies

It also offers practical suggestions for resolving setup problems such as insecure HTTP settings, obsolete components, or excessive permissions.

Enabling Defender for App Service

Defender for App Service can be enabled from **Settings** inside the Defender for Cloud portal, as shown in *Figure 8.7*:

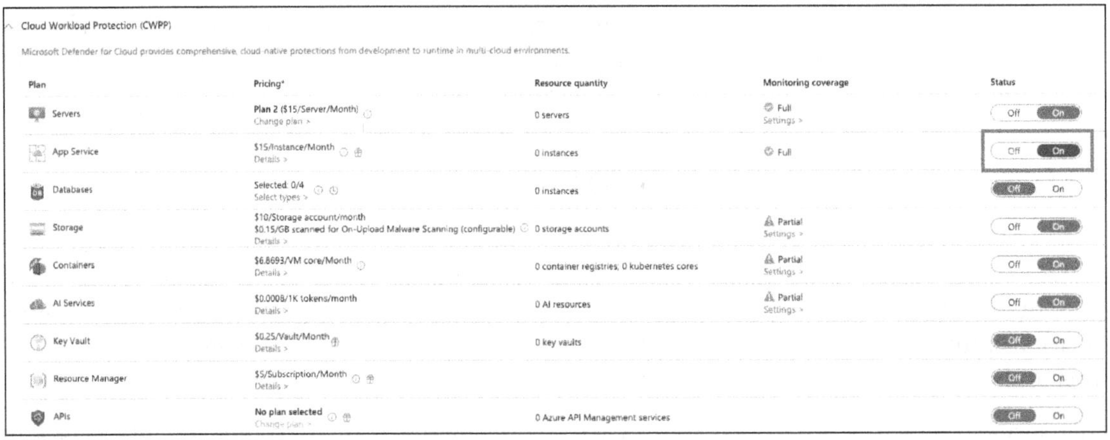

Figure 8.7: Enabling Defender for App Service

Key features of Defender for App Service

Microsoft Defender for App Service is a very innovative application with a lot of security features for web applications hosted on Azure App Service. It has a combination of tools specifically for threat identification, detection of misconfiguration, and enabling proactive response.

These tools serve as a lifeguard for the flight of the cloud's security, especially for a web application exposed on the internet or handling personal information:

- **Threat detection**: Defender for App Service conducts real-time web application threat monitoring of your applications by alerts such as web shell uploads, remote code execution attempts, and suspicious process behaviors. The product application uses various technologies, including machine learning, behavioral analytics, and Microsoft Threat Intelligence, to find abnormal and common attack patterns that target the application's environment. These enable teams to discover possible breaches earlier, thus reducing damage, response time, and improving the result.
- **Custom alerts**: Defender for App Service has built-in features for detection, but it also has an additional warning function that can be customized based on how your app works, how it is designed, and how dangerous it is. In Azure Monitor or Microsoft Sentinel, clients can make their own alerting rules. This lets security respond in a unique way to certain endpoints, APIs, or user actions. This gives you the freedom to make sure that the alerts are useful and accurately reflect the dangers that each app faces.
- **Vulnerability scanning**: Defender for App Service endlessly monitors the application environment for security concerns, probing for configuration errors, unsafe settings, unjustified perms, and old items. Some issues it finds are publicly exposed endpoints, the enforcement of HTTPS, or the weak authentication policy, and it offers guidance on how to remediate these identified issues to secure the application infrastructure.
- **Integration with Microsoft Sentinel**: The Defender for App Service application connects directly with Microsoft Sentinel. This means that you can correlate security incidents at multiple levels and perform centralized incident investigations and automated playbooks that help security teams find out about and respond to attacks quickly and more efficiently than ever.
- **Web shell detection and script analysis**: The service comes with a unique feature that detects web shells and malicious scripts; the most commonly used tools are taken over the web app by hackers after a successful attack. Defender for App Service checks for unexpected script executions and file modifications during the monitoring process, and thus, it can catch exploitation attempts very fast.
- **Platform-aware insights**: As a part of the integrated environment in the Azure platform, Defender for App Service has many contextual features. These include app-

specific resource affected alerts, request metadata, user identity, and recommended remediation steps, which streamline the investigation and incident response.

Best practices of Defender for App Service

Organizations should implement best practices that enhance application security and facilitate early threat detection in order to optimize the protections offered by Microsoft Defender for App Service.

The following methods provide ongoing visibility into possible threats across web apps hosted on Azure App Service and lessen the attack surface:

- **Enforce HTTPS for all applications**: Ensure all web traffic is encrypted in transit by enforcing HTTPS-only communication. This protects data from interception or tampering and is especially critical for apps handling authentication, financial transactions, or personal data.

  To ensure secure communication in Azure App Services, enable the **HTTPS Only** setting to enforce encrypted connections by default. Additionally, configure automatic redirection of all HTTP requests to HTTPS to maintain consistency and prevent unencrypted access. For managing SSL/TLS certificates securely, use App Service Certificates or integrate with Azure Key Vault to automate certificate provisioning, renewal, and protection.

- **Enable Managed Identity**: Use Managed Identities for Azure Resources to enable secure, passwordless authentication between App Service and other Azure services like Key Vault, Storage Accounts, and Azure SQL Database.

  To enhance application security in Azure, avoid hardcoding credentials or connection strings directly in your app code, as this exposes sensitive information to potential leaks. Instead, leverage system-assigned or user-assigned Managed Identities to securely authenticate to Azure services without storing secrets. When assigning resource permissions, apply the principle of least privilege using Azure RBAC to ensure each identity has only the necessary access for its intended operations.

- **Regularly monitor application logs**: Enable and review logs from App Service diagnostics, including HTTP request logs, error logs, and audit trails. This helps detect unexpected behaviors, such as spikes in traffic, unauthorized access attempts, or injection attack patterns.

  To gain comprehensive visibility into application behavior and security, enable App Service Diagnostics, Azure Monitor, and Log Analytics for centralized log collection and analysis. Integrate these logs with Microsoft Sentinel to leverage advanced threat detection, correlation, and incident response capabilities. Configure alerts for anomalous patterns such as repeated failed login attempts or access from unfamiliar geolocations to detect and respond to potential threats in real time.

- **Keep platform and frameworks updated**: Ensure your application stack, including language runtimes, frameworks, and dependencies, is kept up to date to avoid exposure to known vulnerabilities.

  To maintain secure application deployments, integrate automated vulnerability scanning tools into your CI/CD pipeline to identify and remediate issues early in the development cycle. Enable Defender for App Service vulnerability assessments to receive platform-level security insights and recommendations. Regularly rebuild and redeploy applications to ensure that the latest security patches and updates are incorporated, reducing exposure to known vulnerabilities.

- **Restrict app access with IP restrictions and authentication**: Limit access to your app by configuring IP restrictions, service endpoints, or Private Endpoint. For public-facing apps, implement Entra ID authentication, OAuth, or other identity providers.

  To secure Azure App Services, implement Access Restrictions to limit incoming traffic based on specific IP addresses or subnets, effectively controlling who can reach the application. Ensure authentication is required for all users, including those accessing internal admin interfaces, to prevent unauthorized access. For enhanced identity-based security, enable Conditional Access policies to enforce additional controls such as multi-factor authentication or location-based restrictions.

- **Enable alerting for high-risk behaviors**: Configure Defender for App Service to raise alerts for events such as web shell uploads, remote code execution attempts, or unexpected outbound calls.

  To streamline incident detection and response, regularly review alerts generated in Microsoft Defender for Cloud and route them to Microsoft Sentinel or your organization's SIEM for centralized visibility. For high-priority incidents, implement automated playbooks that can take immediate action, ensuring swift and effective mitigation of potential threats.

Microsoft Defender for Key Vault

Secrets, encryption keys, and certificates are the backbone of secure operations in the cloud. They can provide attackers with direct access to sensitive systems and data if compromised. Microsoft Defender for Key Vault offers intelligent threat protection for Azure Key Vault, ensuring that secrets are securely stored and actively monitored against misuse and malicious access attempts.

Microsoft Defender for Cloud has a built-in feature called Defender for Key Vault that lets you find threats, analyze user behavior, and monitor Key Vault access in real-time. It helps businesses stop and deal with bad behavior like mass secret extraction, illegal access, and brute-force attacks. It lets you monitor user behavior and talk to Azure-native tools like Microsoft Sentinel to set up preventative and investigative security controls that are important to protect the privacy, integrity, and availability of data.

Overview of Defender for Key Vault

Azure Key Vault is a resource that stores private keys and manages secrets in the cloud. Defender for Key Vault is made to keep the secrets, keys, and certificates inside safe. The service scans how your keys are being used, looking for patterns and anomalies that could mean an attack or misuse.

Key threats detected include the following:

- Unusual or excessive access to secrets or keys
- Access from unfamiliar IP addresses or geographies
- Access attempts by users or services that do not typically interact with the vault
- Possible credential misuse or automation abuse
- Mass secret retrieval attempts indicate potential exfiltration

Defender for Key Vault sends out detailed security alerts that include information about the resource accessed, who requested it, when it was accessed, and what should be done next. You can send these reports to Microsoft Sentinel to match them with other cloud security events.

Enabling Defender for Key Vault

Defender for Key Vault can be enabled from **Settings** inside the Defender for Cloud portal, as shown in the following figure:

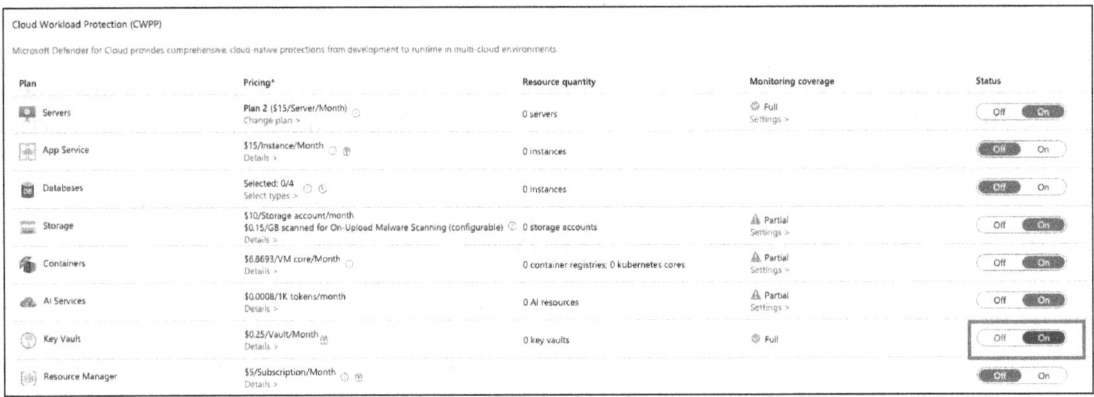

Figure 8.8: Enabling Defender for Key Vault

Key features of Defender for Key Vault

For secrets, encryption keys, and certificates kept in Azure Key Vault, Microsoft Defender for Key Vault protects them from smart threats. It helps businesses find out about odd behavior, keep private data safe, and keep track of who is accessing their files.

The following are key features that make Defender for Key Vault a critical component of workload protection in Azure:

- **Anomalous access detection**: Defender for Key Vault constantly checks trends of access to find strange or unexpected attempts to log in. This includes entries from IP addresses, locations, or identities that are not usually linked to the vault. It helps find possible misuse of credentials, insider risks, or identities that have been stolen.
- **Threat intelligence integration**: The service uses Microsoft's global threat intelligence to show when someone tries to reach a known malicious domain or IP address. This kind of proactive monitoring helps stop attacks like key theft, token abuse, and privilege escalation, especially when they are still in their early stages.
- **Real-time alerting and incident context**: Defender for Key Vault sends out detailed security alerts when threats are found. These alerts include who entered the vault, when, what operation was done, and whether the access was normal or not. For quick incident reaction, these alerts give you insights you can act on and instructions on how to fix things.
- **Integration with Microsoft Sentinel and SIEM tools**: Alerts can be easily added to Microsoft Sentinel or other SIEM platforms, which lets businesses connect Key Vault behavior with more significant security events happening in the cloud. This makes it easier to look into incidents and supports automated response processes.
- **Monitoring high-value operations**: The service focuses on sensitive tasks like getting secrets, encrypting and decrypting keys, making certificates, and changing access policies. This makes sure that acts that could compromise the privacy and integrity of protected data can be seen.
- **Minimal performance overhead**: As a native, agentless solution, Defender for Key Vault introduces no performance degradation to Key Vault operations. It works passively in the background without requiring code or infrastructure changes.
- **Alerts for secret exfiltration and abuse patterns**: Defender identifies patterns consistent with mass secret downloads, brute-force key access attempts, or the use of the vault in ways that deviate from normal usage. These behaviors may indicate malware activity, insider misuse, or automation went rogue.

Best practices of Defender for Key Vault

The following best practices should be used by organizations to get the most out of Microsoft Defender for Key Vault and make their secrets, keys, and certificates safer.

The following recommendations help reduce the risk of unauthorized access, support regulatory compliance, and ensure proper key lifecycle management across environments:

- **Enable logging for all Key Vault activities**: Enable Azure Monitor diagnostic logs and Azure Activity Logs for all Key Vaults to maintain an audit trail of operations, such as secret access, key usage, and policy changes.

  To ensure effective monitoring of Azure Key Vault, stream logs to centralized destinations such as Log Analytics, Storage Accounts, or Event hubs for collection and long-term retention. Integrate these logs with Microsoft Sentinel or another SIEM to correlate Key Vault events with broader security signals across the environment. Regularly reviewing these logs helps identify unauthorized access attempts, unusual usage patterns, and potential security threats, enabling timely investigation and response.

- **Use separate Key Vault instances for development and production**: To enforce isolation and reduce the risk of accidental exposure, maintain separate Key Vaults for development, testing, and production environments.

  To protect sensitive information in Azure Key Vault, apply strict access controls to production vaults, granting access only to essential personnel and trusted services. Ensure that test scripts or automation from development and test environments are isolated and cannot inadvertently access secrets stored in production. Implement consistent naming conventions and tagging policies to clearly distinguish between vaults across environments, reducing the risk of misconfiguration or accidental access.

- **Regularly rotate secrets and keys**: Implement automatic or scheduled rotation of secrets and encryption keys to minimize the impact of potential exposure.

  To maintain strong security hygiene and minimize the risk of credential compromise, use Azure Key Vault's built-in key rotation policies for supported key types. Automate the rotation of secrets using Azure Functions or Logic Apps to ensure they are updated regularly without manual intervention. Additionally, implement mechanisms to notify dependent services of updated secrets promptly, preventing application downtime due to stale or expired credentials.

- **Implement least privilege access with RBAC or Access Policies**: Grant only the minimum required permissions to users, applications, and services interacting with Key Vault.

  To securely manage access to Azure Key Vault, use Azure RBAC or Vault Access Policies based on your vault's configuration, ensuring fine-grained control over permissions. Regularly audit access permissions to identify and remove stale or over-permissioned identities that could pose security risks. For services accessing the Key Vault, leverage Managed Identities instead of embedding credentials in code, promoting secure and streamlined authentication without exposing sensitive information.

- **Restrict public network access**: Reduce exposure by disabling public access to Key Vault and using Private Endpoint to allow access only from within your trusted virtual networks.

To secure Azure Key Vault at the network level, set **Public network access** to **Disabled** to prevent exposure to the public internet. Enforce access through trusted and controlled environments by integrating the vault with a VNet. For additional protection, combine this setup with firewall rules and NSGs to establish a layered security model that tightly controls traffic to and from the vault.

- **Monitor for anomalous and high-risk access patterns**: Leverage Defender for Key Vault alerts to detect abnormal behaviors, such as mass secret access, unfamiliar IPs, or access at odd hours.

  To ensure timely detection and response to security threats, set up automated alerting and incident response workflows using Microsoft Sentinel. When high-severity alerts are triggered, investigate them immediately and take appropriate actions such as revoking access permissions or regenerating secrets to contain potential breaches and protect sensitive assets.

- **Use CMK for greater control**: For workloads with stringent compliance or encryption requirements, use Customer-Managed Keys stored in Azure Key Vault to control encryption at rest for services like Azure Storage, Azure SQL, and AKS.

  To maintain the integrity and availability of your cryptographic infrastructure, regularly rotate CMKs and actively monitor their usage for unusual or unauthorized activity. Additionally, enable soft delete and purge protection on your Azure Key Vault to safeguard against accidental or malicious deletion of keys, ensuring critical cryptographic material can be recovered if needed.

Microsoft Defender for Resource Manager

The ARM layer is the control plane for Azure. It lets users and services set up, handle, and provision cloud resources. Since this level is where all resource management tasks are performed, any breach here can have numerous effects, such as unauthorized launches, changes to the setup, or even switching between services. Microsoft Defender for Resource Manager is a security program that keeps an eye on this critical control plane to find and report any actions that might be harmful or unauthorized.

Defender for Resource Manager works with Microsoft Defender for Cloud to give you real-time insight into operations at the resource level. This helps protect your business from threats like stolen credentials, wrong configurations, insider threats, or automation abuse. It is a key part of IaC standards to keep the governance and orchestration layer of the Azure environment safe.

Overview of Defender for Resource Manager

Defender for Resource Manager secures the ARM control plane, which deploys and manages all Azure resources, including VMs, storage accounts, databases, networking components, and more. To find suspicious changes, unauthorized deployments, or odd access patterns, it continually scans writing activities (PUT, POST, DELETE) throughout the environment.

Common threats and behaviors monitored include the following:

- Modification or deletion of critical resources like Key Vaults, role assignments, etc.
- Deployment from unfamiliar locations or IP addresses
- Usage of service principals or identities that typically do not interact with specific resources
- Excessive or abnormal write operations in a short timeframe
- Tampering with resource configurations or policies

Defender for Resource Manager uses Microsoft Threat Intelligence and behavioral analytics to generate alerts that include rich contexts, such as the operation performed, user identity, timestamp, and remediation guidance. It integrates with Microsoft Sentinel, allowing teams to correlate control plane events with other environmental signals for improved incident response.

Enabling Defender for Resource Manager

Defender for Resource Manager can be enabled from **Settings** inside the Defender for Cloud portal, as shown in the following figure:

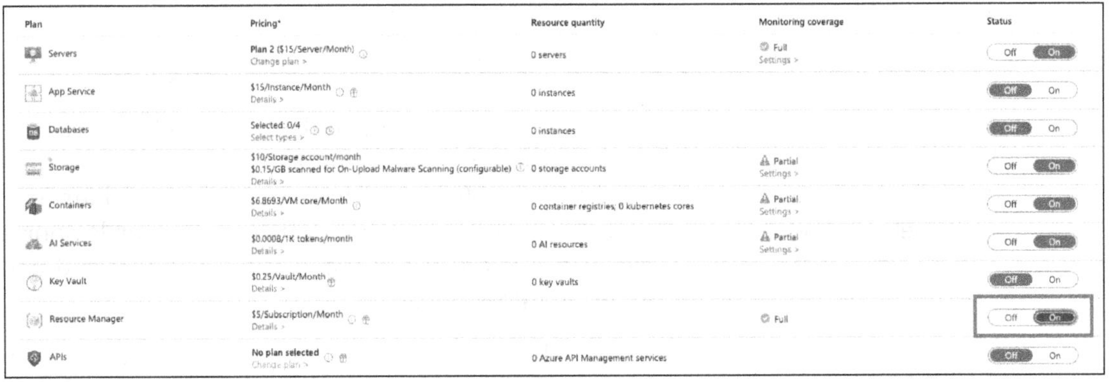

Figure 8.9: *Enabling Defender for Resource Manager*

Key features of Defender for Resource Manager

Microsoft Defender for Resource Manager is the protective resource that keeps Azure control plane secure by tracking and securing the operations that are done through ARM. ARM controls the ways that resources can be created, changed, and removed, so it is very important to the integrity of your cloud environment.

The following are the key features that make Defender for Resource Manager a critical component in workload protection:

- **Activity monitoring**: Defender for Resource Manager continuously monitors control plane activity across Azure subscriptions, tracking **create, read, update, and delete** (**CRUD**) operations. It helps detect unusual patterns in resource changes and provides detailed audit trails for investigation and compliance.
- **Azure Activity Logs**: They provide comprehensive visibility by detecting changes in resource configurations, policy assignments, role bindings, and network settings across your environment. They monitor actions performed through various interfaces, including the Azure Portal, CLI, PowerShell, SDKs, and ARM templates, ensuring consistent tracking of administrative activities. These logs offer detailed insights into who performed what action, when it occurred, and from where, supporting effective auditing, compliance tracking, and security investigations.
- **Threat detection**: Using Microsoft Threat Intelligence and behavioral analytics, Defender identifies unauthorized or suspicious changes to Azure resources.

  Microsoft Defender for Cloud continuously monitors your environment for suspicious behaviors by flagging unexpected deployments, privilege escalations, and unusual API calls. It detects activities originating from unfamiliar IP addresses, geographies, or previously unseen service principals, helping to identify potential threats early. The system also raises alerts for high-risk actions such as changes to role assignments, resource deletions, or the disabling of critical security controls, enabling rapid response to potential security incidents.
- **Compliance enforcement**: Defender ensures that resource configurations comply with organizational policies and governance standards.
- **Microsoft Defender for Cloud**: It helps maintain security posture by identifying configuration drift from established security baselines, ensuring that resources remain aligned with organizational standards. It supports audit readiness by flagging policy violations, missing tags, and other compliance issues that could impact regulatory reporting. Working in conjunction with Azure Policy and Azure Blueprints, it enforces governance controls across your environment, enabling consistent and automated compliance management.
- **Integration with Microsoft Sentinel and SIEM tools**: Defender integrates with Microsoft Sentinel and third-party SIEMs to enhance security operations.

  Microsoft Sentinel enhances cloud security by enabling the correlation of alerts with other activities and incidents across your environment, providing a unified view of threats. It supports custom analytics rules and interactive security dashboards, allowing organizations to tailor detection and monitoring to their specific needs. Additionally, Sentinel automates incident response through playbooks and alert-driven workflows, improving response times and reducing the manual effort required to contain and remediate threats.

- **Visibility into control plane activity across subscriptions**: Defender provides centralized insight into control plane actions across all Azure subscriptions and management groups.

  Microsoft Sentinel helps detect cross-subscription activity anomalies, making it easier to identify suspicious behavior that spans multiple Azure environments. It enables broader analysis of attack propagation patterns, allowing security teams to trace and understand complex threat movements. By centralizing monitoring and response, Sentinel also supports consistent governance and oversight across large-scale environments, improving both security posture and operational efficiency.

Best practices of Defender for Resource Manager

By implementing these best practices, organizations can significantly enhance the security of the Azure control plane, which governs all resource management operations. Defender for Resource Manager not only provides deep visibility into infrastructure changes but also serves as a crucial enforcement layer for governance, compliance, and threat detection.

Combined with monitoring, least-privilege access controls, and policy-driven governance, the following practices help maintain a secure cloud environment, reducing the risk of misconfigurations and unauthorized activity:

- **Use Azure Policy to enforce resource configurations**: Azure Policy helps ensure resources are deployed and managed in alignment with organizational standards and compliance requirements.

  Azure Policy allows you to define and assign policies that enforce organizational standards such as naming conventions, tagging requirements, region restrictions, and allowed resource types. By using policy initiatives (policy sets), you can group related policies to enforce broader compliance goals, such as security baselines or regulatory frameworks. To maintain consistency and reduce manual intervention, non-compliant resources can be automatically remediated using policy effects like **DeployIfNotExists**, ensuring alignment with your governance model.

- **Regularly audit resource activities and permissions**: Periodic reviews of control plane actions and access rights help identify potential misconfigurations, over-permissioned roles, or unauthorized changes.

  To enhance security and detect potential threats, regularly analyze activity logs for unusual write operations or unexpected permission changes that could indicate unauthorized access. Leverage Entra ID PIM to manage just-in-time access and periodically review role assignments, ensuring that elevated permissions are granted only when necessary and for a limited duration. For deeper investigation and context, cross-reference activity logs with alerts from Defender for Resource Manager, enabling a more comprehensive view of suspicious administrative actions across your Azure environment.

- **Enable alerts for suspicious activity**: Configure Defender for Resource Manager to raise alerts for actions that may indicate misuse or threats at the control plane level.

  To protect your Azure environment from high-risk actions, continuously monitor for activities such as disabling security controls, deleting critical resources, or modifying role assignments. Integrate these alerts with Microsoft Sentinel or another SIEM to enable automated investigation and response, streamlining incident handling. Additionally, apply alert tuning to reduce false positives and ensure that your security operations team can focus on high-impact anomalies that require immediate attention.

Microsoft Defender for DNS

The **Domain Name System** (**DNS**) is a fundamental part of any network, translating domain names into IP addresses and enabling communication between services. In cloud environments, DNS traffic can be a rich telemetry source for detecting malicious activity, such as C2 communications, phishing, **domain generation algorithm** (**DGA**) activity, and data exfiltration attempts. To stop such threats from going undetected, Microsoft Defender for DNS, a cloud-native threat security solution, assists in monitoring, analyzing, and defending DNS activity within Azure settings.

Defender for DNS, which is incorporated into Microsoft Defender for Cloud, employs machine learning and Microsoft's Threat Intelligence to detect anomalous DNS query patterns, which are flagged as connections to the domains that are known to be malicious and inform the security teams of dubious activity that could be indicative of early-stage sabotage. Such an improvement in the knowledge of the methods of DNS attacks permits organizations to take preventive and prompt measures to deal with intrusions.

Overview of Defender for DNS

The main task of the Defender for DNS app is to find and protect DNS data coming from Azure resources, like virtual machines and services that use custom DNS setups in a virtual network or Azure's DNS. This program keeps a look at DNS queries. The trends it finds are based on the total number of queries it records and the target addresses of those queries. It may then notify an administrator of an unauthorized query or redirect traffic to another hostname and route. Based on cloud intelligence, the system examines millions of DNS queries to identify hidden malware, tunnelling techniques, and contacts that should not be there.

Key threats and activities it helps in detecting include the following:

- DNS tunnelling is often used for command-and-control communications or secret data exfiltration.

- Connections to known malicious domains, flagged via Microsoft's Threat Intelligence feeds.
- Unusual query volumes indicating botnet activity or misconfigured systems.
- Requests to suspicious or non-resolvable domains, which may signal beaconing or domain generation algorithm usage.

Defender for DNS generates security alerts with rich telemetry, including the resource initiating the query, the queried domain, the timestamp, and suggested remediation actions. These alerts can be surfaced in Microsoft Defender for Cloud or forwarded to Microsoft Sentinel for deeper analysis, correlation, and automated incident response workflows.

Enabling Defender for DNS

Customers having a current Defender for DNS subscription can keep utilizing the service as of August 1, 2023. Defender for Servers P2 will notify new subscribers, though, of questionable DNS activity.

Defender for DNS can be enabled from **Settings** inside the Defender for Cloud portal, as shown in *Figure 8.10*:

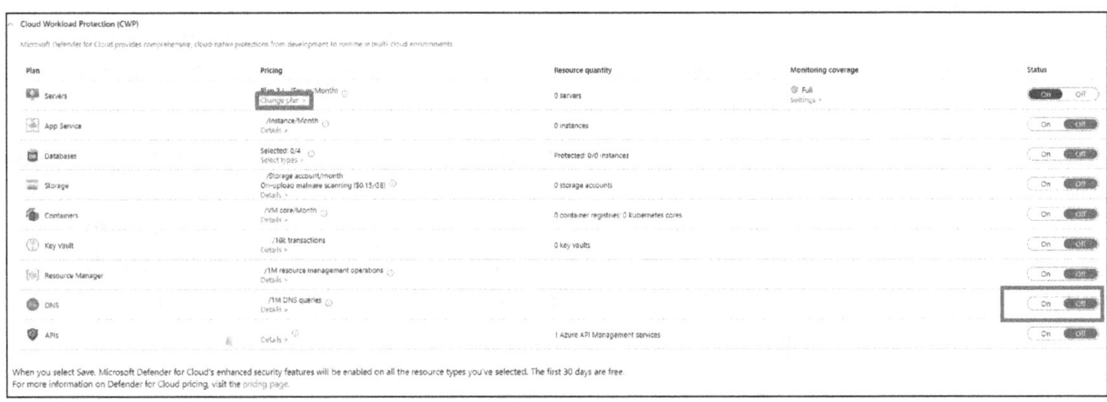

***Figure 8.10**: Enabling Defender for DNS*

Key features of Defender for DNS

Microsoft Defender for DNS is a cloud-native threat detection solution that helps protect your Azure environment by monitoring DNS for suspicious activity. Since DNS is one of the most abused protocols in cyberattacks, for example, in C2 communications, DNS tunnelling, and domain spoofing, securing this layer is critical.

The following are the key features of Defender for DNS:

- **Threat detection**: Defender for DNS scans for unwanted domain lookups and blacklisted IPs using Microsoft's Threat Intelligence and behavioral analytics.

Microsoft Defender for DNS enhances threat detection by identifying connections to known malicious domains, including those used for phishing, malware distribution, or C2 servers. It also detects domain queries linked to botnets, crypto-mining operations, and ransomware activity. When suspicious activity is observed, Defender generates alerts enriched with context such as the requesting resource, the time of the activity, and recommended remediation actions, enabling faster and more informed incident response.

- **Anomalous query detection**: Defender continuously analyzes DNS query patterns to detect unusual spikes, repeated queries to non-existent domains, or high-entropy domain names, which may indicate attempts to bypass traditional detection.

  Microsoft Defender for DNS provides advanced threat detection by flagging rare or algorithmically DGAs, which are often used by evasive malware to avoid detection. It also identifies DNS tunneling behaviors, where DNS queries are exploited to exfiltrate data or establish covert communication channels. Additionally, Defender helps uncover misconfigured or potentially compromised workloads that generate abnormal DNS traffic, enabling security teams to investigate and respond to threats more effectively.

- **Integration with Azure Firewall**: Defender for DNS integrates with Azure Firewall and Firewall Premium features, enabling deep packet inspection, DNS proxy capabilities, and threat intelligence filtering.

  Azure Firewall DNS Proxy enhances DNS-level protection by blocking known malicious **fully qualified domain names** (**FQDNs**) directly at the firewall layer, stopping threats before they reach internal resources. It supports DNS logging and analytics, providing enriched context to Microsoft Defender alerts for more accurate threat detection. Additionally, it integrates with DNS Proxy to route and inspect DNS queries from spoke virtual networks through a central firewall, enabling centralized visibility and control over DNS traffic across your environment.

- **SIEM and Sentinel integration**: Defender for DNS integrates with Microsoft Sentinel, providing correlated insights across DNS, network, and endpoint layers.

  Integrating DNS insights with Microsoft Sentinel enables centralized alerting, investigation, and automated response workflows, streamlining the detection and handling of DNS-based threats. Security analysts gain the ability to trace DNS anomalies back to specific virtual machines, services, or users across the cloud environment, providing valuable context for faster root cause analysis and incident resolution.

- **No agent deployment required**: Defender for DNS is an agentless solution, natively built into the Azure platform.

Azure DNS threat protection is easy to enable across virtual networks, whether you are using Azure-provided DNS or custom DNS solutions, with traffic routed through Azure Firewall or DNS Private Resolver. It operates at the network layer, ensuring that DNS traffic is inspected without any performance impact on workloads, thereby maintaining security without compromising efficiency.

- **Full visibility into DNS activity across virtual networks**: Defender for DNS provides detailed visibility into DNS queries and resolution patterns for resources in Azure, which is critical for detecting stealthy attacks that often use DNS as a primary vector.

Best practices of Defender for DNS

Organizations can improve their network security, find DNS-based threats early, and ensure the integrity of internal name resolution services by using Microsoft Defender for DNS in line with best practices. DNS is often used for attacks like C2 contact, data theft, and domain spoofing, so it is essential to keep it safe and keep an eye on it all the time.

The following are the best practices for Defender for DNS:

- **Use private DNS zones for internal domains**: Azure Private DNS Zones are what you need to manage private domain names. It makes sure that name resolution only happens on your virtual networks and not on the public internet, where you do not want private domains to show up. Hub-and-spoke networks let private zones be linked across spokes for clean and centralized DNS control.
- **Monitor DNS logs**: DNS logs are often overlooked, but they can be gold when it comes to spotting odd behavior. Enable diagnostics and look for things like frequent failed lookups, access to weird or random-looking domains, or sudden spikes in traffic. These could be signs of malware trying to beacon out or exfiltrate data.
- **Connect Defender for DNS to Microsoft Sentinel**: Sending your DNS logs and alerts to Microsoft Sentinel helps you to see the larger picture by connecting DNS events to what is occurring all over your endpoints, identities, and cloud services. With playbooks such as blocking domains or isolating a VM, you can create custom dashboards, configure high-risk activity criteria, and even automate reactions.
- **Route DNS through Azure Firewall or DNS Proxy**: Do not let DNS traffic run loose. Use Azure Firewall with DNS Proxy enabled so you can inspect, control, and block traffic at the network edge. Combine this with threat intelligence-based filtering to stop known bad domains in their tracks before they cause damage.
- **Limit who can talk to DNS servers**: Not every service or VM has to contact the DNS resolver. Lock items down using NSGs or Firewall policies. Especially if an attacker is attempting to exfiltrate data or create a backchannel, this helps stop compromised devices from contacting outside domains.

- **Tune your alerts**: Defender for DNS does a good job surfacing threats, but you will still want to tune your alerts regularly. Not every anomaly is worth waking the team for. Categorize what is normal for your environment so that real threats stand out.
- **Consider blocking suspicious domains**: If there are domains you know are bad or even just shady, do not wait for an alert. Set up DNS blocking or sinkholing to redirect traffic from those domains to a safe endpoint for further analysis or to cut it off entirely.

Conclusion

Workload security in the cloud constantly necessitates proactive threat detection, tiered defense mechanisms across all infrastructure components, and ongoing monitoring. This chapter examined how the workload protection services offered by Microsoft Defender for Cloud provide thorough, integrated security for various Azure resources, including servers, Storage, databases, containers, web apps, secrets, and the control plane itself.

Whether for Servers, Storage, Databases, Containers, App Services, Key Vaults, Resource Managers, or DNS, each Defender strategy has a distinct function in protecting its workload against contemporary threats. They work together to create a unified defense approach that tackles security from both a workload-centric and platform-centric standpoint. In addition to real-time threat detection and mitigation, these solutions offer actionable insights, hardening suggestions, and enhanced incident response interaction with SIEM and SOAR technologies like Microsoft Sentinel.

By using the best practices and guiding principles described in this chapter, organizations can lower their attack surface, react quickly to threats, and guarantee adherence to industry standards.

In the next chapter, we will shift focus to security monitoring, covering threat detection, incident response, and the use of Microsoft Sentinel and Log Analytics for real-time visibility and investigation.

Join our Discord space

Join our Discord workspace for latest updates, offers, tech happenings around the world, new releases, and sessions with the authors:

https://discord.bpbonline.com

Chapter 9
Security Monitoring

Introduction

In this chapter, you will learn skills to master securing Azure resources and operations through security monitoring. You will learn security event monitoring with Azure Monitor. You will explore a cloud-based SIEM solution using Microsoft Sentinel, in which you will learn to configure data collection, perform analytics, hunting, and response automation. To conclude the chapter, you will explore Traffic Analytics.

Structure

This chapter contains the following topics:

- Azure Monitor
- Microsoft Sentinel
- Traffic Analytics

Objectives

This chapter aims to equip readers with the knowledge and skills to monitor and secure Azure environments through effective security monitoring practices. Readers will learn how to use Azure Monitor for tracking security-related events, configure and operationalize Microsoft

Sentinel as a cloud-native SIEM for threat detection and response, and utilize Traffic Analytics to visualize and analyze network traffic flows for enhanced security insights.

Azure Monitor

Knowing resource performance, availability, and security in a cloud-native environment is very significant. Azure monitoring is centered on Azure Monitor, a single channel that constitutes the key to collecting and evaluating telemetry data in networking, settings, and apps.

Overview of Azure Monitor

Azure Monitor is a service for monitoring that enables the optimization of service performance and availability. Additionally, it provides advanced notification of issues impacting the two primary service categories or your resources. It utilizes data from several channels, including virtual machines, containers, and operating systems, to ascertain the customization sources.

The platform supports two primary data types:

- **Metrics**: Numerical values that describe aspects of a system at a particular point in time (e.g., CPU usage, request rates, IOPS).
- **Logs**: Structured data records that capture events, traces, and diagnostics across services.

The key benefits of the platform are as follows:

- **End-to-end visibility**: Monitor what is happening at every level, from infrastructure to applications, using a single monitoring tool.
- **Customized workbooks and dashboards**: Make custom visualizations to keep track of KPIs or look into specific scenarios.
- **Advanced alerting**: Set thresholds for metric or log-based alerts and use Azure Logic Apps or Functions to make automated steps happen.
- **Integrated diagnostics**: Access diagnostics logs and performance counters in real time to help fix and analyze incidents.
- **Integrations**: It works with Microsoft Defender for Cloud, Microsoft Sentinel, Azure Automation, and other ITSM or SIEM tools without any issues.

Azure Monitor homepage

The following *Figure 9.1* shows the Azure Monitor Overview page, specifically highlighting the Insights section. Azure Monitor provides a centralized interface to track the health and performance of your Azure resources. This section offers curated monitoring views designed for specific resource types.

For example, Application Insights lets users keep an eye on web apps in real-time, showing them performance, errors, and how users are interacting with them. Container insights lets you see a lot more about Kubernetes settings by keeping an eye on the controllers, nodes, and containers' health and performance. Monitoring virtual machines and VM scale sets is what VM insights does best. It helps administrators look at performance data, figure out problems, and understand how things depend on each other. Network insights gives you a full picture of the health and functioning of different parts of your network. This helps you fix problems and make the most of your network's resources. Have a look at the following figure for your reference:

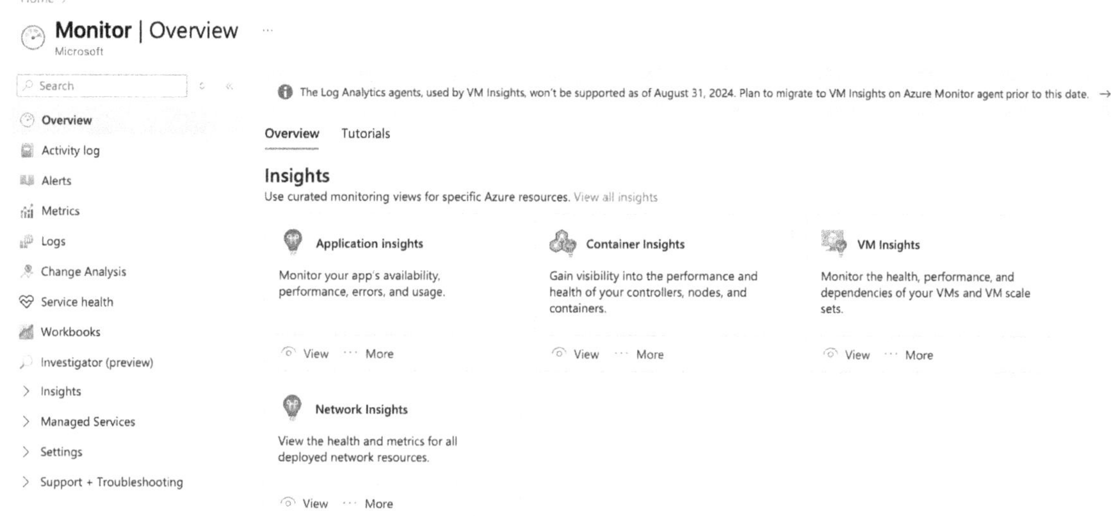

***Figure 9.1**: Azure Monitor homepage*

The upcoming *Figure 9.2* covers the detection, triage, and diagnosis tools available in Azure Monitor. These tools enable users to visualize, analyze, and respond to operational data and events across their Azure environments. The Metrics section lets users build custom charts to monitor resource utilization and performance trends. Alerts can be configured to trigger notifications based on predefined conditions, supporting proactive incident response. Logs provide powerful diagnostic capabilities through query-based analysis of activity and performance data. The **Workbooks** feature allows for the creation and sharing of rich, interactive reports that combine text, charts, and log data. **Change Analysis** is particularly useful for incident investigations, as it helps identify recent modifications that could have caused issues. The **Diagnostic Settings** section is used to route monitoring data to destinations such as Log Analytics, Event hubs, or Storage Accounts for long-term analysis and retention. Additionally, there are options for more advanced or hybrid scenarios: Azure Monitor SCOM managed instance extends monitoring to on-premises environments, and Managed Prometheus collects metrics from containerized workloads using the popular Prometheus framework.

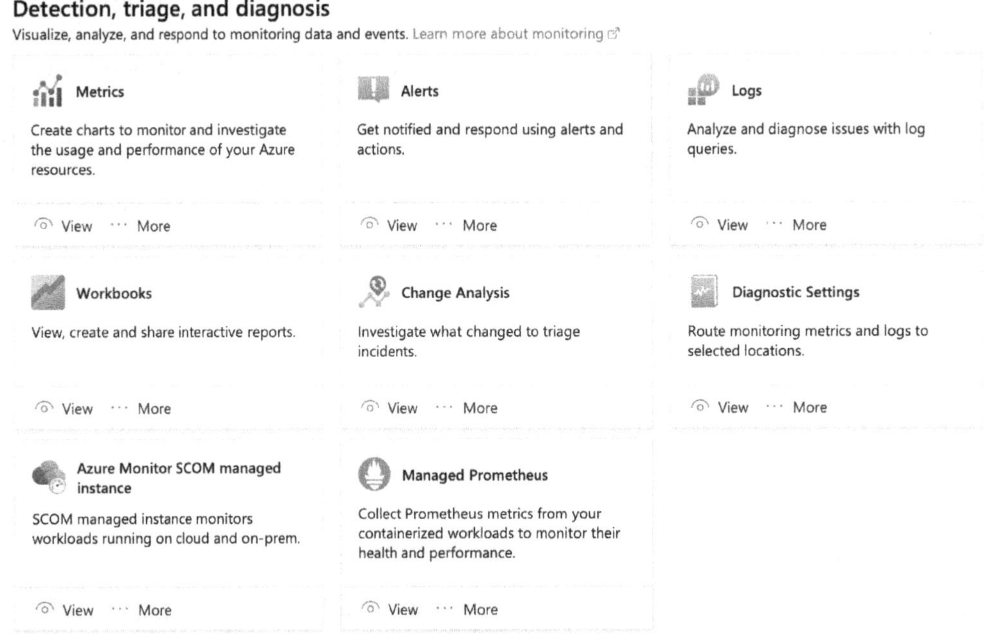

Detection, triage, and diagnosis
Visualize, analyze, and respond to monitoring data and events. Learn more about monitoring
Metrics
Create charts to monitor and investigate the usage and performance of your Azure resources.
View ··· More
Alerts
Get notified and respond using alerts and actions.
View ··· More
Logs
Analyze and diagnose issues with log queries.
View ··· More
Workbooks
View, create and share interactive reports.
View ··· More
Change Analysis
Investigate what changed to triage incidents.
View ··· More
Diagnostic Settings
Route monitoring metrics and logs to selected locations.
View ··· More
Azure Monitor SCOM managed instance
SCOM managed instance monitors workloads running on cloud and on-prem.
View ··· More
Managed Prometheus
Collect Prometheus metrics from your containerized workloads to monitor their health and performance.
View ··· More

Figure 9.2: Various options in Azure Monitor

Together, these sections of Azure Monitor provide a comprehensive toolkit for maintaining visibility, performance, and reliability across your entire Azure ecosystem.

Azure Monitor uses a **Log Analytics** workspace to process and capture the logs. *Figure 9.3* depicts a sample Log Analytics workspace:

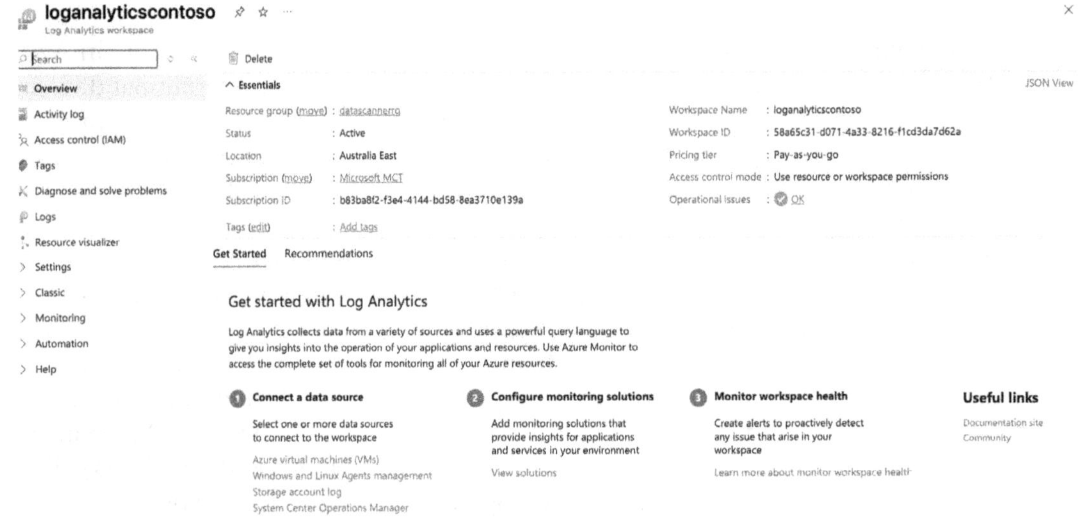

Figure 9.3: Sample Log Analytics workspace

Key features of Azure Monitor

A crucial element of cloud security is the recognition of security incidents. Azure Monitor facilitates collecting, analyzing, and responding to security information from many organizations' sources. This enhances the overall security of the environment.

The following are its core capabilities:

- **Log Analytics**: Log Analytics is the heart of data analysis in Azure Monitor. It collects telemetry and diagnostic data from various sources, such as Azure resources, on-premises machines, and other cloud environments, and stores it in a Log Analytics workspace. Users can write queries using **Kusto Query Language** (**KQL**) to identify trends, investigate anomalies, and correlate security or operational events across environments.
- **Metrics monitoring**: Azure Monitor gets numerical information from the resources it monitors nearly in real time. Metrics like CPU usage, disc IOPS, and request delay are often used to send alerts, keep track of SLAs, and find performance bottlenecks. Since metrics are designed to be easily accessible and visually appealing, they work well for dashboards and quick insights.
- **Alerts**: Alerts that are based on metrics or logs can both be set up in Azure Monitor. These alerts can be set off by fixed levels, dynamically set baselines, or certain event patterns. When the alerts are set off, they can do things like send emails, call Log Apps, use webhooks, or start auto-scaling to adapt to changing tasks.
- **Application Insights**: Application Insights is an **Application Performance Management** (**APM**) service part of Azure Monitor. It enables deep monitoring of live applications, collecting data such as request rates, failure rates, dependency calls, and response times. It provides end-to-end transaction tracing, user behavior insights, and innovative diagnostics to help developers detect, triage, and fix issues rapidly.
- **Workbooks**: Workbooks offer rich interactive reporting and visualization for monitoring data. Users can build custom dashboards to visualize trends, KPIs, and drill-downs across logs and metrics. Workbooks support dynamic parameters, making them useful for both troubleshooting and executive reporting.
- **Diagnostic settings**: Diagnostic settings lets you send platform logs and data from Azure resources to places like Log Analytics, Event hubs, or Storage Account. This lets the data be stored for a long time, processed later, or connected to other SIEM systems.

  Administrators can enable diagnostic settings using the Azure Portal, ARM templates, Azure CLI, or PowerShell. This ensures that logs from critical resources are consistently routed to centralized destinations like Log Analytics for analysis, compliance, and long-term retention.
- **Autoscale**: Resource autoscaling based on monitored metrics is supported by Azure Monitor. App Services and virtual machine scale sets, for instance, can automatically

modify the number of instances to meet demand, enhancing productivity and cost control.

Security event monitoring in Azure Monitor

Another important part of cloud security is being aware of security events. Azure Monitor lets organizations gather, examine, and act on security data from a variety of sources. This helps keep the Azure environment secure in general.

The following are the key components involved in security event monitoring:

- **Activity Logs**: Azure Activity Logs show system-level operations carried out on Azure resources. Control-plane changes, such as resource creation, deletion, updates, role assignments, and policy evaluations, are covered in these logs. Activity logs are helpful for auditing and governance purposes because security teams frequently use language like who did what and when to succinctly explain periods and actors within the environment.

- **Diagnostic Logs**: Diagnostic Logs offer detailed, resource-specific telemetry and operational data. These logs are generated by individual Azure services such as Key Vault, Azure SQL, App Gateway, and Storage Accounts and provide in-depth visibility into the data plane operations (e.g., read/write access, authentication attempts, configuration changes). They can be streamed to Log Analytics, Event hubs, or Storage Accounts for retention and analysis.

- **Integration with SIEM**: Azure Monitor enables smooth integration with SIEM solutions, especially Microsoft Sentinel, to perform advanced correlation, threat detection, and response. Logs collected by Azure Monitor can be forwarded to Sentinel for rule-based detection, behavioral analytics, and incident creation, improving your ability to detect and respond to sophisticated threats across hybrid environments.

- **Resource health and security alerts**: Azure Monitor provides built-in health checks and alerts for security-impacting events. It can detect anomalies like sudden spikes in traffic, unauthorized access attempts, or failing compliance checks, triggering real-time alerts for faster incident response.

- **Log retention and archiving**: Security-relevant logs can be retained long-term for forensic investigations, compliance audits, and historical trend analysis. Azure Monitor allows the export of logs to Azure Storage for archival purposes and integration with external audit tools.

- **RBAC integration**: Access to log data can be governed using Azure RBAC, ensuring only authorized personnel can view or query sensitive security telemetry. This ensures separation of duties and helps maintain compliance with the least privilege access models.

Best practices of Azure Monitor

Implementing security monitoring is not just about enabling services—it is about doing so in a way that maximizes visibility, minimizes blind spots, and supports a strong incident response posture.

The following are some best practices to follow when using Azure Monitor and integrating it with other security tools:

- **Enable Diagnostic Logs for all critical Azure resources**: Ensure that diagnostic settings are enabled on all production and sensitive Azure resources, including Key Vaults, Storage Accounts, App Gateways, Virtual Machines, and Azure SQL Databases. Route these logs to Log Analytics or Microsoft Sentinel for analysis and alerting.
- **Configure custom alerts for high-priority events**: Do not rely solely on default alerts. Define custom alert rules for critical security events such as failed login attempts, privilege escalations, resource deletions, unusual outbound traffic, or changes to NSGs.
- **Use Log Analytics queries to identify unusual patterns or activity**: Build and regularly review KQL queries to detect signs of compromise or misconfiguration, such as sudden spikes in activity, access outside business hours, or geographic anomalies in authentication events.
- **Centralize logs into a single Log Analytics workspace**: Configure all related subscriptions and resource groups to send logs to a centralized Log Analytics workspace for better manageability and correlation. This simplifies cross-resource monitoring and reduces data silos.
- **Set RBAC for monitoring data**: Apply least-privilege access controls to log data using RBAC. Only authorized teams (e.g., SecOps or compliance teams) should be able to query sensitive security logs.
- **Regularly review and update monitoring rules**: Security threats evolve. Periodically audit and update your monitoring rules, alert thresholds, and diagnostic configurations to ensure they align with current risks and compliance requirements.
- **Leverage Workbooks for visualization and reporting**: Use Azure Monitor Workbooks to create customized dashboards and reports that visualize security data for different audiences, security analysts, engineers, and management.
- **Integrate with Microsoft Sentinel for advanced threat detection**: Forward logs to Microsoft Sentinel to leverage its built-in analytics rules, threat intelligence, and SOAR capabilities for a more advanced, automated response strategy.
- **Archive Logs for long-term retention and compliance**: For organizations under regulatory requirements, configure log retention policies and archive logs to Azure Storage for extended periods, which are helpful for audits and forensic investigations.

Microsoft Sentinel

Modern cloud systems produce enormous quantities of security-relevant data. Therefore, a centralized platform to correlate, analyze, and react to threats in real-time is vital. Combining SIEM and SOAR features, Microsoft Sentinel satisfies this demand by offering an intelligent, scalable, and integrated solution. From a single Azure interface, it enables security teams to identify sophisticated threats, investigate issues quickly, and respond quickly.

Overview of Microsoft Sentinel

Microsoft Sentinel is a cloud-based solution for SOAR and SIEM. It offers threat intelligence and sophisticated security analytics throughout the organization. Sentinel's agility and scalability allow enterprises to consume, examine, and respond to vast amounts of data from Azure, hybrid, and multi-cloud environments.

The following are some of its key features:

- **Data collection at cloud scale**: Microsoft Sentinel ingests security data from multiple sources—including Azure resources, on-premises environments, Microsoft 365, AWS, firewalls, endpoint solutions, and more—using pre-built data connectors. All collected data is stored in a Log Analytics workspace, making it easy to search, correlate, and visualize.

- **Built-in analytics and detection rules**: Sentinel includes predefined analytics rules to detect common threats, such as brute-force attacks, lateral movement, and credential theft. These rules use KQL queries under the hood and can be customized to match your organization's environment and risk posture.

- **AI-driven threat detection**: With Microsoft's Threat Intelligence and machine learning models, Sentinel identifies complex and emerging threats that traditional rule-based systems might miss. It also correlates low-fidelity signals across data sources into high-confidence security incidents.

  For example, Sentinel detected a coordinated brute-force attack against Entra ID sign-ins. The incident was raised when multiple failed attempts from different IPs occurred in a short period. The security team was alerted, and a predefined playbook automatically disabled the targeted user accounts, reducing response time and minimizing risk.

- **Investigation and hunting tools**: Sentinel provides graph-based investigation tools to explore the root cause and scope of incidents. Analysts can also perform proactive threat hunting using built-in or custom queries, workbooks, and notebooks based on KQL or Jupyter.

- **Automated response with Playbooks**: Sentinel integrates with Azure Logic Apps to automate alert responses. These playbooks can perform actions like deactivating compromised accounts, sending incident reports, creating tickets in ITSM systems, or notifying response teams in Microsoft Teams.

- **Workbooks and dashboards**: Use Sentinel workbooks to create custom dashboards that visualize key metrics, alerts, and threat trends. Both SOC analysts and executives can use these dashboards to overview the security posture.
- **Integration with Microsoft Defender for Cloud**: Sentinel integrates effortlessly with Microsoft Defender for Cloud to enrich incidents with security recommendations, vulnerability data, and contextual threat intelligence, improving visibility and remediation efforts.
- **Scalable and pay-as-you-go model**: Sentinel uses a pay-per-GB ingestion pricing model with options to reserve capacity for cost savings. This makes it flexible and scalable for organizations of all sizes.

Microsoft Sentinel homepage

The upcoming image showcases the Microsoft Sentinel overview page within the Azure portal. Microsoft Sentinel is a cloud-native SIEM and **Extended Detection and Response** (**XDR**) solution. It is designed to help organizations detect, investigate, and respond to threats across their digital estate. The overview page offers a centralized experience where security teams can gain immediate insights into their environment. The banner at the top promotes the integration of SIEM and XDR capabilities within the Microsoft Defender portal, which enhances security operations with embedded Security Copilot, an AI-powered assistant.

On the left-hand navigation pane, users can access a wide range of features and tools under categories such as Logs, Incidents, Workbooks, Hunting, and Threat Intelligence. This panel is designed to help analysts quickly find relevant data, investigate threats, and build detection rules. For instance, the Incidents section aggregates security alerts and groups them into incidents for triage and response, while Automation allows users to create and manage playbooks that help automate responses to security threats.

The page also indicates that the user is viewing the new overview experience, with an option to toggle back to the previous interface. This new layout aims to improve the visibility and accessibility of critical features by streamlining the dashboard. The empty states in the incidents and automation tiles suggest that no new incidents or automated actions have occurred in the last 24 hours, which can help analysts quickly assess whether further investigation is necessary.

Overall, the Microsoft Sentinel Overview page serves as the launchpad for security operations, combining AI, automation, and real-time analytics to empower security teams in defending their environments more effectively.

The following is an overview of the Sentinel homepage:

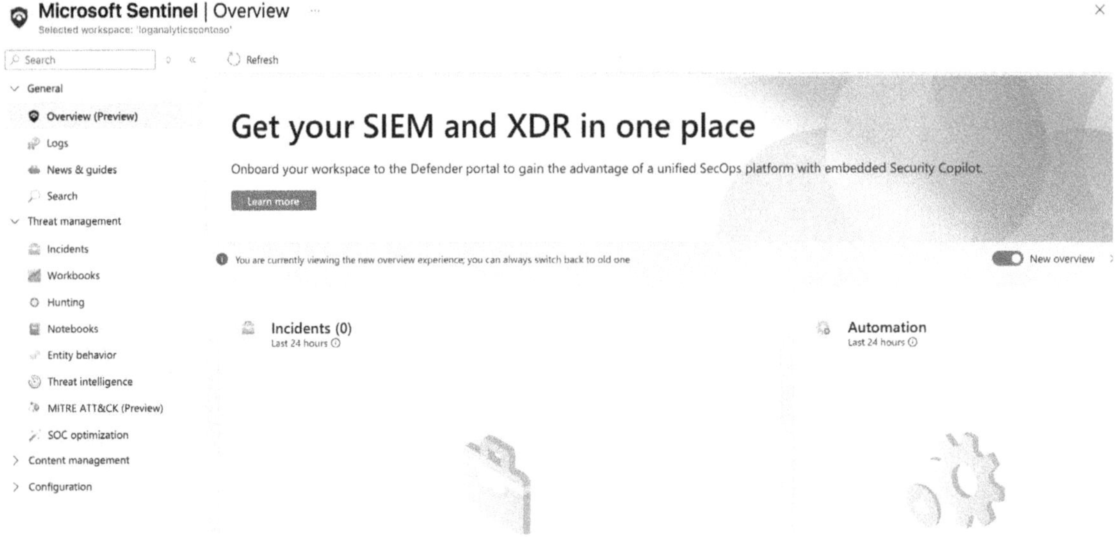

Figure 9.4: *Microsoft Sentinel*

The preceding image displays the Log Analytics workspace overview page for Microsoft Sentinel, showcasing the foundational layer that enables Sentinel to collect, analyze, and query log data. This workspace is named sentinelworkspacecontoso and is part of the DataScannerRG resource group, located in the Australia East region. It is currently in an active state and operating under a pay-as-you-go pricing tier. Log Analytics workspaces like this are critical to Microsoft Sentinel as they act as the storage and processing hub for all ingested data, allowing security teams to run queries, visualize data, and detect threats.

At the top of the page, key metadata about the workspace, such as the workspace ID, subscription details, tags, and access control settings, is displayed.

The **Get Started with Log Analytics** section at the bottom provides an onboarding guide for new users. It outlines the three fundamental steps to effectively leverage the workspace:

- **Connect a data source**: This is done by connecting different services, like Azure virtual machines, storage accounts, Windows/Linux agents, or **System Centre Operations Manager** (**SCOM**), so that telemetry data can flow into the workplace.
- **Configure monitoring solutions**: Users can use predefined monitoring solutions that are suited to certain services or workloads, which gives them more information and alerts.
- **Monitor workspace health**: This step focuses on proactive health tracking, making sure that users can use alert rules and built-in health dashboards to find and fix any problems in their environment.

Log Analytics for Sentinel

Following is a sample Log Analytics workspace that will ingest logs from resources, and then Sentinel uses the logs from this workspace:

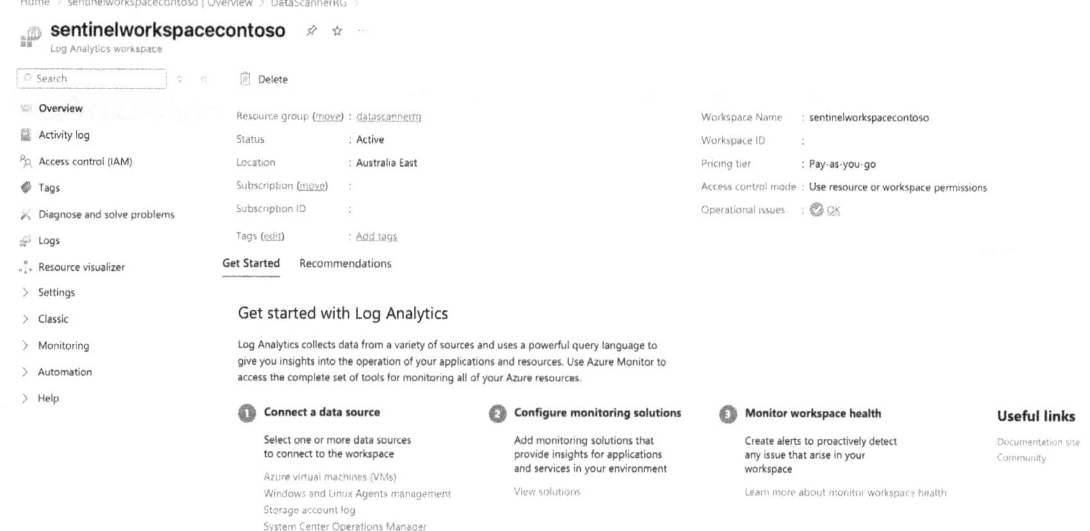

Figure 9.5: Log Analytics workspace used by Sentinel

Key features of Microsoft Sentinel

Microsoft Sentinel offers a rich set of capabilities that enable security teams to detect, investigate, and respond to threats effectively. Its combination of cloud-scale data collection, intelligent analytics, and automation makes it a vital component of any modern security operations strategy.

Here are the key features of Microsoft Sentinel:

- **Data collection**: Sentinel integrates with various data sources, including Azure services, Microsoft 365, AWS, third-party security solutions, firewalls, identity providers, and on-premises systems. It provides over 100 built-in data connectors for services like Palo Alto Networks, Fortinet, Symantec, and CheckPoint. This centralized data ingestion enables a complete and unified view of the security landscape.
- **Analytics**: Sentinel uses built-in analytics rules that apply machine learning and behavioral analysis to detect threats and anomalies across your environment. These rules can identify known attack patterns, suspicious activity, and multi-stage attacks. Analysts can customize or build new rules tailored to the organization's threat landscape. Incidents are generated by grouping related alerts for better context and reduced noise.

- **Hunting**: Sentinel supports proactive threat hunting using KQL. Analysts can craft custom queries to search across large datasets for evidence of suspicious behavior or indicators of compromise. Sentinel also offers built-in hunting queries and integrates with notebooks for advanced threat hunting using Python and Jupyter.
- **Automation**: Incident response using playbooks built on Azure Logic Apps can be automated. These playbooks can trigger actions such as disabling user accounts, isolating machines, creating service tickets, or sending alerts to teams through Microsoft Teams or email. Automation improves response speed, reduces manual effort, and ensures consistent handling of incidents.
- **Investigation graphs**: Sentinel lets you investigate by using graphs to show how things like IP addresses, people, and devices are connected. The scope of an attack and its path through the world can be quickly seen with these graphs.
- **Workbooks and dashboards**: Users can make interactive dashboards that show alerts, trends, hunting results, and success indicators with customizable workbooks. Security experts, management, or compliance teams can use these dashboards to keep an eye on the organization's security and report on it.
- **Threat intelligence integration**: Sentinel supports the import of threat intelligence indicators like IP addresses, file hashes, and domains. These can be correlated with existing data to detect known malicious activity and prioritize investigation based on threat context.
- **User and entity behavior analytics (UEBA)**: Sentinel leverages behavioral analytics to detect deviations from regular user and entity behavior patterns. This helps surface insider threats, account compromise, and unusual access patterns that may go unnoticed.

Configuring data collection in Microsoft Sentinel

Microsoft Sentinel's ability to find threats and monitor them starts with collecting the right data. Sentinel gives you several different ways to connect to sources in the cloud, on-premises, and outside sources to ensure that your whole system is covered.

The following outlines how to configure data collection for optimal visibility:

- **Connectors**: Sentinel provides many built-in connectors to integrate with various data sources. These connectors make it easy to ingest security data from Azure services (such as Entra ID, Key Vault, and Defender for Cloud), Microsoft 365, and third-party platforms like AWS, GCP, Palo Alto Networks, Cisco, Fortinet, and others.

  In the setup wizard for each connector, you usually need to give people access, choose log types, and set up a destination Log Analytics workspace. The **Common Event Format** (**CEF**), Syslog, or REST APIs can be used to set up custom log ingestion on systems that do not have a built-in connector.

- **Log ingestion**: Logs from different sources are imported into a central Log Analytics workspace after connections are set up. This includes audit logs, network logs, login data, and security alerts, among other things. Sentinel can send data in almost real time, which lets threats be found quickly.

  For hybrid or on-premises infrastructure, agents such as the Azure Monitor Agent or legacy Log Analytics Agent can collect and forward logs to Sentinel. Additionally, Event hubs can route large volumes of telemetry data for custom or third-party use cases.

- **Data normalization**: To ensure that logs from diverse sources are meaningful and actionable, Sentinel normalizes data into a standard schema. This makes it easier to query, correlate, and analyze information across different platforms.

  Sentinel uses the **Advanced Security Information Model** (**ASIM**) to standardize key types like DNS logs, authentication events, and network sessions. This consistency improves the reliability of analytics rules, hunting queries, and incident correlation across multiple data sources.

- **Validation and testing**: It is important to make sure the logs are received properly after setting up the data connectors. To see the types of logs, how often they happen, and field maps in Log Analytics, you can use sample KQL searches. This step makes sure that the data can be used for analytics and automation.

- **Access and governance**: Apply RBAC at the workspace level to make sure that only authorized users can log data. This helps people follow the rules for protecting personal data and keeps data private.

Threat hunting and response automation in Microsoft Sentinel

Microsoft Sentinel gives security teams the tools they need to find threats by using automated analytics to look for complex attacks and make responding to incidents faster and easier.

This dual approach enhances the effectiveness of **Security Operations Centers** (**SOCs**) by reducing response time, improving threat visibility, and minimizing manual workloads through the following components:

- **KQL**: Sentinel uses KQL to query log data stored in Log Analytics. Security experts can write their own queries to look for signs of compromise (IOCs), notice odd behaviour from users, find sideways movement, or find patterns of attacks. KQL is powerful and flexible, and it can do things like joins, aggregations, time series analysis, and regular expressions.

  Sentinel provides a library of built-in hunting queries to get started, which can be modified or extended to fit an organization's specific threat landscape.

- **Workbooks**: Workbooks are customizable dashboards that help visualize the results of hunting queries, monitor key security metrics, and track incident trends. Analysts can use them to create interactive views of sign-in failures, alert heatmaps, unusual traffic sources, or threat actor activity. Workbooks support dynamic filters and parameters, allowing security teams to drill down into specific data or pivot between dimensions, making investigations quicker and data-driven.
- **Playbooks**: Playbooks are automated workflows built using Azure Logic Apps. Sentinel alerts or incidents can trigger them to perform predefined response actions, such as isolating a machine in Microsoft Defender for Endpoint, resetting a user's password, sending alerts to a SOC channel in Microsoft Teams, or updating incident tickets in a service management system. By automating repetitive or time-sensitive tasks, playbooks improve response consistency, reduce analyst workload, and help contain threats before they escalate.
- **Incident management**: Sentinel groups related alerts into incidents, providing a consolidated view of an attack chain. Security analysts can assign incidents, track status (e.g., New, Active, Closed), add comments, and collaborate within the Sentinel console. This enables structured investigations and reduces alert fatigue by correlating low-fidelity signals with meaningful security events.
- **Notebook integration**: Sentinel supports integration with Jupyter Notebooks for advanced analysts and data scientists. These allow combining KQL, Python, and Markdown to create sophisticated hunting and investigative workflows. Notebooks are ideal for advanced correlation, hypothesis testing, and documenting hunting processes.
- **Watchlists**: Sentinel supports watchlists, which are custom lists of data such as IP ranges, user IDs, or asset tags that can be referenced in detection rules or hunting queries. These are especially useful for tracking known malicious indicators or VIP users.

Best practices of Microsoft Sentinel

To get the most out of Microsoft Sentinel's threat hunting and automated response, you need to make sure that your detection logic, hunting strategy, and automation workflows stay in sync with your changing security needs and threat environment, through the following methods:

- **Regularly review analytics rules for relevance and effectiveness**: You should review your rules regularly to ensure they are still relevant to current threats and business risks. Turn off old rules, tweak limits to reduce false positives, and change the logic to fit how your organization works. Use the Microsoft and Sentinel GitHub community's analytics rule examples as a starting point on which to build.
- **Use threat intelligence feeds to enhance detection capabilities**: Integrate internal and external threat intelligence feeds, such as those from Microsoft, ISACs, or third-

party providers. Enrich alerts and hunting queries with IPs, domains, file hashes, or behavioural indicators to identify known threats and improve detection accuracy.

- **Enable incident automation to reduce response times**: Implement playbooks for common and repetitive incidents such as brute-force attacks, malware detections, or data exfiltration alerts. Automating the first triage level and response reduces **mean time to respond** (**MTTR**), ensures faster containment, and helps SOC teams focus on high-value investigations.
- **Continuously develop and refine hunting queries**: Treat threat hunting as an ongoing process. Keep your KQL queries updated with emerging threats, red team insights, and recent incident patterns. Store commonly used queries in Sentinel's hunting library and share knowledge across the SOC team.
- **Use tagging and categorization for incident management**: Classify incidents by severity, affected resource type, and threat category to streamline triage. Consistent tagging enables better filtering, reporting, and correlation across incidents.
- **Conduct regular simulation and tabletop exercises**: Test your detection rules and automated responses using threat simulations or tabletop scenarios. Use tools like Microsoft's Attack Simulation Training or third-party red team exercises to validate that Sentinel alerts are triggered correctly and playbooks execute as intended.
- **Leverage UEBA**: Enable UEBA functionalities to identify anomalies in user or asset behaviour. These analytics can reveal sluggish, covert, or insider threats that bypass rule-based detection methods.
- **Monitor playbook performance and failures**: Regularly audit the performance and reliability of your playbooks. Track metrics such as execution time, failure rate, and skipped steps. Keep Logic Apps and connectors up to date to prevent breakdowns in your automated response pipeline.

Log retention in Microsoft Sentinel is managed through the underlying Log Analytics workspace. Organizations can configure default data retention from 30 to 730 days based on their compliance needs. For long-term storage, logs can also be exported to Azure Storage using diagnostic settings.

Traffic Analytics

To find possible security risks, manage bandwidth, and get the most out of firewall flows and network rules, it is important to understand how network data flows. Microsoft Azure Traffic Analytics lets enterprises see how traffic flows in cloud environments. Security and network teams can find strange behaviour, wrong settings, and boost total network security by using flow logs and built-in analytics.

Overview of Traffic Analytics

Traffic Analytics is an Azure cloud-based service that shows you how network traffic flows. It looks at **Network Security Group** (**NSG**) Flow Logs, which record IP data moving to and from Azure resources and information about it. These flow logs are stored in the Log Analytics workspace. Azure Monitor and Traffic Analytics then handle them to get helpful information that can be used.

Traffic Analytics helps organizations in the following manner:

- Visualize the top sources and destinations of network traffic.
- Identify hotspots or unexpected communication paths.
- Analyze traffic distribution across geographies, protocols, and ports.
- Monitor allowed and denied flows for auditing and compliance.
- Discover unused or overly permissive NSG rules.

Components of Traffic Analytics

The following components are needed to enable and use Traffic Analytics in Azure:

- **Azure Network Watcher**: This must be enabled to monitor network activity and to turn on flow logs for your resources.

  Figure 9.6 depicts the **Network Watcher** homepage:

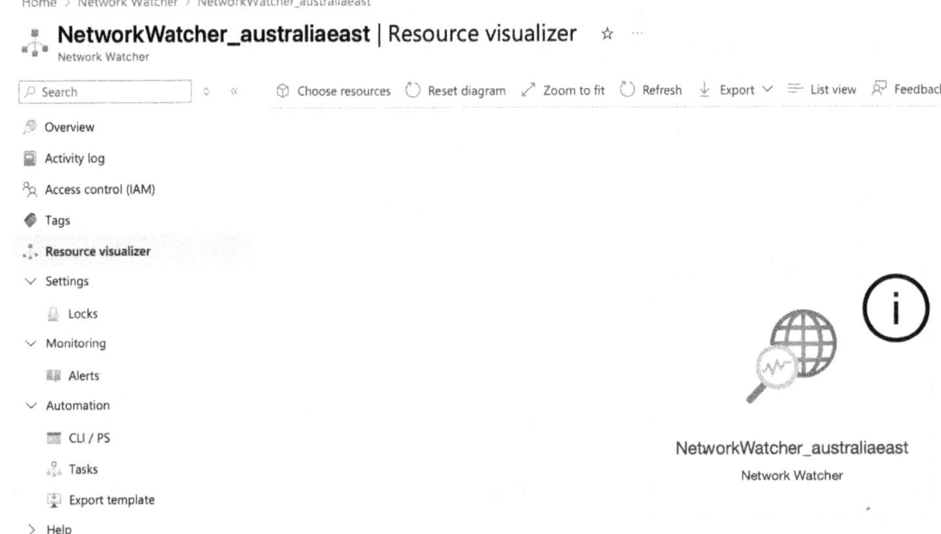

***Figure 9.6**: Sample Network Watcher*

- **Log Analytics workspace**: A central place where flow logs and network data are collected and stored for querying and analysis.

Figure 9.7 depicts a sample Log Analytics workspace:

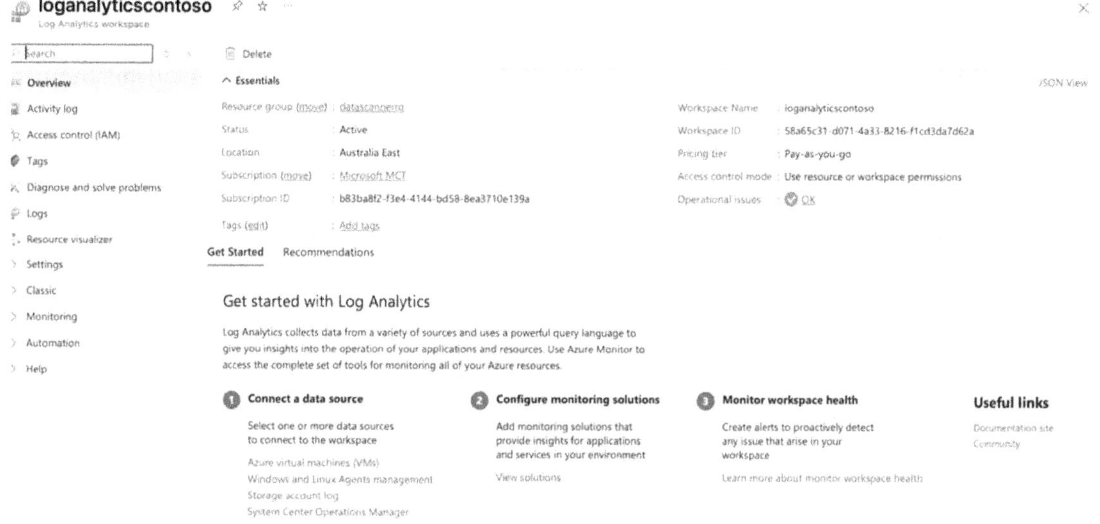

***Figure 9.7**: A Log Analytics workspace*

- **NSGs**: These define rules that allow or block network traffic. Flow logging must be enabled on NSGs to feed data into Traffic Analytics.

NSG Flow logs can be configured from within the NSG configuration page, as shown:

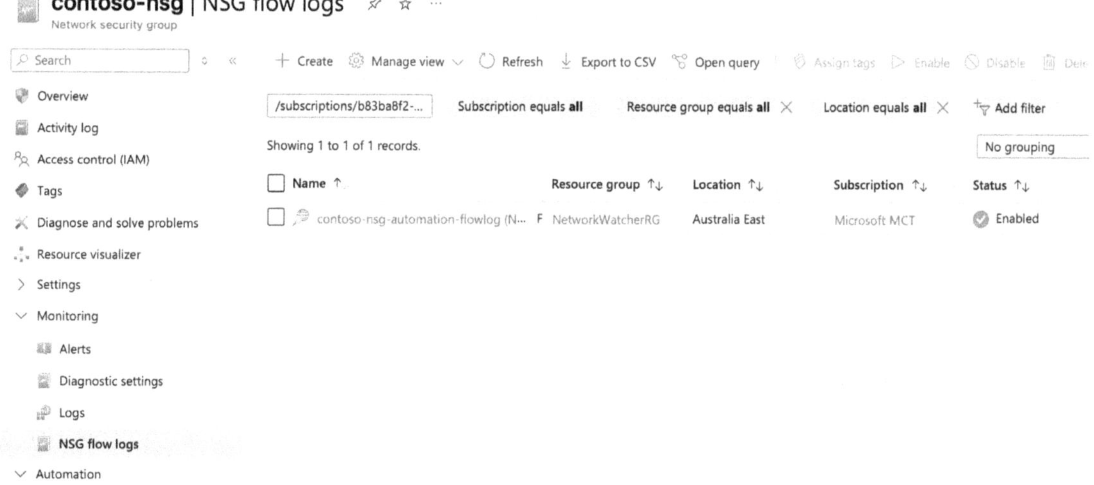

***Figure 9.8**: NSG Flow Logs Configured for NSG*

- **NSG Flow Logs**: These capture detailed info (like IPs, ports, protocols, and status) about traffic going in and out, and are crucial for analytics.

  The data flow for Traffic Analytics typically follows this pattern: NSG Flow Logs are written to a Storage Account, which is connected to a Log Analytics workspace. Traffic Analytics then processes this data to generate insights.

- **VNets**: If analyzing traffic across VNets, flow logging must be enabled on them as well.

  Flow Logs can be configured for a vNET or NSG, as depicted in *Figure 9.9:*

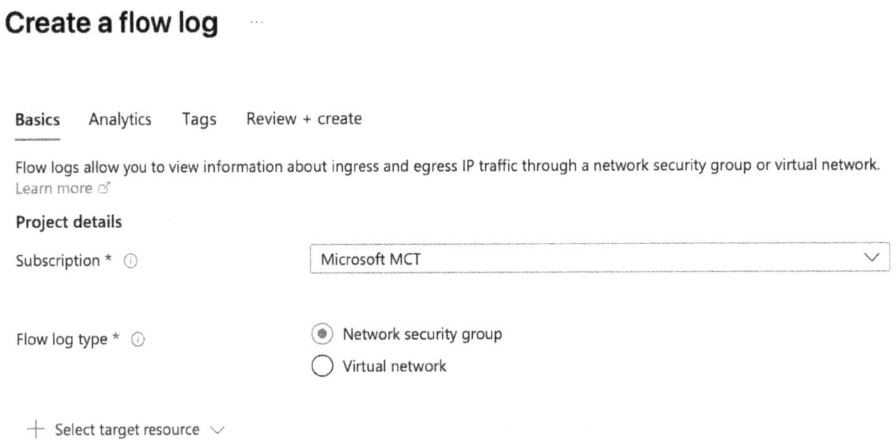

Create a flow log ...

Basics Analytics Tags Review + create

Flow logs allow you to view information about ingress and egress IP traffic through a network security group or virtual network.
Learn more

Project details

Subscription * Microsoft MCT

Flow log type * Network security group
Virtual network

+ Select target resource

***Figure 9.9**: Creating a Flow Log*

Key features of Traffic Analytics

Traffic Analytics offers a range of powerful features to help security and network teams understand, monitor, and improve network traffic flow across Azure environments.

It uses NSG Flow Logs and Azure Monitor to give smart analysis and useful information that can be used to improve both speed and security:

- **Flow analysis**: Traffic Analytics shows how traffic moves between Azure resources, subnets, and destinations outside of Azure. For teams, it helps to know who is communicating to whom, what protocols and ports are being used, and whether data is being allowed or not. These visualizations help you plan out dependencies and find communication paths or lateral movement that were not meant to be there.

  Security teams can build queries in Log Analytics to identify unusual patterns such as failed login bursts, access outside working hours, or unexpected geolocations. These insights can be used to fine-tune alert rules and detect misconfigurations or threats proactively.

- **Threat detection**: By analyzing historical and real-time traffic data, Traffic Analytics can highlight unusual traffic behaviour, such as a spike in denied connections, access from foreign IP ranges, or abnormal port usage. These indicators can point to potential threats like port scanning, brute-force attempts, or misconfigurations that expose resources to the internet.
- **Optimization**: Traffic Analytics finds NSG rules that are not being used, are not being used enough, or are being used too much. This lets administrators make the best use of their security group configurations. This helps lower the attack area by blocking access that is not needed and making the network more divided. Optimizing NSG rules also helps with better speed and makes it easier to report compliance.
- **Geographic insights**: It gives geolocation representations of traffic sources and destinations, which helps businesses find traffic from places they would not expect to see it. This could mean that someone is spying on them or trying to steal their data.
- **Application and protocol breakdown**: Traffic Analytics categorizes traffic by protocols and port numbers, making it easier to understand the nature of communication, for example, whether traffic is HTTP, RDP, SSH, or DNS.
- **Time-based trend analysis**: Teams can monitor traffic trends over time to establish baselines and identify deviations. For example, a sudden spike in inbound traffic during off-peak hours may trigger further investigation.
- **Integration with Log Analytics and Workbooks**: Traffic data is stored in Log Analytics, allowing security analysts to create custom KQL queries and dashboards. Workbooks can be used to build comprehensive visual reports for SOC visibility, audits, and executive reporting.

Configuring Traffic Analytics

Setting up Traffic Analytics involves configuring flow data collection, storage, and analysis pipelines to ensure visibility into network traffic.

Enabling a traffic monitoring solution that brings insights into net your security and performance posture overall is very simple with these steps:

1. **Enable NSG Flow Logs**: To start with, the very first step you should take is to activate the NSG Flow Logs. The logs that are turned on track data about the IP traffic flowing through NSGs. This data includes the source and destination IPs, ports, protocols, as well as whether the traffic was allowed or denied.
    a. In the Azure portal, you can activate flow logs for each NSG under Diagnostic Settings, or you can do it by using Azure PowerShell, CLI, or ARM templates. The flow log version should be set to 2 or higher since it comes with advanced metadata that tracks the details of the VMs, byte counts, and traffic directions.

2. **Storage account integration**: When configuring NSG Flow Logs, specify a `Storage Account` where the logs will be stored. This storage acts as a staging area before the data is processed by Traffic Analytics.

3. **Compliance and long-term audit**: You can configure lifecycle management policies to archive or delete logs based on retention requirements. It is also a best practice to use a centralized storage account for all NSG logs to simplify access and management.

4. **Log Analytics workspace**: Once flow logs are being stored, configure Traffic Analytics to process and analyze them by linking them to a Log Analytics workspace. This workspace enables rich querying using KQL and integration with Azure Monitor Workbooks for visualizations. Sentinel and Azure Monitor can also use this workspace to correlate flow log data with other telemetry like security alerts, audit logs, and threat intelligence, providing a more holistic security view.

5. **Regional and subscription considerations**: Ensure the NSG, storage account, and Log Analytics workspace are in the same region or supported regions to avoid latency or unsupported configurations. Cross-subscription setups are possible but require proper access and RBAC permissions to link resources.

   Note: **Cross-region configurations may lead to increased latency and are subject to Azure region-specific limitations. Whenever possible, ensure NSGs, Storage Accounts, and Log Analytics workspaces are in the same region for optimal performance and simplified access control.**

6. **Verify and tune configuration**: After enabling flow logs and setting up analytics, verify that the logs are being appropriately ingested. Use Log Analytics queries to inspect sample data, check for gaps, and validate the timestamp accuracy. You can also configure alerts based on flow data (e.g., sudden spike in denied traffic).

7. **Use tags and naming conventions**: For larger environments, apply consistent **`naming conventions`** and **`resource tags`** for NSGs and storage accounts to make managing and filtering flow logs easier during analysis. This helps in building targeted dashboards and filtered visualizations.

Best practices of Traffic Analytics

To get the most value from Traffic Analytics, it is essential to implement it in the right way and always throughout your Azure environment.

The following best practices will help you enhance visibility, tighten security, and improve operational efficiency:

- **Enable Traffic Analytics for all critical NSGs**: Ensure that Traffic Analytics is enabled on all Network Security Groups protecting key workloads, including internet-facing VMs, databases, jump servers, and internal tiered resources. This provides visibility into traffic entering and leaving critical zones and helps monitor east-west traffic across subnets.

- **Use flow logs to refine NSG rules**: Regularly analyze NSG Flow Logs to identify overly permissive rules or unused access paths. Remove or restrict regulations that are not actively used and enforce least privilege principles for network access. This helps minimize potential entry points and limits lateral movement in case of a compromise.
- **Integrate Traffic Analytics with Microsoft Sentinel**: By forwarding flow data to a Log Analytics workspace connected to Microsoft Sentinel, you can correlate network activity with other signals like user behaviour, alerts from Defender, and Threat Intelligence feeds. This allows for comprehensive threat hunting and more accurate incident detection.
- **Set retention and lifecycle policies for flow log data**: Define retention policies in the connected storage account or Log Analytics workspace to manage the data lifecycle. Retain logs long enough to support compliance, auditing, and incident forensics, but use tiered storage or lifecycle rules to control costs.
- **Schedule regular reviews of traffic patterns**: To manage the changes in network traffic trends, one of the ways would be by executing either monthly or quarterly review cycles. This information can be utilized to identify the changes in application operations, the presence of unwanted access attempts, or threats. This is especially beneficial after significant infrastructure changes or deliveries.
- **Visualize traffic trends using workbooks**: Build custom dashboards using Azure Monitor Workbooks to track key metrics like top talkers, denied traffic, unusual geolocations, and protocol usage. Visual representations help both security teams and leadership stay informed and aligned.
- **Tag and organize resources for targeted monitoring**: Use resource tags and naming conventions for NSGs and VMs to make flow data easier to filter and analyze. This is especially helpful in large environments where traffic needs to be segmented by department, environment (e.g., dev/test/prod), or compliance zones.
- **Monitor for anomalies in east-west traffic**: In many cyberattacks, lateral movement occurs within the internal network. Key attention needs to be paid to east-west traffic between VMs or subnets, which may not pass through firewalls. Use Traffic Analytics to spot unusual flows or unexpected communication paths.

Conclusion

In today's complex cloud environments, visibility is a key component of security. This chapter explored how Azure provides powerful tools like Azure Monitor, Microsoft Sentinel, and Traffic Analytics that help organizations monitor, detect, and respond to threats in real-time.

The integration of these solutions will achieve a strong, intelligent, and scalable monitoring framework that, in turn, will boost your threat detection and incident response capabilities and strengthen your overall security posture. Following the standards described in this chapter will be the right way of making sure your Azure environment is secured, audited, and resilient to the threats that it evolves.

In the next and final chapter, we will bring it all together with a set of comprehensive security best practices, covering key areas such as identity, network, data, and governance, ensuring you are equipped to design and operate secure Azure environments from end to end.

Join our Discord space

Join our Discord workspace for latest updates, offers, tech happenings around the world, new releases, and sessions with the authors:

https://discord.bpbonline.com

CHAPTER 10
Security Best Practices

Introduction

In this summary chapter, you will learn the best practices for all topics covered in this book. This will include security concepts, identity and access security, network security, compute security, data security, governance and compliance, and security operations.

Structure

This chapter contains the following topics:

- Concepts best practice guidance
- Workload implementation best practice guidance
- Security operations best practice guidance

Objectives

This chapter aims to consolidate and reinforce key security learnings from the previous chapters by presenting a comprehensive set of best practices. By the end of this chapter, you will be equipped with practical guidance and proven strategies to design, implement, and manage secure Azure environments, spanning identity, network, compute, data, governance, and operational security.

Concepts best practice guidance

Understanding and using basic security ideas when building safe architectures in the cloud is very important. These broad concepts help people make decisions and lay the groundwork for how they should be put into action on a technical level. These rules affect how solutions are created, reduce risks, and handle tasks in a shared computer setting.

Foundational security principles

When it comes to Azure, the following concepts are the building blocks of all secure architecture. They are not tied to a specific tool or service. Instead, they are a way of thinking about and managing risk in the cloud. Organizations can better handle changing threats, government regulations, and the practical challenges of cloud environments if they understand and use these basic ideas.

Here are the best practices for a secure Azure architecture:

- **Zero Trust security model**: The idea behind this model is never trust, always verify. No matter where it comes from, every entry request has to be constantly verified, authorized, and authenticated. For this to work well, MFA should be required for all users, especially those with protected accounts. Conditional Access policies should also be used to check sign-ins in real-time, considering the user's risk, the device's compliance, the user's position, and their behaviour. Additionally, Azure supports **Continuous Access Evaluation** (**CAE**), which allows real-time enforcement of policies during active sessions, improving security by revoking access immediately when risks are detected.

- **Defence-in-depth**: Defence-in-depth refers to applying multiple layers of security controls across various parts of the environment, identity, networking, applications, data, and endpoints. If one control fails or is bypassed, others are in place to contain and mitigate the damage. This layered approach can include network segmentation, firewalls, data encryption, endpoint protection, and strict RBAC.

- **Shared responsibility model**: The service provider and the customer are responsible for cloud security. Customers are responsible for keeping their data, identities, and access settings safe. On the other hand, Microsoft is in charge of safely maintaining the infrastructure and key services. To keep your security up to date and avoid making assumptions that lead to vulnerabilities, it is essential to know where your responsibilities begin. *Chapter 2, Securing Identity and Access,* covers the shared responsibility matrix, outlining customer vs. provider responsibilities across IaaS, PaaS, and SaaS. Reviewing this helps clarify security ownership and avoid gaps.

- **Least privilege access**: This principle ensures that users and services are granted only the permissions they need to perform their functions, nothing more. Reducing unnecessary access minimizes the attack surface and helps limit potential damage from compromised accounts. Implementing JIT access and managing elevated privileges through Azure PIM are effective ways to uphold this principle.

- **Security by design**: Security should not be a secondary concern but an essential part of both creation and operations. By using security by design, organizations build in things like threat modelling, secure coding, and automated security testing from the beginning of the solution-building process. This method supports a DevSecOps culture and ensures that applications are made safe and stay safe throughout their entire lifecycle.
- **Visibility and monitoring**: Managing cloud infrastructures requires constant monitoring. Organizations can efficiently identify issues and risks and react by gathering and evaluating telemetry from all systems. This monitoring is centralized by Microsoft Defender for Cloud, Azure Monitor, and Microsoft Sentinel, which also detect vulnerabilities and use analytics to automate incident response.

Best practices

Security is a continuous effort requiring strategic planning, monitoring, and team training rather than a one-time setup.

The recommended practices listed in the following list offer a solid basis for protecting Azure environments while encouraging a resilient and responsible culture:

- **Regularly review the Azure Secure Score**: Azure Secure Score offers a centralized view of your security posture and actionable recommendations. Reviewing and addressing these items helps improve your environment's defences against evolving threats.
- **Educate stakeholders on cloud security principles**: Ensuring that all team members, from developers to business leaders, understand their role in cloud security improves the overall security posture and reduces human error.
- **Use Microsoft Learn to stay updated**: The cloud security landscape constantly evolves. Microsoft Learn and other official documentation offer up-to-date training and resources to help teams stay ahead of new vulnerabilities and best practices.
- **Perform threat modelling during design**: Integrating threat modelling early in the development lifecycle allows you to identify and mitigate risks before they become real issues, supporting a security-by-design approach.
- **Conduct periodic security assessments**: Regular penetration tests, vulnerability scans, and red team exercises help validate your defences and uncover security gaps that automated tools may miss.
- **Enforce security governance with Azure Policy and Blueprints**: Use governance tools to apply and enforce organization-wide policies, ensuring consistent compliance with security and regulatory standards across all Azure subscriptions.

- **Maintain and test incident response plans**: Having a clear and tested incident response strategy ensures that your team can act quickly and effectively during a security breach, minimizing impact and downtime.
- **Foster a DevSecOps culture**: Embed security into CI/CD pipelines and development processes to secure applications from the ground up. Automation helps detect issues early and enforces consistency.
- **Use PIM and JIT for privileged access**: Limit standing administrative access by assigning roles temporarily with approval workflows. This reduces the risk of misuse or compromise of privileged accounts.
- **Enable centralized monitoring and logging**: Tools like Microsoft Sentinel, Defender for Cloud, and Azure Monitor provide visibility into activities across the cloud environment to detect and respond to threats.
- **Verify backup and recovery readiness**: Ensure data backup and disaster recovery procedures are configured and regularly tested. This helps guarantee business continuity in case of data loss or ransomware attacks.

Workload implementation best practice guidance

Translating high-level security principles into real-world protections starts with implementing and maintaining workloads. This section outlines best practice guidance across critical security domains, starting with identity and access, which form the foundation of secure workload access and control.

Identity and access security

Identity is the new security perimeter in the cloud. Properly managing and securing identity and access is critical for protecting your workloads and data. The following best practices offer actionable steps to strengthen identity security across your Azure workloads:

- **Identity management**: Use Entra ID as the central identity platform for user and application authentication. Centralizing identity simplifies access control, improves visibility, and supports integration with third-party services. Apply RBAC to assign users the minimum permissions required to perform their roles, adhering to the principle of least privilege.
- **Access protection**: Protect access to sensitive workloads by enabling Conditional Access policies. These policies allow you to enforce controls such as requiring MFA for high-risk sign-ins or blocking access from non-compliant devices. Passwordless authentication methods like Microsoft Authenticator, Windows Hello, or FIDO2 security keys should be adopted to reduce the risk of password-based attacks.

- **Privileged access management**: Use Entra ID PIM to manage and monitor privileged roles. PIM enables JIT access, approval workflows, and access reviews, helping reduce the standing time of high-risk accounts. Regularly audit privileged access to detect anomalies, revoke unnecessary permissions, and enforce governance.
- **Segregate identities for administrative functions**: Ensure that users performing administrative tasks use separate accounts from their daily accounts. This reduces the risk of lateral movement in case a standard user account is compromised.
- **Enable identity protection and risk-based policies**: Leverage Entra ID identity protection to detect risky sign-ins and user behaviour. Combine this with automated Conditional Access policies to block or challenge access dynamically based on real-time risk assessments.
- **Integrate external identities with control**: When collaborating with partners or contractors, use Entra ID B2B collaboration. Set up access reviews, expiration policies, and Conditional Access to ensure guest identities are governed as tightly as internal ones.

Network security

A well-secured network forms the backbone of your cloud architecture. Controlling traffic flow, minimizing exposure, and enforcing boundary protections are critical to reducing risk and maintaining secure connectivity across workloads. Let us look at its best practices:

- **VNet best practices**: Design your Azure Virtual Networks with security in mind. Use NSGs and ASGs to define and manage traffic rules at the subnet and workload levels. This helps limit lateral movement and ensures workloads only communicate as intended. For more comprehensive protection, enable Azure Firewall to inspect, filter, and log traffic centrally across your environment.
- **Public and private access**: Reduce your public exposure by using Azure Private Link, which allows secure access to Azure services over the Microsoft backbone network, keeping traffic off the public internet. For workloads that must be internet-facing, always enable DDoS Protection, particularly for business-critical or regulated services, to defend against volumetric and protocol-based attacks.
- **Segmentation and isolation**: Use subnets, route tables, and NSGs to segment workloads and isolate critical services from less-trusted zones. Deploy workload tiers (e.g., web, app, and database) in separate subnets to enforce tighter control over communication paths.
- **Avoid open management ports**: Never expose RDP, SSH, or other management ports directly to the internet. Instead, use secure options like Azure Bastion or jump boxes within locked-down networks to manage virtual machines securely.

- **DNS security and resolution**: Use Azure DNS Private Resolver and custom DNS forwarding to manage name resolution securely across hybrid environments. This helps avoid DNS-based attacks and supports split-horizon DNS configurations.
- **Leverage Azure Virtual Network Service Endpoints**: Service Endpoints allow secure and direct access to Azure services from your VNet without requiring traffic to be routed through the public internet. This improves data exfiltration protection and simplifies access control.
- **Implement JIT VM access**: Instead of keeping ports like RDP or SSH open, enable JIT access through Microsoft Defender for Cloud. It only opens ports when needed, for limited periods, and only to approved users, reducing exposure to brute-force attacks.
- **Monitor network traffic continuously**: Enable analytics via Azure Network Watcher to gain visibility into flow logs and NSG rule usage. This helps detect unusual patterns, validate firewall rules, and support forensics during incident response.
- **Use UDRs carefully**: When customizing traffic flows with UDRs, ensure routes do not inadvertently bypass critical inspection points like Azure Firewall or NVA appliances. Misconfigured routes can lead to traffic leakage or security gaps.

Compute security

Maintaining workload integrity, safeguarding data, and avoiding misuse or illegal access all depend on secure computing resources. Enforcing effective compute layer security policies helps limit exposure and protect your environment against threats, regardless of whether you are running virtual machines or containerized apps.

The following are best practices for securing your compute in Azure:

- **Virtual machines**: Protecting virtual machines starts with controlling access. Enable JIT VM access via Microsoft Defender for Cloud to reduce exposure to brute-force and port scanning attacks. This ensures RDP or SSH ports are only open for approved users for limited timeframes. Additionally, secure data at rest using Azure Disk Encryption, which leverages BitLocker (Windows) or DM-Crypt (Linux) with keys stored in Azure Key Vault.
- **Containerized workloads**: Containers introduce flexibility, but they also introduce new security risks. Regularly scan images stored in **Azure Container Registry** (**ACR**) using Defender for Containers or other tools to detect vulnerabilities before deployment. Apply Kubernetes network policies to segment and isolate workloads, ensuring pods communicate only with authorized services.
- **System updates and patching**: Keep your VMs and container hosts up to date with the latest security patches. Use Azure Automation Update Management or Azure Automanage to streamline update deployment and reduce the risk of exploits targeting known vulnerabilities.

- **Use Managed Identities for computing resources**: Assign system-assigned or user-assigned Managed Identities to VMs and containers to avoid embedding secrets in code or configuration files. Azure services like Key Vault or storage accounts can securely authenticate these identities.
- **Hardening the OS and baseline configurations**: Apply security baselines and hardening guidelines such as those from Microsoft or the **Centre for Internet Security** (**CIS**). Tools like Azure Policy can enforce configuration standards, while Azure Defender for Cloud provides benchmarking against best practices.
- **Monitor runtime behaviour**: Use Defender for Servers and Containers to detect anomalies, unwanted changes, or suspicious runtime behaviours like privilege escalation. This adds a layer of defence beyond pre-deployment checks.

Data security

Data is one of the most valuable assets in any cloud environment, making its protection a top priority. Whether at rest or in transit, securing data requires a combination of encryption, access control, and visibility. The following best practices help ensure that sensitive data remains confidential, available, and protected from unauthorized access or tampering.

The following are best practices for securing your data in Azure:

- **Encryption**: Ensure that data is encrypted both at rest and in transit. For databases, enable TDE, which encrypts the storage of the entire database, logs, and backups without requiring application changes. Use Azure Key Vault to centrally manage encryption keys and secrets, giving you control over key rotation policies, auditing, and access control. Use CMK instead of PMK for added protection.
- **Access control**: Limit data exposure by applying Azure RBAC to manage who can access sensitive data resources like storage accounts, databases, and Key Vaults tightly. Assign roles with the principle of least privilege in mind and routinely review permissions. Additionally, it enables dynamic data masking in SQL databases to hide sensitive data in query results for non-privileged users, allowing access to the data structure without exposing confidential content.
- **Data classification and labelling**: Use Microsoft Purview to classify and label data based on sensitivity. This helps ensure that appropriate protections, like encryption, access restrictions, or data loss prevention policies, are automatically applied based on classification.
- **Secure backups and retention**: Protect against accidental deletion, ransomware, or corruption by enabling backup policies with encryption and long-term retention. To ensure resilience, use Azure Backup and configure GRS for critical workloads.
- **Monitor data access and anomalies**: Track data access patterns using tools like Microsoft Defender for SQL and Microsoft Purview Audit Logs. Monitoring access helps detect insider threats, unauthorized queries, or unusual access patterns.

Governance and compliance

Adequate governance guarantees secure and compliant cloud environments that meet organizational and regulatory standards. Enforcing consistent policies, managing resources at scale, and tracking data sensitivity help organizations reduce risk and improve operational confidence.

The following best practices support governance and regulatory alignment in Azure:

- **Azure Policy**: Azure Policy helps define and enforce resource rules across your subscriptions. Use it to prevent misconfigurations, enforce tagging standards, and restrict unsupported regions or SKUs. Leverage built-in policy initiatives aligned with regulatory frameworks such as GDPR, HIPAA, ISO 27001, and NIST to monitor real-time compliance posture. Assign management group-level policies to ensure uniform governance across multiple subscriptions.

- **Azure Blueprints**: Azure Blueprints can automate and standardize the environment setup. Blueprints bundle together key components like policies, role assignments, Resource Manager templates, and resource groups into reusable definitions. This allows teams to rapidly deploy compliant environments that align with internal standards or industry regulations, minimizing the risk of drift over time.

- **Microsoft Purview**: Implement Microsoft Purview to classify data based on sensitivity, track lineage, and manage regulatory data risks. With Purview, you can gain insight into where sensitive data resides, how it is being accessed, and which compliance requirements apply by enabling proactive control and audit readiness.

- **Management groups and RBAC**: Use management groups to organize subscriptions into a hierarchy for scalable policy enforcement and role assignment. This allows consistent governance across business units or environments (e.g., dev, test, prod) and simplifies access control using role-based access across all levels.

- **Resource consistency and naming standards**: Enforce consistent naming conventions, tagging strategies, and resource organization through policies and governance documentation. This improves discoverability, cost tracking, automation, and incident response efficiency.

- **Audit logging and compliance tracking**: Enable Azure Activity Logs and Microsoft Purview Audit Logs to record changes across your environment. Centralized logging supports investigations, compliance reporting, and helps meet data retention and audit requirements.

Security operations best practice guidance

Proactive detection, investigation, and response to threats in Azure rely on essential security operations that maintain constant awareness. Even the most resilient security architecture requires continuous monitoring and threat detection to prevent compromise. This section outlines the key tools and practices facilitating this proactive approach for organizations.

Monitoring and threat detection

Security operations form the frontline of defence in detecting, responding to, and recovering from threats in real time. Effective security operations depend on deep visibility, proactive detection, and automated response mechanisms. The following best practices focus on strengthening your cloud detection and response capabilities using Azure-native tools.

The following tools can be used to ensure that various operations are monitored:

- **Azure Monitor**: Azure Monitor collects metrics and diagnostic logs across critical resources such as virtual machines, storage accounts, Key Vaults, and App Services. This ensures visibility into performance, configuration changes, and potential security issues. Set up custom alerts based on defined thresholds or activity patterns to detect and escalate high-priority incidents such as unauthorized access attempts, resource depletion, or excessive privilege escalations.
- **Microsoft Sentinel**: Microsoft Sentinel acts as your cloud-native SIEM and SOAR platform. Review and fine-tune analytics rules to capture relevant events and reduce false positives. Use threat-hunting queries to proactively search for signs of compromise across your data sources. For recurring incidents, automate remediation steps using playbooks built with Azure Logic Apps, for example, auto-disabling a compromised user or isolating a VM with suspicious activity. Utilize Fusion Analytics Rules in Sentinel for machine learning-based correlation across data sources, and develop proficiency in KQL to build advanced threat-hunting queries efficiently.
- **Traffic Analytics**: Monitor NSG flow logs using Traffic Analytics to understand traffic patterns and detect anomalies such as unauthorized lateral movement, unexpected geo-location access, or port scanning behaviour. This visibility is critical for the early detection of network-based threats and validating security configurations.
- **Defender for Cloud**: Enable Microsoft Defender for Cloud to continuously assess your environment for misconfigurations, weak security controls, and vulnerabilities. It provides Secure Score recommendations and integrates threat protection across computing, storage, databases, and containers. It uses integrated alerts to detect real-time threats such as crypto-mining activity, brute-force login attempts, or malware presence.
- **Log centralization and retention**: Ensure logs from different sources, including Azure Activity Logs, Defender alerts, and audit logs, are ingested into a centralized workspace like Sentinel. Configure long-term log retention policies to meet compliance and forensic requirements.
- **Incident response readiness**: Develop and test your incident response plan regularly. Document roles, responsibilities, communication plans, and escalation paths. Integrate

runbooks and playbooks within Sentinel to automate parts of the response process for faster containment.

Incident response

Organizations must prioritize both preventing and preparing for security incidents. A well-defined **incident response** (**IR**) process empowers them to contain threats quickly, reduce damage, and recover operations effectively. Within Azure environments, response strategies should incorporate preparation, automation, and seamless integration with native tools to optimize detection, triage, and remediation.

The following are the key elements of an effective incident response strategy in Azure:

- **Preparation**: Create an incident response plan specifically for Azure workloads and services. The plan should include detection thresholds, escalation procedures, communication channels, and recovery steps. Assign stakeholder roles and responsibilities, and provide them with advanced access to critical systems and contact lists. Conduct regular security drills to evaluate team readiness and improve the plan.

- **Automation**: Speed is critical during an incident. Use Azure Logic Apps to automate response workflows, such as isolating a virtual machine, deactivating compromised accounts, or notifying security teams. Automation reduces response time and human error. Additionally, the cloud can leverage Microsoft Defender to receive real-time alerts and trigger workflows based on threat severity, resource type, or risk level.

- **Post-incident analysis and improvement**: A detailed post-mortem or lessons-learned session should be conducted once an incident is resolved. Documenting root causes, response actions, and areas for improvement from this session allows for strengthening defences and preventing future similar incidents by feeding insights into playbooks and detection rules.

- **Integration with SIEM and ticketing systems**: Integrate Microsoft Sentinel with incident tracking systems like ServiceNow, Jira, or Microsoft Teams to ensure end-to-end visibility and consistent case management. This allows security teams to collaborate and act efficiently across multiple platforms.

Continual improvement

Security is not a set-it-and-forget-it discipline; it requires continuous evaluation and evolution to stay ahead of emerging threats and shifting business requirements. A mature security posture is built on regular assessments, knowledge sharing, and process refinement. This section highlights practices supporting a continuous improvement culture in cloud security operations

The following are some ways we can continuously improve the security:

- **Audit and review**: Conduct regular security assessments using tools like Entra ID advisor, Microsoft Defender for Cloud, and Secure Score to evaluate current configurations, detect drift, and identify areas for enhancement. Reviews should cover identity, network, data, and workload configurations. Access controls, policies, and monitoring rules should be updated based on these assessments to reflect changing risk profiles and business needs.
- **Training and awareness**: Keep security and operations teams informed about the latest threats, vulnerabilities, and defence techniques through continuous learning initiatives. Encourage ongoing training using Microsoft Learn, Microsoft Security Copilot (where applicable), and external certifications such as SC-200 (Security Operations Analyst) or AZ-500 (Security Engineer). A well-informed team is critical to reducing human error and improving response effectiveness.
- **Feedback loops from incidents and drills**: To improve procedures, regulations, and tools, use tabletop exercises and post-incident evaluations as feedback channels. Update playbooks, detection guidelines, and communication protocols to reflect lessons learned.
- **Security community engagement**: Encourage team members to follow reliable security blogs and newsletters, participate in security communities, or attend security seminars. This contributes to new insights and early detection of attack patterns or zero-day threats.

Conclusion

Security in the cloud is not a one-time configuration—it is a continuous, organization-wide commitment. In this chapter, we brought together best practices from every aspect of the Azure security landscape, spanning foundational concepts, workload implementation, operational readiness, and governance.

By applying principles like Zero Trust, least privilege, defence-in-depth, and security by design, organizations can build resilient architectures prepared to withstand modern threats. From securing identities and networks to protecting data and managing access, every layer of your environment must be aligned with a security strategy.

It is just as important to have operational practices like monitoring, incident response, and continual improvement, which ensure that security remains effective over time and adapts to changing risk profiles. Empowering teams through automation, ongoing training, and a culture of accountability helps ensure that security becomes an enabler, not a barrier, to innovation and agility in the cloud.

As you move forward, remember that the strongest cloud security posture combines sound architecture, intelligent tooling, vigilant operations, and a continuous learning mindset.

Index

A

Access Control 140
Access Control, architecture 140
Access Control, methods
  Microsoft Entra ID Integration 141
  RBAC 141
  Shared Access Signatures (SAS) 141
Access Control, policies
  Access Tier 143
  Immutable Blob Storage 142
  Storage Account Keys 142
Access Control, practices 143-145
AKS Cluster, ensuring 122, 123
Authentication 32
Authentication, architecture 32
Authentication, flow
  Conditional Access Integration 36
  Interactive 35
  Non-Interactive 36
Authentication, methods
  MFA 33
  Password-Based 33
  Passwordless 34
Authentication, practices 37-40
Authorisation 40
Authorisation, architecture 40
Authorisation, practices 44-46
Authorisation, technologies
  Privileged Identity Management (PIM) 42
  RBAC 41

Azure Advisor 202
Azure Advisor, architecture 202, 203
Azure Advisor, characteristics
  Actionable Insights 204
  Customizable Recommendations 205
  Multi-Category Optimization 205
  Proactive Monitoring 205
  Secure Score Integration 204
  Security Recommendations 203
Azure Advisor, practices 207
Azure Advisor, terms
  Automating Remediation 206
  Custom Reports 206
  Efficient Team Collaboration 206
  High-Impact Recommendations 206
  Integration/Governance 206
  Multi-Cloud Visibility 206
  Regular Assessments 206
Azure API Management 130
Azure API Management, architecture 131
Azure API Management, features
  API Gateway Security 133
  Authentication 131
  Data Protection 132
  Network Security 132
  Rate Limit Controls 132
  Threat Detection 133
Azure API Management, practices 134-136
Azure API Management, preventing 136, 137
Azure App Service 124
Azure App Service, architecture 124
Azure App Service, features
  Authentication/Authorization 124
  Backup/Disaster Recovery 126
  Continuous Monitoring 127
  Data Encryption 125
  HTTPS Enforcement 124
  Networking 125
  Secure Configuration 126
  Secure DevOps 127
Azure Architecture 286
Azure Architecture, concepts
  Defence-in-Depth 286
  Least Privilege Access 286
  Security Design 287
  Shared Responsibility 286
  Visibility Monitoring 287
  Zero Trust Security Model 286
Azure Architecture, foundations
  Compute Security 290
  Data Security 291
  Governance/Compliance 292
  Identity Access Security 288
  Network Security 289
Azure Architecture, operations
  Continual Improvement 294
  Incident Response 294
  Threat Detection 293
Azure Architecture, practices 287
Azure Blueprints 183
Azure Blueprints, architecture 183
Azure Blueprints, characteristics
  Change Management 184
  Consistent/Repeatable Deployments 183
  Policy-Driven Governance 183
  RBAC Integration 183
  Subscription Management 183

Azure Blueprints, deploying 184
Azure Blueprints, practices 184
Azure Container 118
Azure Container, deploying 120-122
Azure Container, services
ACI 118
ACR 119
AKS 118
Azure Container Apps (ACA) 119
Azure Database Security 156
Azure Database Security, architecture 156
Azure Database Security, capabilities 164
Azure Database Security, mechanisms
Firewall Rules 157
Microsoft Entra ID 157
SQL Authentication 158
Azure Database Security, practices 162-164
Azure Database Security, principles
Authentication/ Access Control 156
Data Protection 156
Network Security 156
Threat Detection/Auditing 156
Azure Database Security, techniques
Advanced Threat Protection 159
Azure Monitor 159
Azure SQL Auditing 158
SQL Server Audit Logs 159
Azure DDoS 102
Azure DDoS, configuring 102
Azure DDoS, levels
Basic 103
Standard 103
Azure DNS 105
Azure DNS, configuring 105
Azure DNS, types
Communication Encryption 106
DNS Hijacking 106
DoH/DoT 107
Enternal Exposure 106
Performance Availability, enhancing 107
Azure Front Door 96
Azure Front Door, concepts
DDoS Protection 97
Global Traffic Routing 97
High Availability 98
Performance Accelaration 98
Rate Limiting 98
SSL Offloading 97
Azure Front Door, flow 99
Azure Kubernetes Service (AKS) Cluster 122
Azure Locks
about 196
Architecture 196
Practices 197, 198
Use Cases 197
Azure Monitor 264
Azure Monitor, architecture 264
Azure Monitor, benefits
Advanced Alerting 264
Customized Workbooks 264
Ent-to-End Visibility 264
Integrate Diagnostics 264
Integration 264

Azure Monitor, components
- Activity Logs 268
- Diagnostic Logs 268
- Log Retention 268
- RBAC Integration 268
- Resource Health 268
- SIEM, integration 268

Azure Monitor Data, types
- Logs 264
- Metrics 264

Azure Monitor, ensuring 264-266
Azure Monitor, features
- Alerts 267
- Application Insights 267
- Autoscale 267
- Diagnostic 267
- Log Analytics 267
- Metrics Monitoring 267
- Workbooks 267

Azure Monitor, practice 269
Azure Policy 191
Azure Policy, architecture 191
Azure Policy, benefits 192, 193
Azure Policy, features 191
Azure Threat Intelligence 4, 5
Azure Threat Intelligence, features
- Advanced Analytics 5
- Azure Defender 5
- Global Threat Visibility 5
- Incident Response 5
- Threat Indicators 5

Azure Traffic Manager 103
Azure Traffic Manager, ensuring 104, 105
Azure Virtual Machines (VMs) 112
Azure Virtual Networks (VNets) 68
Azure Virtual WAN (VWAN) 90
Azure VMs, architecture 112, 113
Azure VMs, ensuring 116, 117
Azure VMs, features
- Access Management 113
- Disc Encryption 113
- Endpoint Protection 113
- Secure Networking 114
- Update Management 114

Azure VMs, guidelines 114-116
Azure VNets, architecture 69
Azure VNets, practices
- ASGs 69
- NSGs 69
- Subnets 69

Azure VNets, strategies 77, 78
Azure VPN Gateway 84
Azure VPN Gateway, benefits
- Backup Connectivity 86
- Cost-Effective Hybrid Networking 85
- Flexibility 86
- Multi-Protocol 86
- Scalability / Redundancy 85
- Secure Connectivity 85

Azure VPN Gateway, steps 85
Azure VPN Gateway, types
- ExpressRoute 85
- Point-to-Site (P2S) 84
- Site-to-Site (S2S) 84
- VNet-to-VNet 84

C

CAF, architecture 168
CAF, points
 Cost Management 170
 Identity Baseline 169
 Monitoring / Reporting 170
 Policy / Compliance 169
CAF, techniques 171
Certificates 107
Certificates, ensuring 108
Certificates, purpose 108
Cloud Adoption Framework (CAF) 168
Cloud Security Posture Management (CSPM) 9
CSPM 214
CSPM, differences
 Complaint Staying 11
 Misconfiguration Fixing 11
 Multi-Cloud Environments 11
CSPM, practices 216, 217
CSPM, steps
 Automate Remediation 214
 Azure Resource Graph 215
 Custom Compliance Initiatives 214
 Secure Score 214
 Security Posture 215
 SIEM Solutions 215
CSPM, terms
 Clear Remediation 11
 Continuous Assessment 10
 Prioritizing Risks 11
CSPM, tools
 Azure Policy 10
 Microsoft Defender 9
CWPP 220
CWPP, architecture 221
CWPP, benefits 223, 224
CWPP, features 221, 222

D

Data Protection 145
Data Protection, architecture 145
Data Protection, features
 Azure Backup 147
 Snapshots 146
 Soft Delete 146
Data Protection, methods
 Azure Policy 147
 Storage Monitoring 148
 Tagging 148
Data Protection, practices 149, 150
Data Protection, strategies 145
Data Protection, techniques
 Always Encrypted 161
 Backup Encryption 162
 Dynamic Data Masking (DDM) 161
 Row-Level Security (RLS) 161
 Transparent Data Encryption (TDE) 160
Defender For App Service
 about 245
 Architecture 246
 Cloud Portal, enabling 246
 Features 247
 Practices 248
Defender For Containers
 about 240
 Architecture 241
 Cloud Portal, enabling 241

Features 242
Practices 243, 244
Defender For Databases
about 235
Architecture 235
Cloud Portal, enabling 236
Features 236, 237
Practices 238-240
Defender For DNS
about 257
Architecture 257
Cloud Portal, enabling 258
Features 258, 259
Practices 260
Defender For Key Vault
about 249
Architecture 250
Cloud Portal, enabling 250
Features 251
Practices 251-253
Defender For Resource Manager
about 253
Architecture 253
Cloud Portal, enabling 254
Features 254, 255
Practices 256
Defender For Servers 224
Defender For Servers, architecture 224, 225
Defender For Servers, configuring 225
Defender For Servers, features
Adaptive Application 227
EDR 226
Endpoint Integration 227
FIM 227
JIT VM Access 227
Microsoft Sentinel 228
Network Security 227
Security Baselines 228
Threat Analytics 227
Vulnerability Management 227
Defender For Servers, practices 228, 229
Defender For Storage
about 229
Architecture 230
Cloud Portal, enabling 230
Practices 232-234
Defender For Storage, features
Data Exfiltration 231
Data Protection 232
Insider Threats 232
Least Privilege Enforcement 231
Malware Scanning 231
Microsoft Sentinel 231
Ransomware Attacks 232
Security Posture 232
Threat Detection 231
Defense-in-Depth 19
Defense-in-Depth, advantages
Business Security 25, 26
Comprehensive Protection 23-25
Redundancy 23
Scalability 24
Defense-in-Depth, architecture 19
Defense-in-Depth, layers
Application Security 21
Data Security 21
Identity Access Management 20

Network Security 20
Physical Security 20
Response Monitoring 21
Defense-in-Depth, levels
Educate Employees 22
Layered Method 21
Leverage Automation 22
Regularly Test Security 22
Domain Name System (DNS) 257

E

Encryption 151
Encryption, architecture 151
Encryption, frameworks
Compliance 151
Confidentiality 151
Data Integrity 151
Encryption, methods
Client-Side 152
SSE 151
Transit 152
Encryption, practices 154-156
Encryption, types 152
Encryption, ways
Audit Logs 154
Azure Key Vault 153
Key Rotation 153
Endpoint Security 103
Endpoint Security, tools
Azure DNS 105
Azure Traffic Manager 103
Certificates 107
Entra ID 28
Entra ID, architecture 28, 29
Entra ID, concepts
Identity Access Reviews 66
Identity-Based Secure Authentication 65
Reduce Vulnerabilities 65
Risk-Based Access Management 65
Session Management 65
Entra ID, features
Centralised Identity Management 30
Conditional Access 31
MFA 30
On-Premises Directories 31
Entra ID Identity 55
Entra ID Identity, architecture 58
Entra ID Identity, capabilities
Identity Governance 60
Risk Detection 59
Risk Policies 59
Entra ID Identity, features 59
Entra ID Identity, strategies 61
Entra ID Identity, types
Guest Accounts 56
Managed Identities 58
Service Principals 57
User Accounts 55
Entra ID, roles
Built-In 44
Custom 44
Entra ID Tenant 52
Entra ID Tenant, concerns 52
Entra ID Tenant, practices 54, 55
Entra ID Tenant, scenarios 54
Entra ID Tenant, validating 52, 53
Entra ID, ways
Compliance/Regulatory Guidelines 30

Protection Unauthorised Access 29
Zero Trust Principles 30
ExpressRoute 86
ExpressRoute, benefits 90
ExpressRoute Connectivity, models
Any-to-Any 88
CloudExchange Co-Location 88
Point-to-Point (P2P) 88
ExpressRoute, implementing 89, 90
ExpressRoute, models
Direct 89
Service Provider 89
ExpressRoute Peering, options
Azure Private 87
Microsoft 87
ExpressRoute Private Access 83
ExpressRoute, types
Local 87
Premium 87
Standard 87

G

Guest Accounts 56
Guest Accounts, features 56
Guest Accounts, practices 57

H

Hybrid Connectivity 82
Hybrid Connectivity, factors 83
Hybrid Connectivity, solutions
Azure Virtual WAN 83
Azure VPN Gateway 82
ExpressRoute 83

K

Key Vault 193
Key Vault, architecture 194
Key Vault, features
Auditing/Monitoring 194
Automate Certificate 194
Centralized Management 194
Role-Based Permissions 194
Secure Storage 194
Key Vault, practices 195

L

Landing Zones 185
Landing Zones, architecture 185
Landing Zones, deploying 187
Landing Zones, features
Automation/IaC 186
Connectivity Networking 186
Identity Access Management (IAM) 186
Pre-Build Controls 186
Standardization/Scalability 186
Landing Zones, practices 187

M

Managed Identities 58
Managed Identities, features 58
Managed Identities, practices 58
Management Groups 180
Management Groups, architecture 180
Management Groups, features
Consistent Policy 181
RBAC Scale 181
Resource Visibility 181
Scalability/Flexibility 181

Tree Structure 180
Management Groups, guidelines 181
Management Groups, illustrating 182
Microsoft Defender 207
Microsoft Defender, configuring 208, 209
Microsoft Defender, features
Agentless/Agent-Based Scanning 213
Compliance Monitoring 212
External Attack Surface Management (EASM) 211
Hybrid/Multi-Cloud Support 213
Inventory Management 210
Recommendation Engine 213
Secure Score 210
Threat Detection 213
Microsoft Purview 176
Microsoft Purview, architecture 176
Microsoft Purview, features
Access Based Security 177
Data Categorization 177
Data Flow, tracking 177
Data Governance 176
Data Lifecycle 177
Growth Insights 177
Microsoft 365 177
Policy Governance 176
Microsoft Purview, practices 177-179
Microsoft Purview, preventing 179
Microsoft Sentinel 270
Microsoft Sentinel, architecture 270
Microsoft Sentinel, capabilities 273
Microsoft Sentinel, components
Incident Management 276
KQL 275
Notebook Integration 276
Playbooks 276
Watchlists 276
Workbooks 276
Microsoft Sentinel, ensuring 271, 272
Microsoft Sentinel, features
AI-Driven Threat Detection 270
Automated Response 270
Built-In Analytics 270
Data Collection 270
Investigation 270
Microsoft Defender 271
Scalable 271
Workbooks/Dashboards 271
Microsoft Sentinel, outlines
Connectors 274
Data Normalization 275
Governance Access 275
Log Ingestion 275
Validation/Testing 275
Microsoft Sentinel, practices 276, 277

N

NSG/ASG, comparing 70
NSG/Azure Firewall, differences 77

P

Password-Based/Passwordless, comparing 35
Private Access 78
Private Access, options
  Azure Bastion 81
  Azure Private Link 79
  Service Endpoints 79
Private Link/Service Endpoints, comparing 82
Privileged Identity Management (PIM) 42

R

RBAC 41
RBAC/PIM, comparing 42
Resource Graph 189
Resource Graph, architecture 189
Resource Graph, deploying 190
Resource Graph, features
  Azure Monitor 190
  Continuous Resource 189
  Data Analysis 189
  Fast/Efficient Querying 189
  History Analysis 189
Resource Graph, practices 190

S

Secure Application Access 61
Secure Application Access, components
  Azure AD 64
  Conditional Access 62
  Entra ID 61
  Single Sign-On (SSO) 61
Secure Score 46
Secure Score, architecture 47
Secure Score, configuring 47, 48
Secure Score, elements
  Identity Protection 49
  Microsoft Defender Integration 49
  User Behavior Insights 49
Secure Score, ensuring 48
Secure Score, implementing 50, 51
Serverless Services 127
Serverless Services, architecture 128
Serverless Services, features
  Azure Functions 128
  Logic Apps 128
Serverless Services, implementing 129, 130
Service Principals 57
Service Principals, features 57
Service Principals, practices 57
Shared Responsibility 6
Shared Responsibility, architecture 6
Shared Responsibility, illustrating 7, 8
Shared Responsibility, practices 8
Shared Responsibility, preventing 8, 9
Shared Responsibility, principles
  Customer Responsibilities 6
  Microsoft Responsibilities 6
  Responsibility Distribution 6
Simple Azure Network 70
Simple Azure Network, configuring 71, 72

T

Threat Landscape 2
Threat Landscape, architecture 2

Threat Landscape, elements
Advanced Persistent Threats (APTs) 3
Cloud-Specific Threats 4
Ransomware Attacks 3
Supply Chain Vulnerabilities 3
TLS Certificate Rotation 108
TLS Certificate Rotation, practices 109
TLS Certificate Rotation, services 108
Traffic Analytics 277
Traffic Analytics, architecture 278
Traffic Analytics, components
Azure Network Watcher 278
Log Analytics Workspace 279
NSG Flow Logs 280
NSGs 279
VNets 280
Traffic Analytics, features
Flow Analysis 280
Geographic 281
Log Analytics 281
Optimization 281
Protocol Breakdown 281
Threat Detection 281
Time-Based Trend 281
Traffic Analytics, implementing 281, 282
Traffic Analytics, practices 282, 283
Traffic Filtering 72
Traffic Filtering, tools
Azure Firewall 72, 73
Azure Route Server 75, 76
NSGs 74
UDRs 75

U

User Accounts 55
User Accounts, features 56
User Accounts, practices 56

V

VWAN, benefits 91, 92
VWAN, implementing 91
VWAN, practices
Azure Application Gateway 94
Azure DDoS 102
Azure Front Door 96
Azure Resources 93
Public Access Consideration 93
Secure Public Access 94
Web Application Firewall (WAF) 100
VWAN, types
Basic 91
Standard 90

W

WAF, architecture 172
WAF/CAF, comparing 173, 174
WAF, parts
Cost Optimization 172
Operational Excellence 173
Performance Efficiency 173
Reliability 173
Security 173
WAF, practices 174, 175

Web Application Firewall 100
Well-Architected Framework (WAF) 172

Z

Zero Trust Security Model 11
Zero Trust Security Model, architecture 12
Zero Trust Security Model, breakdown
- Application Security 15
- Data Security 14
- Identity Access 13
- Network Security 14
- Visibility / Analytics 15

Zero Trust Security Model, configuring 17, 18
Zero Trust Security Model, deploying 16
Zero Trust Security Model, principles
- Assume Breach 13
- Least Privilege Access 13
- Verify Explicitly 12

www.ingramcontent.com/pod-product-compliance
Lightning Source LLC
Chambersburg PA
CBHW061801210326
41599CB00034B/6838

* 9 7 8 9 3 6 5 8 9 1 3 1 7 *